THE WELLSPRING, FANNIE'S STORY

DIANA WIENER

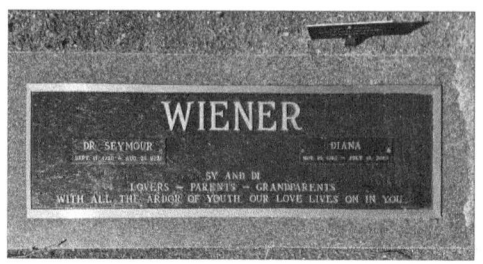

**To Fannie's descendants:
With all the ardor of youth, her love lives on
in you.**

Copyright ©2026 by Diana Wiener
All rights reserved. No part of this book may be reproduced in any manner whatsoever without written permission except in the case of brief quotations embodied in critical articles and reviews.

THE WELLSPRING, FANNIE'S STORY

Introduction

In the summer of 2000, my mother visited with us in Montague, a rural township in the Delaware River Valley, where New Jersey's state boundary intersects with those of New York and Pennsylvania.

One evening, she regaled my brother, Dickie, and me with tales of her father's Hungarian family. After a few hours, Dickie began an entertaining project. He sketched a descendant tree while our mother recalled her relatives. She never knew her grandfather, Samuel, who had died eleven years before she was born. But she remembered her grandmother, who died when my mother was nine. She had *known* her.

The first leaf on the tree: Fannie Bruder Freed.

In September 2001, aged sixty-six, Dickie died. Amongst his papers was that tree. It sat on my desktop for a few weeks, until one day, with some time on my hands, I visited Ellis Island's website. In less than an hour, scanning immigration databases, I found the ship on which Fannie had arrived, the *SS Maasdam*. I discovered a genealogy website. I thought: *This family tree thing will be fun, and easy. All the information is on Ancestry.com!*

For the next nine years, obsessed with the tree project, I plodded steadily through a labyrinth of research databases. There were dead ends and "aha" moments.

One day, I felt Fannie's presence, her hand guiding mine on the keyboard. I told my husband, "Sy, my great-grandmother is channeling me, asking for her story to be told."

The research and this narrative are dedicated to Fannie and Dickie, my silent and ever-present co-authors.

PART ONE

1

The story is global: invasion, conquest, and religious tyranny. It is of exodus, world war, disease, economic innovation, and depression. It is the continuum of human events blending gradually into its unending, repetitive story.

The singular story is of Fannie Bruder. It is personal, yet universal. A woman's story. A love story. Love for her husband, for her children, for life.

The contemporary world into which my great-grandmother was born was shaped by eight hundred years of conflict and contradiction between the Hungarian State and the Jews.

Semi-Nomadic pagan communities of Magyars lived in yurts on the Eurasian Steppe. Feared warriors, superb horsemen, archers, and saber wielders, the men served as mercenary fighters in Germanic, French, and Italian conflicts. Having seen what lay beyond, the idea of nationhood took root.

In the last decade of the ninth century, more than a hundred communities allied, electing seven leaders and a titular head, Prince Árpád. When three Turkic tribes fused into the coalition, they were ten. Ten arrows, On-Gurs: The Hungarians.

Thousands of men, women, children, cattle, sheep, pigs, and twenty thousand horses crossed the Carpathian Mountains. In their westward sweep, the Hungarians seized more than a hundred thousand square miles of middle Europe. The territory included the Danube and Tisza Rivers and forested, hilly lands rising north toward the Carpathians, and to the south and east, a great Basin covered more than half the terrain.

Among the conquered settlements were communities of Jews who, after expulsion from England, Spain, and the Germanic lands, had lived there for six hundred years,

At the beginning of the second century, the Holy Roman Emperor, Pope Sylvester II, crowned Prince Árpád's great-grandson, István, King of Hungary. As a Catholic Apostolic Kingdom, paganism was abandoned.

Hungary's royals enacted terror and tolerance of the Jews in cycles for the next eight hundred years. At times, restricted to residing in cities, Jews were identified by a piece of red cloth worn on the left side of their outer garments.

The royals and archbishops intended to exterminate the Jews, but the nobles, objecting to the loss of their labor force, opposed the slaughter, suggesting systematic cultural extinction. The privilege of peddling products or provisions in marketplaces outside of cities was offered to Jews converting to Christianity. Decrees forcing secularization accomplished the gradual desertion of the ancient teachings.

Beginning in 1541 and for more than one hundred fifty years, Ottoman Muslims occupied large portions of the country, including Óbuda, later known as Budapest. When the Austrian Habsburg Empire defeated them and claimed the land, a dual monarchy, Austria-Hungary, was established, an arrangement deeply resented by the Hungarians.

The Habsburgs, counseled by the archbishop, double-taxed the Jews, prohibited land ownership, farming, and living in cities. In the mid-seventeenth century, those refusing conversion were expelled, with the exception of Yiddish-speaking extended families living in virtual slavery on aristocratic land. Ignored by their titled lords, they continued practicing extreme orthodoxy, undisturbed.

In 1848, following a series of uprisings, the house of Habsburg was dethroned by revolutionaries led by patriot Lajos Kossuth.

Hungarians of Croatian, Serbian, and Romanian ancestry led by priests and officers loyal to Emperor Franz Joseph's Habsburgs, rebelled against the Hungarian government. Early on, the Hungarian insurgents won many skirmishes, but a year later, they were routed by the armies of the Russian Czar, an Austrian ally.

In a gesture of peace, Hungary's Constitution was restored. Some civil reforms and political rights were granted to the peasantry. Full citizenship for Jews was offered on condition they accept a confession of Christian faith. Assimilation demanded secularity, including the shaving of their beards, and conducting business on Saturday, the Jewish Sabbath. The cultural extermination of Hungarian Jewry was at hand.

In 1867, Austria-Hungary became a dual monarchy, sharing a common Emperor and military, yet separately governed by two parliaments: one in Vienna, the other in Budapest. Second only to Russia in land mass, the Empire was the third most populous in Europe.

Eager to join the European powers, the country was determined to modernize industry and bring the near-illiterate peasantry into the nineteenth century.

The Jews were eager, too. Eager to prove they were Hungarians.

My great-grandmother's life began on April 1, 1862. She was born in her mother's bed in a small house on Veres Útca, in Nagy Karolyi, a city of twenty thousand souls one hundred sixty miles east of Budapest.

Fannie

Six babies were stillborn before she carried me to term. On that rainy Tuesday, a precipitous labor had begun at daybreak. After a dozen contractions, the midwife, Jennie, urged, "Push, Sarah, push!"

Mama bore down, and Jennie, sitting on a chair at the edge of the bed, placed one hand on the top of my head and the other on my shoulders as they emerged from my mother's warm body. Her skilled hands held me firmly, guiding my arrival into the cool April morning. Jennie had attended thousands of births. There were no wasted motions.

I lay quite still on the bloody linen, masked by a caul, the thin membrane of my amniotic sac. Wiping my body clean, Jennie's experienced fingers carefully flayed the caul from my face.

Enfolded in a linen square, pressed against her ample bosom, I dangled upside down while she massaged my throat to encourage a clear airway.

After a few sputtering coughs, I was laid upon the bed. I made no sound, yet Jennie was unconcerned. She felt my energy, zest for life. She said, "It's a girl, Sarah."

Mama cautiously asked, "Is she alive?"

"Sarah, dear. She is beautiful. Good fortune will be hers, born under the caul. I've placed the membrane on a scrap of linen to dry. In a week's time, it will resemble a crisp parchment, a keepsake."

Working quickly, Jennie removed two linen strips and a knife from her surgical box. Tying and knotting the linen a few inches apart on my umbilical cord, she cut between the two, releasing me from my mother's tether.

Opening my eyes, and inhaling deeply, I cried.

"Thank God," Mama whispered.

"She's of good weight and very long; she'll be tall."

Jennie removed the soiled linen. Swaddled in a cotton blanket, I was placed in Mama's arms.

Mama examined my face. "She is perfect, Jennie. Her scent is of my own body. What an extraordinary discovery."

When the detritus of birth was removed and Mama wore a clean gown, Jennie went into the parlor. "Úr Bruder, come and welcome your beautiful daughter."

My Papa, Sándor Bruder, well over six feet tall and stout, not fat, was thirty years old when I was born. His signature was the felt hat he wore outside the house; keeping his thick, wavy, brown hair in check. God forbid a hair was discovered clinging to a chicken or in the ground beef he sold! On this day, his hatless curls were in wild disarray, as was his sense of control, under the circumstances. His large presence, along with a tendency to raise his voice and gesture by hand for emphasis, had caused breakage of glass or pottery bowls in the past. I tell you this because it was impossible for him to enter a room quietly.

When invited, he treaded softly into the bedroom, cautiously approaching the gift Mama was offering him, me.

Mama told me that as he neared the bed, the heel of his shoe slid on a spill Jennie had overlooked. Losing his balance, he grabbed for the bedpost to steady himself, making an awful commotion. Both women laughed out loud.

"I'm sorry, Sarah, for the noise."

Addressing the midwife, he stuttered, "Thank you, Jennie, for bringing my beautiful wife and daughter through the ordeal. Of course, I was never worried, not for a minute. Thank you, thank you."

Before leaving the room, Jennie said, "Úr Bruder, you are welcome. I'm so very happy for you both; finally, you're a family."

"Jennie! Is this her caul?"

"Yes, Úr Bruder, it's rare and a lucky omen. For centuries, it's been a protection for those at sea, a talisman. Although your daughter has been born in a land-locked country, you never know what the future will bring, so keep the membrane. It's her birthright."

Papa fought to hide a smile. "Jennie, you're a superstitious witch. Don't worry, I promise to keep the parchment." He laughed out loud before saying, "If the Croatians ever return control of Fiume to Hungary, perhaps we'll take a cruise on the Adriatic. With the caul in my daughter's pocket, we won't fear sinking!"

"Úr Bruder, you are mocking me." Jennie finished repacking her surgical box and brought Mama a cup of tea. To Papa, she said, "I'll check on the chicken fricassee before I leave; it will be ready in one hour. Please remember it's cooking; don't let it burn. Goodbye, Sarah, Úr Bruder."

Papa nodded goodbye. Mama said, "Thank you, Jennie, and bless you, dear."

"Sándor, here she is." Turning my face toward Papa, she whispered, "Isn't she lovely? Look, her eyes are open. She's saying hello to her Papa."

Cradling me in the crook of his arm, Papa wept. "My gyönyörű—beautiful—child, my Fannie, named to honor my own mother, may she rest in peace and bless your life. Finally, our home is complete."

Turning to Mama, he said, "Thank you, my dearest." Swaddled in my bunting, I wriggled against Papa's shoulder and slept soundly all the while he sat next to Mama on the bed.

"I love you, my Sarah. I never thought I would love anyone as I do you. I am the happiest man in the world."

Mama spoke softly, "I had given up hope of ever bringing a child to term, to life. Fannie is the reason we are here on this earth and why we'll never die. She'll carry our spark into the next generations." Sitting up against the pillows, she lifted the teacup to her lips. Papa waited for her to speak again.

Papa's bottom lip quivered, tears sliding down his cheeks. "Sarah, I'm sorry."

"Shh, my dearest. It's all right to weep. After losing so many babies, we never thought this day would come. Yet, it has, and we must not take the gift and responsibility lightly. Raising this child is a duty we must both commit to. I will nourish her, nurture her, love her. I'll teach her all I know, respect her, always be her champion. As a father, Sándor, you must protect her, love her, but there is more. She will judge all men by your actions, so you must keep your good character.

We must encourage her dreams and teach her to give and receive the one thing in the world that matters most, Sándor, love."

I made small, squeaking noises, my mouth agape, head turning from side to side. "She's searching for my breast, Sándor. Give her to me." Papa witnessed, with reverence, the powerful force of maternal instinct.

As the others on Veres Útca, our small house was built of brick with a veneer of white stucco, roofed with wood shakes. The front door opened directly into the parlor, Papa's domain. Reflecting his personality, the furnishings were purposeful and oversized: a settee and his upholstered chair occupied the center of the room, their bulk obscuring the pattern of a large rug. There were potted plants, kerosene lamps, a bookcase, and a few small tables. Mama's artwork adorned every wall, softening the room's masculinity. Yellow bricks, laid in a herringbone pattern, oiled to a high shine by Mama, covered the floors throughout. A narrow hallway led to two rooms at the rear of the house. To the left was my parents' small bedroom, with barely enough floor space for a chifforobe and matrimonial bed. To the right was the large kitchen, with wood stove, cupboards, ice box, china sink, a wall-hung water tank, and an oak table with two benches.

The kitchen door opened onto a rear yard, fenced all around to keep the neighbor's dogs away. Mama's garden was planted to receive as much sun as the huge oak tree would allow and as far from the sanitary as possible.

I slept in a cradle next to Mama's bed for a year when Papa raised the roof over the kitchen. Behind the stove, he installed a narrow set of stairs to reach the lovely little bedroom in which my childhood was spent. Pushed against the wall under a small window; I stretched out on a feather-filled mattress atop a drawer base which held my clothes. Shirtwaists were hung on six wooden pegs on the adjacent wall. Above the pegs, two shelves painted deep blue held my special rag doll and books. In winter, through the window above my cot, all the yards of our neighbors were in my sight. When the oak came into leaf, I enjoyed the privacy of a birds-eye view, peeking through the greenery, invisible to the world.

My parents were fortunate to live during those times, yet it was *my* generation who benefited in ways never known before. I was a full citizen of a modern Hungary. The reform era had given the Jews freedom to work anywhere and speak Hungarian, although, in the house, my parents still spoke German.

Papa taught me to read two years before I entered óvoda—kindergarten—in 1868. Coincidentally, it was the first-year Hungarian law required all children to attend nondenominational public schools. Occupying separate classrooms, the girls wore white dresses with green aprons, the boys' white shirts and green short pants.

Papa told me, "Fannie, as a child of the new Hungary, your future is unlimited. Let your natural intelligence shine." Mama said, "Do your very best, darling. Never be afraid to ask questions if you don't understand." My reading was so advanced, that, the following year the headmistress placed me with the second-grade class.

Papa was a serious man, though not particularly a religious one. We did not observe the Sabbath, and Mama did not keep a kosher kitchen. We attended synagogue only for very special events, a wedding or funeral. A few of my father's cousins became Catholic when their children entered secondary school. It seemed logical to ask, "Should we convert, Papa?"

"Our people have been secular for generations. My relatives fought in the war against the Ottomans, and my own father, Aladár, was one of the first Jews to enter Debrecen, a patriot and an agnostic. We're Hungarians. My focus is on my family's welfare first, then that of my neighbor. God knows of my integrity without attendance at synagogue or any church."

Papa had developed powerful upper body strength lifting animal carcasses at Bruder's Fine Provisions, where he sold fowl, beef, and pork. Customers came from outside our neighborhood because he offered accurate scales, top quality meat, and fair prices. He had a helper, József Schler. Mama said the boy's limited intelligence had been caused by a difficult birth. József washed the butcher blocks, rendered the fat in a cast iron pot over a fire at the back of the shop, kept the straw-covered floors clean, and made deliveries to the restaurants Papa supplied. They worked from dawn to sunset, Monday through Saturday.

Mama had deep brown eyes, like mine. She wore her light brown hair in braids, pinned at the top of her head like a crown. She was a short woman, reaching just to Papa's chest. Playfully, he would lift her off the ground to bring them face to face, and she squealed with delight when he nuzzled her neck. My parents' demonstration of love was unusual for that era. Papa never forgot her birthday or praise for her cooking. A practical man, he marveled at her creativity and encouraged her intellect.

Mama taught me to sew and keep house. We prepared her grandmother's recipes for paprikash and strudel. These skills were a daughter's birthright.

Mama was a painter. She taught me about pigments, the magic of blending primaries to produce nuanced tints. I watched her carefully clean her brushes; listened to her describe how the artist attempts to stimulate all the viewer's senses even when the model was as pedestrian as a still life. "The apple is a sturdy and useful fellow, Fannie," she told me. Pointing at the fruit, she continued, "You see how he stands guard and allows the soft little grape to lean on him? See the drop of sunlight reflecting on the leaf?" I nodded, and she went on, "Now, look at the apricot, her furlike softness inviting the viewer to imagine biting through her skin and drooling while devouring the sweet wetness of her flesh!" My bewilderment was palpable, I suppose, because Mama laughed out loud when she saw the utter incomprehension on my face. I was ten or eleven. I had no understanding of sensuality but sensed I would learn to appreciate that conversation someday.

She hung her framed landscapes all over the house, with the exception of the parlor, where painted roses climbed every wall from floor to ceiling. Though eager to emulate her, I possessed no creative bent. I was a reader, hungry to learn what lay outside my room, my city, my country.

My life's plan was determined by Papa. I was his adored daughter, yet in many ways, he regarded me as a son. At his shop, I learned the anatomy of animals, the craft of butchery, the importance of proper bookkeeping, how to sharpen knives at the whetstone wheel.

He acknowledged my intelligence and encouraged my academic drive yet never hinted of a daughter's limitations. He didn't tell me opportunities for my future were confined to a narrow reality: motherhood, sales clerk, or academic spinsterhood. I was blissfully unaware that Papa's insistence that I attend school beyond the age of twelve was to improve my prospects for marriage to a business or professional man, a man whose proper household I'd manage, and whose enlightened children I would bear.

As my last year at elementary school approached, the headmistress recommended preparation for admission examinations offered by Debrecen's Gymnasium. As valedictorian of my class, my acceptance to the eight-year secondary school came as no surprise to my teachers, or to Papa. All was going according to his plan for me.

At the end of August 1874, my parents brought me to Debrecen, a city of fifty thousand, Hungary's capital during the Revolution of 1848.

Papa's older brother, Ezekiel, and his wife, Eva, owned a large flat whose windows overlooked a small park just a few blocks from my school. Their only child, my cousin, Abraham, welcomed me with love.

Leaving home was an adventure I embraced with confidence. Papa had nurtured my independence. Mama, by example, taught me that love and appreciation for the arts kept life in balance.

The time had come to learn what lay beyond my birthplace. Would I find my own way or fulfill the destiny designed for me by others?

Samuel

The son of a vineyard tender, I was born on Christmas Day, 1859, on the outskirts of Tolcsva, a small village in the mountain's northeast of Budapest.

The house, on the southern edge of the vineyard, was a ramshackle place clad with wood shakes that had weathered over the years to a deep chestnut brown. Originally built as a one-room cabin in which vineyard laborers sheltered during unexpected weather, my father added two rooms as the family grew.

After decades of foot traffic, the earthen floors were so hard packed they resembled the slate teacher used at school. A brick hearth as tall as Papa and as wide as two rain barrels occupied a corner. A wood stove squatted beside it. There was no plumbing indoors. A hand-cranked water pump with a washtub occupied a small enclosure outside the front door.

Much of our family life: meals-schoolwork-conversation-handwork, and games—was enjoyed at a large, rectangular, oak table Papa had made. Side by side, on the opposite wall, were two settees built from rough planks unused for fencing. Generous cushions covered with dark green wool hid all the spills and baby spit-ups. Three wall-mounted oil lamps on each wall assured the place was never gloomy. Tintypes of our grandparents hung over the hearth. Brother Izak's charcoal-on-wood portraits of Mama, Papa, and our dog, Angyal, hung on nails above the settees.

In 1849, Abe was born. During the next seventeen years, when Rozsa came, Mama was either expecting a baby or nursing one. We were eight children: Abe, Etel, Izak, Kati, the twins Sali and Hani, me, and Rozsa.

When Abe and Izak were sixteen and thirteen, I was six. Beginning in early spring, they helped Papa dig a cold cellar into the side of the hill in back of the house. It was difficult shoveling that hard earth, and the boys emerged each day sweaty and covered with grime. Mama wouldn't allow them through the door until they stripped naked and washed with water from the rain barrel. Hilarious laughter emanated from that hole in the ground. All the siblings found humor in everything and considered themselves experts in everything. Having no construction experience of any kind, by winter's first snow, the cellar proved them right, they were experts. That construction was the shining achievement of my brothers' year, their engineering bona fide. They had dug the hole, cut, and installed the wood trusses, fashioned a vent from scraps of metal, and installed the shelves that held Mama's jars of fruit jams, pickled meats, smoked fish, and whole eggs preserved in brine. They had built the boxes that stored straw-covered root vegetables. The boys used bits of iron scraps discarded from horseshoes to fashion wall hooks for Mama to hang braided wreaths of garlic, their bulbs swollen with fat cloves.

Thinking of those boyhood years, the cellar is vivid in remembrance. After moving the heavy wood planks that kept rain and animals out, one walked down the incline into the storage room. The oil lamp's light reflected golden in droplets of water clinging to the glass jars; water drawn from the moist, subterranean atmosphere. The wet earth permeated with the aroma of straw and vegetables smelled so clean, I thought it to be a delicacy I wished to taste. To be honest, I did taste it once. Sadly, my romantic expectation didn't change the reality that it was dirt, after all.

My parents shared one of the bedrooms with baby Rozsa. The older girls occupied a small room behind the stove. My brothers and I slept on a straw mat in front of the hearth. In winter, we never lacked for warmth, all snuggled together. Escaping the crowd in milder months, I slept in the shed, with Fulop, the horse. Teased that I smelled like my stablemate, I didn't care. The stall offered me room to stretch my long legs. The chicken coop built against the wall outside Fulop's shed proved an annoyance, the racket made by those birds woke me before sunrise every morning.

Leaving school when he was eight, Papa had learned to read and write. Once he told me he had hoped to be a writer, which explained the stories he invented for our amusement. He said his life, in the employ of the estate, had been wasted. Having resigned himself to the way things were, what else could a poor boy have done?

He told me, "I want you to *be* something, to have it better than me. Your generation will be city dwellers; they'll not waste their lives cultivating other men's vines while working a few rocky rows of cabbages and potatoes to feed their children."

About thirty Jewish families attended the synagogue in Tolcsva. For those in the outlying areas, a traveling rabbi led Holy Day services at one of the farms. Papa was not observant, so we rarely attended. We spoke Hungarian and German. Mama also spoke Yiddish but did so only sparingly: in the company of her family, when she was angry with Papa, or the times she chose to express her opinion without inviting criticism.

Papa told me, "Praying for a better life is all well and good, son, but you must make yourself ready for prosperity. Get an education, live an honest life, raise a family, and love a woman." Yes, Jakob Freed was a romantic, and a progressive, too. All his children attended the local school, including my five sisters.

Papa's brother, Adar, had a sweetheart living in Tolcsva, Mahle Rosenberg. Her cousin, Amalia was a petite, dark-eyed girl who loved to read. A meeting was arranged at Mahle's house, and Papa said he fell in love with Mama the moment he first saw her, even before she spoke a word! They were married and rented the small acreage to get a start on life; it was never intended for a lifetime.

For a month, my father served as apprentice to the vineyard's overseer. Having learned to "read" the vines, he was accepted into the employ of the landowner, a descendant of Hungary's earliest aristocracy. In exchange for his labor, he earned a small salary. He was also given the use of the house, shed, and adjacent farming plot. He toiled in all weather for almost all of the year, except during the snows of January and February. From early spring through November, pruning and securing of the vines demanded continuous activity. Harvesting was ongoing from late summer through fall, from dawn to sunset.

Our family's vegetables needed planting and tending, too. All the children worked the field and learned to chop and stack wood to prepare for winter. It was a grinding, laborious life, and Papa fell asleep at the dinner table often. From the beginning, Mama wanted to go back to town, near her people. but Papa had no skills of use in the little town. Then the babies came. Providing food was a relentless endeavor for both my parents, foiling any opportunity for change.

A quiet, introverted woman, Mama lived a peasant's life. Her people were observant Jews, not like Papa's. She found comfort in lighting candles on Sabbath and fasting on Yom Kippur, but having married a man who was not a believer, she kept her religious practices to a minimum. She gave birth to eight children, sewed, washed, cooked, kept chickens, and weeded our vegetable garden. In a state of perpetual exhaustion, there was little time for small talk, so I barely remember a conversation with her. Her interior nature ran counter to my outgoing personality, causing me to suffer a sense of guilt for my overt optimism and social inclination. All the children helped with every task. I was next to the youngest. I wanted to keep up, but never could. I was tall and skinny, with little muscle mass. For that, I felt guilty, too.

In March of 1871, Mama died. Papa said it was pneumonia, though I believe, at fifty-two, she was just used up by life, too tired to go on. Abe, Etel, and Kati, all newly married, lived in Tolcsva. Izak, who worked in Debrecen for the university's groundskeeper, came home for the funeral. Barely nineteen, he was engaged to the daughter of the owner of a dry goods shop.

Abe and Papa met with the rabbi to arrange for Mama's burial, which was held the next day in accordance with Jewish law. Mama had a brother and sister living in town, and they were very sad. I remember their helping prepare Abe's house for the Shiva. The mirrors were draped with cloth. Wooden boxes on which the mourners would sit were placed in a row near the hearth. For seven days, morning and evening prayers were recited honoring Mama's memory. Ten men, a minyan, were required to chant the prayers. There was never a problem meeting that requirement, as Mama had been born in Tolcsva. Every family knew her and came together in prayer for her.

The Jewish rite of passage into manhood is celebrated at age thirteen. Presented to the congregation, and permitted to read, in Hebrew, from the Torah, he is accepted as a Bar Mitzvah, Son of the Commandments. At twelve, I was not counted among the praying men but stood when they stood, sat when they sat. Papa, of course, was tallied among the men. Unable to read the Hebrew text, he recited the prayers by echoing the rabbi's prompts.

Papa cried for days but returned to his responsibilities. The functioning of our household and seven-year-old Rozsa's welfare fell to Sali and Hani, then sixteen.

I was to receive elementary school certification at the end of May and had anticipated entering Gymnasium in Debrecen in August. For months I had been studying with a rabbinical student, preparing for my Bar Mitzvah. With Mama's death, plans and lessons ended. Papa needed me to care for Fulop and the chickens, chop wood, plant the garden, and earn a few pennies outside the house.

For the next three years, until 1874, I worked for Gitel and her husband, Jozsef, at their dairy farm two kilometers east of our house. It was common knowledge that Gitel was the most talented baker in Tolcsva.

Always, there were bowls of rising dough, bread and pastry baking or cooling, and the floor covered with flour. Gitel, herself, was always covered in flour, too. A large, handsome, woman with a ready laugh, her personality was more in line with mine than my own mother's. I loved her enthusiastic bear hug that left me gasping for air. The kitchen's aromas were pure love. Her pies, pastries, and braided loaves were delicious expressions of Gitel's own innovation. She shared her knowledge of the art and science of baking with me, and also her most important secret: "Use lots of butter, Samuel. Lots of butter!"

Three mornings a week, pushing a cart filled with cakes through the streets of Tolcsva, I followed Josef's milk cart. My pay was ten percent of the take. If the cart sold out, Gitel added another two percent. The housewives tipped me a kreuzer when I paid them a compliment. "Jó reggelt, Asszony Asboth, that's a lovely shawl." Every coin was saved for books I'd need in Debrecen.

At the end of the summer of 1874, my cousin Max and I left the mountains; we were almost fifteen. Izak had no room for us in his flat in Debrecen, so we rented a bedroom from the Mishpucha (family) of his wife, Katrina. To pay our way, we worked in restaurant kitchens, weeded private gardens, swept for shop owners, shoveled manure for the livery. There was no time for social pleasure and little time for class preparation. Most nights, I fell asleep with pen in hand and head resting on a book. For five years, this marathon of school and work consumed my life. I didn't bemoan my fate; self-pity wasn't part of my nature. I was young, simply doing what had to be done.

A distracted student, I demonstrated no aptitude for mathematics or science; I was a dreamer. Although it didn't excite me, it seemed inevitable I'd become a teacher. This was a disappointment to Papa. "There's no money in it, no future, Samuel."

Having begun Gymnasium late, I was three years older than my classmates, which, aside from my poor grades, contributed to my low social standing. At the end of 1879, just before my twentieth birthday, the headmaster summoned me to his office.

"Samuel, your class begins preparation for final examinations next month. I'm sorry to say it's not likely you'll receive certification. Having come into the program late and, at the same time, shouldering the responsibility for your own sustenance." After a pause, "Academic success is simply out of your reach. I'm sorry, Samuel. There seems no purpose in your continued attendance here. You are a fine young man.

I'm confident you'll discover a vocation that will fulfill your desires. Good luck, Samuel."

He was right, of course. Thanking the Headmaster, I resigned from school, accepting the reality that after five years of effort, there would be no certificate, no graduation.

Max was always the better student. He had a good head for business, especially the ledgers. He was hired as assistant bookkeeper at a button factory even before graduation the following spring.

I wanted a career or trade that would inspire and support me. Without Gymnasium certification, even had I *wanted* to teach, I could not qualify. I enjoyed cooking, yet spending life bent over a restaurant stove did not appeal.

By chance, I discovered my calling. Finding work as a sweeper in the cutting room at The Gentleman's Emporium, G. Balázs, Tailor, I learned to appreciate the "hand", or feel, of the finest woolens. The Master Tailor, Almos Horváth, took note of both my suggestion for updating old patterns and attention to oiling the sewing machines. My eagerness to learn every aspect of the garment earned reward. After a few months, under Horváth's watchful eye, I proved myself worthy for promotion. The Master allowed me to prepare the fabric for patterning, spreading the material across the cutting table's length. There were several fabric layers one atop the other. There could be no wrinkles, snags, or imperfection of weave anywhere within the strata, or the whole of it would be rendered unusable.

"Excellent work, Samuel. You have a real gift for the tailoring art. A respect for the fine materials and craft needed to dress a European gentleman."

It wasn't long before I was pinning the patterns, making ready for the cutters. The goal was to position the templates on the fabric in the most economical configuration, resulting in the least wastage. An error meant the difference between profit and loss.

My future had begun.

2

The Age of Enlightenment: philosophical ideas of individual liberty, tolerance, constitutional government, and separation of church and state dominated eighteenth century Europe. Self-determination influenced every societal class. Challenging both royal houses and sacred hierarchy, schisms occurred in all religious groups as rational thought challenged dogma.

The Age ended in 1800, when European territories, to varying degrees, had adapted to modernity and secularity.

In the German states, an urban, affluent Jewish class formed, but not so in Hungary. Magyar nobility fiercely protected its power, property, and privilege.

In 1848, Revolutionary leader, Lajos Kossuth, brought the Holy Crown and half the Parliament to the new capitol and "Guardian City of Liberty," Debrecen. It was in this city that Hungary's independence and the dethronement of the Habsburg monarchy were declared. When the Revolution was lost, so was Debrecen's status.

The Hungarians remained opposed to the dual monarchy, and civil unrest continued to plague the Habsburgs.

In 1887, The Austro-Hungarian Compromise granted autonomy to the Hungarian government. This included Jewish emancipation, even permitting a Jewish Congress to meet in Budapest. The Jews split into two groups: the modernist Neologs and the traditionalist Orthodox. Many declined both groups, establishing the Status Quo Congregation. This faction was not governed by a rabbinical chain of authority and accepted all congregants as long as they declared themselves Jewish. The three levels of Judaism remained a feature for generations.

Barely affected by modernization, the northern, most backward regions remained strictly Orthodox and allied with the Sephardim Hasidim, whose isolation and radical ideology were rejected by mainstream Jewish communities.

The Neologs accepted Magyar policy. Keen to integrate, they identified with Hungarian patriots, abandoned speaking German, and accepted secular education. The Neologs retained rituals, dietary restrictions, and the Sabbath, laymen delivered churchlike sermons in modern language.

The city of Debrecen lies one hundred thirty miles east of Budapest. Embracing the Protestant Reformation, first as Lutherans then Calvinists, Catholics were expelled, and their churches occupied for one hundred fifty years. The Holy Roman Emperor, Leopold I, offered the city a limited self-government *if* the Catholic Church were permitted to return. With this compromise, the city became known from that time as the "Calvinist Rome."

As for the Jews, in 1814, after centuries of expulsion, the Enlightenment's influence enabled one hundred eighteen Jewish men to enter Debrecen. Among them was the fifteen-year-old child of an itinerant peddler, Fannie's grandfather, Aladár Bruder.

Ten years later, Aladár's son, Ezekiel, was born, followed in 1832 by Fannie's father, Sándor. The brothers were raised with no religious affiliation, encouraged to discover their own spiritual paths. To satisfy his wife's Neolog family, Ezekiel attended services once a year, for Yom Kippur. Sándor abandoned religion altogether.

In 1874, Debrecen's population of fifty thousand included two thousand Jews. Sandor's twelve-year-old daughter, Fannie, entered Debrecen's Gymnasium. She lived as a guest in her uncle's house for the next eight years.

Fannie

I lived with Papa's elder brother, Ezekiel, and his family. Both brothers were six feet tall, Papa stout, and Ezekiel very slender. Ezekiel was fastidious about his appearance, oiling his hair and waxing the tips of his twisted mustache each morning. He also had a splendid beard, which he kept clipped close to his face. Papa sported no facial hair and kept his unruly mop under a green felt hat when not in his own house. Uncle Ezekiel owned a tobacco shop near the train station. His wife, Aunt Eva, was a rotund woman of good disposition with dark, almond-shaped eyes. Their only child, my cousin Abraham, had been raised, as was I, in a household of comfort.

I arrived in Debrecen six months after my twelfth birthday. Abe, in the eighth form at Gymnasium, was fifteen. We enjoyed that special closeness of first cousins, love without sibling challenge. Abe introduced me to the great city's culture: library, concert halls, public gardens, and the shopping district. Best of all, at the Debrecen Theater, we attended performances of Shakespeare's "Hamlet" and "A Midsummer's Night's Dream," both translated to Hungarian by the great poet, János Arany.

The women's Gymnasium occupied a square city block. Four brick structures, each designed for a specific purpose, defined the perimeter around the central courtyard. One building accommodated classrooms, another the administrative offices. The third held the library, physical exercise areas, science laboratories, and the dining hall. The last provided dormitories for the boarders.

Scoring well on the entrance examinations had earned me a full academic scholarship and living with relatives saved Papa ten forints a month, the fee for room and board. I entered in the fifth form, joining classmates from all levels of society and all parts of Hungary. There were girls from aristocratic families and some from small villages, including two Jewish girls, both boarders. All students took luncheon together in the dining room. The food was terrible, usually a thin beef broth with day-old bread or porridge with a few raisins. Occasionally, a chicken ragout or noodles and cottage cheese were served, both filling and tasty. As you can imagine from the description of the meager menu, the cost for Day Girls, like me, was very reasonable: only sixty-five Kreutzers a month.

Class duration was one hour; six classes each weekday and three on Saturday. Allowed five minutes to reach their next lecture, students hurried through the corridors between classes to be seated and ready as lessons began. At the front of each room, the teacher's lectern, on an elevated platform, provided an unobstructed view for every student. Ten benches, arranged in two rows, were fixed to the floor in a neat procession extending from platform to rear wall. Benches one and two, at the front of the room, were reserved for those achieving excellence. Students were seated according to grade ranking, in descending order, the poorest intellects at the last row.

In all the years at Gymnasium, I never vacated the first bench, always receiving grades of either one or two in every class. The school year was divided into quarters ending with exams and holiday, or summer break. In the early forms, I studied geography, history, Hungarian literature, Latin, and mathematics. In the upper forms, English, French, German, and science were added. Religion classes, befitting the city's history, taught Protestantism. Catholics and Jews were expected to attend instruction in parish or synagogue classrooms on their own time.

At Uncle Ezekiel's, I resided in the small room above the entrance foyer; my window overlooking the busy street. It was not unusual to be awakened in the night by the snort or whinny of a horse being reined to a stop on the tram route.

For winter holiday and summer hiatus at home, I rode the train unaccompanied, a real city girl. Papa and Mama never tired of hearing of my life in Debrecen. Their little house was empty without me, but Papa forbade my guilty feelings. He scolded, "Your education will secure your future; your absence here is a sacrifice we gladly make." I didn't quite understand how, with neither burning ambition nor special talent, education would secure my future. As always, I accepted Papa's reasoning; he knew best.

It was heaven, returning to my room above the kitchen, sleeping on my featherbed, and looking through the oak tree's limbs and leaves, but I was no longer a resident of Nagy Karolyi. With limited resources, its quaint distraction was confining. I was happy to return to Debrecen.

Uncle Ezekiel's row house had a rental flat on the ground floor. When I first arrived, it was occupied by a young couple, Andres, and Anna. Their daughter, Katrina, was born near the end of my first school year. Eager to help the new mother with all the work a baby requires, I learned to wash diapers, force cooked vegetables through a sieve, comfort, swaddle, and sing lullabies. Never having had the opportunity to be close to a little baby, I was fascinated with her development, thrilled to care for her when Anna needed to run an errand. It was so easy to love a baby. Katrina was so dependent and trusting. I learned how nature endows babies with intelligence and a sense of humor. All a mother need know was already in her heart, a protective instinct, and the capacity to love. I knew I would have a large family someday.

For five years, I applied myself to schoolwork, excelling, as Papa wished. Everything in my life was done at Papa's behest to benefit Papa's plan for my life. At seventeen, the powerlessness of childhood awakened my consciousness. My friends at school and I questioned the legitimacy of parental and societal tyranny. Sadness, joy, apprehension, impatience, anger. These emotions appeared, unexplained, making life unpredictable and confusing. Aunt Eva told me, "It's your age, dear Fannie. You're becoming a woman. Your body and mind are growing up. Don't be afraid, it's natural." Abe and I grew even closer, sharing the suffering one endures as they leave childhood behind. Abe was admitted to the University Law School, class of 1882. I was so proud of him. I had only three years left to receive certification. Then, what will happen? Only Papa knew.

The summer at home had been a sweet relaxation, quickly faded to memory as the winter hours in Debrecen filled with demanding, upper-level course work.

Marking my eighteenth birthday, Aunt Eva was preparing to serve Sunday afternoon tea with an apple torte when the front doorbell rang.

"See who is at the door, Abraham," Uncle Ezekiel said.

I could hear happy greetings exchanged as Abe led two young men into the parlor. The shorter fellow clapped Abe on the back and said, "We were on the way to the park, passing right in front of your door. I thought we'd see if you had your nose out of a book on a Sunday afternoon!"

The speaker was Max Better, Abe's former Gymnasium classmate, a boy I had met at a performance of the school's orchestra. I didn't recognize his mate.

Abe said, "You're in luck, we're celebrating Fannie's eighteenth birthday!"

Introducing his friends to Aunt Eva, they kissed her hand in greeting then turned to me.

Rising to welcome Max, I said, "So nice to see you again."

He responded warmly, "Fannie, what a treat for us! Are you still smarter than Abe? Forgive the interruption of your celebration, but accept my congratulations for the day."

Max made a little bow and kissed my hand. I laughed at his enthusiasm.

Smiling, he said, "Dear girl, when last I saw you, three years ago, you were a child. Now, you're a lovely young woman!"

He paused, then added, "Oh, please excuse my poor manners; this is my cousin, Samuel Freed." Stepping in front of Max, the fellow moved very close to me. I was completely unprepared for the scent of him. The mixture of shaving soap and a musky maleness was so pleasing, I drew a deep breath to capture the aroma.

"Hello, Fannie. I hope you'll accept my wishes for happiness and all you desire as an adult." Surprisingly, this stranger reached for, kissed, and held my hand. I was stunned and confused.

A heat rushed to my face, blushing my cheeks, my hand trembled. Removing my hand from his, I managed, "It's nice to meet you, too, Samuel."

He was very handsome: tall, with deep brown eyes. A small mustache drew attention to this boy's lips, an anatomical focus that, to my recollection, had never before engaged my interest. Somehow, they suggested a gateway through which I was passing.

Polite, yet persistent, I felt his presence enfolding me as in a velvet cape, dismissing everything and everyone in the parlor and the world beyond.

A week later, with Aunt Eva's permission, Samuel and I walked along Piac Útca, Park Street. Although the April sun was bright, the breeze at our backs held a chilly edge as we made our way along the tree-lined avenue. Several times, our elbows touched, forearms brushing against one another. I shivered, but it was not due to the coolness of the air. All my senses were heightened by his nearness, my face flushed with excitement.

I said, "It's a lovely day, Samuel. I can't think of anything I'd rather be doing than walking with you."

A bit formally, he replied, "That your Aunt Eva has allowed us this time together is a gift, a great gift, Fannie."

Polite conversation was a superficial exchange. I could find nothing interesting to say. Truth be told, the nearness of him muddled my thinking.

"Aunt Eva is enjoying having a daughter in the house. This morning, before you arrived, she fussed over what I'd chosen to wear and how I was arranging my hair," I giggled.

Stopping abruptly, he turned to face me.

Taking my hands in his, he stared directly into my eyes and said, "I am a man, dearest Fannie, a grown man. You are the woman my father told me I would find in this world; I knew it the moment we met. I want you to be with me always. I love you."

I couldn't breathe. My heart seemed to swell, filling my ribcage. My lungs simply couldn't expand. I could see only his face. People strolling the promenade had to avoid the island we had created on that spot. They milled about us, as the surf surrounds a lighthouse.

Perhaps a gypsy's cards might have predicted these forces rerouting my life, but the circumstances were unexpected and extraordinary. We found ourselves in a world within a world, a reality insistent upon complete surrender. His words were exactly what I anticipated, what I knew to be true.

What would become of us, what *could* become of us? I heard his words, how he called me "dearest," his handsome face, his manliness. That beautiful moment of Samuel's declaration was overshadowed by my immediate, conditioned response. What will Papa say? Instinctively, I sensed disapproval.

I said, "I feel as you do, Samuel, but I'm inexperienced. Of love and romance, I know only what I read in books, and that didn't prepare me for you. I've been raised by a very strong father, who invested in me a certain expectation and responsibility. It's not clear what purpose my education will provide, but whatever my life's path, living in Nagy Karolyi is required. He will not accept you. I know that, for certain. I cannot deny my attraction to you, Samuel." I hesitated, "This liaison will be forbidden. I know it."

It was as if I were speaking a foreign tongue. Samuel looked puzzled.

"Why would you think that, Fannie? I am a young man with a trade, I'm young and strong. I love you. What could your father find wrong with that?"

I said, "I pray you are right, but our love doesn't fit my father's plan or timing. And Papa is not accustomed to compromise."

He said, "Clear that dark cloud from your mind. I will win him over, and your mother, too. There is nothing and no one in this world that will stand between us and our life together. Trust in me, Fannie."

The next few moments passed in silent contemplation of the journey ahead. There was no reason to anticipate a jaunt. More likely, it would be a trek. I knew my Papa, Samuel didn't. He had no idea of the storm clouds looming on our horizon.

We ended the day with a coffee. At my front door, I whispered, "Until next week, my dearest." Samuel kissed my hand and held it to his cheek for a moment.

The next Sunday, at an open-air café, we shared a strudel. As I leaned close to him, so as not to miss a word, Samuel told lively stories of his family, always with an amusing twist. He listened as I described my solitary and indulged childhood, my stories so obviously in contrast to the anecdotes of the creative and resourceful siblings he lived with in that small house in the mountains. I was bookish, quiet. Throughout my early years, there had only been one or two classmates I would call a friend.

He made me laugh. The way he wove a tale or expressed an opinion about the world was amusing, charming. He engaged in conversation with waiters, shopkeepers, and street cleaners, always ready to hear another point of view. We spoke for hours, our faces inches apart, our gaze connected, unguarded.

Every moment of the week, frustrated by how slowly the days passed, I thought only of Sunday with Samuel. Attending a university orchestra concert, we whispered goodbye to Abe and left before intermission. Listening to Mozart was a waste of the precious time we had together. Hurrying down a stairwell to leave the building, we stopped for a moment, enjoying our escape. Laughing, and out of breath, leaning on the wall, our foreheads touched. A moment later, wrapping his arms around my waist, he brought his lips almost to mine.

"Is it alright if I kiss you, Fannie?"

Trembling, I answered breathlessly, "Yes, please."

Never having kissed a man before, I was surprised to find my mouth soft and eager to taste his lips. At first, I didn't close my eyes, wanting to see his reaction to my offering. His eyes were closed, his expression one of concentration, savoring the moment. After a few seconds, my lids closed, allowing my mind to focus on my body's response. My lips softened; my breath quickened. I felt an urgency, the need to press myself against him, to relieve an ache, a physical yearning.

Three students running down the stairs brought our embrace to an end. Drawing apart, we studied each other's faces. The intimacy had changed us. We were lovers, no longer children. I thought, "Anyone looking at me will know I am not a girl anymore."

After our sixth Sunday encounter, Aunt Eva wrote to Mama. I received Papa's post a week later:

May 17, 1880
Fannie:
Mama and I oppose your involvement with this friend of Abraham's. I am very, very displeased at your lapse of common sense and intelligence. My plans for your future will not be deterred by a careless flirtation. I'm disappointed you have allowed this stranger to turn your head. Your future husband deserves a virtuous, educated, woman. Don't jeopardize your life.

Papa

I didn't reply, thought it best to wait a week hence, on my next visit home.

Mama met me at the train. "Where is Papa?" I asked. She replied tensely, "He's busy at the shop. We'll talk about it later."

At the house, she busied herself with dinner preparations. Her discomfort barred any conversation, so I went to my room to write to

Samuel. Hearing the front door slam shut, I ran down the stairs to greet Papa.

He stomped into the kitchen, nodding curtly to Mama. I stepped forward. He turned away, there was no embrace, not a word was spoken. At table, a sense of foreboding cast a pall on the scene. With no appetite, I pushed the chicken around my plate, managing to swallow only a small bit. Finally, I said, "Is it your intention never to speak with me again, Papa?"

Mama rose to clear the table, escaping the imminent confrontation. Papa did not look at me all the while his booming voice ricocheted from floor to ceiling, walls, and cabinetry.

"I will speak with you when I am ready to do so," Papa said. "Not today or tomorrow. In fact, I don't anticipate any conversation with you before you return next week to Debrecen and that scoundrel." He stood and left the room.

I looked to Mama, who whispered, "When I'm finished in the kitchen, I'll come upstairs, darling." Tension and anger were thick in the air. I did not cry, though. I was on a precipice, my life separating from my parents.

Mama sat on the bed and cradled me in her arms.

She said, "He will never approve a marriage to Samuel, whom, he feels, has taken advantage of your youth and naïveté. Fannie, I have never seen your Papa so angry. It is as if a thief robbed him of everything dear to him."

"Mama, I have not been stolen away. I am the same. I'm sorry to have caused you and Papa so much worry, but Mama, I love Samuel."

I would not discuss a compromise, would not apologize. Neither would Papa; we were at an impasse.

It is a simple truth, young love. Intense, it allows no distraction. The need for each other trivializes all else. The larger truth was waiting for me when I returned to Debrecen; I did not control anything.

Papa commandeered my life through Uncle Ezekiel.

"I have received a letter from your father, Fannie. He's asked me, demands, I close my door to Samuel, and he will bring you home if you continue this defiance. I like Samuel, so don't be angry with me, but I cannot deny my brother. Until Sándor decides otherwise, Samuel is no longer welcome here, can no longer visit or contact you. I'm sorry."

Fighting back tears, I said, "But, Uncle, I beg you to speak with my father. You know Samuel. You can vouch for his character and sensibility."

Softly, Uncle Ezekiel said, "I'm sorry, Fannie. I cannot do what you ask." He left the room, the discussion ended.

Aunt Eva, sitting on the settee, tried to comfort me. "Fannie, you're as my own daughter. You are at a crossroad in your young life, no longer a child. My advice is: follow your heart, be honest with yourself. If this *is* your love, it will all work out in the end."

I leaned against her bosom, sobbing. I said, "There's no turning back. I'll complete my studies, as I promised Papa. Then, I *will* marry Samuel. Surely, my parents will allow it by then."

I persuaded Uncle Ezekiel to allow one more afternoon with Samuel, so that he may learn from my lips of Papa's edict.

Without ordering, we left the coffee shop on Piac Útca and walked directly to the underpass at the park.

I said, "There is nothing to be done to change Papa's mind. There is also nothing to be done to change mine."

He said, "I'm heartsick. There must be a way to find a compromise. In the meantime, we'll meet in secret. I cannot bear the thought of being apart."

Under the stone bridge, we held each other, kissed. Those stolen kisses awakened my sensuality. His fingertips lightly skimmed the ribs above my waist tracing the outline of my breasts. Turning my torso, I caused his hand to cup my breast directly. I felt an exquisite ache as a heat rose from my pelvis to the place of his touch

He said, "We will find a way, dearest. No matter what forces are against us, we will prevail."

I said, "I love you, Samuel. I would give up everything, and everyone I have ever known to be with you."

We invented a science class study group, and Uncle Ezekiel was none the wiser, and Samuel and I met at the park on Wednesday and Sunday.

Isolated by our forbidden hunger, there was no haven. Elopement seemed the only solution. We decided to escape to Budapest at the end of the school year. Obsessed with unfulfilled passion and the details of flight, our daily commitments began unraveling.

Samuel, preoccupied at work, was unable to sleep through the night. I lost my appetite and couldn't focus on schoolwork. After I received a poor grade on an easy history section, Papa was furious and arrived in Debrecen on an afternoon train.

Abe found me reading a book in the park a few doors from the house. "Your father is here. You had better come quickly, Fannie. He has barely spoken to my parents; and when I entered the parlor, he didn't greet me, just barked 'Find her.'"

I hurried back to the apartment. The mountain of a man that is my Papa seemed even larger and more imposing. The starched white collar barely contained his neck, which, in flushed anger, seemed ready to burst the fabric.

"I don't know you anymore, child! You're casting aside your studies, your life, for a stranger who will surely ruin your future."

I tried to argue, but Papa wouldn't let me speak, his voice a raspy whisper.

"I'm warning you, Fannie: if you don't give him up, I'll stop paying for school and bring you home. Think about what you're doing. You believe him to be a man of good character. As of this day, I've received one letter of introduction, yet he hasn't made the trip to Nagy Karolyi to state his intention in person. He is not respectful."

"Papa, to be fair, you never gave him the courtesy of a response, so what was he to do? I promise I'll finish school, but I will not come home to marry a boy of your choosing. I beg you and Mama to think about how happy Samuel makes me. Papa, I love him."

"If you're thinking of running off to marry, we will sit Shiva for you."

It frightened me to think my parents could cast me off, give me up for dead.

I said, "Papa, I want your blessing, not your condemnation. I am the headstrong daughter you raised. Please don't say hurtful things. I will follow my heart, and I hope you will, too."

Aunt Eva tried to ease the tension. "Sándor, will you stay for dinner? Ezekiel will be home in a few minutes. Perhaps a little schnapps with your brother will stimulate your appetite and calm the scene."

In measured tones, Papa replied, "It's no use, Eva. My rage will not be stifled by a little schnapps. What's more, I hold you and my brother partly responsible for encouraging this from the beginning!"

"But, Sándor...." Papa interrupted her, "Enough, Eva. I'll not stay for dinner. I've said what I've come here to say, and now I'll return to Sarah on the evening train." Without a further word to any of us, he rushed out the door to hail a carriage.

I knew my own mind. I knew my own heart. Papa always said that Hungarians believe to love and be loved is the only reason for life. I'm certain he believes that to be true. Now, he must learn to accept that I've found a love of my own.

For a few days, there was a strained atmosphere in the house, but soon things returned to normal.

Abe consoled me with a wry comment. "Don't worry, Fannie. Love will win the day. The only question is: When will that day come?"

Aunt Eva mentioned she had received a letter from Mama, who was very unhappy about the rift. Apparently, Mama was using all her powers of persuasion to convince Papa that he was being unreasonable, that he could not decree love. He didn't accept correction well, but Mama is a romantic and put up a fight for my happiness.

Abe, our go-between, delivered our love notes and pretended to be my escort when, in actuality, he was delivering me to a concert, the library, or the city gardens where Samuel would be waiting. It was an anxious time, hiding from my family, who imposed upon us a guilt we did not merit. I'm not certain that my aunt and uncle were unaware of the deceit. Trusting me, they never pried, scolded, or moralized about standards of behavior.

In spite of Papa's threat to end my studies if we didn't break it off, Samuel and I met secretly for the next year. Thanks to Mama's starry-eyed persistence, Papa apparently decided it best not to inflame my entrenched position, so he pretended Samuel didn't exist. He and I were back on speaking terms, with one verboten topic: Samuel.

Dominated by deception, my daily activity demanded cynicism and dishonesty, devices I had not known I was capable of. Never before had I lied to my parents or to anyone else.

The intense pressure began to take its toll upon my constitution. I lost my appetite, withdrew from my uncle and aunt in dark moodiness, slept fitfully. The burden of my lies weighed heavily upon my conscience. By the end of summer, preparing to enter senior year, an overall discomfort, headaches, pain on swallowing, and fatigue, forced me to take to my bed. A few days later, along with nausea and fever, there appeared flat, red spots on my face, hands, forearms, and then my trunk. The spots developed into small blisters filled with fluid.

Aunt Eva sent Abe to the Kenézy hospital to fetch Dr. György. Before entering the flat, the doctor covered his nose and mouth with a handkerchief tied about his head. I vaguely remember his presence and examination. I'm sure he did not palpate or otherwise touch me; only his practiced eye observed my signs and symptoms. I opened my mouth when instructed to do so, and, holding my tongue with a scrap of linen, he thrust it from side to side, to observe my gums and throat. "This is very serious," he told Eva. "She has smallpox. The blister's clear fluid will turn into pus. Sores have also developed in the mucous membranes of her nose and mouth. Scabs will form in a week or so, eventually leaving deep, pitted scars when they fall off."

Aunt Eva began to whimper, "I've drawn the curtains as she complains the light is an irritant."

"Darkness is soothing. You should be aware that blindness is a common result of the pox. You are all at risk of contagion. I recommend her immediate admittance to the hospital, where several cases, isolated from the public, are receiving good care. There is no cure. She's young and will likely survive the crisis, after which she'll retain immunity to the pox for life. We can only keep her comfortable, offer broth and warm tea to nourish, and apply cold compresses to reduce fever. Cover your nose and mouth when in her presence. It is believed the cause is airborne."

Abe was sent on the evening train to bring the news to my parents; a post would take too long. Persuading a hackie to risk infection, Uncle Ezekiel paid a double fare to transport me to the hospital.

All the while my kin were attending to what appeared to be my last needs, not one of them summoned Samuel. In a fevered state, there is little I remember of the hospital. Conquered by the malady, I felt abandoned, forsaken.

Doomed.

Samuel

Following a lunch of boiled potatoes and fish at The Halász bistro, Max and I walked toward Kicsit park. One couldn't help but notice lilies of the valley emerging from soil around tree trunks. The lilies heralded the return of millions of sweet-smelling, stark white flowers soon to show themselves in window boxes and landscapes. Residents were out for an afternoon stroll; it was brisk and sunny, the first day of April.

Max smiled at me. "Let's stop and visit Abe Bruder. He lives just down the street!"

I said, "Max, you haven't seen him for a year, since he began law studies. I'd feel uncomfortable intruding on his family. Let's just go on to the park."

"Oh, no, Samuel. I'm certain Abe will be happy to see us!" We climbed the front steps of the row house, and Max rang the bell. Abe answered the door. Max was right; he *was* delighted to see us. "Well, well, well! I can't believe my eyes! Max, my old chum!" He embraced Max, then shook my hand enthusiastically. "And Samuel! What a wonderful surprise to see you both. Come in, come in."

With some uneasiness, I followed Max and his former classmate into the parlor.

Abe said, "You're in luck. We're celebrating Fannie's eighteenth birthday!"

Over Max's shoulder, I watched her approach. In spite of her youth, she moved with a woman's confidence across the carpet. She and Max exchanged greetings. Impulsively, I stepped in front of him, between them, compelled to draw closer. She smelled like apricots. Her eyes were deep brown and met mine without hesitation. She wore no powder or rouge, just a touch of tinted beeswax on her lips. Oh, I could barely contain myself, so eager was I to kiss, to nibble that gloss from the fullness of her mouth.

I tried to be glib, though I'm sure I looked a fool to her. It was difficult to breathe, standing so near. Without thinking, I reached for, and held, her hand, uttering some nonsense. As she stepped away, I allowed my fingers to graze the sash at her waist. It was unbearable. I thought I'd explode. I wanted her, this marvelous girl-woman.

I contributed little to the conversation of school and world affairs, dumbstruck by her presence. Although it seemed an eternity, it was less than an hour before Max became aware of my discomfort. We thanked our hosts for the tea and sweets, kissed Abe's mother's hand, and made our exit.

Obsessed with thoughts of her, I enlisted Abe's help to gain his mother's permission for Fannie to spend Sunday afternoon with me. We walked along Piac Útca, and I tried my best to converse, to ignore her nearness. When I could stand it no longer, there on the boulevard, I declared my love. "I want to spend the rest of my life with you." She wasn't surprised. It was as though my stumbling confession and proposal were expected, an obvious fact. Her feelings were in accord," she loved me, too.

"There is a weakness in our grand plan," she said. "Our destiny is not ours alone to chart. My father will not accept you. I know he will forbid this."

I couldn't comprehend why her father would reject me as a suitor. I loved Fannie; she loved me. I had a bright future.

I told her, "Not to worry, my dearest. This is love, and it conquers all." The world had tilted on its axis for us both.

Six blissful Sundays at café or concert deepened our ardor. In detail, we related stories of our families and friends. When we kissed for the first time, there was nothing left to fear. Love was ours. The one greatest love in the entire world.

Then, Eva wrote to Fannie's parents about our courtship.

Her father was furious. To him, she was a baby. He would not tolerate a romantic interest.

"Absurd," he wrote Eva, "Fannie must not be distracted from her studies."

I wrote to Bruder, declaring my intentions, assuring him I would never take advantage of his daughter.

"We will wait for her Gymnasium certification and, I hope, with your blessing, become engaged." Giving no response, Bruder made his contempt for me obvious.

We ignored his displeasure. Parental disapproval cannot deter young lovers, who are driven by an inescapable chemical force. We believed he would eventually relent, yet I was in a state of perpetual agitation, unable to sleep through the night, waking every hour or two.

Bruder wrote to his brother, demanding he offer no encouragement to our liaison. All encounters were forbidden. He traveled to Debrecen to have it out with Fannie, whose studies were suffering under the stress.

I *wanted* to be present, to speak with him, plead our case. Fannie told me her father made it clear I was unwelcome.

There was an ultimatum: Give me up or come home. He underestimated the independent daughter he had raised; Fannie would not concede our love. For Sándor Bruder, that was the moment he knew his influence was lost, his child grown. His opposition had driven us closer, even more determined to overcome his tyranny.

As I was unable to present myself legitimately, Fannie and I continued to meet on the sly. We had one supporter, Abe, who facilitated our meetings and note exchanges. Taking advantage of every opportunity for privacy, whether in shadows under a stone bridge or a library stairwell, we kissed and pressed against one another desperately. Our bodies were on fire, but there could be no relief. As a last resort, we began planning an elopement.

Fannie regained her class standing, and her father paid the administrative bills. He gave our love no credence. To his thinking, it simply didn't exist; consequently, there was no problem. Apparently, he had decided to play a waiting game, hoping our fire would burn itself out. Of another era, his own youthful passions must have, long ago, been forgotten.

As her senior year was to begin, Fannie fell ill. Abe came to my workplace to tell me she had been hospitalized with smallpox.

At the stroke of six, ending the workday, I ran through the city, reaching the northeast sector in less than twenty minutes. Not only was I refused entry to the hospital's quarantine ward, even the flowers I bought were not permitted. The nursing sister promised she would tell Fannie I had visited. I asked, "Will she survive, be disfigured, is there pain?" The sister offered no answers. With no standing to inquire after Fannie's treatment or medical status, I was asked to leave the facility.

A week passed before the doctors allowed Bruder, who had hired a private livery, to rescue my beloved from curtained isolation at the windowless end of a hospital hallway.

Requesting a two-week leave from work, I left for Nagy Karolyi immediately. Upon arrival, the stationmaster directed me to the nearest synagogue. I found the Rabbi in his study, making final preparations for Sabbath. He listened to my desperate story of love and illness before leading me to a small house at the rear of the building. As we entered the kitchen, the rebbetzin was removing a challah from the oven. Bruder was not a congregant in their Orthodox synagogue, but they knew of his butcher shop. After insisting I have a bowl of soup, the rebbetzin arranged for my lodging with one of their congregants.

The five-minute walk to Bruder's shop allowed me time to organize my approach. I was not going to grovel yet could not appear demanding. My mother said I was "charming," and I was known for my optimistic disposition in Tolcsva. I'd simply state the facts: Fannie needs my love at her bedside. My presence will give her hope, the will to live.

It was almost four in the afternoon when I reached the shop. Through the window, I observed one customer, a woman, standing at the butcher block, preparing to pay. Bruder, removing a pencil from behind his ear, wrote a few numbers on a brown paper package tied with string. As she counted out her coins, I pushed against the door. A bell suspended from the frame's header tinkled, announcing my entrance. I held the door for the woman and turned to Bruder.

"May I help you, sir?" Bruder asked.

"I am Samuel Freed."

He made no reply, turning instead to direct his helper to a task in the rear of the shop. "Josef, refill the ice boxes in back." Without another word, he walked around me and bolted the door.

"Well, Freed, why do you come here? Can you be so dim-witted you haven't yet realized you are not welcome? What do you want?"

"Úr Bruder, I beg you...let me visit with Fannie."

"Go away. She's quarantined and contagious."

My voice caught in my throat, so near was I to sobbing. It was clear my charming disposition wasn't affecting Bruder in the least.

"Please, listen. Fannie and I love each other. I am here to demonstrate my willingness to sacrifice my work, even my life, for her. She must not despair, not lose hope. Please let me see her. I beg you."

"Go back to Debrecen. Fannie's in the care of her mother. There is no need for the agitation your presence may cause her."

He unbolted the door and held it open for me. There was nothing further to be said. Without another word, I left the shop and located my lodgings.

The next evening, Saturday, Fannie's mother answered the door at the house on Veres Útca.

"Azzony Bruder, please tell Fannie I'm here."

Bruder's voice boomed from the parlor, "Mama, close the door."

Before closing the door, Sarah whispered, "I'll tell her, Samuel."

I continued to present myself, daily, hoping for a change of heart. Unhappily, the door remained barred to me.

I learned later that my persistence gained sympathy with Fannie's mother, who pleaded with her husband on my behalf. "He's kind, and considerate. He's not cowed or intimidated by your bluster. He wants to take care of Fannie, nurse her at the bedside. This man is begging you to let him see the woman he loves. How can you be this callous? I know Fannie has told you she loves him. Perhaps, when she recovers and learns you sent him away, she'll hate you."

On the fourth morning, before daybreak, I paced in front of the shop, waiting for Bruder to arrive. At dawn, as a light rain fell, I watched him approach.

I said, "Good morning, Úr Bruder."

He gave no verbal response. His hooded eyes radiated malice, and I noted a muscle in his jaw begin to twitch. He unlocked the door, and I followed closely behind. He was a large man with an intimidating presence, but I was neither submissive nor combative.

"Please, Úr Bruder, let me speak from my heart. My father is a farmer, a simple man who raised me to be responsible and to respect the woman I love. I've completed secondary school and am apprenticed to one of Debrecen's finest tailors. The Master assures me of promotion to First Apprentice soon, perhaps on my twenty-fourth birthday in December."

He walked behind the butcher block. Above it, metal hooks hung from the ceiling, one with a heavy linen fabric draped over the tip, his butcher's blood-stained apron. Eyeing me with hatred from beneath the brim of his hat, he tied the fabric around his ample midsection. Slowly, he began scraping the edge of a fillet knife against a leather strop fastened to the block.

Uncertain of his intent, I watched him cautiously. I had to find a way to turn his rage into resignation, if not friendship. I was not his physical equal, but as a younger and well-built man, I could account for myself in a tussle. I would not be cowed. I squared my shoulders, assumed my full six-foot height, and without animosity returned Bruder's look. For a long moment, we faced each other, both understanding a compromise must be found for the sake of Fannie's love.

Doggedly, I plodded on; "Fannie and I love each other. We want to marry. Our dreams are in your hands. Please, Úr Bruder, allow me to see her."

It was as if a page had turned. His gaze no longer threatened. Laying the knife upon the block, his voice softened. "Alright, Samuel. Come tomorrow morning. We'll see how things progress after that."

At eight the next morning, Sarah Bruder welcomed me into the house, leading me through the kitchen. "Samuel don't be alarmed when you see her. Scabs all over her face, she's lost weight, her cheeks sunken. I bring her broth or tea every hour, but with the sores in her mouth, it's difficult to swallow. I insist and do get her to take a little, maybe just a thimbleful. I don't know what her body is surviving on. I'm so frightened we're going to lose her."

Following Sarah up the narrow stairs, I saw Fannie in the little bedroom resting on the white featherbed of her childhood. I stood mutely at the top of the stairs, and the sight of the sickbed and my beautiful Fannie suffering upon it was very distressing. The sun's rays, filtered through the oak leaves, covered my beloved in a dappled pattern of light. Under a crisp, linen sheet, she wore a white cotton gown, her hair secured with a remnant of paisley fabric. A damp cloth covered her eyes, her hands encased in bandages to prevent scratching at the lesions on her arms and face.

Sarah Bruder brought me a cup of tea and quickly left.

Moving closer, I could see how pale and thin she was, wasting away. I leaned over and softly called her name. "Fannie. Fannie, my dearest, please wake up. I'm here now, and my love is the medicine that will bring you back to me." She made small, whimpering noises. Tears ran a track down her cheeks. As I lifted the cloth covering her eyes, the sunlight caused her to wince.

Hurriedly, I tried to replace the protection. She brushed my hand away, whispering, "Leave it off, my darling, I want to see you." Squinting, she looked deeply into my eyes. "I knew you would find a way, Samuel."

Through my tears, I managed to say, "We will never be separated again, Fannie. You will recover and we'll be together always, my love. You are my life. Without you, there is nothing."

Kneeling beside the bed, I wrapped my arms around her as best I could, and we both wept.

With no space for a chair, I sat on the floor beside the bed. I spooned soup and read poetry. Her face was covered with black scabs. Morning, afternoon, and evening, I gently washed the crusts with warm milk and then applied a paste of crushed garlic, the Rebbetzin's secret remedy. Before leaving for my lodging, I spent a few minutes with Bruder, hoping to win him over. He was courteous, not warm. It was clear, for the love of his daughter, he was learning to accept a situation over which he had no control. Fannie improved every day, but it was expected the pox would leave her face deeply pitted.

After a fortnight, I returned to Debrecen.

At parting, Fannie told me, "Papa said you may make a good husband, after all."

Even with the favor of Fannie's youth, months of complete bedrest were required before she regained full vigor. Much improved by mid-March, she could not prepare adequately for certification examinations on the first of May. In April, Eva packed Fannie's clothes, books, and personal articles into two wooden crates. A drayman collected them for shipment to Nagy Karolyi. There was no reason to return to Debrecen.

For the next ten months, every Sunday, I rode the early train to visit Fannie, returning to Debrecen by midnight. We began planning our wedding, anticipating the lifetime of love fate surely had waiting for us.

Bruder may not have valued me as a son, yet, grudgingly, he recognized I would provide for and love his daughter for as long as I lived. As for Sarah Bruder, my romantic future mother-in-law, she was certain that my love, alone, had cured the pox and healed her daughter's face, on which only a few fading scars could be seen.

3

Moses received the Commandments from God, establishing the moral principles of human behavior and the basis for western civilization's system of justice.

Hebrew: You shall not murder.
Catholic Catechism: You shall not kill.
King James Protestant Bible: Thou shalt not kill.
Islam Quran: If anyone has killed one person, it is as if he had killed the whole mankind.
Orthodox Christian Archdiocese: You shall not kill.

All these faiths declare murder to be a sin against God, yet for centuries, Christians and Muslims have indoctrinated their followers with a libel against the Jews. They validate the Hebrew's faithful adherence to every commandment *except* "Thou Shalt Not Murder." The charge is specific in its interpretation. They claim the Jews practice ritual murder to obtain the blood of non-Jews for use in the baking of Passover matzo.

In the post-Enlightenment era, blood libel accusations continued in various locations. In particular, state-supported looting and burning of Jewish villages, called pogroms, were retribution for the murder of six-year-old, Gavriil Belostoksky. In 1820, the boy was canonized by the Russian Orthodox Church, delivering the highest credentials for perpetuating the myth.

A fourteen-year-old Catholic peasant girl lived in Tisza-Eszlár, a Hungarian river village thirty-six miles south of Debrecen. In April 1882, Ezster Solymosi disappeared. After an unsuccessful search, Győző Istóczy, a Member of Parliament, spread the charge of blood libel. Eszter's mother demanded the county notary, Jozsef Bary, investigate. No corpse, blood, or evidence was found at the synagogue. Still, twelve Jews were arrested.

Bary questioned Samuel Scharf, the five-year-old son of the cemetery's caretaker. Leading him with suggestion and bribing him with sweets, the boy 'confessed' he had been hiding in the synagogue and saw Eszter's murder. He said he watched the elders, his father, and fourteen-year-old brother, Móric, cut the girl's neck and drain her blood into a copper pot.

Móric was arrested and pleaded innocent, but beatings by the local safety officer convinced him to name co-conspirators. Three more Jews were arrested.

Two months later, Eszter's body washed up on a riverbank twenty miles west of Tisza-Eszlár, near the village of Dada. At first, Eszter's mother denied the corpse to be her daughter's, then admitted she recognized her clothing. At the burial in Tisza-Eszlár's Catholic cemetery, the priest distributed pamphlets provoking mob justice.

Károly Eötvös, a member of Budapest's House of Deputies, came forward to defend the Jews. Louis Kossuth, the leader of the failed 1848 Revolution, was a powerful voice for reason. In exile in Turin, Italy, Kossuth published opinion pieces in Hungarian newspapers calling ritual murder a medieval prejudice. Professors from the University of Budapest examined the exhumed body and found no evidence of ritual murder, no cut neck.

With only Mórics Sharf's coerced confession, the case could not be supported. After more than thirty lower court hearings, in July 1883, the Supreme Court unanimously acquitted and released all the prisoners.

Demonstrations calling for a retrial were held in Budapest and in the villages. The martyred girl's grave became a pilgrimage site. Had there, in fact, been a murder? Eszter's death might have been accidental. The truth will never be known, and the case remains a festering Hungarian wound.

Resurfaced, the ancient propaganda revealed its tenacity, brutality, and timeless appeal. Also exposed was the hypocrisy inherent in contemporary Hungary. Citizenship and personal liberty had been granted to the Jews by a modern-day government. The reality: Jewish equality was inconceivable in the hearts and minds of the people.

The Tisza-Eszlár affair forced my great-grandparents to examine the precarious situation of Hungarian Jews. The affair, and the violence it precipitated, altered the course of Fannie and Samuel's lives, changing the destiny of generations yet unborn.

Fannie

"This morning, Moshe delivered chickens from his family's farm in Dada. He says the day Solymosi's body washed up on the bank; two men fishing downstream were arrested. One was a local farmer, the other Moshe's cousin, a rabbi visiting from Budapest. The men were forced to dig a hole in the earthen floor of their cell. One policeman and Jew-hating volunteers threw them into the pit. Planks of wood, held in place with stones, sealed the opening. The men were left for two days. When dragged from the cavity, they begged for their lives, saying they were innocent."

Shocked, Mama held her kitchen towel to her mouth, her face ashen. "What did they do to them?" Papa continued, "The rabbi's head was held under the water in the rain barrel until he passed out. Throwing him to the floor, they waited for him to breathe and questioned him again. His head was returned to the barrel after each denial. In the end, he was drowned. The dead man and his cousin, still alive, were buried in the cell vault they had been forced to dig. There was no investigation."

Mama began to weep. "Oh, my God, Sándor. How can this be happening in modern times?"

Papa said quietly, "Things will calm down, eventually. We must be careful not to provoke the Gentiles. Just mind our own affairs, keep to ourselves."

For the rest of the week, there was unease in the house. Not wishing to encourage Mama's sense of the dramatic, Papa had little to say at dinner. For the rest of the evening, in his parlor, there was no discussion of the turmoil. Papa sipped a glass of schnapps and read his newspaper. Mama crocheted while I read a book of János Arany, the Hungarian Shakespeare of ballads. I mouthed the delicious words without a sound because Papa would not approve of so much as a whisper: "In dreams and in love there are no impossibilities..."

One Sunday, Samuel told me, "In Debrecen, crowds gathered at the courthouse and St. Anne's Catholic Church. They demanded the execution of the Jews who murdered Solymosi."

Optimistically, I said, "I read that a gathering of students at the Calvinist College stood in silent vigil, with signs demanding the government arrest the blood libel fanatics and release the Jews. That's good news, Samuel. There *are* good Hungarians, too."

"There were less than twenty students, Fannie. Only a handful of "good" Hungarians. And, another thing. No police came to protect them when a gang of louts beat them with sticks. The students ran for their lives, and I doubt they'll congregate again. I can't say whether the majority of the people agree with the students yet remain silent behind closed doors, or the majority of the people are simply Jew haters."

"I'm frightened, Samuel. I worry about you alone in that big city. Would you consider moving in with Uncle Ezekiel and Aunt Eva? At least someone will know that you've arrived home after a day's work."

"I'll be alright. I can account for myself in a fight, Fannie. Anyway, who's to know I'm Jewish? I walk with purpose, head high, eyes ahead. I appear a young, prosperous city dweller. I'm tall and dressed in the latest fashion." He added, laughing, "They'd have to pull my pants down to find out!"

I didn't find that humorous.

I worried about Samuel in Debrecen, yet an incident in Nagy Karolyi forced me to confront the grave reality of our situation. An anonymous letter had been pushed under our neighbor's door, demanding, "Murderous Jews! Go back to Poland, where you belong." Tamas Farkas owned a dry goods store on Magtár Utca. 'Go back to Poland?' Tamas is a descendant of generations born in Zemplen County, near the village where Samuel was raised.

Thugs prowled the streets in the Jewish neighborhoods after dark, eager to encounter and brutalize anyone out and about. A meeting at the synagogue was attended by over a hundred men. Groups were organized to escort shopkeepers to and from their workplace and patrol our streets through the night.

Papa appeared unworried, but Mama begged him to close his shop before dark.

He told Mama, "It's alright, Sarah. Everything will return to normal once the Jews are released. This is not olden times. Modern laws will end the issue of ritual murder once and for all. I have faith in Parliament and the judges. It's the nineteenth century, for God's sake! There's no place for such belief." He paused for a moment; his face red with anger. "And, the world relies on money, commerce. The Jews provide economic and cultural benefits to the government. And don't forget, the imprisoned accused are innocent. These things take time. Justice will prevail." Mama kept quiet while he raged and vented his support for modern Hungarian society.

Powerless in the public arena, we found security in our home, with family. In our little world, life's blessings continued. There was a wedding to arrange!

Seventy years earlier, Grandmamá Einhorn designed and sewed her wedding dress by hand. My Mama wore it when she and Papa were married. Now, Mama altered it for me, adding three inches to the hem and opening two darts at the midriff.

Influenced by Queen Victoria and Napoleon's Marie Louise, the dress was of sheer white muslin embroidered with silk cross-stitch and knots. Floor length, it had a high waist, belted under the bosom, square neckline, and short sleeves. The semi transparent gown overlaid an underdress, for modesty.

Mama and Samuel's sister, Etel, kept a brisk correspondence for months, coordinating arrangements.

On Sunday, August 3, 1884, Papa fastened his mother's amber bead necklace around my neck and escorted me to the garden, where I would become Samuel's wife.

The white oak's leafy branches towered over the crocheted wedding canopy under which we stood. Mama's sister, Clara, and her two daughters, Uncle Ezekiel, Aunt Eva, and Abe; Jakob Freed, all of Samuel's siblings, and Cousin Max, witnessed the ceremony.

Rabbi Strauss read our Katuba, the Hebrew marriage contract. From under my veil, I looked beyond the rabbi at Mama and my sisters-in-law to all the women standing in the garden with white lace squares covering their heads. Filled with love for Samuel and me, and remembering their own wedding days, many eyes glistened with tears.

Drawn to Mama's gaze, we nodded. Both of us understood if it wasn't for her belief in the triumph of love, this day might never have come to pass. Wordlessly, I mouthed, "Thank you, Mama." She answered with a smile.

Even with no understanding of Hebrew, the melodies blanketed me, as they had for millions of women for thousands of years. This day, at this moment, I entered the sisterhood of the Jewish matriarchy. When the Katuba had been read and we signed our names, we drank wine from a silver cup. Samuel placed a gold band on my finger. Only then did he raise my veil to kiss my lips. We were man and wife.

A glass wrapped in white cotton was placed on the ground. Samuel smashed it to pieces with his heel. Some say it's a symbolic reminder of the destruction of the ancient temple; others that despite the joy of the moment, it is an occasion to reflect upon the fragility of man's mortality. Everyone shouted, "Mazel Tov!"

As a wedding toast and an inspiration for me, Rabbi Strauss quoted lines from King Solomon's brilliant poem, A Woman of Valor. "She is more precious than rubies and the heart of her husband trusts in her. She does him good every day of her life. She faces whatever may come with wisdom and loving kindness. Her children rise up to call her blessed. Wherever people gather, her deeds speak her praise." His arm around my waist, Samuel held me close as we listened, blissful.

He kissed my cheek and whispered, "You are more precious than diamonds, my darling. Our future shines bright in your reflection. I'll love you through eternity."

Following the luncheon, our guests bid us a happy future, each placing a forint or two in my purse.

Our parents came along with us to the train depot.

My new father-in-law, Jakob, hugged Samuel and turned to me. "Take good care of each other. Never go to bed angry. Always love each other." I kissed his cheek and said, "I promise to love Samuel for all time."

Mama hugged me, whispering, "Be happy, my darling. Love each other."

Papa shook Samuel's hand. "I have given you my greatest possession. Take care of my girl." To me, he said, "I love you, dearest daughter. Be happy and live well. I am here if you need me, always."

"Thank you, Papa. I know you're unhappy we are going to Debrecen, but distance cannot remove you from my heart, where you will be every day." I kissed his cheek, leaving his embrace to take Samuel's hand and walk across the platform.

Samuel lit the oil lamp on the bedside table, keeping the wick tightly wound to maintain the softest glow upon the linen. Quickly undressing, he climbed between the sheets. Reclining against the pillows, he appeared as a young prince observing his realm. I turned my back to him and removed my shirtwaist and undergarments. Slipping into the white lace nightdress Mama had sewn, I walked slowly toward the bed.

The long wait over, we celebrated our passion with ardor, tenderness, and grateful tears for the triumph of our love. I discovered, with Samuel, satisfaction, and fulfillment in the sensuality of my body. Physical love was everything I'd hoped for. A blending of hearts, bodies, and minds, fearlessly trusting the exposure of our very souls to one another.

In the morning, after coffee, I opened the window to watch my new husband walk purposefully or, perhaps, "swagger" is a better descriptive. After tidying up, I left the flat to explore the neighborhood. The shops were varied and well-stocked. Introducing myself to the local merchants as "Azzony (Mrs.) Freed, the new tenant in the building on the square," I had arrived at womanhood, married.

I set about making our two-room flat a home, sewing curtains from claret-colored lining fabric Samuel brought from The Emporium. I embroidered floral borders on our pillow casings, scrubbed the windows until they appeared unglazed! Like children, we played at house and found joy in the wonder of being together. Every day was brilliant, never dull. We were a real wife and a real husband, making a brand-new life together where there had been none.

I served Mama's recipes by candlelight at our little table. Most evenings, dessert was enjoyed in the afterglow of love making.

Inside our nest, the world was bliss. Outside our walls, although the Supreme Court had acquitted the Jews almost a year earlier, Hungary still roiled over the Tisza-Eszlár murder. It was a rare day to find the Debrecen-Értesitő newspaper free of anti-Jewish editorial comment and accounts of vandalism and assault. Lest they be mistaken for a Jew, city dwellers hurried from work to the safety of their homes, their silence an approval of the bias.

We no longer spent Sunday afternoons relaxing at a café or walking the promenade. Groups of toughs roamed the boulevards and walked brazenly through coffeehouses, threatening clientele with their very presence. Tenants in our building assumed we were Jews. At best, when meeting a neighbor in the stairwell or courtyard, I might receive a terse "Szia," a hello, but nothing further—not even a comment about the weather. There was no tip of the hat, no "Jó reggelt, good morning," at the bakery or other shops.

But, how did they know we were Jews? The building was not in a Jewish neighborhood. We didn't affiliate with any synagogue, did not observe the Sabbath, and did not frequent kosher shopkeepers. We wore no adornments with Hebrew lettering or a Star of David, did not speak Yiddish. We were Hungarians; born, raised, and educated. Why did Samuel and I threaten our neighbors so viscerally? Why did this fear and hatred, loathing reside within our fellow-countrymen?

One afternoon, I visited Zsófia Kovács, the milliner. "Hello, Fannie! How's married life?" I replied, "All is fine, thank you. I stopped by for a few hatpins, Zsófia." Casually, she mentioned, "Such a pleasant surprise to have met your husband, Samuel, at The Emporium. He's designing a fur-collared winter coat for my husband. My brother-in-law swears by the attention to detail you Jews are blessed with and highly recommended your husband. When Samuel said he lived with his new bride only two blocks from my millinery, I said, 'My goodness! I know your wife, Fannie!'"

Zsófia must have thought it her duty to inform the local merchants that I was a Jew. Neither she nor the others refused to serve me, my contamination was kept at arm's length. No matter when I entered a queue, I was the last to be served.

One day, the grocer said, "Those figs are on reserve for another customer." It was a lie. I asked myself, "Why is this happening?"

Unreasonably rooted in their beliefs for centuries, they detest and fear our tribe. So, I learned, firsthand, how prejudice is passed from one to another, no explanation needed. At last, I recognized, as my ancestors had done, that I had never been a part of the society into which I had been born.

In October, I knew I was with child, and our attention focused on the joyous mystery of the new life our love had created.

The Emporium closed for three days at Christmas, giving us an opportunity to celebrate Samuel's twenty-fifth birthday with my parents and to bring the news of my pregnancy. Immediately upon arrival, Samuel happily declared, "Papa Bruder, you're going to be a Grandpapa!"

Mama embraced both of us, and Papa clasped Samuel's hands between his. It was midafternoon, but Papa set the glasses out for a celebratory brandy. "We drink to the future! To a healthy and happy life for us all: my Sarah, my beautiful Fannie, our Samuel, and my grandchild!"

Clearing the dinner dishes, I told Mama, "I want midwife Jennie to attend the birth if she's available." Mama said, "I'll be sure she enters your name on her calendar for next summer. She'll be thrilled to hear the news. Oh, my darling, I'm so happy. A Grandmamá!"

The pregnancy was uneventful. I felt healthier than ever before in my life. At the end of June, I traveled to Mama's to await my confinement. On July 24, 1885, a four-hour labor began. Jozsef was sent from the butcher shop to summon Samuel in Debrecen.

I relaxed through the ordeal, "listening" to my body's instruction. In the late afternoon, with little fanfare and no complication, Albert was delivered in Mama's bed by Jennie, now well into her sixties.

On the eighth day, a male child enters the Jewish community through the Covenant of Circumcision. The Bris is an ancient ritual in which the foreskin of the penis is removed to identify members of the tribe. Assimilated, secular, and ignorant of Jewish dogma, I felt it a pretense. I told Papa, "We're Hungarians. We know nothing of Judaism, nothing at all. This is a barbaric ritual promoting the idea that

Jews are special, chosen, by God. By inference, non-Jews are unworthy, and these secret rites feed into the hatred. Further, this disfigurement does not foster assimilation. My Jewish son will be instantly identifiable, putting him at risk in these perilous times."

Papa won the argument, insisting on participation in religious tradition at life's events: birth, marriage, death. "You were married by a rabbi, weren't you, Fannie? Remember, no matter how tightly we are woven into the national fabric, in the end," he paused for emphasis, "We are Jews." Surprisingly, Samuel sided with Papa. At first, I thought he wished to avoid a scene and then remembered a compelling moment at our wedding. I had experienced an intense spiritual pleasure, taking my place among the women. Perhaps Samuel was identifying with the centuries-old patriarchy and its connection to his own son. Mama, too, didn't agree with me. So, I yielded to the pressure and seduction of tribalism. Apparently, belonging to a religious denomination did not require complete immersion or fanaticism. I was authentic even with the thinnest of credentials, an accident of birth. I could call myself an agnostic, atheist, even pagan. I was a Jewess, nonetheless.

A single chair stood at Mama's linen-covered kitchen table, around which the men gathered. The seat was reserved for the Sandek, godfather, who held the baby's legs immobile while the foreskin was removed by surgical knife. My father-in-law, Jakob, was given that honor. The women gathered in Papa's parlor, with the door closed. I could hear Rabbi Straus and Mohel Rosenthal, the Rabbi trained to perform the rite, chanting prayers in the next room. I wanted to see what was happening, but Mama and the others wouldn't allow it. Women were strictly segregated from men in all Orthodox services. To comfort me, some of the women related accounts of their own experiences and how to care for Albert's petzel in the days ahead.

Aunt Eva said, "Cover the wound with a clean cloth. Don't allow urine to soak the area for too long. After two or three days, expose him to the air. Usually, there is little discomfort for the baby; his mother is more distressed!" Mama and the others laughed, but I found little amusing in subjecting my baby to this surgical mutilation.

Hearing Albert cry, my breasts began to lactate. I tried to leave the room, go to him, but was led back to the settee. To calm my anxiety, I was told the baby was kept comfortable, anesthetized by sucking a wine-soaked bit of cloth during the procedure. After ten minutes, we heard a chorus of "Mazel Tov!" from the men, declaring the ordeal over. The women opened the door and began preparing a celebratory lunch.

Papa came to find me in the parlor where I was nursing the baby. "Fannie. I must tell you what happened!" "What is it, Papa, is the baby alright? Did something go wrong?" "No, Fannie, everything is fine. Your husband had to leave the room! Samuel almost fainted when he saw the Mohel's scalpel. Abe and I had to help him to a place with no direct view of the table!" He continued, laughing. "And then, he drank two glasses of vodka. I think he's drunk." When it concerned Samuel, Papa was always ready to find fault. I said, "Papa, can't you be supportive of Samuel just once? Of course, he was nervous. That tiny baby is his son, Papa. Even with your bloody vocation, you may not have been able to watch gruesome surgery performed on your son, either. Fortunately for you, I was a girl." I closed my eyes to signal my displeasure, and he treaded softly from the room. A moment later, Samuel joined me on the settee. We fell asleep, with Albert swaddled tightly in a cotton blanket, content on my bosom.

The aroma of onion and cabbage sautéing in butter soon filled the house. Mama added a little sugar before tossing cooked noodles into the pan, releasing a subtle sweetness to the dish so typical of Hungary's cookery. Quartered chickens, onion, spicy paprika, and broken fresh tomatoes simmered on the stove. A little cream would be added to the paprikash before serving. Stewed squash, tomatoes, and peppers fresh from Mama's Garden sent their fragrant message of community and love. Of course, there was tea, apricot and cherry fruit soup, and Mama's strudel. Delicious!

Two days later, we returned to Debrecen. The baby was unbothered by the wound, which healed in less than a week. My milk was plentiful and nourishing. My body healed rapidly from the trauma of childbirth. All the same, for no apparent reason, I felt a great sadness and wept without provocation. The weight of physical exhaustion bore down on every minute of the day and night. I was overwhelmed. There was no personal time to bathe or care for myself. The endless cycle of shopping, cleaning, meal preparation, washing clothes and diapers, and nursing almost continuously smothered me. Some days, I never dressed or bathed at all, lying about in despair.

On Sunday, Samuel helped with meals and the baby's care, but my spirits were down. "Why did we have a baby? This world is too dangerous for us to offer a child a happy life." "Fannie, darling, everything will return to normal. The Jews have been in Hungary for centuries; we'll be here tomorrow. You mustn't worry about these things. Just concentrate on taking care of Albert and me. That's all you need do."

My nerves were always on edge. I begged Samuel not to go to work, fearing he'd be murdered. Worried, Samuel wrote to Mama, asking for her help.

Arriving on the next evening's train, she took charge of the scene. There was barely room for our little family, yet we didn't mind the inconvenience. I needed my Mama. "Fannie, it's common to have a few gloomy weeks after giving birth. Don't be alarmed; it will go away." I confessed, "Mama, I'm so downhearted. I brought a child into a world in which he will never be welcome. A superficial civility thinly covers the Gentile's loathing. Even our building's janitor, Adorján, doesn't accept me. He says, 'Good morning, Madame. How is the little darling today?' I'm suspicious of the brawny dolt and his seemingly friendly nature. But, Mama, why should I question his intention? I was always trusting of the world, happy. Everyone can't hate us, can they? Will I ever be myself again?" "Samuel is secure in his employ, and you will be alright. Everything will return to normal, even Papa says so. Be patient, my darling."

Mama stayed with us for a month. She left when Albert was sleeping through the night, and I began to regain my confidence.

It was autumn, a time to put things in order, to make our nest secure for the storms to come. Albert had a robust appetite and curiosity for his world. I loved him more than I knew was possible. I loved him so much it could bring me to tears.

Cousin Abe moved to Budapest, working as a law clerk for Eduard Szeyffert, the State Attorney General. In Debrecen, we all missed Abe's presence, so Samuel and I dined with Uncle Ezekiel and Aunt Eva every Sunday. Eva's spirits were buoyed by Albert, her surrogate grandchild. We attended a Passover celebration at the Neolog Synagogue to which they belonged. The congregation was lively and offered activities other than worship: current event discussion groups, even cooking demonstrations. That Samuel worked on the Sabbath, we spoke no Hebrew or Yiddish, and didn't observe the rules of Kashrut/Kosher, were of no consequence to the Neologs. The majority of the membership was of young families with whom we shared the insecurities of public sentiment and suspicion. We joined the congregation during the summer of 1886. Conversation and companionship with other young women made life in Debrecen so much easier, so much happier.

On May 4, 1887, the careless use of petrol in preparing charcoal caused a fire in Nagy Karolyi. Destroyed were Count Karolyi's family estate and mansion, twenty-five large workshops, and two hundred twenty-five other buildings.

Bruder's Fine Provisions and our house escaped the flames. Papa served on the bucket brigade, saving the city administration building. The fire smoldered for more than a week, displacing hundreds of citizens. Fifty-three people died from inhaling smoke, as did four children trapped in an attic room. At the time of the disaster, Mama was in Debrecen, caring for Albert while I awaited the onset of labor for the birth of my second child.

On Friday, May 6, Morris, weighing a robust ten pounds, was born at the Debrecen hospital. Eight days later, his Bris and naming took place at the Neolog Synagogue in a room designated for such rites.

Papa arrived on the morning of the celebration, in time to serve as Morris' Sandek. In spite of his oversized self-confidence, he was uneasy. "Fannie, he's like a little chicken. I'm afraid my big paws will press too tightly on his legs and injure him for life. This is a terrible responsibility!" When it was over, fighting back tears, Papa carried the blanket-wrapped baby to me. "Thank you, Fannie. I am blessed that you are my daughter."

In an adjacent Kiddush room, we celebrated with schnapps and a lunch of salads, herring, and fresh baked challah bread. Uncle Ezekiel, Aunt Eva, Abe, Max, and a dozen couples from the congregation attended. As a wonderful surprise, Jakob Freed and Samuel's sisters, Rozsa, Sali, and Hani, made the trip from Tolcsva.

My stress was not lessened having had the experience of Albert's Bris. I hoped the next child would be a girl.

Thankfully, I suffered no difficulties after Morris's birth. Healthy and energetic, I welcomed the tasks of wife and mother. The baby was placid, happy to nurse and sleep. At two years old, Albert, only a baby himself, delighted in fetching blanket or diaper, if needed. It was in his nature to be the responsible big brother and my helpmate. Afternoons, the three of us napped together in the big bed.

After dinner, with the boys asleep, Samuel and I talked about the worsening situation at The Emporium. He told me, "No matter that I avoid responding to the vitriol, it's a hostile environment. The only other Jew, Andrew, has decided Hungary is too dangerous, and is moving his family to Croatia."

At the retirement of the Master Tailor, his position was awarded to a lower assistant. Samuel was furious, and deeply offended. "Regardless of promises made, I've been betrayed. Balázs accepted my resignation without a protest." "I hope you haven't made a reckless decision, Samuel. We've built a life here, with Uncle Ezekiel, Aunt Eva and our Neolog friends. There's no guarantee another location will be an improvement."

"My mind is made up. We're moving to Budapest to live among our own. I know you'll worry about your parents; nevertheless, we must do what is best for *our* family, you, me, Albert and Morris."

"I understand, my dearest. You've been treated unfairly. I'll go wherever we'll all be safe. I trust your decision."

Samuel

I was happy, in love, anticipating my wedding, beginning life with Fannie. I'd built a good reputation as First Assistant to the Master Tailor. My future was bright.

The Tisza-Eszlár affair cast a pall over every Hungarian, Jew, and Gentile. The upheaval and violence caused by Solymosi's death stirred the entire country. Voices from Debrecen's university and government called for calm and reason. On the other hand, newspapers condemned the accused. One editorial claimed, "Using technicalities in the law, the Jews are getting away with murdering Christian children. Where is the justice for Ezster?"

Blood libel, ritual murder? How could anyone living in nineteenth century Hungary take it seriously? As the case was thrown out of the lower courts, the uneducated and indoctrinated peasants grew more intense in their hatred and violence.

My family in Tolcsva feared for their lives. Father hid behind doors braced with furniture, holding tightly to his hunting rifle. One Sunday afternoon, men with whom he had lived in peace for decades put a torch to the subterranean storage cellar and stole his chickens.

For myself, I felt no panic. My workplace was stable, and the Master showed no signs of bias. The salesmen, fabric buyers, and office workers were an outspoken lot, given to overheated opinions about the Solymosi case. Thankfully, they had little contact with the cutters and tailors, who kept mind and hands focused on work. Believing sanity would win out, I refused participation in the venomous dialogue of the day.

Only one other Jew was employed at The Emporium, Andrew Tóth, a mild-mannered bookkeeper, easy prey to the rowdy sales group. "Why don't you go back to wherever you came from, Tóth?" They laughed in his face when he said, "I'm named for King Andrew III. I'm a native-born Hungarian, not an immigrant."

Tóth told me, "Samuel, we're moving to Kopács, in Croatia. My brother-in-law offered me a job at his small factory. My family is here, but the safety of our three children comes first. The Christians want to kill us all. You should leave, too. You're young, just starting out. You must accept there's no future here for us." "We were hated before. We just didn't know how much. I must believe the courts will condemn the libel charges and people will come to their senses. They're not all peasants, you know." "Yes, I know, Samuel, not *all*. Just *most*."

On the train to Nagy Karolyi, four mill workers were seated in my compartment. Conversation quickly turned to Ezster and the Jews. I focused on my newspaper.

"We should throw the foreman in the river. Why should that Jew give orders to men like us?" His mate replied, "He forgets who he is. Look at history. They've been thrown out of every country; they caused the Black Plague. Why does Hungary let them run all the businesses?"

"There's a family on our street. Why can't they stay with their own kind? The government should never have let those murderers leave the estates, should have left them as slaves." The red-haired man said, "Men like us, not the courts, should be deciding what to do with the Jews who killed Ezster; the whole mess would be over already, the filth hanging from trees." Feigning sleep, I rested my head against the window, keeping my eyes closed until we reached Nagy Karolyi.

Fannie was fully recovered and planning our summer wedding. She worried about me, suggesting I move in with her uncle. In reality, neither Debrecen nor Nagy Karolyi was safe for Jews. Threats and vandalism plagued the small town. Sarah was begging Bruder to close his business before dark. She asked me, "Is it worth the risk just to earn a few forints? Every evening, with a nervous stomach, I stand for two hours at the parlor window, watching for him. Will you talk to him, Samuel?" "Mama, he has a Gentile clientele loyal to his shop. Many stop for meat on their way home from work. His door must be open or lose their business for good. You and Fannie are worried with good reason, but don't panic. Your men are smart and strong; we'll be alright."

Fannie and I sat on the settee, my arm about her shoulders. I turned to kiss her. Preoccupied, she didn't respond. "I understand you're worried, but like your father, I must work. I can't hide under my bed. I skimp on everything, so we'll have money for rent and furniture after the wedding. My lodgings are the cheapest I can find. I've given up the occasional beer. Every kreuzer and forint that can be spared is put into the leather pouch hidden behind my chifforobe. My life is work, sleep, and visiting you on Sunday. On this one day, I don't want to hear how dangerous it is in Debrecen. I need you to focus on *us*. *We* are the center of the universe, not Ezster Solymosi!"

"I'm sorry, Samuel. Being confined to this house with Mama agonizing about being murdered in our beds has taken its toll. I promise not to cause you any more worry. And Samuel, I trust you know how to conduct yourself safely in the city."

The women made an effort not to dwell on the menace. They busied themselves with wedding preparations, and the months passed quickly.

Assistant Takás tailored my wedding suit of dark grey English wool. The Master himself did the final fitting, then generously offered the fabric and manufacture as a gift.

On Sunday, August 3, 1884, in the Bruder's garden, we stood under the canopy crocheted by my Grandmamá for my parents. I was the third of my siblings to be blessed under this Chuppah. The four corners, tied to long poles, were raised to create a symbolic roof for our home, under which the rabbi, Fannie and I, and our fathers stood. My brothers, Izak and Abe, and cousins, Abe, and Max, were honored to support the corners.

The Ketubah was read, and Fannie and I signed our names. The Seven Benedictions were recited, and after the rabbi blessed the wine, I drank from the silver cup before bringing it to her lips. Placing a gold ring on the index finger of Fannie's right hand, I declared: "With this ring, you are consecrated to me according to the law of Moses and Israel." Raising her veil, I kissed her lips. We were man and wife. With one firm, stomping motion, I smashed the glass, and everyone shouted, "Mazel Tov."

My brother, Abe, played his fiddle, and, after lunch, Fannie and I took the evening train to Debrecen, arriving at our flat as the tenth hour was announced by church bells all over the city.

Lighting the bedside lamp, I undressed quickly. The handsome, wine-colored nightshirt Max had given me as a wedding gift lay in a heap on the chair. Sliding naked between the sheets, my eyes became accustomed to the shadows where my wife, her back turned to me, disrobed. Having waited four years for this night, I resolved to relish every moment.

I held out my arms to her and she came to sit on the edge of the bed. I kissed her forehead, eyelids, her mouth. "Samuel, I don't know what to do, what is expected of me. I hope I won't disappoint with my ignorance."

"My darling, don't worry," I said. "Our love will guide us. There is no text, only desire and joy."

She removed her nightdress and lay beside me. Her skin against mine transmitted an extraordinary sensation. My every pore was excited by her smoothness. Our kisses, gentle at first, became demanding in our lust. There was nothing awkward about our movements. We were lost in each other's taste, smell, and touch. At first, her fingers traced the muscles of my back. Then, increasing the tactile intensity, her hands pulled me closer. When I entered her, the temperature and moistness of her body caused me to stop breathing. We looked into one another's eyes. We were coupled, one single body. I felt I had been devoured.

She whispered, "Samuel, we are a concert of harmony and rhythm. I love you so." Unable to bear another movement, we were grateful for the release of erotic tension. Lying in each other's arms, I could feel her excited heartbeat return to a normal pace.

"Are you alright, Fannie? Is there discomfort?" She giggled. "Not at all, husband. It was thrilling. I feel I've descended from heaven." Smiling broadly, she said, "I'm starving. Is there anything to eat in the icebox?" I laughed, "There's only the wedding cake we brought back with us. Oh, there's brandy to help swallow that dry pastry!"

Naked, and in bed, we ate cake with our fingers and shared the liquor from a coffee cup.

"Samuel, must you work tomorrow? Perhaps you'll send a message you're unwell and we can spend the whole day in bed!"

Dawn's light brought reality into the room. I was a man with a wife to protect, be responsible for, and the only place in the world she was truly safe was in our own bed. I kissed her sleeping eyelids. "Good morning, wife. Stay in bed. I'll dress, make coffee, and leave." She smiled, pulling me to her, arousing me again. I whispered, "I'll be late to work." She raised the sheet to expose her body. Why would I resist? This is what I had hoped for.

Wrapped in my nightshirt, she prepared coffee. Watching her at a wifely chore, I was a husband swelling with happiness. With a farewell kiss, I left for work.

Our two-room flat was Eden, a sanctuary at the end of my day.

Fannie navigated the neighborhood, finding grocer, baker, and butcher. Each evening meal was delicious, the table spread with cloth and set with candles. She was eager to hear of my day and to make love.

On the very first morning, she met the woman from the next flat, Mrs. Kardos. Smiling back at her icy stare, Fannie said, "Hello, I'm Azzony Freed." Without a word, the woman walked away. "Why do they hate us, Samuel? How are we different from anyone else?" "It's been this way for centuries. There's nothing we can do to change things; to hell with the outside world!"

Two months later, Fannie was pregnant, and we were ecstatic.

At work, there was ugliness. Bigotry was tolerated where it had not been before. In the employee cloak room, two buyers were chatting. "Did you see how Rosenstadt tried to Jew me down this morning?" The remark was not whispered, was not taken to task. The others remained silent, unperturbed. Even with Jewish representatives in the Legislature and families titled by the Crown, it was clear Hungary's tolerance had ended with Tisza-Eszlár.

At Christmas, we celebrated my twenty-fifth birthday and the news of the baby with Bruder and Sarah. In the kitchen, the women chattered about babies and birthing. In the parlor, Bruder and I shared stories of street violence we dared not tell the women. It was decided Fannie would spend June and July with her parents to be near midwife Jennie.

Spring was a busy season at work, fashion demanded new suiting.

Bruder's helper, Jozsef, came to fetch me when Fannie entered her confinement. I arrived two hours after Albert was born, on Friday, July 24, 1885.

"Samuel, I don't want our son circumcised. This ritual has no logic. Give me one good reason why he should be mutilated?" "Fannie, no matter what you believe or don't believe, we've been born into the tribe. I agree with your father that traditional rituals should be observed. As the child's father, I don't want to argue about this."

So, it followed that Albert received his Hebrew name and the mark of a Jewish man.

Rabbi Straus intoned, "Welcome Avraham ben Schumuel ha-Kohein." Albert, son of Samuel, of the tribe of Kings, wore a white gown. The child was placed upon a pillow, which I carried around the room, presenting him to each of the men.

My father took the baby to the table. As Sandek, his task was to hold the child immobile. He removed Albert's gown and laid the naked baby on the cloth.

I stood between Abe and Bruder, behind my father's chair.

Rabbi Straus began praying. Mohel Rosenthal removed his scalpel from a small case. When a bit of wine-saturated cloth was placed near Albert's mouth, the baby immediately began sucking on it. Then, using a piece of cotton soaked with a boric acid solution, the Mohel swabbed Albert's penis.

Turning to Abe, I said, "I need to sit down. I feel dizzy and nauseous." Abe and my father-in-law laughed and steered me from the table to a chair at the end of the hall. Bruder said, "You're a tailor, Samuel, not used to the sight of blood. This will be over in a few minutes, and your son will sleep from the wine. You also need something to calm your nerves. I'll bring you some schnapps." I had two small glasses of vodka and hung my head between my legs. It was embarrassing, but I was thinking, "Fannie was right. Why do this to a little baby?"

A lunch was served, for which I had no appetite. For most of the afternoon, I slept on the settee with Fannie and Albert.

Suffering a bad headache, I was relieved not to have to return to Debrecen for another two days. This was too much excitement for all of us.

Our lives were upside-down, with no night or day. Exhausted from lack of sleep, I watched Fannie struggle to cope with her new duties.

"Please don't go to work today, Samuel. I'm so tired, and I worry I'm doing everything wrong. Maybe I wasn't meant to be a mother." She began to cry. "Oh, Samuel, I'm so afraid when you're not home. What if you are set upon by thugs? What if I accidentally drop the baby on the floor?"

I did my best to comfort her, but I couldn't stay home. Describing Fannie's misery, I sent Sarah a post. Eva helped for a day until Sarah arrived.

She told me, "Don't fret. Melancholy is not uncommon after a confinement. Giving birth tests every system of the body; it takes time to correct itself. Fannie will come around, I promise you."

She was right, of course. After a month, Sarah returned to Bruder.

We dined with Eva and Ezekiel every Sunday and were included for Passover at their Neolog Synagogue. I told Fannie, "I know it's important to make friends, but I am not going to services, nor will I stop working on Saturday." She said, "I know you won't, dearest. I think, though, since we've been ignored by the neighbors, we need this community. *I* need this, Samuel.

"There are no requirements for membership. We'll be social members, not praying members. The leadership is alright with that."

How was I to argue?

In 1887, a fire destroyed most of Nagy Karolyi. Fortunately, Bruder's shop and house escaped the flames. Sarah was with us at the time, caring for Albert while Fannie awaited confinement with our second child. On Friday, May 6, ten-pound Morris was born at the Debrecen Hospital.

Bruder arrived at the Neolog Synagogue on the morning of Morris' bris. This time, taking the seat at the head of the table, pale and uncomfortable, he was the Sandek. My father, and sisters Rozsa, Sali, and Hani came from Tolcsva.

We were a family of four, and Fannie suffered no melancholy.

"The fönök Balázs told me Master Horváth is retiring, and Takás, my assistant, will be promoted, not me. Balázs had the nerve to say my work has been shoddy. He said Úr Molnár, the bank president, had complained to him about a collar facing not lying perfectly flat. Takás will complete the tailoring of his new evening jacket, the one I've already cut and pinned! Molnár has been my customer for three years. This is not about my work, it's about my Jewishness.

"Regardless of my talent and promises made, I've been betrayed. I'll not accept the treachery. I told him, 'Please don't insult my intelligence, Úr Balázs. I'm grateful for having been in your employ for seven years. Horváth pledged I would succeed him, a pledge *you* are not honoring. I cannot remain here, subordinate to my own assistant. I'll finish the two garments on my workbench and resign my position.' Oh, he was *so sorry* about the *misunderstanding*, yet promptly accepted my notice without further discussion."

Fannie agreed moving to Budapest would be safer, where almost twenty percent of the population were honfitárs, lanzsmen. "I feel I'm abandoning my parents, Samuel. They'll never move to Budapest as long as Papa keeps the shop. And Mama is fifty-four. Who knows how much longer she'll live?"

I told her, "They're a train ride away. Your mother will come, and we'll visit them. I've already spoken to your father about moving. He said he's 'too old to start over,' but 'we must do what's best for our family.'" Fighting tears, Fannie leaned on my shoulder. "There's no family in Nagy Karolyi, only neighbors and customers. We're all they have." "I will not live my life cowering to the bigots at work. I know you love your parents, but we must do what is best for our family, you, me, Albert, and Morris."

Amidst all the uncertainty, one option was clear: there was relative safety among the lanzsmen in Budapest.

4

Vienna was the cultural and intellectual center of the Habsburg's dual Austro-Hungarian monarchy.

The constitutional union was formed in 1867 as a concession to the Hungarians after their failed War of Independence. Only foreign affairs and the military remained common to the "co-equals." All other government responsibilities were administered by each state individually.

Architecturally, Budapest, the city on the Danube, rivaled Paris' grand boulevards, promenades, and bridges.

Budapest thumbed its nose at Old World society. Vienna was regarded as the dowager aunt to Budapest's contemporary young woman. Its free-spirited, nonconformist music halls, cabarets and coffeehouses resembled those of Berlin.

The glorious Ungar, the equestrian conqueror gazing from the Steppes toward the great plain was the true Hungarian. This mythology did not include the Jews.

By the final decade of the nineteenth century, Budapest had transformed from a German-speaking small town into a Hungarian-speaking metropolis. Twenty-three percent of its four hundred fifty thousand inhabitants were Jews.

The term "Judapest" was coined to infer the ethnic influence over the city's cultural life. Derogatory and toxic, the label implied a putrid foreign infiltration. Although the majority of Budapest's Jews had eagerly adopted conversion or secularization to attain equal opportunity, an unequal result evolved.

A well-defined code of behavior was followed between Jew and Gentile. At every social level, the Jews practiced "tapintat," tactfulness, a mask of incomprehension and silence when anti-Semitism was encountered.

Although a large Jewish middle class developed, their interactions with non-Jews related primarily to business. Social classes mixed only in the vibrant Bohemian, music hall and cabaret nightlife. Avant-garde vignettes and parodies of Jewish life were all the rage. In the spotlight of caricature, assimilation's façade was revealed.

An enlightened, progressive Gentile glimpsed the world of the "other," like visiting the city zoo. An evening's entertainment of tongue-in-cheek, anti-Semitic parody advanced the misguided bon vivant's notion of tolerance. This big-city sophistication, also popular in Paris and Berlin, did not foster empathy or inclusion; it stoked xenophobia.

"Judenwitz," Jewish jokes, were published in magazines, delivered in coffeehouses. Like music hall performances, they were outlandish observations of a universe existing in the center of the city, yet outside the mainstream.

"The Jewish Ambassador" joke, circulating at the time, expressed the double-edged truth:

A representative of Parliament is asked, "If they establish a Jewish state in Palestine, all Jews will be expected to go there, including you. No matter how great a patriot you are." "I have no intention of going," he replies. "I cannot live anywhere but here." His host persisted, "And if you have to?" "If I have to, I will go, still. I would hope to have enough influence to have myself immediately appointed Jewish ambassador to Budapest."

The ambassador joke says in plain language that Jewish citizens are not legal "enough" to resist expulsion and live outside the national embrace. That all Jews were visitors, ambassadors, existing on the scraps of Hungarian citizenship and declaring it full assimilation. The joke circulated through all the European capitals. Everyone laughed, including the tapintat-practicing Jews.

In 1882, the Tisza-Eszlár ritual murder trials fueled two years of anti-Semitic violence. The tragedy was a decisive incident in both the history of Hungary and my own family, but it was not the *only* incident.

In the spring of that same year, fleeing pogroms, more than twenty thousand Russian Jews took shelter in Galicia, a northern Austrian province. Ironically, although not within its territory, the presence of these refugees in the monarchy contributed to a parliamentary crisis in Hungary.

Mór Wahrmann, a Liberal Member of Parliament representing the Jewish district, said, "A Civilized free nation must not forcefully chase back refugees to a place that expelled them so violently. Regardless of religion, they should be allowed to settle in the country."

At the beginning, there was compassion, until the question of Hungarian-Jewish loyalty was incongruously linked to the refugee problem.

Gyozo Istóczy, a Conservative Member of Parliament, advocated expelling all Jews to Palestine. He founded The Alliance of Non-Jews to advance his Semite-free Hungarian vision. Suggesting the patriotic spirit of the Jews was compromised by the refugees, he muddied the waters. "Do they align with the Russian Jews or Hungary?"

Opposed to sanctuary or aid, he combined the Russian immigrant dilemma with Hungarian-Jewish allegiance.

Istóczy contended, "It is well-known that the Jews murder the children of Orthodox priests for ritual purposes. These actions have caused the peasants of Russia to rise up against, and chase the Jews out of their own homes." In a sinister move of propaganda, the perpetrators of the pogroms were converted into victims acting in self-defense.

Függetlenség, the Conservative newspaper, agitated public opinion. Depicting Hungarian Jews as ritual murderers and financial and moral supporters of the accused Jews of Tisza-Eszlár and the Galician Russians, journalists declared patriotism was simply not born in the bones of the Jews.

The Alliance of Non-Jews declared "Jewish-ness" to be a root too deeply embedded in the soul to be completely driven out.

While Parliament's Liberals argued for the support of any persecuted religious group, its Conservatives promoted a connection between the immigration issue and the Tisza-Eszlár blood libel case.

In the end, the government agreed to allow Hungary to serve as a conduit through which the Russian Jews were allowed to pass, unmolested, on their way to America, Palestine, or elsewhere.

While the Liberal government appealed to reason and equality, anti-Jewish agitation rose to a fever. In Parliament, the battle was won by the Conservatives, who, dismissing Budapest as a liberal sewer, placated the rural population's distrust and disconnect.

In this political climate, Fannie and Samuel sought refuge in the Jewish Mecca, Budapest.

Samuel

Eight treadle-powered sewing machines bolted to the wooden floor spanned the width of the workshop. At my station nearest the window, the machine was flanked on my left by a large basket to hold garments ready for the hand-finishers. On my right stood a metal cabinet with drawers containing my tools: shears, thread, steel needles, pins, bobbins, tape measure, marking chalk, thimbles, thread wax, a small can of engine lubricant.

Shelves along the rear wall held fabric, with patterns stored in cabinets below. Four large cutting tables occupied the rest of the cavernous space. Separated from the workshop by floor-to-ceiling glazed walls, my boss, Fönök Balázs' corner office desk allowed him an unobstructed view of the cutters and tailors.

Upon entering the workshop, my gaze went directly to Balázs. Seated at his desk, peering over his pince-nez, he scrutinized my approach. A short, stout man of sixty years or so, his bald pate a shiny egg sitting in a nest of oily brown curls connecting his ears. A sallow complexion attested to years of six-day work weeks with few holidays. His greying, brown mustache was carefully tended, waxed, pointy ends hanging below his chin. A cold cigar stub tightly clenched in his teeth, he adjusted the eyepiece at the bridge of his nose while waving his hands rapidly, motioning me forward.

Pointing toward the wooden stool in front of his desk, he cleared his throat. "Sit, Samuel, sit. We need to talk about your resignation." He paused to relight the cigar.

I began earnestly, "Úr Balázs, I wish to apologize for my untactful remarks on Saturday; please forgive me. Most importantly, I don't want to leave on a sour note after the generosity you've shown me. You have been a strict, yet sincere, mentor. Were it not for you, I may never have found my calling. You've known me since I was twenty, so I'll speak plainly. Since I'm aware that The Emporium's reputation is affected by my interaction with customers, I understand why I was not promoted Master."

Balázs blushed, shifting in his seat. "Samuel, it pains me to see what's becoming of Debrecen. I thought it impossible to reverse the strides made by the government since Independence, but I read the newspapers. I hear the vicious, unfounded attacks. You know I hold no hostility toward you, or anyone, based on religion. I'm a lapsed Catholic myself; who am I to judge?

"I'll be honest with you, Samuel. There *have* been decisions made over the last months to satisfy resistant customers. They made it clear they did not want you to serve them. I'm truly sorry I bent under their pressure. It was unfair and reflects my cowardice, yet I must think first of my family, employees, and The Emporium."

"We can't change the times in which we live, Úr Balázs. I bear you no ill will; I understand. My concern now is to provide for *my* family; to keep them safe. Fannie and I have decided to move to Budapest, where we believe we can live our lives with less tension. I'll need a letter of recommendation from you to find a position there. May I expect one?"

"Samuel, I wish the best for you. This entire affair pains me more than you'll know. You were a boy when I first met you. A boy with a charming manner, a quick wit, a creative mind; not a hint of laziness. You never disappointed me; you were one of the best business investments I ever made. For that, I thank you."

He sighed and crossed the room, arms reaching to embrace me. It was with mixed emotions that I responded to his gesture. This man had been like a father to me. I respected him and, yes, loved him. Yet there would be no denying he had yielded to the anti-Semites. It was an uncomfortable moment, necessity demanding I stand mute, accept the injustice with a small protest. It was a moment I'll always remember. No matter my effort or talent. As a man, born a Jew in Hungary, I was politically emasculated.

Returning to his desk, he said, "I'll write, today, to one of the finest suiters in Budapest. The proprietor, Kálmán Korda, is married to my cousin. He's half Jewish, serving a Jewish clientele. It's Budapest, Samuel. You'll meet all kinds of people there. You'll be happy you made the move, and I'm confident you'll be hired on my reference."

I managed a blank facial expression, tapintat. "Thank you, Úr Balázs, and God bless you for all you did for me."

In a week's time, I received correspondence from Balázs's cousin-in-law, offering an immediate position at The Budapest Gentleman, Fine Tailors. My positive response was in the next post, advising Úr Korda I'd begin my employ in ten days.

I rode the train to Budapest after work on Saturday, reaching Cousin Max's flat in time for breakfast coffee. The next day, I visited eight flats and put a deposit on one near the Király Synagogue.

Still unmarried, Max was bookkeeper for the owner of several commercial buildings along Park Útca.

"I'm going to America, Samuel. I want a better life, a life without fear."

"Max, you're exaggerating. It's probably true the only place in Hungary I am assured of work is here, in the ghetto; still, haven't we always lived in the shadows? We might not have seen it, but it's always been thus. Fannie and I can't just pick up and move to the other side of the world."

He replied, "You believe your own lies, Samuel. The whole of Eastern European Jewry is on the move. America is the answer. Europe has never accepted us and never will. If you were honest with yourself, you'd admit that moving here offers only a little more acceptance. I know you'll come to your own decision without my influence. You can't deny Hungary hates the Jews; your father was attacked in his home by neighbors he knew for decades. Every day, assaults on shops and innocent people are carried out in broad daylight, with no police interference, the laws ignored."

"Max, please. I don't want to hear these things. I have to believe this move will solve our problems. There are over a hundred thousand Jews here. You're proof this place tolerates us. You earn a good living, working for a Gentile."

He laughed, "My boss won't dismiss me while my ledgers are immaculate and my pay low; on the other hand, he hates and distrusts me. I've done nothing to deserve such contempt. The violence is escalating while legal protections are disappearing. I see only a bad outcome, and I'm leaving. My family urges me to move back home to Tolcsva. Even your brothers laugh at me. They say I'm running away for no good reason. They don't believe I'll leave, but I'm going. In spite of the incident at your father's house, they won't accept that hate is in every corner of this country. Hate is forever, not a fleeting reaction to the Solymosi affair.

"I've started organizing papers for an exit visa. I don't care how long it takes to find a position in New York; I'm leaving as soon as I can, before the pogroms start in Hungary."

I listened and agreed with everything he was saying yet kept quiet. We were as close as brothers; he *knew* his words would resonate and cause me to question my direction.

In a measured voice, he said, "You owe Fannie and your sons the opportunities they will never find here. Samuel, there's no limit to a man's ambition in America, even for a Jew."

"I can't think about America, Max. I can only think of the immediate safety of my family. Budapest is the answer, for now."

"Samuel, you must listen. We've got to get out of here!"

"I'm no fool, Max. The assaults are on my mind every day. I worry about Fannie venturing to the bakery. I worry if I leave work after dark. Balázs *is* Hungary. Maybe not *eager*, but *ready* to go along with the hatred. He betrayed, sacrificed me to save his own skin. He is the Hungarian soul, Max; my termination was a reasonable business decision. I worry that my new fönök in Budapest will treat me fairly. I trust you, Max. Your observations weigh heavily on my mind."

"We'll go together, as we did when we left Tolcsva. We thought Debrecen would be the answer; it wasn't. Now, you believe Budapest is the answer. I've been here for three years and can tell you it is not the refuge you think. We're hated here, too. The government is in turmoil over the Russians and the Jewish "loyalty" question. We live in a ghetto in a city that is, itself, a ghetto. Yes, there are many of us, but we live in our place; they live in theirs. Assimilation is a lie. They demand we give up our traditions and heritage to be citizens. We do that, and they still refuse to accept us as patriots. We will never be pure-bred Hungarians. They want us to prove that we're not Jews. That's impossible. How can we prove that, Samuel? Think about it, and you'll know I'm right. You and I are still searching for our future, and it's not in Europe!"

"Max, I don't have enough money in reserve to fund a venture that will require hundreds of forints."

"Samuel, dearest cousin, I will help you."

I returned to Debrecen on the evening train. My thoughts, Max's arguments, would not be drowned out by the screeching of the wheels against the track. What will Fannie say about this? My eyes closed to avoid conversation with the other passenger in the car; my head bobbled against the window. Sleep was out of the question.

A week later, the night before moving to Budapest, Fannie and I talked about our situation.

"Dearest, the possibility exists that Budapest is not the answer." Then I related my conversation with Max.

She listened quietly, thoughtfully. "Samuel, let's see how life is when we move. We haven't even left Debrecen, and Max has convinced you to go to America. I love him, but we must make our own decisions, and we've decided on Budapest."

In my own defense, I raised my voice. "I am not convinced by Max! The future of our family will be decided by you and me."

She interrupted, "We have no family in America. My parents are aging. It's difficult to move to the other side of the country; the other side of the world is impossible."

She added, "Also, although we see them only a few times a year, we celebrate family events with the Freeds. Your father is not well, and neither is Rozsa's husband. Who knows how long they'll live? The Freed nephews and nieces are our son's only cousins. It's not right to remove our boys from their grandparents, aunts, uncles, and cousins. Can we be so unkind, so selfish, as to abandon all of them? How can we even think of leaving our Motherland?"

"Let's not go to bed angry, Fannie. We'll work out a plan that's best for us. First, Budapest, then, we'll see.

I spent a sleepless night, certain in the morning that this move would prove to be a short stay on our life's journey. I kept that to myself. No need to trouble Fannie, although I was certain she would support whatever lay ahead.

The Budapest Gentleman dominated the large corner space on Andrassy Útca in District V. Employing thirty people, The Gentleman enjoyed a fine reputation for excellent service and tailoring. I was hired on for six months as provisional Master, pending satisfaction with my work. The clientele was the affluent middle-class Jews; the bourgeois, i.e., professionals, men of commerce and banking; even Mór Wahrmann was suited by Korda's. The clientele lived in huge apartments in districts whose rentals I could not afford, enjoyed reserved seating at the opera and fine restaurants. They considered themselves successful Hungarians, the equal of upper-class Gentiles. As such, their businesses exploited lower-class Jews, with whom they felt no kinship.

In April, I was welcomed by Korda to permanent status at work. My colleagues were hale fellows who respected my talent, yet I wasn't happy. Life in the city was hectic. Always, there was a sense of urgency, my workload never permitted more than an hour of rest during the ten-hour day. I felt weighed down by life and responsibility.

Fannie was enthralled with the city's pace, eager to discover and enjoy the culture it offered. She embraced an optimistic view of things, with an open mind to new experiences. I was the serious partner. Exhausted as I was on Sunday, she insisted I find the strength to visit places of interest with her and the boys. Of course, she was right; that's how a family builds its bonds.

Max came to dinner, and the conversation was, as always, of his escape. Planning to leave in the fall, he was deciding when to book passage. The conversation made me restless, a growing anger at my own procrastination.

"Thank you, Fannie. Dinner was delicious!" Max lit his pipe, sucking on the stem. "You're welcome, dear Max. It's been interesting to hear how much time and money it takes to make the journey. I do wish you the best of everything and have to confess I'm wondering if we may eventually be leaving, too. I'm discovering a lot about this beautiful city. How we're confined to a place in society and a Jewish neighborhood. It's terribly sad to learn my love and pride for Hungary are not reciprocated by our countrymen. Even here in the modern capital."

I almost choked on my torte! "Fannie, are you thinking we should leave?"

"I'm thinking, Samuel, just thinking."

A month later, the day after Morris's first birthday, the gravity of our situation was brought into close focus. Leaving The Gentleman, my colleague and I were set upon by galoots. They beat my co-worker with a chain and clubs. I defended myself but lost a tooth to the ruffians before they ran into the shadows.

Budapest had appeared to welcome us. It was an illusion. "Judapest," as Max described it, had strict rules, a double standard that kept Jews in line.

There was no defense for remaining. The Jews had no legal standing. Max was right; there could be no good ending.

I sat on a wooden chair in the kitchen, steeling myself against the pain. Holding my chin, Fannie washed the blood from my mouth, her face a portrait of sadness.

"We are going to America. You agree, don't you, Fannie?"

"I see no alternative. I don't want to raise our sons here. America is big, Samuel, very big. There's plenty of room for young, hard workers like us. We'll survive...no, *thrive,* there. Do this for all of us. Go with Max."

What an extraordinary woman the fates had led me to. I loved this woman so deeply. How fortunate I was to be loved by her. Fannie stood before me holding the cotton rag now stained brown-red with my blood. I put my arms about her legs, leaned my head on her belly, and cried softly. Her arms around my shoulder now, she swayed slowly back and forth. "I love you so intensely yet cannot find words to express it. You are my world, my dearest." I felt her surrounding me, protecting me, transferring strength to me.

My father-in-law visited us once while we lived in the Capital. Sarah stayed with us: he lodged at a hotel. Bruder loved his grandsons in his own way, yet had no experience with infants or small boys. Although he brought small gifts, he neither engaged with Albert nor bothered with Morris, whose gibberish was not yet understandable. To Bruder, children resided in a woman's domain, a place in which men had no function or purpose. Then, there was the inescapable fact that Fannie loved me, had given birth to *my* children. Bruder resented my being their father.

At leave-taking, he said, "I will say this once, so it can't be said I didn't: I am against your plan, totally against the whole thing. It is irresponsible in the extreme to consider leaving your family, traipsing off to America."

He expected no argument, so I didn't respond.

Max paid a premium to have a travel broker bribe his way through my visa process. By mid-August, exit papers, tickets for the train to Le Havre, and passage on the Hamburg-American Line's Hammonia were stacked on the dresser.

Korda was not happy with my resignation, although giving six weeks' notice did take the sting out of his anger.

A week before departure, we went to Tolcsva. Spending two days with my kin was bittersweet. All were aware it was probable we'd never see one another again. Abraham and I got drunk and cried for hours, reminiscing about our youth and our mother.

My father, as always, had a few words of advice: "Always ask yourself if you are a good man, Samuel. Ask yourself if you are doing whatever it takes to keep your wife and children safe. Love your wife; put her above everything. She is the reason you'll have a good life; it's not your employment, it is Fannie that will give you the courage to overcome adversity to find the joy in living."

Fannie packed two bags for me: one held clothing, toiletries, an extra pair of shoes. The smaller sack contained my tools: fabric shears, tapes, chalk, patterns, a pin cushion.

In the morning, tearfully, we made love. Our movements were subdued, somehow obligatory. It was farewell, not a joyous coupling.

I said, "I'm sorry, dearest."

She cried softly against my shoulder. "Samuel, I know everything will be for the best, but I'm so very sad that you're leaving me. Never forget I love you."

Hiring an open livery, I paid close attention to the landscape of Andrassy Út. I wanted to later recall, in detail, this beautiful avenue. Albert sat on my lap, Morris on Fannie's. There were no words between us during the heavy-hearted ride to the train station. I was anxious about the moment I would board the train with Max. Would I change my mind? Could Fannie and I bear the pain of separation? Would we see one another again; when?

Max waited on the platform. He embraced Fannie, kissed the boys, and clapped me on the back.

"Well, Samuel, this is it! I barely slept last night, checking my luggage and papers over and over. Are you ready?"

I attempted nonchalance, "I'm ready and have absolutely no second thoughts about the decision. Fannie is still solidly behind the venture, so I'll try to be as strong as she!"

A whistle blew and the motorman called, "All Aboard!"

Fannie and I were silent, my arms enfolding her. If I spoke, I feared a torrent of tears would be unleashed, but I managed to say, "My dearest, I love you more than life," and kissed her, inhaling her scent.

I kissed Morris' head, then knelt to face our three-year-old eye-to-eye. "Albert I'm putting all my trust in you. Take care of Mama and the baby."

I knew he couldn't have understood what I was saying to him, but he was aware it was a solemn moment. "Yes, Papa, I'm the big brother."

Across the European continent, a fever burned in the Jewish breast, an urgency to escape the recurring, wretched saga, and I was one of them. Now, there was a sanctuary...America.

Fannie

Albert was two years and six months and Morris only six months when we moved into the three-room flat in the Terézváros district, joining the majority of lower-middle-class Jews. From comestibles to dry goods to clothing to tinkers-ware; all was available on Király Street, the noisy, bustling heart of our neighborhood.

The city was alive with an energy I never felt in Debrecen. It was beautiful and a testament to the newest engineering marvels. I had not been prepared for the scope and size of the place, the wide boulevards, the ornate buildings, and the bridges.

The autumn weather was perfect for getting acquainted with the city. Albert squeezed into the pram with his little brother, and I walked the promenade of the Danube. On Sunday, with Samuel, we explored; one time crossing the Chain Bridge to enjoy a lunch of hard-boiled eggs and berries on a grassy knoll. On another, visiting the park and railway station designed and built by the Paris Eiffel Company. Although we had no money to frequent them, restaurants, cafes, and coffeehouses were in abundance on all the major thoroughfares and their immediate side streets.

My daily routine was fairly set. The mother of two young boys, I washed, ironed, cleaned, shopped, cooked. My tasks would be the same in Nagy Karolyi or Debrecen, but in Budapest, I was compelled by some inner force to observe the city itself. Only the most inclement weather could keep me from walking Király Street, where I watched a mime perform on the sidewalk or purchased a bag of apple fritters cooked in a street vendor's pot of oil over a coal-fired brazier.

The shops I frequented in Terézváros District were Jewish owned. It had only been twenty years since Jews were permitted, mandated, to speak Hungarian, so the language of commerce was still almost entirely German and Yiddish.

I asked myself, "If this is the liberal, assimilated, modern democracy, where is the rest of humanity, the Gentiles?" Even in Nagy Karolyi, we intermingled with non-Jews at the library or greengrocer or an outdoor concert. Here, everything was available in our segregated neighborhood. One never had to leave for shopping or cultural activities. Were we insiders or outsiders? There was little diversity; it existed only as a mirage. We were in a house of mirrors, a city within a city. The Jewish Mecca proved to be as anti-Semitic as Debrecen, though without its honesty.

Through the winter, Samuel suffered periods of melancholy. Putting down the newspaper one evening, he said, with disgust, "We are kept on a tight leash, living in the "free" city. We're not any more welcome than in Debrecen. Those Jews accused of Ezster Solymosi's murder are innocent, yet people still believe, somehow, in our collective guilt. Those burned out of Russia take refuge in Austria, and it becomes an excuse for violence against Hungarian Jews. All over Europe, the poor can't find work, yet Hungarians say it's *our* fault."

"You're being a bit dramatic, Samuel." I tried to lighten his mood. "We're still safer here than in Debrecen. If we stay in the neighborhood. And, Papa says all this hatred will soon be over, things will be back to normal."

Through clenched teeth, he spat out, "Back to normal? 'Normal' is uncertainty and pretense for the Jews here!"

When I learned Max had pressed him to go to America, I begged Samuel not to make a hasty decision, to wait and see. I promised to consider emigrating if life in Budapest proved unsafe.

Now, without words exchanged, I knew he had reached a decision. Undoubtedly, he was researching the costs, developing a plan for departure. I also knew when he was ready to discuss them, I would hear the details.

My new friend, Lidia, was a widow who lived with her twelve-year-old daughter, Magda, in the flat next to ours. She worked in the office of her father's furniture factory. Born in Budapest, she was familiar with every part of the city and knew its history, its cosmopolitan, cultured world. I learned about the coffeehouses and social clubs, the bawdy entertainment enjoyed by the modern age. She learned from me, too: of being raised outside the ghetto.

Lidia's brother was employed as a clerk at the Attorney General's office, so I mentioned Cousin Abe, who worked there for some time. She said, "I'll write to Johan and ask if he knows your cousin."

Abe and I had been in correspondence with one another since he left Debrecen three years earlier. Still unmarried, he was a young professional, hoping to establish himself as upper middle class. He opened his own law office when, after the blood libel trial, the Attorney General's office terminated the employ of Jews.

I invited him to dinner, including Lidia at the table, hoping they might find an attraction. I was sure Aunt Eva would approve of my playing Cupid. Happily, they were drawn to one another and discovered a common thread. Lidia's brother and Abe were colleagues.

The following Saturday, Abe, Johan, and Lidia went to the Muvesz coffeehouse on Andrássy Út. With Samuel at work until eight, and Magda tending to the children, I accompanied them, visiting the mysterious and unconventional atmosphere of the city's heart.

The Muvesz's walls, covered in deep red cloth, were hung with rows of gilt-framed posters of renowned music hall entertainers. Along the rear wall, upholstered benches surrounded tables accommodating parties of six or eight people. Tables for two or four, placed at random, surrounded a clear space reserved for dancing or spontaneous entertainment. It was not unusual for patrons to move their seats to an adjacent conversation. As we entered, my attention was drawn to the din, punctuated by voices expressing passionate points in debate. Some men wore top hats. Women's hats were positioned to conceal half their faces; eyes peeking seductively from wide-brimmed, feathered constructions. Fashion dictated accents of scarves or gemstone necklaces. All women wore powder and lip rouge, some with black, penciled "beauty" marks on cheek or chin.

We ordered strong coffee, chocolate mousse, and a bottle of brandy. Lively discussions were taking place around us: the Jewish bourgeoisie exhibited their pretension visibly annoyed by the raised voices of Russian refugees, their guttural language stoked by vodka. A group of swells in one of the booths decried the snobbery of Vienna, the treachery of the Conservatives. A young man wearing a cape played piano on a raised platform at one end of the dance floor. When he played from Strauss's operetta, "The Gypsy Baron," a few patrons joined him in song. At the table next to us, a woman put down the pipe she had been smoking to stand and play a violin! I found it hard to breathe. Was it the smoke-filled air or the stimulating environment?

Abe said, "These are not good times. Legal protections for the Jews are being rescinded by Parliament. Budapest's Mayor feigns ignorance of police assaults. A woman was thrown into the Danube in front of the Parliament building, and no one came forward as a witness. Beatings, rapes, and broken windows go unreported; it's known there will be no justice if the victims are Jews."

Jonah added, "Enrolment of Jews at Gymnasium ended last year. No public education laws had been changed; it was just *known* Jews need not apply."

I begged them, "Please let's not dwell on the dreadful elements of political affairs! Tonight, I wish to enjoy every moment of the coffeehouse experience. Can't we speak of other things?"

The men laughed, "Fannie, there's nothing more interesting than the predicament we're in, the future of our country, and our brethren," Abe said.

I sighed in resignation. The men were single-minded. They had no children to focus on, to consume their attention, to attest to the love in this world. It so dampened the spirit.

A fellow at the next table passed a newsletter to Max, who read it and remarked, "This is written by Theodore Herzl. He was born in Hungary a few months before Samuel but raised in Vienna, where this was published. It describes the anti-Semitism raging at Warsaw University, where he attends the School of Law.

"Herzl is calling for the Jews to organize to protect their rights. I agree with him, but I think to do that, we'll need an army of our own, and that's never going to come to pass. Some of my friends say the goal is to leave Europe, establish a Jewish country."

Lidia said, "I agree with that. The truth is, every Jew wants to leave Europe. My mother's sister's family is going to America. All they talk about is where they are in the process; how many more stamps and seals they need for visas, how much longer it will take to save for the ticket, which steamship line offers the cheapest fare."

Turning to Lidia, Abe said, "You might suggest they use a travel broker to be sure they have all the documents needed." He went on, "So many educated people I know are leaving. Although I wish them well, I know I can't do that. I'm a Hungarian, a child of the Motherland, in spite of her problems. I believe in the law, that government will stem this insanity."

Lidia said, "Let's not be so melodramatic! I want to dance!" Pulling Abe by the hand, she walked to the center of the floor and began a few elaborate moves that might have been a grand waltz. Jonah and I laughed and finished our brandy. It appeared my Cupid's arrow may have found its mark!

At home, Samuel was asleep on the settee. Eager to share the experience of my evening with him, I kissed his cheeks to awaken him.

"Oh, Samuel, this city is so exciting! The coffeehouse is the world in miniature, rich and poor, Jew and Gentile; all enjoying freedom and camaraderie. It was amazing to hear the animated talk in German, Hungarian, Russian, and even Yiddish!"

"It's not reality, Fannie; it's an escape from reality. Those people have nothing in common; they're not 'together'."

I was deflated. It had been such a lovely evening. "Well, at the very least, *our* table was together."

The day after Morris' first birthday, Samuel was assaulted. After work, walking to the tram with Gabor, five men set upon them. They beat Gabor with a chain and clubs. Samuel managed to fight them off, escaping with only a cut lip and one lost tooth. As I cleaned the blood from his face, he said, "Not one of them was more than fifteen years old!"

Later, lying in the darkness, he asked, "Do you believe Hungarian Jews will ever be free? Are we brave enough to leave our families and chase a dream? What if America hates Jews, too?"

A global social rearrangement was in process. Emigration, once an absurd idea, had become too rational to ignore. The decision to leave was not an easy one, but Samuel and I agreed the risk and sacrifice were worth a new life; we would give it our all. "Go with Max, Samuel. Find the place for us."

I dreaded bringing the news to my parents, knew they deserved to hear its in person, not through correspondence. But there was no opportunity for a trip to Nagy Karolyi; Samuel had to work. Mama was planning a visit in June; I'd wait until then.

An hour after arriving at the flat, Mama asked, "What is it, Fannie? I can see you are fretting over something. What is it?"

"I wanted to wait until dinner, with Samuel at the table, but it won't wait, Mama. I've already kept it inside for a month! We've decided to go to America."

Stunned to silence, she sat on the settee. After a moment, she began to cry. I sat next to her, held her hand. "Mama, you know we must go. Hungary is no place for the Jews, no place to raise the boys. Please don't be angry. Think about coming with us, a new start in a new country!"

"Papa will be furious. I pray he doesn't have a heart attack. How can we live without you, without the boys?"

It was a very sad few days with Mama; sadder still when she boarded the train, burdened with the daunting task of telling Papa.

A week later, I received a letter written on butcher paper. Papa's handwriting was bold, his uppercase letter pointed.

Fannie:

Mama is melancholy. I find her sitting in the kitchen in the middle of the night, crying. I've grown to like Samuel, but do not approve of, nor will I remain silent, about this decision to upend the family.

To be very honest: I have affection for Samuel, and I love my grandsons. But YOU are my life. Losing you will kill me.

What spell has he and others in Budapest cast upon you? You have abandoned all logic and reasoning. I beg you to change his thinking about this escapade; tell him you refuse to leave your country, your parents.

He's behaving as a single man, without regard to his responsibilities. Leaving you behind with a three-year-old and a baby at the breast is immoral. How will you live while he's gone? Who knows how long it will take for him to find work and save enough to send for you? If he wishes to go off on a quest, that's his choice; you and the boys can come home, to us.

Please, Fannie, I beg you not to go along with this

Papa

I responded immediately, by postal card:

Papa dear:
I love Samuel, and we are committed to the journey. Think of a future where your grandsons will have opportunities, live in freedom. Please. Come with us. Your loving daughter,
Fannie

We had some savings, perhaps enough to sustain me for three months. Max, leaving in October, already had papers and tickets. Determined to have Samuel join him, Max made us a generous loan, immediately bringing Samuel to tears and joy at the same time.

Optimistic that his education and experience would secure a position on arrival in New York, I began to wonder how the future would unfold. How long will it take for a post from America to bring me money to pay the bills? I began to realize I'd likely need to find work to help out.

Leaving had been a seductive, intellectual speculation. What had not been fully contemplated was the interim period, when we would live apart. He would leave in less than six months' time. Now, my focus shifted to the price we were about to pay. When would I see him again? How long will it take to put aside enough for us to come? A year, two?

Mama visited twice before Samuel's departure. She suffered shortness of breath, and her legs cramped when climbing stairs. The doctor said it was heart trouble. The train trip was difficult for her, exhausting, and our cramped flat on the third story offered little comfort. She came to be with us, aware time was fleeting. Papa came only one Sunday and stayed in a hotel overnight.

The last weekend in September, we went to Tolcsva. The mountainous landscape was beautiful, as the vineyard leaves had gone yellow, red, and umber. We stayed in town, with Etel, her husband Hersko, and their five children. During the two-day visit, I barely held

Morris. The happy, blonde, eighteen-month-old was passed, lovingly, from one to another: aunts, uncles, and cousins.

Kati and the twins, Sali and Hani, even Rozsa, were all married and lived within a few minutes' walk from one another. Four of my sisters-in-law had produced seventeen children!

No longer able to work the grapes, Jakob's fingers resembled the vines themselves, all gnarled and inflexible. He lived in town with Rozsa and her husband, Josef, a Hebrew school teacher with chronic lung problems. They had no children.

Fortunately, good weather permitted an outdoor celebration at Sali's large yard, for the crowd could not be accommodated in any of the family's parlors.

Abraham traveled from Debrecen with his wife and three children to see his brother one last time. They drank too much wine. By mid-afternoon on Saturday, both drunk, they hung onto each other's shoulders to remain upright. It was quite the maudlin spectacle: the men embracing, kissing, and crying. All the while, they recalled incidents of their youth and remembrances of their long-suffering mother, Amalia. In tight embrace, they bawled, expressing the probable truth: they'd never, ever, see one another again. The Freeds were a dramatic group: there were no subtleties here. They had perfect timing when delivering a story's punchline and laughed with, and at, one another.

What a lively bunch they were, with a handful of conversations taking place at one time. Each family member followed and commented on all threads of discussion, including the children, who were not separated from the adults at table.

Albert knew he was witnessing a spectacle. "Mama, there are so many stories told at the same time!" Samuel was so happy to be among his kin, and I was overwhelmed with the good cheer and enjoyment freely shared between them. There was no pretense in this group. It was expected, and accepted, you would keep up with the conversation, jokes, anecdotes, and instruction about some topic of which you had no knowledge; be it astronomy, history, music, or politics.

"Charming" was the adjective I would use to best describe their collective wit, native intelligence, and natural ability to welcome all ages and personalities into social discourse.

There is no doubt that Kati's cabbage rolls were the most delicious I have ever tasted. She mixes the chopped beef with uncooked rice, grated onion, eggs, and plenty of ground pepper and salt. After parboiling the cabbage, balls of the meat are tightly rolled in the leaves then laid closely together upon a bed of chopped onions in a large iron pot. She covers the rolls with stewed tomatoes mashed to a pulp and seasoned with brown sugar, salt, pepper, lemon juice, and raisins. The pan is covered tightly and remains for six hours in the wood-burning oven. The sauce develops a dense, sweet-and-sour flavor that awakens your tongue and brain together: Divine!

A little tipsy from the wine produced from grapes in the fields he had tended for decades, Jakob raised his glass. "To my beautiful family, a toast. Egészségedre! To our continued good health and spirit." Everyone cheered.

My eyes filled with tears as he continued. "Let us all pray for Samuel's safe journey to America and that he finds the life he seeks!" Everyone cheered.

Pausing for effect, he added, "If not, he can always come back here!" All present either laughed, cried, or embraced each other. The demonstration of deep love between the siblings and Jakob made me keenly aware of what I had missed, growing up an only child. We feasted all afternoon, catching the last train to Budapest at eight in the evening.

His papers were in order. They were sailing on the *Hammonia*, from Le Havre, on Sunday, October seventh.

For several days, I busied myself packing his clothing and carefully wrapping his tailor's tools in soft chamois cloth to protect them from moisture.

Monday, October 1, was mild, almost summer-like. Anxious and fearful, we made love as the sun rose; it was unnatural and unsatisfying. Samuel said, "I love you, dearest. Our love makes everything possible. Don't lose hope or faith in me. We will be together in America before too long."

Embracing at the station, we said our tearful goodbyes and whispered loving thoughts. He wept, kissed Morris's head, and told our three-year-old son, "Albert, I'm putting all my trust in you. Take care of Mama and the baby."

I turned to leave, unable to bear watching him turn his back to me and walk with Max toward the waiting locomotive.

5

The decision for Samuel to emigrate without Fannie banished them both to solitary lives led on different continents, exiles.

Imagine being struck deaf, dumb, and blind. Not to hear or be heard; not to set eyes upon nor be seen, by your beloved for five years.

The survival of their love relied only upon the written word.

The symbol of the Hungarian Royal Postal Service is a tasseled horn under King István's Holy Crown. The service, well organized under the Habsburg Monarchy, included defined delivery routes and offices in every city and rural district of Hungary.

In addition to postal services, wired telegraph messages were available throughout Europe. Called the eighth wonder of the world, Morse Code transmissions connected the continent to North America through the Transatlantic Cable. Promoting global commerce, transcontinental wiring was, for the most part, used only in emergency by the common man.

During the nineteenth century, letters and postal cards were regularly exchanged between family and friends near and far. Written greetings, invitations, sharing special events or everyday comings and goings were considered conversation. Receiving the compliment of a fine hand was high praise. Penmanship was regarded an important skill, a measure of one's social standing and cleverness.

At the end of one's workday, penning a letter made for a relaxing evening's diversion. A writing box held glass ink jars, lead pencils, dip-pens, and steel points, or nibs. Dip-pens were slender cylinders of polished wood, glass, or stone with a slit in the bottom to accept a steel point.

A single page, folded to create its own envelope, was sealed with wax or a bit of flour-and-water paste. Envelopes selling for a few coins at stationery shops were required for letters of several pages.

Fannie would have penned Samuel's Pennsylvania address in a bold hand under a twenty-five Kreutzer stamp, her address jotted on the back.

The letter's journey began at the Budapest station's new post office, where a service clerk ink-imprinted the stamp with date and city before sorting it to a sack tagged for the mail car on the Monarchy's Railway. All international letters and packages were obliged to move through Vienna, the monarchy's portal to the world.

In Vienna, after an entry and exit date ink-imprint, the piece forwarded to a German rail line. Imprinting, sorting, and forwarding were repeated at the border and cities along the route. By the time a letter reached a packet ship at a coastal depot and crossed the Atlantic Ocean, four weeks might have elapsed.

In New York, ink-imprinting and sorting actions were repeated before the Lehigh Valley Railroad's mail car carried the letter from Jersey City, New Jersey through Philadelphia and on to Allentown, the central postal district for Carbon County. Sorted for its final thirty-mile rail trip, the sack containing Fannie's letter would have been collected at the Mauch Chunk depot and carted by wagon to the Lehigh Avenue Post Office. There, it was imprinted and sorted to the general delivery, awaiting Samuel's collection. Of course, mail traveling from Mauch Chunk to Budapest would also have taken a similarly long journey.

October 25, 1888
My dearest wife:
Saying goodbye broke my heart.
The train to Hamburg was tedious but without mishap, and Max and I slept for most of the ride.

The Hammonia left Hamburg on October 7^h. She took on more passengers at Le Havre, crossed the Atlantic, and reached New York on the 19th. Conditions were bearable, not comfortable. The single men's steerage housed mostly ignorant, dirty louts, a few drunks, and some who were seasick for the entire crossing. I wasn't, and neither was Max!

Upon reaching New Jersey's coast, wireless contact was made with the immigration center at Castle Garden. Quarantine and customs officials boarded to clear the ship for arrival; however, with many in the queue, our ship remained at anchor for the night. The next morning, barges towed us into the Bay, passing so close to Lady Liberty, I could have thrown a stone at her feet.

A tugboat's horns saluted, and Max and I hugged and cried with joy.

It took about four hours to pass through immigration. Officers were available to converse in all the European languages, including Hungarian! The obviously infirm were taken to hospitals, and the rest simply declared themselves healthy.

Seven questions were asked: name, nationality, age, occupation, country of origin, final destination in America, and whether we had any money. Our papers were stamped, and Max and I, along with the majority, simply walked onto the streets of New York. A few were detained at the Garden to await deportation. They were without either funds, an American sponsor, or a trade. Agents of the railroad lines ushered the people leaving the metropolis, at no cost, onto ferries crossing the Hudson River to the New Jersey westbound train terminals.

We exchanged forints for dollars and left the customs building. Commerce in the neighborhood caters to the newly arrived. Men with painted adverts hanging from their shoulders circulate, directing people to lawyers, travel agents, and employment brokers. Walking the area, we bought grilled sausages and sweet potatoes from a street vendor. For the rest of the afternoon, sitting on a pier, we were entertained by harbor activity. Barges laden with bricks and materials delivered their loads to one of the islands facing us. In broken English mixed with German, I asked a fisherman on the pier what was being built. He told me it was a new immigration center, the island named Ellis. Judging by the unending queue of ships bringing Europe's poor, I can't imagine how many thousands the new center will welcome. In the evening, we returned to the Garden to spend the night on the hard benches.

The next morning, we met with an employment broker and learned our prospects were good, even excellent, if we were willing to leave New York City. There is less competition for jobs away from this crowded place.

At Gymnasium, I applied myself to English, thinking it was the language of the new world. And here I am! Today, I can say the lessons of those years changed our life, Fannie. Understanding and conversing (albeit at the level of a four-year-old) set me apart from others with similar credentials but no English.

Max was hired as bookkeeper for a factory in Philadelphia, Pennsylvania. It's a big city between New York and the Capital of America, Washington.

There were several openings for experienced tailors. I took the one offering the highest salary, in a mountain town, Mauch Chunk, Pennsylvania.

Max and I were so happy, jubilant really. We never thought we'd find good jobs the first day in America. Everything moves quickly here. There's no time to waste; decisions are made with little study, right on the spot.

Our employers paid all fees and travel expense. That was a relief, as we had no idea how far the little money we had would take us. We signed Letters of Employment that say we accept the salary and swear we have represented ourselves honestly and are able to meet the requirements of the position. The broker sent his courier to the Western Union company to telegraph our names to our employers. We were given vouchers for rail tickets, then walked to the New Jersey-bound ferry slip and boarded.

Since Max and I were taking different lines, the trip across the Hudson was our last adventure together. We promised to correspond, made our farewells, and he left to find the southbound train platform. It was sad to watch him walk away.

I'll end this letter here and post it immediately. You'll find six dollars enclosed, which will be most welcome, I know. When I'm settled, I'll wire the money directly to Budapest! The modern world is a wonder, isn't it?

I began writing this letter on the train but abandoned the undertaking until I found lodgings and some privacy. I'm staying at a traveler's rooming house, which I'll describe in my next post.

Kiss the boys and tell them their Papa loves them more than life itself.

To you, darling: I love you with all my heart.

I know we'll weather the trials ahead, the loneliness. Our decision to start life anew is the right one. I'm very happy to be here, where every man is free.

Your loving husband,
Samuel

November 1, 1888
My dearest wife:

I still haven't received a letter, although I'm not surprised, it has a very long way to travel.

I'm told Mauch Chunk winters are long, cold, and snowy, like Tolcsva. Oddly, this autumn has been mild. I wake to frost in the early morning, but afternoons are comfortable, and the mountain's trees still bear yellow, orange, and red leaves.

The original natives named the place, which translates to "Mountain of the Bear." There is only one town of 5,000 persons, which the Lehigh River splits in two; Mauch is upper class and Scottish-Irish. Across the river, in East Chunk, the German immigrants live.

Mainly, men work for the railroad or industries relying on transport to Philadelphia, New York, and across the country. It's a center for distributing coal and lumber, and there are two foundries: one producing stoves, the other sewing machines. With all these goods to prepare and load onto the trains, a large workforce is employed, mostly unskilled and barely literate Germans.

Millionaires summer here in mansions along the mountain ridges, atop a deep gorge. It's called the "Switzerland of America" for two reasons: the alpine terrain and local banks flush with profits of commerce.

I am working at D.G. Bertsch, Merchant Tailor, on Market Square, near the train station. I read the daily newspapers and study an elementary school

English primer. Happily, I've been able to converse with sufficient fluency in only a month. No real conversations, of course!

Earning $7.00 a week, a $2.00 raise is promised upon completion of a year with satisfactory performance. My work is already well received. European credentials, and attention to detail justify competitive pricing with New York and Philadelphia; earning Bertsch a good profit from my labor and experience.

I share a bedroom with a newly arrived Austrian fellow who snores very loudly and never changes his socks, not a good arrangement. There's little privacy, but it's cheap. $2.50 a week includes a bed, drawer chest, daily breakfast, and the dinner meal on Sunday.

Since arriving, my mood has been triumphant, euphoric. I am in good health, secured good employment, and found a place to live. All objectives on our agenda!

I'm hoping you're faring well and not melancholy without me.

I wired five dollars by Western Union Telegraph yesterday. I'm curious to learn how quickly the funds reach you, so be sure and tell me in your next post. Try to put as much aside as possible, my dearest.

Kiss my sons and tell them I love them more than I can say. Keep me in your conversation each day. I am fearful they'll not remember me…

My darling, as I sign my name, I feel you close to me. I love you with all my heart and pledge my enduring affection.

Your own, adoring,
Samuel

December 15, 1888
My darling Samuel:
Finally, after almost two months, I received your letter of October 25th, and was relieved to hear about the journey and how nicely you are set up.

If you can wire eight dollars a month, I think I will manage quite well. Three days after you sent it, the telegram was delivered to my door! I claimed payment that very afternoon at the office on Király Út. What a relief, and how convenient and up to date the telegraph is! I still don't understand how thousands of tapping signals can travel at the same time through a cable all the way to America, under the ocean! The dispatcher allowed Albert to place his hand on top of his own while tapping the Morse code dits and dats on the wire. Albert asked to learn the code, and the dispatcher told him, "When you learn to read, come, and visit me again. I'll teach you." Wasn't that nice? After counting the money twice, I tipped him three Kreutzers.

We have a new savings account at the bank. I call it our "journey" account. Hopefully, it will grow quickly.

We are all well, and the boys have already grown so much since you left. Albert is learning the alphabet, and his numbers. Morris is a placid baby, happy the day long. He loves music, Samuel. I wish you could see how he closes his eyes in contentment when I sing, or we encounter a street musician when out and about.

The house is terribly empty without you, my dearest. I miss you and love you. I yearn for your kiss and caress.

I admit to you now that I worried how I'd manage the household by myself. But I've learned my responsibilities are not terribly difficult to deal with.

I did plan to find employment to help out, but it seems life always brings surprises.

Perhaps I should say "Thank you" for the gift you left when we parted in October...I'm with child again, a July birth expected.

Of course, I feel very well. Please don't worry.

Mama paid a visit. Her health is about as it was. She's short of breath, her ankles are swollen, and she naps for a good part of the day. Even so, we baked and cooked and talked for hours on end, and she was happy to be with her grandsons. Papa is still working ten hours a day, six days a week, and Mama frets about his health, although he complains of no aches or pains.

On the first of each month, Papa sends me money. He doesn't want me to worry, and I don't either, so I gratefully accept the gifts. Don't be angry, Samuel; we need his generous help.

The weather has been dreadful. Today, it's very cold and snow is piling up in the street.

The Christmas season has begun its display all over the city. Fronting the Parliament building, a giant tree is being decorated with garlands of berries and nuts. An angel carved of wood sits at the top. The scene is so beautiful, it's sad to dwell upon the hatred in the world.

I know you are hoping to hear life for Budapest's Jews is easier, safer. I wish I could spare you the truth. Nothing has changed since you left. I am always aware of where I'm walking and who is behind me on the street. I never venture out alone after dark. The police brutalize Jews walking to synagogue. There is no protection from petty thievery or insults. A man spit on Lazlo as he was closing his shop for the evening. Hungarian freedom is guaranteed by law; still, we live along its margins. It's depressing to live this way, but we are all becoming inured to the fear.

No matter how difficult the sacrifice, we must leave Europe. There never will be a time when we'll be completely safe here.

I'll close now, with thoughts of you in my heart. Your sons send kisses and love for their wonderful Papa's happy birthday. Even the baby in my belly sends you his/her love.

  Yours eternally,
  Fannie

To: Mr. Samuel Freed
c/o D.G. Bertsch, Merchant Tailor
37 Market Square
Mauch Chunk, Pennsylvania
United States of America
July 12, 1889
Dearest:
Rudolf Elmér born 7:00 this morning Budapest Jewish Hospital. He is healthy, as am I

He resembles your father.

Dispatched with all my love to you, my darling.

Fannie, Albert, and Morris.

From: Azy. Fannie Freed
Király Út 17
District VI
Budapest, Hungary
July 17, 1889
My darling wife:
How can I express my joy at receiving the beautiful news?

I am on top of the world, knowing you have survived the ordeal, and our son is healthy and perfect. I wrote his name, Rudolf, and date of birth, July 12, 1889, on the back of the tintype I carry of you and the boys. It makes me feel he is part of the family, even though I have not yet seen his face.

You are remarkable, Fannie, and I am blessed to have found you, to love you.

I pray you can forgive my absence at this most important of moments. I hope I can forgive myself.

It's almost a year since I left you to bear it all. Who knows how much longer it will be until you are here?

I've been calculating how much money you'll need for the journey. My guess is it will take almost two hundred dollars, an enormous sum. I don't think we'll be able to save enough in a year, as we'd hoped. Maybe it's best not to think about traveling before Rudolf is two years of age. Do you agree?

I'm not taking this as a setback, Fannie. There was no way to know what the cost would be for future travel, as prices for passage and paperwork are not fixed. We'll have to keep saving, and when you are able to travel, the real costs will become clear.

I'm very concerned about our situation, living apart and impoverished. When we planned a year's separation, it was a sacrifice I felt I could bear. Now, I don't know if I can live away for an indefinite period. Should we abandon the scheme, should I come home?

What a bad choice you made when you fell in love with me.

It's good that your father is helping, though you know I'd rather it not be the case. I'm certain his low opinion of your husband has only worsened as his contributions have become necessary.

Do you still respect me as a man; love, me, Fannie? Do you still want to manage everything without me?

I didn't intend to have a letter beginning with such joyful news become a melancholy ramble, but I am compelled to tell you what is in my heart.

I rarely allow myself these doubtful moments, yet the birth of our new son illuminated the miserable reality that we are living in a situation I, alone, have orchestrated for all of us: myself, you, and three little ones. I am guilty of causing all the pain. Forgive me.

By nature, you know I'm an optimist, and despite what I've written here, I still believe America is the prize on which to focus.

My responsibilities are clear. I remind myself that we'll have the rest of our lives together, years and years of loving one another.

My dearest one, thank you…for the greatest gift a man can receive, a healthy child conceived in love.

I am yours, always, my love,
  Samuel

SENT BY INTERNATIONAL PARCEL POST
October 20, 1889
My dearest Samuel:
I hesitated to send another package to you after the last took more than two months to reach you, but I'm giving it another try!

That said, I'm praying it reaches you by Christmas day, your 30th birthday!

Regarding the photo of me and the boys: Abe arranged for a family sitting at the passport office. His friend, Henrik, the manager, was happy to contribute to the birthday celebration box, waiving his thirty-cent fee. Abe provided the velvet-covered frame as a gift to you, making sure to remind me several times to credit his involvement in the undertaking. It was an exciting experience for all of us, dressed up in our best clothes and trying to get everyone to sit perfectly still for at least a minute!

I know you'll revel in the images of your sons. Aren't they handsome, dearest? You will note little Rudolf's striking resemblance to your father. Of course, he's asleep in my arms in the photo, but I assure you, his deep brown eyes communicate the Freed family's intelligence.

I've begun inventing "America" stories at bedtime and reading from an English book I purchased. Pieces of paper with English words are pinned and pasted everywhere in the house: Bed, Chair, Table, Water, Stove, Lamp, and Shoe. It's a game Albert and Morris love, and they're learning so quickly!

Albert's charcoal drawing is a portrait of me. Please acknowledge his skill in your next post. Morris attempted to sketch an apple. A circle with a very long stem, it's really not a bad likeness for a two-year-old, is it? At first glance, it appears to be a round boat with a very tall mast!

The handsome etui is made of the finest French leather, the cost borne by my Mama, who sends greetings and wishes for the birthday milestone. Papa gave me one hundred Forints to add to our savings account, claiming it's a donation in honor of your birthday. He will not change, Samuel. But, in spite of his opposition, he is helping us leave Hungary; to leave him. No matter the depth of his frustration at having no control, he still demonstrates his love for us.

I knitted the single-breasted grey wool sweater. I visited The Budapest Gentleman where Kálmán Korda insisted I accept ten exquisite, tortoise-shell buttons. In addition, he gave me a fine English wool remnant, suggesting I use it to line the sweater's button placket. All as a gift, Samuel, and with his very best wishes! It might be a good idea to send him a note of thanks.

There is a jar of apricot preserves, a taste of home, for you so far away. I pray it didn't break or open on the journey.

I will say goodnight and that I love you with all my heart, my darling. Please take good care of yourself, and dream of making love to me...

    Yours eternally,
    Fannie

January 1, 1890
My own Fannie:
What a splendid "Birthday Box," carrying your letter and treasures from my loved ones in Budapest!

The parcel arrived on the 23rd, two days before my birthday. A messenger was sent from the Railroad Depot office informing me a package had arrived. The European Parcel Post is much more efficient than the companies here. It took almost as many days to come from New York's port of entry as it had from Budapest and across the ocean! Yet, it was wonderful to realize both my hands and yours held that box! And, all things considered, twenty-four cents was a small price to pay for a parcel of four pounds.

All my colleagues at D.G. Bertsch begged to see what was in the box, but I waited until that evening to open it in my room. It was a treasure I needed to savor alone.

The apricot preserves made the journey without breakage. The instant a spoonful reached my tongue, I was reminded of the taste of your skin, my dearest. I miss you so very much.

TO ALBERT: My dear boy, I am sending you all my love, and thank you for the wonderful drawing of Mama. It is held by a tiny easel on my bedside table. I think you have the gifted eye of an artist, Albert (no doubt inherited from your Grandmamá)! I am still relying on you to take care of Mama and your brothers. Be a good boy, and remember I am proud of you, and I love you.

TO MORRIS: Dearest son, from across the ocean, I'm sending you a kiss and hug. Thank you for the wonderful drawing of an apple. I keep it next to my bed so I can see it every morning when I awaken. Listen to Mama and be a good boy.

Fannie, thank your mother for the leather etui. I have filled the little box with my thimble, a small pair of scissors, several needles (sharps and darning). And, I am most grateful for your father's generosity. Of course, I'm happy that you have them to count on, dearest. I pray they remain healthy, and I'll see them again. Really, I bear your Papa no ill will. I wish he could see our situation is difficult but necessary.

I love the sweater. The buttons are very special. At D.G. Bertsch, we charge five cents for each button of that quality. I'll write a note of thanks to Kórda; it was very kind of him.

I miss Abe. I can visualize him selling Henrik the idea of stealing time and materials from the government office! Is he still calling on Lidia? Abe is more a brother than a cousin to both of us. He was our love's advocate, our champion, and for that we must always love him. I'm not surprised at his thoughtfulness, providing the perfect frame for my most wonderful gift of all: the photo of you and our sons.

The photographer captured your beautiful smile, and I cherish every detail of the image. The velvet-lined wooden booklet in which the photo is mounted fits neatly into the pocket of my overcoat, enabling me to carry it wherever I go. I refer to it several times a day and say goodnight to you as I retire.

Today is the first day of the last decade of the nineteenth century, the fin de siècle. The modern world promises a bright future for you and me and our boys. Here in Pennsylvania!

Wherever we are, we will be together, of that I'm certain. Together and loving each other as we have from the very first moment. Take care of yourself and the boys.

My dearest darling, you are my life.
Samuel

March 29, 1890
My dearest Samuel:
It is times like these that make our separation more than difficult.

Your sister, Etel, has written me of the death of your dear Papa, Jakob, and also of Rozsa's husband, Hersko.

It has been a very cold winter, full of snow. Pneumonia ran rampant through the mountain villages. Papa and Hersko, whose lungs were always weak, became infected. Although Rozsa and your sisters cared for them lovingly for a week, on March 26th Papa passed away before noon, followed by Hersko two hours later.

They were buried in the Tolcsva Jewish cemetery. I was unable to attend the funeral. I know you'll understand that while I'm still nursing Rudolf, I could not manage the trip.

I wrote to Rozsa, offering our deepest sympathy to her and all the Freeds. You know I loved your father, Jakob, as my own. He was an affectionate and kind man who always made me feel beautiful. He accepted our love when my own father would not, and for that I hold him very, very dear.

I've tried to put these words in the kindest, gentlest way possible, but I'm at a loss. I cannot console you, cannot hold you in my arms and cry with you; only words must suffice.

My dearest, please know I am there in spirit and love you more than ever. Soon, soon, we'll be together. We must believe that and carry on.

Your loving wife,
Fannie

May 1, 1890
Dearest:
Learning of my father's death was a shock. I am inconsolable. Perhaps I could have been of some help if I were closer at hand.

Why am I here? What price must we all pay for my decision to leave the homeland and my family? A decision I, alone, engineered?

My father loved life. He was a gentle and considerate soul. He accepted everyone for who they were, saw in each person a unique gift. How guilty I feel today for not being with him during his illness. How guilty I am today not being at the graveside saying the mourner's Kaddish with my brothers and sisters.

I am in self-imposed exile. From how many more life events will I be absent?

How can you love me? I have proven a selfish, unworthy man, walking away from my ancestry and the family I have fathered. Leaving to chase a dream, the wisp of a cloud.

I weep for my father and aspire to emulate his quiet wisdom. He sent me off to America with his blessing.

I cannot reverse my actions now, for in spite of my despondency, I know two things:

I love you more than life, and America is the future.

Your beloved,
Samuel

September 25, 1890
My dearest one:

Can it be two years since you left? I am missing you so very much, Samuel. Although I'm grateful for each sunset, knowing another day has passed, I don't know how much longer I can bear our separation.

I don't usually carp about life, not wanting to burden you unnecessarily, darling. Yet, I have to admit raising the boys alone can be tiresome. Some days, I feel I am not more than a scullery maid. I'm weary of this husbandless life. It's not often I am downhearted, but we never really thought we would still be apart after two years, did we? I promise that tomorrow I'll begin skimping more than ever to hurry our escape!

With one-year-old Rudolf beginning to walk, and sleeping through the night, I am feeling a bit of a respite—although he's still nursing throughout the day. Albert is very mature for six, truly my helpmate. He's reading at third grade level, two forms above his peers. At four, Morris remains such a baby, still requiring an afternoon nap. How will he stay awake for a full day at Óveda next year? Perhaps, we'll be in Pennsylvania by that time. Is the age for entry into kindergarten five years, as it is here?

After supper, a bath, and a bedtime story, the little ones are asleep by seven. For the next two hours, usually I'll enjoy a cup of tea and read. Once a week, Lidia visits and we play hearts. More often than not, I win. She has very little card sense! She and Abe have parted company. I don't understand my cousin. He's so charming and successful, and out most evenings at cabaret and concert hall. Sadly, he never seems to find the right woman. Lidia is very fond of Abe, but after a frenzied beginning, he lost interest and withdrew. Aunt Eva visited with him last week and spent a day with me and the boys. The conversation was a never-ending complaint about not yet being made a grandmother by her only son.

Hungary has changed little in two years, my darling. Daily assaults on the Jews are still commonplace. No one bothers to report a crime in the Jewish Quarter. A blaze was started in the courtyard of the house behind Lazlo's shop. No hooligans were apprehended, no one bore witness to the crime, no investigation was conducted. Thankfully, nothing was destroyed, as neighbors doused the flames with water taken in buckets from the horse trough. The fire brigade did not respond. What terrible people the Hungarians are. Why can't we just be allowed to live in peace?

On a happier note: Yesterday, I received the parcel you sent, having been in transit for only three weeks!

It was lovely looking at all the picture postcards of Mauch Chunk, the Lehigh Valley Railroad, and the Statue of Liberty. The photo taken at the baseball game was grand. Albert was being helpful in pointing out which face belonged to you, but Morris took offense. "I remember Papa! You don't have to tell me which man is Papa! I'm not a baby, Albert!" Both boys were thrilled to receive the hand-tailored baseball suits, knickers, and shirts, with their names on the back. Albert quickly realized the numbers below their names were their birthdays, 24 and 6! The fabric is so soft; I've never seen anything like it. It would be helpful if you'd sent a book about the game, as we have no idea how it's played. And, on the subject of books, those included are marvelous. The Adventures of Huckleberry Finn will be the first I'll read, followed by Uncle Tom's Cabin. The boys are very excited to learn of life in America. And last, but first in my heart: I love the cameo pin. It is so lovely. It's the color of an autumn leaf, and offsets my brown shirtwaist perfectly. Thank you, dearest.

We are all well, and you are in our hearts every moment.

I will love you forever, my Samuel.

    Eternally,

    Fannie

December 1, 1890

My dearest Fannie:

I am so happy today, after just returning from Philadelphia and two days with Max!

I'm enclosing photos taken in front of Independence Hall and the Liberty Bell. Also, you'll find a small leaflet explaining about the Constitution and the Fathers of America. Read it to the boys, so they'll begin to understand about where they will live: the only country in the world with laws guaranteeing individual freedom.

Max is keeping company with a Jewish schoolteacher, Sarah Zimmerman. She's very short and petite of frame, with dark brown hair and eyes. She's very intelligent, and Max is so in love with her.

Sarah's mother died when she was born, and her father (a pharmacist) died last year, leaving Sarah a modest house in a Jewish neighborhood near the city's center. They are to be married next summer, at which time, Max will move into her home.

I am planning to attend the wedding, as I will have the honor to sign their Ketubah. I will be the American representative of our family in Tolcsva.

I miss you so, my dearest. Seeing Max and Sarah together was bittersweet. I was happy for them; nevertheless, their love was a powerful reminder that I am adrift, without my beloved.

We must stay strong and believe we'll reunite next year.

Sending you all the love in my heart, I sign my name,

    Yours alone,

    Samuel

February 21, 1891

Samuel, dear:

It was grand to hear the news of Max and Sarah's engagement. I, too, have news of a wedding!

Your sister, Etel, invited me to Tolcsva next month for the wedding of her son, Ignacz. Since Mama is already here in Budapest for a few weeks, she will come with me and the boys. What fun it will be to see all your brothers and sisters. I'm hoping the weather will be mild, but even at the end of March, it will most likely be cold and full of snow.

Rudolf had the croup. He is not yet two, and I worried he might die. He ran a high fever, and I thought about bringing him to the Jewish Hospital, but you know they offer nothing more than I could do at home. For two weeks, I spooned chicken broth into his mouth every hour; I slept with him under a steam tent fashioned using basins filled with boiling water under a wool blanket. After the steam, I patted his back to dislodge mucus. Once the crisis was reached, his little body began to mend itself. After two long weeks, he is recovered. He is tall and lanky, Samuel. Although he appears frail, his body is strong and manages to fend off these childhood diseases. Still, I worry about him. Morris has always been so robust and is rarely ill. Albert is the tallest and most well-built boy in the second grade. No matter what illness is passed around the school, his case is usually light. He's a natural-born leader, full of confidence and intelligence. He's a boy you can count on to do the right thing. We are very fortunate, Samuel. Our sons are good boys, and smart boys, too.

I am well, just lonely for my husband. I'm managing our money and saving what I can.

I'll close now; it's almost ten, and I'm very tired.

Be well, my darling, and think of me. I love you so.

 Eternally,
 Fannie

May 6, 1891
My dearest Fannie:
I pray you and the boys are well and remembering me today.

I would give anything to be with you all, celebrating Morris' 5th birthday. Tell him how much I enjoyed the drawing he sent me in your last post. I knew immediately it was the Chain Bridge and the Danube.

Albert's note was welcome, too. Read this to him, Fannie: *Thank you, son, for taking care of Mama and your brothers. It is a great comfort to me, knowing you are reliable.*

I have good news to report. For the last month, I've been working for G.F. Burnhauser, the most prestigious establishment on Broadway. I had been speaking with G.F. for two months about changing my situation, and he persuaded me with an offer of $12 a week!

As Master Tailor, I work six days, beginning at eight-thirty in the morning until eight in the evening. I take thirty minutes for luncheon and enjoy a late afternoon dinner break. During the summer season, I will work on Sunday, but $4.00 extra pay will make it worth the labor.

The location is excellent, flanked by the courthouse and the First National Bank. Only two doors away is The American Hotel, where judges, attorneys, and businessmen lunch. Summer residents and tourists enjoy afternoon tea and take evening meals in the tin-ceilinged, elegant dining room.

Everyone walking on Broadway is obliged to pass our windows, and they often stop to admire the fine European woolens displayed. I can say, without boasting, we cater to the most influential clientele in all of Carbon County!

My darling, with this advancement, you may safely begin to secure travel documents. I'd guess it will take almost a year to get everything in order before you can book a crossing.

I'm enormously happy with how things are developing.

I know I've told you there are no Hungarians or Jews that I know of living in East Chunk. My neighbors are all German: Catholic or Lutheran.

I am lodging with a German family on North Street; $5.00 a week pays for my own bedroom and includes Sunday dinner.

They are a serious Prussian family. The household is clean, yet joyless. Herr Pfennig works for the Lehigh Valley Railroad, loading the coal car behind the steam engine. His fat Frau, Gerta, blond hair braided in loops around each ear, is an excellent cook. Their two sons, also fat, are obedient dullards. There is little conversation at the dinner table, and I make no contribution to family or political discussion.

Actually, as long as the board is paid each week, the Pfennigs have no interest in my life or views of the world, which suits my desire for privacy and solitude.

The Lutheran minister, occasionally a guest at Sunday dinner, gives me a wide berth, never directly inquiring about my affiliation; I politely decline any talk of that nature. Since I don't attend his church, he may assume I am Catholic or perhaps an atheist, but religion is not discussed. When he blesses the food, I respectfully bow my head, without uttering thanks to the Savior.

We exchange superficial greetings and converse in generalities, no politics, or philosophies at dinner. Although he may suspect I'm a Jew, to his credit, he accepts me as the enigma of North Street.

On a basic level, I relate to my neighbors as an immigrant, believing steady employment and raising a family defines life's fulfillment. My only deceptions are not mentioning my education or knowledge of Budapest's culture and being a Jew. I would prefer not to hide these things, except these laborers don't believe education or culture benefits anyone's life, and anti-Jewish remarks are part of their normal discourse.

I have made the casual acquaintance of a German-Jewish tailor, Jonas Sondheim, a bachelor of around 60-years-old who owns his own shop on Susquehanna Street and lives in rooms on the upper floor. Occasionally, we find ourselves together at a lunch counter and engage in talk of new fabric or fashion. He may believe I'm a lantzman but has never asked me directly. The newspapers report a synagogue is being organized ten miles north of here, in Lansford. I'm not interested. I don't make a public declaration of my birthright, and I know nothing of the Torah. We were secular Hungarian Jews and will remain thus in America.

Fannie, my dearest, I am a happy man in spite of missing you so terribly much.

It has been difficult for all of us, yet at this moment I can see the sun on the horizon.

I am very proud to have steady employment at a fine location and earn a good salary. The added prestige of Master Tailor printed on my business and calling card is an important accomplishment. I hope you are proud of your husband.

I'll say goodbye now, with thoughts of you in my heart. I miss you, my dearest one.

Kiss my beautiful, brilliant sons. Tell them their Papa loves them.

  Always yours,
  Samuel

January 1, 1892

My darling husband:

1892!! Another year has passed! Life continues on its path regardless of our dreams and wishes.

Lidia and her sister, Ersebet, spent last evening with me and the boys. Only Albert managed to stay awake until midnight and greet the New Year. The other two begged to creep under their covers by eight. Were you celebrating with friends in America? Write and tell me how you spent the evening.

We toasted to those we love who are absent and ate a marvelous chicken paprikash midnight dinner, prepared following my mother's recipe. Served with spaetzel, the flavors reminded me of our wedding feast. For a moment or two, I relished the memory of our first night together, another delicious memory. How I would love to have been welcoming the New Year with you inside me.

Now, for my exciting news. I have secured a position selling gloves at a small specialty shop on Vaci Út. I work on Thursday, Friday, and Saturday from ten in the morning until eight in the evening. Ersebet cares for the boys while I'm at work, and other than sharing our dinner on those evenings, she refuses any compensation. What a dear friend.

Not to be vain, Samuel, but I've become a very good saleswoman. Several well-to-do customers have requested my service, even offering me a few Forints for my attention. In spite of needing the extra money, I decline graciously, as it is a practice frowned upon by the shop's owner. To be fair, the bookkeeper has included an honorarium in my pay envelope several times during the holiday season.

The boys are well, and we speak of you every day. Their English vocabulary is quite remarkable, and you will be so proud of them. Albert has taken over as the "Papa" in many ways, even calling me "Fannie, dear" on occasion.

The winter has been very mild, and for that, I'm grateful. There isn't a great deal to report to you, my darling. Life goes on, and I have become inured to a celibate existence. That does not mean to convey I'm happy about it. Only that I have made peace with it!

There is some sad news to relay. Uncle Ezekiel has undergone dramatic surgery for cancer of the mouth and tongue. He has been in the Jewish Hospital for two months. Sadly, the surgery was brutal and disfiguring, and in addition, he is unable to eat or drink normally. Nurses have fashioned tubes of animal muscle, which bypass his oral cavity and through which liquid nourishment is forced by syringe. He appears to be starving to death. Aunt Eva is at the bedside all day. She lodges with Abe, who is despondent about his father's condition. The physicians do not hold much hope for recovery. Papa has come to see him but had to be removed from the bedside as he wailed with grief when the nurse exposed the ravages of the disease and surgical assault. Aunt Eva most likely will remain in Budapest with Abe when Uncle is ultimately liberated from his suffering. A good and loving man, we are all praying for the end of this painful and tortuous end-of-life journey.

Forgive my ending this letter with such sadness, Samuel.

We must focus on the future now. Life is short, dearest. I am hoping to be at the new Ellis Island Immigration Center next year. I read it opens today!

I send all loving thoughts to you for a year of blessings, my darling.

Yours eternally,
Fannie

SENT BY INTERNATIONAL PARCEL POST
March 10, 1892
My dearest Fannie:
I am enclosing this letter in the parcel you ought to receive by April 1st, your thirtieth birthday!

Can it be twelve years since the first moment I saw you? The beautiful, beguiling girl is a woman now, my woman. How the gods smiled on me. I love you, my darling, more than life itself.

Now, for the story behind the gift: The amber beads were owned by Lafayette Lentz, the proprietor of The American Hotel, with whom I share a lunch on Tuesdays. He's an affable man, whose family emigrated from Essen, Germany almost thirty years ago when he was five. Always in good humor, this stout man, a head shorter than I, greets hotel and dining visitors with *a huge smile under a handlebar moustache that reaches his ear lobes! After mentioning my intention to find something very special to commemorate your birthday, he offered to barter the beads for a plaid woolen vest. Fannie, amber is the hardened resin of trees that lived more than forty million years ago in the northern part of Germany, bordering Poland. Just imagine the strength and resilience of these little drops, the lifeblood of an ancient pine tree has found its way to you!*

Have a beautiful birthday, darling. Embrace and kiss Albert, Morris, and Rudolf in my absence. Share this with them: The little bits that seem to float in the yellowish-brown beads are parts of the tree and insects trapped in the resin before it hardened!

Like you, Fannie, amber is timeless and resilient. beautiful and magical!

I am yours forever,

Samuel

The cholera pandemic of 1829 was spread by trade routes from India to Asia, Africa, Russia, then to Europe. By June 1831, Hungary registered over one hundred thousand deaths.

In 1854, Dr. John Snow, a British physician, found a link between cholera and contaminated drinking water. Snow is considered the Father of Epidemiology, the cornerstone of public health.

Developed nations began investing in clean water supplies and sewage treatment facilities in the mid-1850's, eliminating the pandemic in most major cities of the world.

In spite of Snow's discovery and its remedies, the cause of the disease remained unknown. From 1881 to 1896, the fifth cholera pandemic began in India, spread throughout Asia and Africa, and reached parts of France, Germany, Russia, and South America.

In 1883, German-born Dr. Robert Koch investigated an outbreak of cholera in Egypt. Retuning to Germany with cultured samples, he identified the bacillus causing cholera.

In 1892, the last serious cholera outbreak of the century cost the lives of almost nine thousand Germans in Hamburg.

Fannie and Samuel had been separated for four years, when a few reported cholera cases in areas served by river commerce spread panic through Hungary. This event accelerated the urgency for the family's emigration to America.

October 7, 1892
My dearest Samuel:
Four years ago today, you boarded the Hammonia *for New York. How unperturbed we were, believing I'd be with you in a year's time.*

As each year ended, with blind faith, we believed I would be in America in only a few more months. There were times of deep melancholy as the calendar's pages were discarded without hope of reunion. I am feeling blue today, though I know the world will keep moving forward with no regard to our unhappiness. We live one day at a time, daring not to dwell upon the reality of our separation, whose length was unknown from the start. We have been fortunate, Samuel. Aside from Rudolf's croup and a few childhood fevers, we have enjoyed good health for all this time. We are young and hale. Never once were we faced with an infirmity or catastrophe to derail our plan. Now, I'm worried. Before you become agitated...let me say at this moment, we are well. You'll understand my trepidation as you read on.

Beginning last month, Hungary is under siege. Not by an invading army but an enemy for which there is no defense. We are part of a cholera pandemic that began in India. Especially vulnerable are children and the elderly. I worry for the boys and my parents. I worry I shall never see you again, that we will all die.

With the cholera spreading rapidly through German cities—thousands are dying in Hamburg!— I began to question the safety of Budapest. But, now, we are learning the spread is along the Danube and Tisza rivers, the disease mysteriously following the floating timber trade. As it turns out, Budapest's enormous population is more or less isolated from the country, and port ac-

tivities have been terminated, sealing it off. We are instructed to boil water for drinking and cooking, and strictly adhere to sanitary measures like handwashing and using only toilets connected to the city's sewage treatment system.

As of today, none of us are ill; we are all quite healthy. Nothing is permanent, though, as conditions are apt to change in a moment. There is no place to hide from disease. No one can say why some are afflicted and others in the same household withstand the onslaught. It is almost dreamlike, living in this transitory world.

When I'm at the glove shop, I tie a handkerchief around my nose and mouth. I've taken to wearing gloves when fitting customers to avoid contagion. Commerce has dwindled, people fearful of exposure to strangers. I only work on Saturdays now, so it is difficult to make ends meet, let alone save a few Forints for the oatmeal tin. Many of Budapest's shops have shortened their hours of business, and public schools have suspended all classes.

Abe and Aunt Eva were to visit last week but did not, sending a note of apology. I believe they feared the children might harbor contamination on their hands. For now, we are content to replace a visit with written correspondence.

I urge you, my dearest, to find a way to end our exile. Life is fragile, and we must do everything possible to fulfill the vow we made so many years ago.

I beg you, Samuel. Rescue us from this existence.

Eternally,

Your Fannie

SENT BY INTERNATIONAL PARCEL POST
November 18, 1892
To: Azzony Fannie Freed
Király Út 17
District VI
Budapest, Hungary

Dearest: Received your letter of October 7th today. I am frantic with worry. Telegraph the state of your health when you receive this, and wire every week until danger is past. I will do everything possible to bring you here.

Your loving husband, Samuel

From:
Samuel Freed
C/O G.F. Burnhauser
Broadway
Mauch chunk, Pennsylvania
United States of America
December 1, 1892

Darling: Your letter traveled for six weeks. Once the information reached me, not knowing if any of you had fallen ill during that period of silence, I was out of my mind with dread. The delay in receiving this news of your daily life strips away any pretense that we live in the same world. The simple remedy, a weekly telegraph until the danger has abated, has been a blessing. German language newspapers available here in Mauch Chunk, are causing an upheaval amongst the immigrants, many having lost family in Hamburg.

As a castaway for so long, I've experienced triumph without loving praise and celebration. I've experienced melancholy and despair, with no one to embrace and console me. I receive accounts of my family's daily life many weeks after the events. I'm living every day with regret for the predicament we are in.

Fannie, dearest, I am working six days a week, stinting in every possible way. My life is work and sleep, work, and sleep. Still boarding with the Pfennigs, I live as a celibate monk. In the evening, I retire immediately after dinner. My only conversations and fellowship are with my coworkers. Lafayette Lentz and I attend an occasional performance at the Opera House, using complimentary tickets given him by the actors and musicians who are guests at his hotel.

I promise you I'll find a way to earn additional money. There is nothing that will prevent you and the boys from coming to me next year.

I have been invited to Max and Sarah's during the Christmas work recess. It is only for three days, but I welcome the opportunity to escape this little town.

Please, my dearest, stay strong. I know you will be here in only a few more months...no matter what I have to do toward that end!

Your adoring husband,
Samuel

SENT BY INTERNATIONAL PARCEL POST
January 30, 1893
To: Azzony Fannie Freed
Király Út 17
District VI
Budapest, Hungary
Dearest: I am wiring $100.00. Make all necessary arrangements immediately. Hire a travel broker to assist. The funds are a gift from Max.
Your loving husband, Samuel
From:
Samuel Freed
C/O G.F. Burnhauser
Broadway
Mauch Chunk, Pennsylvania
United States of America

April 15, 1893
Dearest Husband:
We are all well, and the mild weather continues. All vestiges of snow are gone from the city, and the courtyard linden already displays green bulges at the end of each twig. Spring cannot come and go soon enough for me.

I miss you so. How can I describe my longing for your touch? Each night, I look at your tintype and try to remember the taste of your kiss, the touch of your caress. It has been too long, my dearest. Can you believe that our dream will be a reality in only three months?

Thanks to the generosity of Cousin Max and his dear Sarah, our bank account holds two hundred and seventy-five dollars! In addition, the oatmeal tin is filled to the brim with coins. Isn't it wonderful that my employ allowed me to contribute, even in a small way, to our expedition?

Your sister, Rozsa, paid us a visit last Sunday to introduce her soon-to-be husband, István Rivke, a riverboat man who works on the Danube's ferries just north of the city.

They're so happy together and are readying to leave for America, to a town on the Hudson River, north of New York City! Won't it be nice to have family nearby?

Now, to our latest progress: Bence Politzer, our broker, has attended to all the details. His two percent commission on documents and bribes was a bargain. Procuring the papers is a full-time job for someone with experience. I could never have done this alone. His hire has lifted a great weight from my shoulders.

The polished walnut box Max gave us as a wedding gift holds proof of citizenship, sealed and certified documents of births, marriage, education certification, residency leases, and character references. Bence arranged for my visit to the notary for signatures when his proxy was not sufficient. Otherwise, his repeated visits to government offices secured our identity and medical papers.

Remaining items on the list, are exit visas for Hungary and rail tickets within the monarchy, Budapest to Vienna to Prague. Tickets needed on the Rhine and Dutch Railroad will have to be purchased as we enter Germany and Holland. I'm sure I'll manage with the help of written instructions Bence has organized, which include solutions for emergencies or problems that might be encountered enroute.

We are booked on the SS Maasdam, sailing from Rotterdam on Saturday, August 5th, arriving in New York about the 12th. Now that you have our dates, you'll need to find a flat and learn how you can find us at Ellis Island, where, I hear, thousands mill about in transit.

Two weeks ago, I received a birthday gift from Mama: a tapestry purse of strong construction. I'll use it to hold our documents during the journey. Our sons are thrilled to begin the adventure with a fortnight in Nagy Karolyi in July!

Never having been to sea, I'm hoping we'll make good sailors. The boys' attention is fixed upon sea stories and all things nautical.

I'm barely able to concentrate on the business of daily life and would leave today if that were possible.

Soon, soon, my beloved...we will be together again. I am yours, always.
    Fannie

Postscript: Seventeen weeks until we stand on American soil!

SENT BY INTERNATIONAL PARCEL POST
July 12, 1893
To: Azzony Fannie Freed
Király Út 17
District VI
Budapest, Hungary
Happy 4th Birthday to Rudolf!

Twenty-four days until you all depart from Rotterdam. Has it all been a dream?

My dearest one, I pray you and our sons have a safe journey.
Until we meet at Ellis, I love you, my darling wife. Samuel
From: Samuel Freed
C/O G.F. Burnhauser
Broadway
Mauch chunk, Pennsylvania
United States of America

6

Fannie

As daylight overtook darkness, the linden tree's branches came into focus. No breeze stirred its leaves, foreshadowing another day of extreme heat.

I anticipated an uncomfortable day on the rails, followed by a fortnight filled with drama. No matter, this farewell visit could no longer be postponed.

It was July 12, 1893, Rudolf's fourth birthday, an occasion we'd celebrate in Nagy Karolyi.

Our three-room flat faced the rear courtyard, sparing us the noise of Budapest traffic. The rent was cheap, and the landlord was sympathetic to a husbandless woman with young sons.

A settee and two chairs occupied the parlor. The kitchen had a washtub, small icebox, a two-burner gas stove with oven, and a large cupboard. The small bedroom accommodated a wardrobe and bed, under which the chamber pot and extra mattress were stored by day.

Albert entered the kitchen carrying his clothes and began washing at the tub. I wasn't surprised to see him up early. As self-appointed head of house, the eight-year-old was readying himself for the responsibilities of our journey.

He scurried out of the kitchen to wake his brothers. When he returned to the kitchen, I kissed his forehead, then filled the kettle and lit the burner.

Keenly observing me packing a small rucksack with provisions, he scolded, "Mama, don't forget salt for the cooked eggs and a knife to spread the jam." A minute later, he giggled, "Oranges and tejkaramella candy!" As he reached for the caramels, I waved his hand away. "Not for breakfast, my son. These are for the stop in Debrecen."

"I know, I know."

From the bedroom, Morris's voice crackled with annoyance. "Sit still, Rudolf! I can't tie your bootlaces if you move your legs. We have to hurry, or we'll miss the train."

Clearing away the uneaten breakfast, I accepted that the boys had little appetite on this exciting morning.

Albert managed the rucksack while I dragged the large, upholstered bag two long blocks to the livery stand. The hackie doused his overheated horse with a pail of dirty water, while assuring me the beast would survive the trip to Central Station.

Heat waves shimmered in the air column as we plodded our way through the glass and iron structure. Dwarfed by the grand scale of Eiffel's design in this public space, we felt smaller still at the sight of the black steam engine. The Colossus stood at idle, its power in check.

Readying the train for departure, motormen, porters, ticket takers, and furnace stokers exerted themselves in the extraordinary heat.

Albert let out a startled cry, jumping out of the way as a burst of steam from under the giant wheels rushed across his path. Over the hiss of the vapor spray, he shouted, "Mama, it's the sound of a giant flute!"

In an empty second-class compartment, each of the boys found a window seat. The car began to move, at first very slowly. Then, as it left the station, an ear-splitting whistle made known the beast was set free upon the rails. In its belly rode our family. Abducted by the powerful age of steam.

The engineer harnessed the throttle, and soon we were forging ahead at great speed. I was a bit unnerved. Of course, the boys were thrilled.

Albert said, "We're on a ship to the moon, Mama! I love zooming like a shooting star. Makes my belly feel jiggly, ready to run or jump or something, not knowing what's coming next; I'm an explorer discovering a new world!"

Morris asked, "Mama, how long is the trip?"

"We reach Debrecen by late afternoon: then there's a two-hour wait for the connection to Nagy Karolyi. We'll be riding the train for about eight hours."

"I wish we could take the train all the way to America, Mama!"

Rudolf asked, "Will Grandpapa have tin soldiers for me, like those he sent on Morris' birthday?"

"Let's wait to see what they've prepared for you, Rudolf. Try not to be impatient." The child hung his head piteously, as if abandoned by the world. What an actor this boy was! "Rudolf, that's enough of your theatrics."

During the morning hours, we dozed, but not Albert. The clackety-clack of the wheels didn't lull him to sleep. As always, he felt the need to shoulder responsibility for our safety and possessions. It was just his nature. We lunched on eggs, bread, and jam and drank from the jar of tea. A man joined our compartment for a few hours and captivated the boys with card tricks. Rudolf said, "I want to do that. I bet people would pay a coin to watch the magic."

The windows were open, yet the in-rushing air offered no relief. We sat silently within that virtual oven, miserable. Unbuttoning the boy's collars, I swabbed their necks with a moist towel. Rudolf's face was puffy and red, his lips pale and dry. I feared he would die of heat exhaustion and insisted he finish the last of the tea.

Just after the noon hour, the train delayed at a small junction. To fill my jar with water and purchase a cup of chipped ice, I ventured out of the car. Rivulets of perspiration streamed from scalp to neck, my hair a wet helmet.

Adding to the discomfort, a long-sleeved, muslin cotton shirtwaist covered me from neck to ankle. Not a single thread of white cotton stocking was visible between hem and high buttoned, leather shoes. My corset, a contraption of muslin fabric, whale bone stays, and cotton lacings, was an unbearable capitulation to fashion. It was no wonder that women often fainted in public, swaddled in layers of cloth, their lungs and torsos trussed and bound.

It was best to conserve energy, so I advised the boys to sleep, drink water, and keep movement to a minimum.

The journey offered little energy for conversation and considerable opportunity for reflection. After years of stinting and saving, everything was arranged and paid for. I thought of my darling Samuel and the years of our separation. When I was downhearted, he had been optimistic. When he questioned our plan, I was stalwart, just as a supportive loved one should be.

At 5:00 p.m., we arrived at Debrecen, and even at day's end, the heat was unabated.

The local line to Nagy Karolyi operated older trains on a track at the farthest point of the property. Although I knew it would be a slow go, with two hours until departure, it was comforting to know we had plenty of time to traverse the station.

I dragged the bag, carrying Rudolf on my hip. At my side, travel-weary, six-year-old Morris quietly struggled to keep up. Responding to my promise of a cool drink in the main concourse, he summoned his strength, and soldiered on. His wavy hair and muscular build were so like my Papa, but that's where the resemblance ended. A sensitive boy, he had a kind, old soul. A quiet observer of the world, his sweet smile and deep brown eyes endeared him to strangers and family alike.

We followed our navigator, Albert, still pulling the rucksack, through the maze of track and platform. Soon, we neared a kiosk selling periodicals. In front of the racks of newspapers, a vendor stood beside a wheeled, metal box filled with a large block of ice. For only one Kreutzer each, the man filled a paper cone with shaved ice bits and topped it with our choice of fruit preserves: cherry, apricot, or grape. Climbing onto a bench to enjoy his treat, Rudolf lost his grip on the cup, spilling most of the cherry ice on the floor. He whimpered softly as I cleaned his knickers with my hanky. Before I could buy another, dear Morris gave Rudolf what was left of his own treat.

When we arrived at the local rail line, the sun was low in the sky. After waiting in a short queue to purchase tickets, we boarded the center wagon of a three-car train. Many empty compartments were available, as bookings to Nagy Karolyi were not in great demand.

The motion of the car and the late hour drained the boys of their high spirits. With Morris's head resting on Albert's shoulder, both fell into a deep sleep. Rudolf, too, nodded off, his head cradled in my lap.

Leaning my forehead against the window, I tried to doze for a few moments, but there was much on my mind. It had been almost five years, and I feared the unknown. A tintype photo was all I had to remind me of Samuel's face, and the written word had replaced the tone of his voice. Had our love endured? Could I adjust to a new country, a new language, new neighbors, with no kin nearby? Could our little family make a normal life now that there was a father and husband in the house?

I hoped Papa would not upset himself trying to prevail upon me, one more time, to stay in Hungary. Sometimes, he referred to me as a widow, and it grieved me that he could be so overbearing and hurtful.

The sun set at eight, just as we arrived. I pinned my hat into place, smoothed my shirtwaist, and although I knew it was the heat that flushed my cheeks, I hoped Mama would say I had a healthy glow. So exhausted were they, the boys could no longer stand on their feet, making it necessary to hire a hansom to bring us to Veres Útca.

I prayed the two-week visit would be a time remembered with love and laughter for all of us and vowed not to argue with Papa.

The passage of time expands and contracts in concert with the demands of one's responsibilities. At first, those summer days dragged on slowly, the inevitable end of our visit far off in some future place. Mama took care of everything: meals, laundry, and housekeeping. Her every waking hour was spent with the boys, allowing me to enjoy mindless, lazy afternoons reading a book or napping on the bench under the white oak. Such solace was a luxury I hadn't experienced since the duties of motherhood, part-time sales work, and worry filled my life.

From the cast-iron stove, Mama's signature bouquets stirred memories of my childhood: baking apples, sweet and sour cabbage soup, paprikash, goulash, and sweet pastries.

On our last day, Mama's widowed sister, Caterina, and her daughters, Mina, and Hinde, came from Satu Mare. Their husbands sent letters expressing "bon voyage", but they could not leave their rabbinical studies for a family visit. That was alright with me, as every time Papa and the two Orthodox men were together, they inevitably would begin arguing about religious dogma. In the end, the husbands would leave in a huff, and Mama and Caterina would whisper affectionately to one another, apologizing for the disrespect their men had exhibited.

Mina brought her nine-year-old daughter, Mali, a dark-haired beauty. Hinde led her six sons, all under twelve years of age, from the train station to Mama's door in a single line. Watching them walk the center of the street toward the house, Hinde reminded me of a mother duck leading her hatchlings, Aaron, Barak, Judah, David, Ezekiel, and Isaac.

My sons and their cousins delighted in the tumult and general good fellowship of the gathering. They listened intently to the stories of olden days: Mama and Papa's wedding party, family holidays at Grandmamá Einhorn's, trips to the mountains, and how Papa managed to open his own butcher shop.

The parlor was full of joy that evening. Everyone found seating on furniture or floor to witness an entertainment they would not soon forget: Papa's three grandsons amusing and beguiling their kin before leaving their world forever.

Albert drew a sketch of the vessel that was to bring us to America, and Papa pinned it to the parlor wall so all could see.

Albert, standing on an ottoman to view and be viewed, began, "The *Maasdam* has four masts, but we won't need wind to cross the ocean because there are no sails. The Holland Line uses only diesel engines now."

Those listening responded with "oohs" and "aahs."

As Albert's lecture continued, I envisioned the inspiring teacher I hoped he might one day become.

"In Pennsylvania, the miners dig out a special kind of coal from the mountains, one that makes very little dust when it burns. It's call anthracite coal, and my father sent a lump of it to us."

Papa was so proud of his grandsons, but his pride brought him to tears when they demonstrated their command of English. I suppose it was bittersweet for him; their facility with the new speech revealed their intelligence, but they were learning this language to replace Hungarian.

The Freed trio stood at the center of the parlor; all eyes riveted upon them.

Albert continued, "My father sends us books from America, and Mama reads them to us in English! Then she pins little pieces of paper with English words written on them to label practically everything in our flat. That's how we learned English words."

Albert put his hand on Papa's chair. "Ez egy szék. This is a CHAIR!"

Papa laughed and clapped Albert on the shoulder. "Good boy!"

Morris lifted his foot and shouted, "Ez egy cipő. This is a SHOE!"

Papa said, "So smart, Morris. You're a real Yankee!"

Not to be outdone, Rudolf ran to the kitchen. Returning to the focal point with a very large glass of water, he kept everyone mesmerized as he drank every drop very slowly, for maximum impact.

Pointing to the inside of the empty glass, the boy declared, "Ez volt a vi. This WAS WATER!"

Everyone applauded and Rudolf took a bow! Mama moved from the doorway to cover his face with kisses. She appreciated his creativity, his artistry.

The last day caught me by surprise; there was no leisure in our walk through the park nor at dinner. Time was moving faster now. It seemed only a few minutes elapsed between the serving of cold beet soup and dessert of stewed apricots, raisins, and prunes.

Reclaiming my maternal duties, I checked the house for overlooked items, packed our bags, organized toiletries. Time was foreshortened as my mind focused on the return to Budapest and beyond.

After dinner, I joined Papa in the parlor. He poured each of us a brandy. I observed my father as he walked across the room. He was wearing the green brocade jacket Mama and I had bought the year before to celebrate his 60th birthday. Even in the dusky light, I noticed his chest and shoulders didn't fill the coat as they once had. He was still a strong presence, my Papa, but, somehow, he seemed smaller, his manly strength diminished by the body's natural decline.

We spoke of the days of this visit, special moments I would recall later in distant places.

Mama put the boys to bed and joined us for a little while. Striking a safety match taken from an embossed tin box on the bookshelf, she began lighting the room.

A pair of ruby glass wall sconces flanked the settee upon which I lounged, and a pink corona radiated across my gown when she lit their mantles. Papa's serious expression was revealed as the brass floor lamp next to his chair came to full glow.

Papa offered Mama a brandy. She declined.

"Goodnight, my darlings. I'm tired after the day's excitement and must go to bed. Your train leaves at noon, so I plan to awaken early to iron the boys' shirts and prepare a breakfast of crêpes with cream. I want them to remember their Grandmamá's table full of goodies!

"Fannie, you, too should get to bed soon. You'll need all your energy for the days ahead. I am worried about the trip, yet at the same time, I'm confident you'll bring the boys safely to Samuel on the other side of the world." Mama's eyes began to tear, and she daubed at them with her hanky.

"Goodnight, Mama. Please try not to worry. I'll make the journey safely and build our American home with love, as you have raised me to do. I love you so, Mama, and pray we'll be together again before too long." She turned toward me as I stood to embrace her. We remained coupled this way for a few long moments before she quietly closed the parlor door behind her.

I returned to the settee. The room was silent. Papa and I sipped our brandy.

The lamplighter climbed his ladder to spark the streetlight outside the parlor window. Almost immediately, tiny flying insects rode the shaft of light through the window, settling on the deep claret cabbage roses Mama had painted on the walls of the room. As I had done as a child, my eyes followed the advance of stems, thorns, and buds from the "bed" in the dark wooden floor all the way to their pruning by a cerulean blue picture molding at the ceiling. There were bookcases along one wall, and two potted ferns stood beside a pair of straight-backed, cream-colored, wooden chairs near the street-facing windows.

Taking a deep breath of the familiar, smoky, gas residue, I settled back into the cushion, my shoeless feet tucked under the hem of my gown.

In all the preceding days, Papa had never once hinted at his opposition to our move, and I had successfully avoided any argument. But, at this moment, the world slowed, and time expanded to allow Papa to open his heart, to give vent to his anxiety.

"My dearest child, I love you and only want what I think is best for you and my grandsons. Fannie, this is the last time I can try to dissuade you, urge you, to cancel your plan.

"Firstly, these times are not unique. I've seen rejection of the Jews before. I've also seen acceptance.

"We were fortunate to have lived in the era of Reform. I built a successful business, own my house, and you attended a fine secondary school. We weren't given access to education as a token. All of Hungary has benefited from Jewish integration.

"Jewish bankers, doctors, lawyers, and university professors may have lost their positions because of the Tisza affair, but anti-Semitic intensity is on the wane."

He sank back into his chair, pausing for an introspective moment.

I was not accustomed to arguing with Papa. He was Papa. But this confrontation had to be engaged that night; the air had to be cleared between us. I sat upright, determined to maintain my composure and respect.

"Papa, by acknowledging the cycles of intolerance, you make the case for a future of struggle, oppression, and segregation, that the law of this land does not always apply to the Jews. In Budapest, where we enjoy the strength of numbers, violence has abated, but outside the city, incidents are still reported.

"At this moment, people are traveling west across Europe to a country built by immigrants. And it's easy to join them; all we need is money. Not only is Hungary allowing us to exit; she is glad to be rid of us.

"When Samuel's cousin, Max, decided to go, we listened to what he had to say. The truth was plain to see if you didn't hide from it, didn't make excuses for our countrymen's loathing. Have you forgotten the attack against Samuel's father, Abe's dismissal from his government position, newspaper editorials, bigots speaking on street corners? And, do you deny the brutality of the police and the unapologetic hatred of our neighbors? These realities made our decision. We choose not to live our lives, nor raise our children, here."

Papa interrupted, dismissing my remarks with a wave of his hand.

"Aside from politics, the trip is too dangerous for a woman alone with three small children. You might be assaulted, robbed, even kidnapped. Trains can run erratically, causing you to miss your sailing, with no recompense. Steamers have been lost at sea. You or the boys might die of disease carried by your fellow steerage travelers. If any of you are ill arriving in New York, you could be turned back, deported. Is it worth all these risks?"

Offering no pause for reply, Papa went on.

"Samuel is a tailor, working in a small village. He earns a few dollars a month. After five years, you were unable to save enough for your passage; you barely scraped by. Without Max's help, you would still be unable to leave. At this moment, America is in a deep economic depression, which will affect Samuel's earnings. People won't buy new clothes while things are bad. It's not like a butcher shop, where no matter what, everyone has to eat.

"Perhaps, to shield you from despair, he hasn't been truthful about his situation. What if he's destitute there in Pennsylvania? What if he doesn't come to New York to meet you? What would you do, with no one to give you shelter, no one to pay for your return?"

His face flushed, but Papa's voice remained calm.

"I'm angry at Samuel for leaving you and the children to fend for yourselves. Is this a trustworthy man, a responsible man? This man promised me he would provide for my daughter and then abandoned her. I can't make peace with his disregard for your safety and comfort, his selfish response to America's propaganda. I understand there's no quick path to prosperity, but he's been there five years and still works for another man, hasn't established himself. Why, he's no better off now than he was in Budapest.

"You must face the reality that you don't even know Samuel Freed anymore. You married him nine years ago yet haven't seen him, lived together for five of those years. People change. He was not yet thirty when he left, and the hardships he encountered surely have altered him. You too have changed. You lived in Budapest, exposed to art and music, met intelligent, worldly people. Maybe *you* will no longer find *him* attractive or charming; you, too, have matured. You must worry that you no longer have anything in common. He resides in another country, has adopted other values, speaks another language, and it's likely he's been unfaithful. Maybe he already has fathered another family there in Pennsylvania."

Heaving a great sigh, Papa sank into the cushion of his chair, spent. He stared into his glass, and after allowing a moment to pass, I responded. I lifted my chin and directed my gaze to his eyes, composed and confident.

"Papa, I love you very much, and it saddens me that after all these years, you still haven't made peace with my decision to marry Samuel. I beg you at least to consider my point of view. Please, Papa, on this night, my last in this house, our differences must end.

"I love Samuel. I believe I was born to love and be loved by him. We are a pairing of souls. I know he's waiting for me, unchanged. The years of separation have been difficult, but we live each day anticipating reunion. No matter what the economic conditions are, I have faith that Samuel will sustain us. We're young and strong, and we'll give our children the gift of the promise that is America."

My hands trembled as I stood to refill my glass. I needed a distraction, a moment to regain control.

Papa continued with renewed vigor. "For five years, I've been sending money each month to help you. Even though I didn't approve of the scheme, I never insisted you return here to live; that was never a condition for my support. I helped my daughter and my grandsons, not Samuel. If you leave, I won't send you money, even though I'll worry about your welfare.

"The sensible thing would be for you and the boys to live here. I've been thinking how easy it would be to add another two rooms to the house, accommodating all of us. To earn your way, you can keep the books at the butcher shop.

"Most important, Mama and I will be with our grandsons, and you'll be welcomed back into the circle of your childhood friends.

"Fannie, life will go on, and your current status will improve as you embrace the correction of your course. Always, we've helped and loved you; you belong with us. I read of the millions migrating from Europe. What have the Slavic pogroms to do with you? Why are you compelled to join these strangers?

"Abandonment is grounds for divorce. If you stay, you can make a happy new life, perhaps marry again, have more children."

Caught by surprise at Papa's chutzpah, I walked to the window and drew a breath of the evening air. Arguing with Papa would serve no useful purpose, would only escalate the disagreement; so why do it? Having calmed down, I returned to the settee.

"Papa, although I never asked you for money, your monthly gifts demonstrated your love, and I can never express how much it was appreciated. By supporting us, you did what you thought was right, and I accepted the money as a gift, never considering it a debt to be repaid by choosing you and Nagy Karolyi rather than Samuel and America."

Papa's trembling voice increased in volume, reclaiming control of the conversation's direction.

"And, what of the boys? Albert barely remembers Samuel's face. Morris was an infant at your breast, and Rudolf has not had a father since the day he was born. How can you make such demands on these little ones? Torn from everything familiar, they'll be lost in America.

"Mama and I are old. I can't bear to think that we will never lay eyes on you again. It's not too late; you're still on Hungarian soil. Please, Fannie, don't go."

I remember feeling I would faint, hearing these words from Papa. He had given his presentation a great deal of thought; his arguments were perfectly structured.

Determined to find a position without anger, I lowered my voice, softened my tone.

"Papa, I know how deeply you love me. You've unburdened your heart tonight, carefully building your arguments about the present and future of Hungary, my life, my marriage, and what is best for my children. Of course, you're entitled to your opinion, as am I.

"I do agree that Albert, Morris, and Rudolf should know the love of their grandparents. The only difference is that *my* dream is for you and Mama to join *us*, come to live in America. Unfortunately, I know you are inflexibly rooted in the old soil, so I hold little hope that my dream is possible."

Signaling I would brook no interruption, I thrust my palm toward him and said, "And yes, the sacrifices have been many, and there will be more during the voyage and later. The boys and I were impoverished, yet I managed without my beloved at my side. The thought of you and Mama dwelling far from me is painful, so I try not to think about the separation. My choice has been made, so a devoted correspondence will have to suffice.

"Papa, we have less than one day to spend together. I beg you to love me enough to let me go with your blessing. I want to leave with the hope that we *will* embrace one another again. I love you and Mama, but I must go and live my life."

Both of us sat in silence for a few moments. I left the settee and sat on the floor at Papa's feet. Resting my head on his lap, I cried softly, my arms hugging his legs. He put his hand on my head, stroking my hair and repeating, "Én is szeretlek, az én kislányom." *I love you, my little daughter.*

There was nothing left to be said, and after a while, turning down the lamps, we went to bed.

The next morning was a blur of activity and farewell. Neighbors and friends came by with small gifts and well wishes for the journey. To keep them amused on the train, Papa gave each of the boys a pair of tin soldiers, their uniforms painted in the colors of the Royal Hungarian Crown Guards.

Into my bag, Mama tucked a jar of apricot preserves and two brown paper packages. One held apple and raisin strudel, the other a lovely shawl she had crocheted. "This will ward off the chill on the boat deck. When you wrap it around your shoulders, it will be as the embrace of my arms." We held each other closely, my mouth nuzzling her neck, my kisses and Mama's body talc intermingling. I breathed deeply of her soft, powdered skin, tasted the sweetness of her mixed together with my briny tears. Our murmurings were poignant whispers still strong in my memory: "Goodbye, my darling." "Don't forget us." "I love you." "Write often."

Papa pressed a small purse heavy with forints into my hand, his face contorted in anguish. To overcome his emotion, he began a long-winded speech about guarding my valuables, ending with: "Sew them into your corset."

Then, he reminded me it was absolutely essential the children always hold onto my skirts. I was to pay particular attention near train tracks and the ship's deck rail, "They can be swept overboard by the slightest gust of wind."

There was more fatherly advice about the exchange of forints to marks and guilders on the black market. Finally, his arms enfolded me in a powerful hug.

"Én is szeretlek," he said. *I love you.*

"Én is szeretlek, Papa."

The locomotive's whistle announced the departure for Debrecen, where we would connect with the express train to Budapest. The boys and I stood at the compartment's open window, our fingertips caressing Papa and Mama's for as long as we were able. The train, gaining speed, generated enormous clouds of steam, engulfing my parents and Nagy Karolyi. My knees began to tremble, forcing me to take my seat. I knew I would never return to this place again.

Mama later wrote how they remained on the station waving at the train until it was out of sight. I opened the little purse Papa had given me. It was full of forints and one thing more: a folded scrap of linen tied with string. Opening the little packet, I found the talisman for protection on the seas: my desiccated caul.

The passage of time was squeezing, squashing, compacting. The train sped northward toward Budapest. The hours seemed minutes. Racing into the future, I was not afraid.

7

Built in 1827, the French Compagnie du Chemin de Fer de Saint-Ètienne a la Loire was the first public railway in Continental Europe, connecting Saint-Ètienne to Andrézieux.

The single, cast-iron track transported goods in wagons pulled by horses on a towpath. Five years later, after buying two steam locomotives, the company opened the line to passengers.

In 1832, the Austrian Empire opened the second intercity railway on the continent. An eighty-mile-long, horse-drawn railway connected Linz and Bohemia, the westernmost and largest region of the Czech territory. Five years later, Salomon Mayer von Rothschild financed the Emperor Ferdinand Northern Railway Company, a steam locomotive-driven line between Vienna and Krakow. The first railway in Hungary, a nineteen-mile track running from Budapest (then Pest) to Vác, at the foot of the Carpathian Mountains, opened in 1837.

The development of the railway system through Europe facilitated the movement of large numbers of migrants. At the same time, ocean-going steamers were being built to accommodate the steerage crossing to America, South Africa, and South America.

The migration presented an opportunity for investors to reap profits from not only rail and shipping businesses but also vertical silos of attendant, related, and codependent niches: travel brokers, lodging houses, storage facilities, transit-linking port and rail terminals, sundry shops, medical and dental providers, money exchanges, and translation services. All along the route, immigrants were targets of swindlers and scams.

Railway and shipping companies formed liaisons. Competition was keen, as was innovation.

Representatives were employed in cities and small towns throughout Europe, promoting their connections and experience to aid the migrants. They performed many services: guidance for obtaining exit papers, purchasing rail tickets, lodgings on stopovers, accommodations at port, and sailing documents. They even sold luggage designed to accommodate and organize basic necessities for so complicated a journey. Agents and brokers were commissioned handsomely by both the migrant *and* the rail and shipping lines they promoted. Often, they received a "taste" from the lodging houses and medical personnel they recommended.

Special, segregated trains were put into service to move the refugees through to their port destinations quickly and with as little interaction with the German and Dutch populace as possible.

Fannie, Albert, Morris, and Rudolf began their westward trek from Budapest on Sunday, August 30, 1893.

Fannie

It was as if a giant funnel had scooped up Europe's poor, and through the small end, the flotsam came tumbling out onto the trains streaming toward the North Sea.

We were to sail from Rotterdam on the SS *Maasdam* on Saturday, August 5th. Rail travel offered new trains, precise schedules, and the latest innovations for comfort and machinery. It seemed illogical and an unnecessary expense to add an extra day of travel, but it gave me peace of mind to plan for six days on the rails.

On Sunday, July 30th, we boarded the cheapest ride, the overnight MÁV train. Departing Budapest at ten o'clock, we arrived in Vienna at six on Monday morning.

From the time we entered Austria until reaching Ellis Island, Hungarian was spoken only to one another, as it was not a language universally understood. Traveling through a Germanic landscape; Austria, Germany, and Holland, it was convenient to speak their tongue.

After detraining in Vienna, I hired a livery for transport to a boarding house in the Jewish quarter, arranged for by Bentz, our travel broker.

Esther Weitz, the property owner, showed us to a room at the rear of her second-floor row house. The breezeless August sun poured through the only window, which seemed no larger than my handkerchief.

The woman stood in the doorway, observing my reaction to the tiny room. I imagined that prior to having been pressed into immigrant service, it might have been a storage closet.

The room did not offer a clothes cupboard nor a wall-mounted shelf upon which to put garments. It was simply bare walls and a limp mattress covering all but a foot's breadth of floor space around its perimeter. The cushion appeared wide enough for two adults to lie upon, just barely. It would be generous of me to describe the pad as anything more than a collection of cotton lumps confined within a striped, fraying muslin cover. Rejecting the place never entered my mind, as we were all so tired, and it was paid for. To Esther's credit, the linen was clean; three goose-feather pillows well-stuffed. An indoor toilet and sink were just down the hall.

"Mama, will we all fit on that bed?" Albert asked.

I nodded, "I believe we'll make the best of things here, Albert. We must eat and sleep to restore our strength. Tonight, on the train to Prague, sitting upright on stained seats, we may look back to consider this little room luxurious."

Standing in the door frame, no, *filling* the door frame, Esther surveyed us. By any measure, she was large. Broad-shouldered and fat, she stood at least six feet in height. Her dress was ill-fitting, especially across the upper torso, which presented more as a big belly than breasts. Her dominant feature, a bulbous nose with a very large mole at its bridge, kept one's gaze riveted there, distracting a bit from her conversation. Her manner of speech was rapid-fire and to the point, perhaps to keep you from staring at that mole.

"Well, put your bags down under the window and follow me, boys! I can hear your empty bellies grumbling from all the way over here!"

The boys were agog with her aura, her persona.

Directly across from our room, a narrow stairway led to the kitchen. In single file, we followed her bulky form, its mass brushing the walls on either side.

The center of the kitchen held a table and eight wooden chairs. And the stove! Oh, my, what a stove! The tiled floor supported a four-legged device made of cast iron enameled a pale green color. Two coal-burning ovens, both large enough to fit an entire goose, sat one atop the other on the left side of the cooker, and five gas-fired burners were fitted on the right.

Esther steered the boys to the table. In the center, heaped upon a large platter, were vanilla crescent cookies, slices of coffee cake, and glazed pastries. She filled three tin mugs with milk, sliding them across the highly varnished wood precisely to where each of the boys sat.

"Come boys, eat. You'll remember how my cherry-cheese pastries melted on your tongue for the rest of your days!"

They were entranced by her manner and watched every movement as if they were at a traveling circus.

"Danke, Frau Weitz," Albert said

"Danke, Frau Weitz," Morris and Rudolf chimed in unison.

Carrying my coffee cup, the brew topped with cinnamon and shlagsahne, I was drawn to an open door near the stairway.

Looking out to the yard, I saw eight boxes painted bright blue set upon the ground in two neat rows reaching from the doorstep to a wooden fence at the end of the plot. Green and red bell peppers, pole-climbing beans, salad greens, parsley, mint, and sage grew in profusion, the boxes overflowing. The lovely vision of August's bounty reminded me of my Mama's Garden, and I wept.

Esther crossed the room to surround me with her large body, rocking me from side to side. "Weine nicht, alles wird gut in Amerika sein, Fannie." (Don't cry, all will be well in America). It was a kind gesture from this stranger, but I found no relief.

This was the first of many moments of grief I would suffer for the loss of the sight of my mother's face, her touch, her smell. In that moment, I felt the depth of my injury. Gradually, I would become aware of the chronic sense of loss crouching on the edges of my consciousness and would weep during all the remaining years of my life for the Mother I had abandoned.

After a short while, to assure the children I was alright, I sat at the table and engaged Esther in conversation. "What made you open your home to the Jews passing through, Esther?"

She threw back her head. and a roaring laugh escaped her open, long-toothed mouth. "Forgive me, Fannie. I'm no philanthropist, you know. There's no need to flatter me. I'm a businesswoman. My house is my business. The stream of immigrants needing a place to stay for a few hours between trains is making me a good living. So good, in fact, I no longer cater to my old customers. I work with brokers from all the shipping lines. Those boys can count on me to provide a clean room. although I can't say I can count on some of that ilk for honest business practices. I've had travelers show up with receipts of payment, but the money never reached me. You understand, I can offer no pity. If I have the room, they'll have to pay right then. What they already paid is lost. If they don't have the money, well, they'll have to sleep on a bench at the station."

I said, "It's a hard business you're in, having to turn away families who are tired and hungry. Poor people who were victims of swindlers."

"Well, in the end, it's not my problem. I have to take care that I'm not fleeced, don't I? There are thousands coming through Vienna who could be escaped Russian convicts. Over the years, I've learned to size up my guests in the first five minutes, and I'm not often wrong about whose word I can trust. I only want to do business with honest people, and I don't care what language you speak, how poor you are, or what you did for a living. Before this migration, many in the oldest profession rented under my roof, sometimes for a month, often for years. For the most part, they were good women, just trying to get by doing the only work they knew how to do. Truth is, I don't care what my bedrooms are used for as long as I can bank a few gulden or forints in the end!"

I was more than a little shocked by what she was intimating. "Esther, the boys."

Laughing out loud again, she said, "Oh, if they don't know what I'm meaning, it won't corrupt them. If they *do* know what I'm meaning, they'll not be offended or shocked!

"So, Fannie Freed and sons. Finish your morning meal and off to bed with you. The evening train to Prague departs at ten. You'll want to wake up for a meal by seven, at the latest. There's a cheap dinner available at the café just next door if you don't want to pay a small donation to enjoy the cabbage soup and flanken I'm cooking. Now that I think of it and because my heart's as big as my you-know-what, I'll throw the meal in with the lodging!"

Back in our little room, we stripped to our underwear, carefully folding our clothes in piles next to our baggage on the bit of floor space under the window.

Guardedly, Albert asked, "Mama, Frau Weitz is nice, isn't she?"

"If you're worried she'll rob us while we sleep, I don't believe she will. She's a good woman, Albert, just making a living. And think about her kindness, offering to feed us dinner at no charge."

Without a word, Morris yawned and fell backward upon the mattress.

Albert found his grown-up Papa voice: "Move over, Morris! You can't take up the whole bed."

They arranged themselves crossways on the mattress. Albert stretched his legs akimbo to claim a wider share. Rudolf's torso clung to the very edge, his legs hanging over onto the floor. Already asleep, there was no complaint from him.

Spreading my crocheted shawl on the narrow bit of floor available, I said, "I'll take a pillow and lie here so you'll have plenty of room."

And there was. And they did.

Even as young as they were, they had good character and were kind. I was sure they'd mature to be good men. That afternoon lying on the lumpy mattress in Vienna, I listened to their breathing. My heart swelled with love for them. I felt Samuel's presence, giving me strength and confidence. "We're coming, my darling," I whispered.

In spite of daylight filling the room, we slept until sundown, awakened by the aroma of sweet and sour cabbage wafting up from the kitchen.

Esther was a marvelous cook, accustomed to preparing meals for her clientele at all hours. A large oak sideboard was laid with the dinner meal. Slices of thick-crusted pumpernickel bread filled a basket, a tub of butter at its side. A black iron pot rested on a towel; a large ladle perched on its lid. The dining table, covered with a white cloth, had been set for four with napkins, bowls, utensils, three metal cups filled with milk, and one beer stein at my place.

Esther, wearing a stained apron (which may have been a tablecloth) of checkered red and black design, welcomed us enthusiastically.

"Well, Fannie Freed and sons have survived the hotbox back room! You have three hours to eat and relax before you must be at the station. The train to Prague is never late and leaves the station at exactly ten o'clock. Sit down, boys. Fannie, help me serve them."

To better organize and secure our small parcels, Esther gave me a wheeled box pulled by a length of rope. Tying the large carpet bag on top, the consolidation made our movements so much easier.

Leading the way to the front door and down the steps to the street, Esther said, "Goodbye and viel glück, Fannie Freed and sons! Send me a postal card when you reach America!"

"Auf Wiedersehen, Frau Weitz, und danke!"

With a farewell wave of hands, we began the ten-minute walk to the station, Albert pulling the wheeled box.

Our tickets, prepaid by Bentz, were in hand, allowing me to bypass long queues at ticket windows. The majority of Russians and Poles traveled through Vienna, so it was no surprise to learn the night train to Prague had been oversold.

Undaunted, I was determined we'd be on that train. First, we had to find a car with four empty seats, no small task. Rudolf and Morris held my skirts, so as not to be separated, and we made our way, slowly, through the throng rushing this way and that, Albert still pulling our baggage.

Six passenger cars had been added to the train. To accommodate the added weight on the rails, two dining, and one lavatory car had been sacrificed. We were unaware of this upon entering the car, but luckily for us, Esther had provided a box with cheese, bread, fruit, and a jar of tea to get us through the night. The inadequate number of lavatories made the trip a living hell. As they were filthy and always occupied, I took to helping the boys use the empty tea jar as a urinal.

Leaving the wheeled cart on the platform, Albert and I carried the bags to the end of the train, where we managed to find three seats in a compartment already occupied by a family of nine who had not bathed since leaving the Russian Pale! Rudolf sat on my lap, and all three passed the night in the sleep of the innocents, with not a care in the world.

I barely slept at all, jostled and uncomfortable. I worried our luggage, on the overhead shelf, would be rifled through or stolen if I were not alert.

After eight hours and traversing one hundred eighty-five miles, we reached Prague at six on Tuesday morning.

When the doors opened, the crowd charged the platform, coursing as rapids down a sloping riverbed toward the terminal. Railway security personnel stemmed the human tide by locking the metal gate through which the departure area was accessed.

Swept along with the crowd, I realized we needed to exit this melee or risk being trampled. Managing to steer the boys, and our luggage, to a bench in the main concourse, we rested for an hour. Using the lavatory and washing our faces, we ate what remained of the fruit. At a kiosk, I bought sausage, bread, and a jar of tea.

Two hours later, we made our way to the departing train. A large presence of Bohemian police, some on horseback, circulated in the terminal. That caused me to wonder about the possibility of a riot developing. Hundreds of transients deprived of proper sleep and nutrition might react viciously to a conceived slight or jostle. Someone stepping on another's toe or picking up the wrong piece of luggage could result in chaos. There was no common language to bind these travelers. In fact, divisions of tongue, country, history, and religion were exacerbated in this place.

The boys and I held an advantage over the Slavs. As German speakers, we read the signage, were able to ask directions. The Slavs milled about, isolated, exhausted, and confused.

Our cultural understanding and efficiency of movement were rewarded as we arrived in the vanguard and secured four seats in a compartment with a German couple returning home after a Viennese holiday.

A sense of smugness at outplaying the Slavs filled me. I remember thinking, *as a German-speaker, I'll have no problem learning, for the entirety of the trip, how to navigate the obstacles.*

That false pride disintegrated by 10:00, the hour of departure, when a dozen unwashed Russians shoved at one another to enter the coach. Standing shoulder to shoulder in the space between seats, their hands clutched the luggage racks for balance. Still, at the few stops between Prague and Nuremberg, more people crowded in. For eight hours, we sat in silence, miserable. During the last hours, I counted twenty-three persons in our coach, fitted with seats for ten.

In the Nuremberg terminal building, we waited for three hours at the information booth for Bentz's representative, but he never arrived. Representatives of charitable organizations circulated amongst the crowd. One of them, a volunteer for the Nuremberg Clerical Association, arranged for us to spend the night on cots in the basement of a Catholic church. The next morning, we were served a breakfast of gruel, fresh bread, milk, and coffee. Grateful for their kindness, I put four forints in the collection box.

At noon on Wednesday, we departed for Frankfort, arriving at nine in the evening. Upon detraining, a sign informed us the midnight train to Cologne had been canceled.

In fact, two Cologne-bound trains were sent to the yard for repair and maintenance, causing me a great deal of distress. We were marooned in Frankfort until service was restored. If we did not reach Rotterdam the day before the *Maasdam* sailed, we might be denied boarding!

Near to 1:00 in the morning, with the boys asleep on the terminal floor, we were rescued by a member of the Frankfort Jewish Refugee Organization, a philanthropy providing aid for migrants. They arranged for us to spend that night with the Kohens, who generously provided us with baths and breakfast the next morning.

Thursday, the train departed Frankfort at noon, reaching Cologne at 8:00 in the evening. That was not to be the end of our day, though.

Scheduled to leave at midnight, we managed to survive four hours seated on wooden benches before boarding for Rotterdam.

People stormed the car doors. Albert, swift and clever, pushed onto the train in advance of our party and weaving in and about the crowd, staked out seats. Almost immediately, every available inch of the car was occupied with passengers sitting on the floor or standing, where they remained for the seven-hour ride.

Finally, at half past midnight, our last train ride on the European Continent was underway.

After a few kilometers, the bathrooms were unusable, and it was impossible to reach the dining car through aisles clogged with people and baggage. The stench of the unwashed, the smell of food decaying inside their bags, was nauseating.

In spite of all the hardships we had endured, my mood on that last rail was one of contentment. We had come all that way, overcome difficulties, kept our valuables, remained optimistic, never despaired. No matter the discomfort of the train, my sons and I were satisfied with life and with this adventure.

Six days and eleven hundred miles on the rails ended at Rotterdam early on Friday morning, August 4th.

We stood with our luggage on the platform, taking in the crowded scene, oddly full of energy.

Squatting, I faced my sons. Looking into their eyes, I said, "We've made it, boys. We are explorers, discovering new worlds. I'm so proud of you. You were wonderful. I love you all so much. Tomorrow, we'll begin the ocean voyage. And, then, with you and Papa in America, we'll be a whole family again." We all kissed and laughed. We were happy.

A horde of runners rushed us. These young men earned a guilder for each guest or family they delivered to hotels and boarding houses.

Our prepaid tickets on the SS *Maasdam* included lodging at the N.A.S.M. Hotel, owned by the Holland-America Line. To serve its clientele, men wearing striped caps of red, white, and blue emblazoned with the letters N.A.S.M., pushed hand trolleys through the crowds.

"Transport to Holland-America Hotel!" "Transport to Holland-America Hotel!"

Hearing the call, Albert ran to fetch the lad, and we joined a dozen of our fellow-travelers placing their baggage onto the trolley.

Unencumbered, we followed the group out of the terminal to a waiting horse-drawn omnibus whose doors bore the red, white, and blue stripes of the flag of The Netherlands.

By royal decree, a Board of Control was appointed to set rules and standards for hygiene and services at transient lodgings in Holland and on Dutch ships.

In 1893, across from the Holland-America wharf, the Netherlands-American steamship Company (N.A.S.M) Hotel opened its doors to emigrants. Able to accommodate eight hundred guests, they charged half the rates offered by houses competing for the trade.

The company's ticket agent, baggage clerk, and sundry shop, were located in the lobby; dormitories, dining halls and lounge areas were on upper floors. The hotel was built to process large numbers of people staying only a day or two before sailing for America and to do so economically.

On the top floor, a physician, oculist, and two nurses staffed the fifty-bed infirmary. They were available for any medical emergency and examined the guests at no charge, checking for infectious eye or other diseases that could prevent them from boarding. There were isolation barracks, where those suffering with contagion could be quarantined.

From the 1880s to the 1920s, the Holland-America Line carried more than ten percent of all steerage travel to the New World. Known for the quality of its services and cleanliness of its ships, the line was known as "The Spotless Fleet."

Fannie

Checking into the hotel raised our spirits and renewed our resolve. That very afternoon we visited the agent's office, where our papers and tickets were checked and found in order.

"Present yourselves at eight tomorrow morning at the pier. Nothing is sold onboard. You must take everything you might need with you. Mattresses and pillows are provided; however, you must bring your own blankets, bedlinen, and towels."

He continued, "Tableware is also your responsibility. You will want to purchase tin mugs, plates, knives, forks, and spoons. And I suggest you bring a utensil for the collection of vomit, as seasickness is a common problem. The hotel's shop stocks all these items at the same price you'll find at the market across the road; so, save your energy and haggling skills.

"Remember to visit the resident doctor today to avoid problems boarding the ship. You'll be much more comfortable if you check all but one bag into the cargo hold, as steerage space is very limited. Tickets with all certifying stamps must be attached to each passenger's clothing, where they can readily be seen by the ship's crew. There's a bowl with safety pins in the hotel lobby. Take as many as you need, they are provided for you at no cost.

"I want to mention how lucky you are to be traveling now; an adult ticket will increase to twenty-six U.S. dollars on the first of September. It's hard to keep up with demand, and we expect to add six new ships to the line by 1895. So, on behalf of the Company, Mrs. Freed, I wish you and your sons bon voyage and viel glück in America."

Dinner at the hotel was delicious: spaetzle, potted meat, glazed carrots and pickles—a local specialty—and a small slice of chocolate cake for dessert. As a special treat to celebrate our last European night, each boy sipped a bit of beer to toast our voyage, continued good health, and their Papa. At seven, we retired to the dormitory to finally rest without worry.

By the time we arrived, at 8:30 a.m., the morning fog had burned off, leaving a cloudless sky. The quay was bursting with activity. Seamen presented themselves for work, and the ship's mate checked rosters and inventories. Horse-drawn carts laden with barrels, crates, and baggage were offloaded onto barges.

At the top of the quay, a signboard listed the day's schedule of departures in Dutch, German, and English:

Saturday, August 5, 1893
Holland-America Line (N.A.S.M.)
SS Maasdam
Rotterdam-New York
Departure: 8:00 p.m.

First and second-class passengers made their way to tenders. In the area designated, more than two hundred steerage travelers milled about the dock. We heard Hungarian, German, Romanian, Turkish, Dutch, Yiddish, and Russian all around us, and surprisingly, the conversational tones were subdued. I feared the tenders would be stormed if the group was confined in this hot place for too long. I needn't have worried, though; the crowd remained quiet, tempers crumpled by exhaustion.

Perched on my hip, red-faced and limp from the heat, Rudolf nodded off against my breast. Morris sat on the luggage, seriously observing the scene. Albert, my sentinel and protector, stood at the ready, lest one of the brutish, filthy men invade the space we had claimed. There are many who look like moving rags, pulling a shabby collection of bundles and boxes along.

Two fiddlers began to play, and a group of young men and women sang and danced. For this contingent, responsible only for their own welfare, the trip was a gay adventure.

The stoic families, some with as many as eight children, stayed alert, guarding their precious possessions with steely determination.

Spouseless women traveling with children represented one third of the passengers. To our sisterhood, this venture was tedious and dangerous. For the children's sake, we kept a sunny countenance, but uppermost in our thoughts was that in one week's time, we'd be met by husbands most hadn't seen for years.

The last group numbered fewer than a dozen. They were the elderly: men and women over sixty. Stooped with fatigue, they stood mute and distracted; their careworn faces offered testimony to the great effort they had made to reach this place and to the anxious, gnawing suspicion there was no reserve of strength needed to adapt to American life. The journey was unquestionably meant for those who enjoy youthful resilience!

Waiting in that place, the reality of my position became clear. At first, my thoughts were positive, self-congratulatory, declarations about how I had managed all the details of the trip. I reflected on my optimistic nature, my loving and maternal ministrations, and how fit and attractive Samuel would find me.

Standing amongs Europe's debris, my thoughts darkened. I would never see Papa and Mama again nor any of my kin. Looming large was the possibility that our reunion may not work out, that we would suffer through a loveless life in an alien world, in poverty. Or, perhaps we'd be forsaken at Ellis Island. Despite the day's sun and heat, I shivered, and it took all my courage to push the gloom away.

Finally, after queuing for two hours, we inched forward and boarded the tenders. Fifty or sixty of us stood on the flat scow, which moved at a snail's pace to avoid jostling the passengers. To keep from falling into the sea, we kept our balance holding onto nautical ropes installed around the perimeter. The shuttle made its way through the channel, to Hoek van Holland, known as "The Hook," the final spit of land at the entrance to the North Sea.

Nearing The Hook, I observed the *Maasdam* for the first time, and she appeared ancient. Originally designed as a sailing ship, sleek and narrow, she measured forty feet abeam and four hundred twenty feet in length. Only three years earlier, to increase speed and profit, the ship had been fitted with steam engines and boilers. An odd combination, she had a single funnel but also four soaring masts, now useless relics. I was surprised how small she was. Where would we all fit?

A few men began to argue about the ship's seaworthiness and whether it could survive a hurricane. Since storms were always a possibility on the Atlantic in August, this was a very real concern.

To be truthful, until then, the prospect of a disaster at sea was so remote, it had caused me no apprehension. Then, once in play, the scenario could not be "un-thought." This sudden fear, combined with my other negative musings, caused a bilious nausea to rise in my throat. In my mind's eye, the *Maasdam* was a floating coffin.

At that moment, thoughts of Samuel and our participation in the migration seemed irrational. Papa became my focus, unraveling what was left of my self-assurance. The whole scheme had been driven by vanity and the shortsightedness of youth. My invulnerability was overstated, childish. How could I have become infatuated with the American fantasy?

I hadn't thought it all through; not taken seriously the risks to which I was exposing myself and the children. And, as for Samuel, Papa was right. Why should *he* be held blameless after leaving us alone for all this time? Why should *he* be excused for placing upon me all the responsibility for our trip across the Atlantic Ocean?

Sadly, at this point, what options did I have? There was no turning back.

At first, I thought my corset was laced too tightly, as a sudden dizziness and extreme shortness of breath overcame me. A few seconds later, awash in perspiration, my heart pounded so strenuously, I feared it would burst. A creeping dread infused my body, climaxing with an overwhelming desire to flee this place and to do so *now*.

"Keine sorge, kleiner mutter (don't worry, little mother). The ship will withstand a hurricane." A tall woman and young girl stood beside me at the ropes. Henriette Luther introduced herself and her sixteen-year-old daughter, Josephine.

Forced to gather my wits, I managed to respond calmly, "Danke shoen, Dame. I know it's foolish, but I'm worrying about everything at this moment."

"Your distress is obvious to me *and* your sons. You must get a hold of yourself, mustn't panic. We haven't been informed of bad weather, have we? After many crossings, the Master and his crew are experienced handling the unexpected at sea. Josephine will take care of your middle boy, and you can concentrate on the little one."

Taking charge, Henriette took my bag and placed Morris's hand into her daughter's. I adjusted Rudolf more securely on my hip, and Albert, always up to the task, protected our rear. Now, alongside the ship, we made our way, in single file, to the gangplank that hung suspended between tender and ship.

Master Albert Pohjer stood at the rail observing each passenger as they stepped onto the deck and into his care. I was unaware of his watchful eye, concentrating only on Henriette's voice coaxing me forward on the plank.

"We must simply follow the crowd, Fannie. We're all going to the same place. Stay right behind me, and we'll be alright."

Through a hatchway marked "emigrants," a steep, narrow stairway descended sixteen feet below deck to an area between the forward mast and midships. Nearly in free-fall, we gripped the handrail for dear life. Waiting to progress on that ghastly and precarious ladder, I again felt unwell.

Stumbling out of the hatchway, the undirected crowd came to a halt, cramming itself into an even tighter clutch. While waiting to move forward, the stifling heat and noxious fumes caused me to gasp, making it impossible to breathe normally. Feeling the need to escape, yet remaining rooted to the spot, I knew there was no way out.

Henriette hailed one of the stewards, who came to our aid.

"Madam, I assure you the fumes of the bilge, cargo, and humanity will improve as the vessel gets underway. It's apparent you're at the end of your tether, so, if you and the children will follow me, I'll lead you to Section 2, forward steerage. That's the women-with-children quarters."

Hefting Morris up to his shoulder, he led us to our dormitory. "Try to claim the forward-most bunks, the ones against the bulkhead wall. Although farthest from the lavatory, it's a bit quieter and more private. I'll keep you in my sight for the first few days, as you accustom yourselves to the routine. If you have any trouble, look for me; my name is Dieter."

The room was clean and well-lighted, revealing twelve triple-tiered bunks bolted to the deck. At first, I thought them jammed one against the other, but at closer look, there was just enough floor space between them to allow access to the beds. Walking quickly to the end bunk, we secured our territory.

Thankfully, the mattresses and pillows were in good repair and had been disinfected with a solution of formaldehyde, acetone, and alcohol. Each bunk was two feet wide and offered about the same for headroom, making it possible only for the smallest children to sit upright upon them.

Opposite, on the wall of the vessel's hull, was one porthole, promising circulation of fresh air once we were underway. The floor space between the beds and the porthole wall barely allowed a single person to pass, yet we soon accommodated to the claustrophobic conditions.

A large lavatory adjoined the dormitory, with plenty of hot and cold water, all for our cabin's exclusive use.

Henriette and I put our baggage on two adjacent top bunks, assigning the ones below to the children. I began to feel my old self and thanked Dieter with a tip of one guilder as he left to help another family group.

After placing linen on the mattresses and tying our tin utensils to a rope fastened to the bed rail, I rearranged our clothing and toiletries in the suitcase, stowing it under Rudolf's bottom bunk.

A length of canvas served as the interior cabin wall, separating us from the large space amidships, designated as the salon for our class. It was sparsely furnished with wooden chairs and a few small tables scattered about. Until lowered at mealtime, long tables and benches were suspended from the ceiling by pulleys.

At 2:00 p.m., we queued at the salon for inspection by the medical officer. Standing at the door, the chief steward held a bowl filled with folded bits of numbered paper. Luckily, both Henriette and I drew a "1," which meant we were to attend the first seating for meals.

Moving in a slow procession, the doctor gave us the once-over. Every now and then, the line came to a halt, allowing him a closer look at an individual appearing ill. Smallpox vaccinations were administered to those unable to show proof of inoculation, and tickets received certifying stamps.

Later, the tables and benches were lowered to the floor, and the stewards wasted no time dishing out the dinner meal: vegetable soup with rice, boiled potatoes, and cold sausage with bread. There was plenty of water, coffee, and milk for the children.

After washing our tableware at the lavatory sink, we went up on deck. The last light of day cast dark shadows in corners, but the shore was not yet eclipsed.

Dieter stopped to chat, telling the boys that to become good sailors, they had to find their sea legs. "Keep your feet firmly planted on the deck and allow your body to absorb the motion. Never fight it. When the deck falls, bend your knees a bit; when the deck rises, straighten your knees and push with your heels." Practicing the sea legs lesson, we became aware of the soft tidal movements that gently rolled the anchored ship.

First-class passengers strolled their elevated deck, stopping to gawk at the continental discards milling about at the base of the funnel and masts. All on board were in high spirits, and it was taken kindly when some sweets and fruit were tossed to the steerage children.

The sun slipped below the horizon; the anchor hoisted. The ship's lamps were aglow, the whistle blew, all aboard cheered, and we steamed into the North Sea, leaving The Hook in darkness.

The salon offered music and dancing until 9;00, after which only a handful of passengers lingered, enjoying hushed conversation or a game of cards played under the light of a kerosene lamp. In the darkened dormitory, many dialects whispered thanks to Heaven above for the blessing of their arrival to this place and prayed for His continued protection on crossing the great ocean.

It is hard to describe the exquisite relief I felt, lying on the bunk, finally ending this day. Under my bedclothes, I loosened, but did not remove, my corset. The fabric purse containing our valuables and my caul was securely stitched there, as Papa had advised.

Only sleep could repair the toll of the stressful exertions endured during these last weeks, and I wholeheartedly welcomed that sweet oblivion. Rocked by the sea and comforted by the engine's lullaby, I sailed into unconsciousness.

In the morning, we awoke at anchor at Boulogne, France, where an additional sixty passengers came aboard, bringing the manifest total to four hundred forty-five persons.

8

After the War of Independence from Britain, Thomas Paine said, "America is becoming the asylum for the persecuted lovers of civil and religious liberty from every part of Europe."

In 1790, the Congress passed the first Naturalization Act: "Any alien, being a free white person, may be admitted as a citizen of the United States." In the early years, only about six thousand people emigrated annually.

Following the war of 1812, record numbers of British, Irish, and Western Europeans came to America, causing Congress to pass the Steerage Act of 1819. This required ship captains to keep detailed passenger records and provide humane conditions for those on board.

Between 1820 and 1880, millions came to America; 2,800,000 emigrated from Ireland, almost all escaping the potato famine. Nine percent of the total population of Norway left their country.

Why did they come? Geographers and sociologists define it this way: Pushes and Pulls.

"Pushes" are forces that prompt voluntary exit: war, drought, famine, disease, poverty, racial or religious bigotry, and political intolerance.

"Pulls" are the attractions of the destination: better economic conditions, political freedom, religious tolerance, opportunities for education.

Between 1880 and 1930, over twenty-seven million people entered the United States, twelve million through Ellis Island.

On Saturday, August 12, 1893, pushed by religious intolerance and pulled by political freedom and opportunity, my great-grandmother stepped from the deck of the SS *Maasdam* onto American soil.

Fannie

There are few conditions more favorable to the rapid growth of friendship than those made on shipboard. It was as if the world itself was our cabin, and with childlike trust, harmony and understanding took root amongst strangers.

Family influence, national allegiance, economic station, religious affiliation, even illiteracy, miraculously dissolved; abandoned on the European continent. The natural development of democracy and unity was welcomed for the good of all.

I observed that most of the women in steerage knew very little about their destination. Some believed they would find gold growing on bushes, and others thought the country no bigger than Germany or France. Several held currencies sent by relatives from America but couldn't fathom the values of nickels, dimes, and quarters. Terrified of being cheated of their small sums, they implored the stewards, again and again, to explain the coinage.

Dieter told them, "In America, a loaf of bread will cost a nickel." *That* was a fine example. *That* could be understood. "Zo," a woman from the Netherlands declared, "in Hengelo, a chicken for soep—soup—may cost five times a loaf of brood. Dat is slechts vijfentwintig cent. That is only twenty-five cents! An American chicken will cost twenty-five cents. A quarter! Danke, Dieter!"

In our cabin, seventy-five women and children, speaking the native tongue of more than a dozen countries or one of more than twenty dialects of those tongues, found a way to communicate.

Although German dominated, short phrases learned on international railway cars, words borrowed from signage, animated pantomime, even rudimentary drawings were forged into a verbal stew by the mothers. Quicker to adapt, the children bounded over lingual barriers.

On Sunday afternoon the sun shone warmly on our faces, encouraging a sense of well-being. We stood away from land, and the *Maasdam* forged ahead at maximum speed, fifteen knots. Hope was high, and hearts were light. It was remarkable that in only a day or two, we had settled into the ship's routine for meals, lavatory use, and sleeping on those narrow bunks. Our legs mastered the rhythmic movements of the sea, and the boys had no difficulty playing about the ship.

In the early evening, a group gathered around the main mast to hold a Sunday church service, their hymns filling the air with joy and gratitude for divine protection. I marveled at, even envied, their pious community. In times of duress, how comforting it must be to rely upon heavenly salvation and the power of an all-knowing patriarch.

At nine, the watchman made rounds, sending all the women below. Before returning to our bunks, we lingered for a few moments to view, in awe, the spectacle of our surroundings. There was no visible light from any landmass. The ship floated on an endless, moving cushion of inky waves, their white caps reflecting the moon's light. A canopy of deepest black spanned the heavens, the constellations so clearly visible they seemed to hang just above the masts.

After the children were asleep, Henriette and I lay upon our top bunks, facing one another across the narrow gap. In very quiet tones, we shared the stories of our lives. She was forty-eight and raised a Lutheran, yet we had much in common. She, too, had been left behind, waiting for passage money. Her husband, Hans, and their son, Erik, left Germany two years earlier, finding work in Akron, Ohio.

Aside from Henriette and me, when midnight bells rang, only a few in the cabin were still awake. Two women near the entrance to the salon whispered in German. I glimpsed the reflection of an older woman's silhouette pass the porthole, making her way to the lavatory. A baby whimpered, rooting for his mother's breast.

Both Henriette and I wept at the recounting of my city life, her farm life, for the families we would never see again. It was remarkable, given all the people and places we had left behind, and in spite of the insecurity of our marriages, we both held dear the image of a good life in America. By the time we fell asleep, a strong affection for one another had developed, the bonding of surrogate sisters.

Midmorning on Monday, the ship began rolling and pitching, for which we were unprepared. The sky was obscured by low, thick clouds. Borne on a brisk breeze, a salty spray moistened our faces. By midafternoon, the sea was green-gray and lumpy, with waves breaking over the starboard rail. On the leeward side, a safety rope stretched aft. Clinging to this, we made our way to the hatch and went below. Few returned topside.

Waves were level with our porthole, secured by a steel rod bolted to the hull, preventing an accidental opening. The berths began to fill with groaning collections of white-faced, seasick wretches. Albert and Morris vomited until their stomachs emptied. Rudolf and I lay together on the top bunk. We felt queasy but didn't suffer the extreme nausea of our mates. Odors between decks were foul in good weather; and now, with people soiling themselves or clutching bile filled buckets, the air was putrid.

Wet hatchway stairs and decks were treacherous to navigate, yet once or twice, I carefully made my way to the open air just to breathe deeply for a few moments. A few men and women lay about the deck, obstacles around which the deckhands maneuvered to sweep the vomit and coal dust into the sea. By late afternoon, all passengers were instructed to go below, as the gale was becoming a hurricane.

Few sat at the dinner tables. At least twenty persons lay upon the floor clutching their cramping bellies, too weak to crawl to their cabins. Albert and Morris shared one lower berth, covered with a blanket. To secure them, I tied a rope across from one side rail to the other. In the same manner, I fastened Rudolf and myself into the upper bunk. This was a precaution taken after witnessing an injury to one of the young mothers during a sudden lurching of the ship. Two bones in her arm had been broken when she was thrown into the steel hull.

Tin tableware rattled against steel bed frames, a metallic counterpoint to the melancholy moaning of our cabin mates. The roar of the wind and creaking of the boat as it strained in its perpendicular climb to the top of a wave brought many to hysteria. During the seconds of free-fall into the trough, dishes crashed in the kitchen, and the lights went on and off several times.

Children were crying and women prayed. Overwrought, some fainted. Others appeared catatonic. Preparing for the end, women held tight to rosary beads, chanting, "Hail Mary, Mother of God;" and others, in Hebrew, wailed "Adonöy hu ho-Elohim. G-d is the Lord."

The storm intensified through the night. More than a few times, she rolled so far, I was certain the *Maasdam* would be swamped. Miraculously, she righted herself, and Captain Pohjer led her into the next wave. I was aware of each moment; all the same, I wasn't afraid. I put my trust in the captain, the certainty I would see Samuel again, and in the power of my caul.

Throughout the night, I gripped the desiccated tissue in the palm of my hand. For centuries, sustained by legend, superstition, and magic, men believed this talisman protected those in peril on the seas. Who was I to whistle into the wind?

Dieter stopped by several times, his presence a comfort. "I've brought water and biscuits to help calm your stomachs. This is a big storm, but I've been in worse. I can assure you we'll make it through.

"The captain told the crew we'll soon be entering the eye, and you'll be amazed at how flat the sea will become."

Albert asked, "How long will we be in the calm?"

"No one can say for sure; it can be a few minutes or a few hours. It's an amazing sight, nature's force suspended."

I asked, "Might we go topside to witness the event? It would be instructional for my sons."

"I would deny having given you encouragement, but it *is* a once-in-a-lifetime sight. All the same, it's a mixed blessing; the calm reminds us we're only halfway through the hurricane's orbit. On the bright side, I'm sure by morning, it will all be blown away."

In all those hours, I heard not a word from Henriette. She and Josephine clung to one another under a blanket on the middle bunk, both seasick and in silent dread of our imminent sinking.

In the midst of the reeling and rolling, the bone-jarring motion of the ship, and the banshee cries of the wind, a small and trembling voice reached me. "Mama, are we going to die?

I could not respond quickly. Jumping from the bunk could result in a slip or fall upon the deck. It was necessary to ensure each handhold and placement of foot to reach the floor and sit between the bunks. Amazingly, Rudolf appeared beside me, having managed the treacherous descent all by himself.

The boys lay trussed in the bunk, holding each other. Morris's eyes were tightly closed, his face buried in the crook of his brother's arm.

Through tears of despair, Albert hiccoughed his words: "Mama could a giant wave turn us upside down, or one of the masts break and split the ship in two?"

Squeezing into the adjacent lower bunk, Rudolf and I bumped heads as the ship tossed to starboard. Finding that funny, he laughed out loud. I laughed, too, and told the boys, "Look at Rudolf! The storm hasn't dampened his sense of humor! We're not going to die. Even a matchstick floats upon the largest wave, and the *Maasdam* will, too. We only have to keep our heads about us for a few more hours. Tomorrow the sea will calm, and in a few days, you'll tell the story of this night to your Papa.

"So, to pass the time—let's pretend we're characters in a sea adventure book and not be frightened. Can you imagine that?"

"Yes, Mama, I'll be Captain Albert. Morris can be Dieter, and Rudolf will be an engine-stoker. And you. You'll be a first-class passenger."

"Mama, I have to pee." During the storm's drama, this necessity was not only a challenge, but it offered distraction. I untied the bed restraints and one of our tin cups. With my help, Morris managed to stand. Center stage, he played it for laughs, mugging to the approval of his brothers. We all cheered, and then Albert and Rudolf gave it a go. The relief was physical and emotional for all.

Sleep was out of the question, so the four of us maneuvered onto one lower bunk and each character reported their view of the storm: the captain, the steward, the engine-stoker, and the first-class passenger. The role-play allowed us to feel in control of the ship and better about our chances for survival. After a while, the game grew tiresome, and we recited stories and poems.

"My favorite is *Treasure Island*, " Albert declared. "But that might not be good for tonight. I'll tell about *Aladdin and the Wonderful Lamp*. The best thing is I think his name is Arabic for Albert!"

Morris chose *The Brave Little Tailor*, "Once there was a poor tailor, like my Papa, who won the King's only daughter. He killed giants and even a unicorn. Although they were stronger, the tailor was smarter than all of them." After a moment, he added, "he married the Princess, and that's the end."

Rudolf knew only one story, *Little Red Riding Hood*, and told it with perfect inflection. Gregarious and theatrical, he included frightening grimace and ominous voice where appropriate. Sweetly, he chirped, "Grandma, what a big mouth you have." Narrowing his eyes and parting his lips to show his teeth, he snarled, "The better to eat you with, my dear!" His brothers cheered, "Hurrah, Rudolf!" What a boy.

At my turn, I went on about America, all the wonders we would see: big cities, cowboys, the Statue of Liberty. After retelling the story of Samuel and me falling in love, I repeated anecdotes they never tired of hearing: accounts of family visits to Tolcsva and Nagy Karolyi, picnic lunches in Pest.

When the gray dawn appeared, Rudolf was snug asleep, his head upon my lap, feet across the legs of his brothers.

I perceived a tonal change in the screaming wind, the storm's power waning. Shifting Rudolf so the length of his body lay upon my torso, the other two straddled my hips. With my arms encircling them, we were, all of us, secure within the maelstrom. Under the mantle of my son's bodies, a fragile sleep carried me off; but not before I thought of Papa and Samuel.

The hurricane dispersed, as did the tempest within my breast; doubt and uncertainty scattered with the wind on the Atlantic Ocean. My heart and mind were in accord; I *knew* my love was waiting.

The early morning light weakly penetrated the filthy porthole glass. With almost everyone sick, the cabin air was fetid, but from over the canvas wall, I heard the crew arranging tables and benches and smelled coffee brewing. I reasoned if the crew is casually going about its business, the worst was over.

There was little movement until the middle of morning watch, well after eight bells. Only a few ventured to the lavatory, which was in dire need of a good cleaning.

I began straightening up the area around our bunks and sorting clothing, soiled from clean. The boys awakened hungry; we made our way to the salon.

Dieter served us tea, dry toast, sliced apples, and a dollop of oatmeal. "The clouds are scudding fast off the port bow, and I imagine all will return to normal by afternoon. I'm honored to serve under our Captain. God bless him." He stood at attention for a moment. Addressing the boys, "I have to say you all were good sailors. Especially, I'm proud of you, Rudolf. When I made my rounds, most times I found you asleep without a worry in the world, and you and your Mama were the only two people below-ships who were not seasick!"

By noon, the sea was smooth, an intermittent light rain fell, the wind gentle. In order to swab the cabins and scrub the lavatories, the stewards carried and dragged the sick topside. Appearing barely alive, the green-faced passengers sprawled upon the deck or leant against the masts and railings. Protected under canvas shelters fashioned by the crew, children's limp bodies were covered with blankets.

In the open air, we ate oatmeal, cheese, and bread, while our shipmates related their experiences during the dreadful hours just passed.

On Wednesday morning, following instructions of the crew, all passengers assembled on deck. Outside the wheelhouse door, the officers, all in white, stood in a neat line flanking Captain Pohjer. Flashes of sunlight bounced off the brass buttons on their epaulets. They appeared as Gods of Deliverance.

The sun shone equally upon us all: those in first-class reclining on their deck chairs, and the soiled and fatigued steerage mishmash. In spite of our lethargy, slowly, we rose to our feet and began to applaud. Transcending language, we saluted Captain and crew, displaying our gratitude.

The captain stepped forward, addressing us in German. "Schönen tag, good day! The SS *Maasdam* suffered no ill effects from the storm, whose wind registered one hundred sixty kilometers per hour. The blessing is that although tossed from our charted course, the weather carried the vessel along at a good clip, sometimes exceeding twenty-five knots."

The Navigator was called upon to expand on this information. "After recalculating our position and modifying our bearings, I'm happy to report we are steady on course for New York. If all goes well, we will sight New Jersey's coast on Friday evening, a day ahead of schedule."

Next, the First Mate spoke to us. "'Tag, Schiffskameraden, shipmates! Tomorrow, all passengers will undergo a mandatory medical inspection. Persons who are ill may be singled out for quarantine at our destination." A moan passed through the steerage crowd below.

Raising his voice, the Mate continued, "This is precautionary and does not mean you will be sent home. On Friday morning there will be a final medical examination and briefing in your respective salons outlining the procedures for disembarkation.

"Although we'll be ready to move through New York Bay on Friday afternoon, we plan a Saturday arrival at Holland-America's quay. "It is not uncommon to find a long queue waiting for processing. I am fairly certain we can anticipate remaining at anchor off Sandy Hook, New Jersey, for the night."

The crowd began muttering amongst themselves but fell silent when Captain Pohjer stepped forward again. He was a broad-shouldered man, well over six feet tall. In spite of a youthful appearance, I'd guess his age at fifty-five years. A closely trimmed beard covered cheeks and chin, joining with a narrow moustache to complete a blond circle around his mouth.

"Meine freunde, my friends, our actual time of dockage will depend on weather, customs personnel, and marine traffic.

"As a final word: I am grateful to the crew for their seamanship and also thank you all for abiding by their instructions during the ordeal. The *Maasdam* has proven herself a safe and sturdy vessel, and I am honored to be her captain.

"Thank you all for having chosen the Holland-America Line for this momentous voyage. I wish you all much good fortune in America and I will address you each in your own language: Good luck, viel glück for the Germans, veel geluk for the Dutch, Udači to the Russians, tashi delek for the Hungarians, noroc to the Romanians, İyi şanslar to the Turkish, and zol zein mit glick is the best Yiddish I can muster. Good luck to all!"

The captain retired to the wheelhouse amidst cheers from passengers and crew alike. It was a grand day to be alive. A moment or two of silence ensued. We had survived the storm physically and emotionally. The Old World was gone. Today, in the New World, it was time to rejoice.

Two violinists began to play The Wilhelmus, an unofficial anthem of the Kingdom of the Netherlands. Almost one third of the passengers and all the crew were Dutch Nationals. It was beautiful to hear them sing, with passion and patriotic pride. An accordion player struck up a lively folk tune. Excited squeals of pleasure on the steerage deck caught the attention of all on board. At least fifty women and girls on both decks donned brightly painted clogs, and the ship reverberated with the drumbeat of their Klompendansen.

The joy was infectious. The boys and I joined in, clapping to the rhythm, stamping our feet, and smiling broadly. Next, a few Russian passengers commenced playing harmonica, violin, and tambourine. A cheer rose from the Slavs, recognizing the Khorovod, a folk dance where a young man moves about in the middle of a circle with a shawl, finally giving it to a special girl. The circle and the larger crowd responded to the music by clapping, stomping, and moving energetically.

As with the Klompendansen, passengers on both decks joined the fun and enthusiasm!

Samuel

"Hello, Samuel!" Lafayette Lentz's booming voice reverberated from the tin ceiling, ringing out above the dining room's hubbub. I responded with a wave while making my way toward the least desirable, but the *only* unoccupied, table at the luncheon hour—in front of the kitchen door.

Joining me at table, Lafayette used the cotton huck towel draping his forearm to swat a few crumbs from the seat cushion. Pulling the chair clear from the table he said, "Sit, my friend!"

"I'll just have a bowl of vegetable soup with rye bread, Lafayette. I don't have much time. Oh, and a stein of beer."

With prices too dear for my pocketbook, it was a rare occasion to take my lunch at The American Hotel. Today, though, I had good news to share with the friend who had made it possible.

Always alert to greeting clientele and keeping an eye on serving staff, his eyes darted around the room before he set the stein on the table and sat down opposite me. "So, Samuel! What did you think of the lodgings?"

"I'm ecstatic. The place will be perfect. I'm sure Fannie and the boys will be happy. It's an American story: On the very day of arrival from Europe, an immigrant family moves into a house!"

He clapped me on the shoulder and said, "I told you Gunther Hartmann would have a vacancy for you. He owns practically all the two-family row houses in East Chunk."

I said, "I think you exaggerate his holdings, Lafayette. Not that I wish to minimize his business or highlight your gift to embellish, but he told me he owns two houses on West Sixth and another two or three in the neighborhood."

Lafayette laughed so heartily; he sprayed his huge moustache with spittle. "Ach, Samuel, you know me too well!

"Gunther and I own three commercial buildings here in downtown, and that's no lie. He's a born money-machine. He owns a little piece of the lumber yard, the stable on Susquehanna Street, and at least two acreages he leases out for farming. We've known each other for years, and my chef has been serving him dinner here every night since his wife died two years ago. So, now, tell me."

"Thanks to your reference, the lease is signed, and for only $9.00 a month, including one coal delivery. It's a street-level apartment on West Sixth. You know the layout: two bedrooms, a parlor, a kitchen, and a sanitary in the yard. He told me he plans to install indoor toilets next spring.

"I can't find words enough to thank you, Lafayette. You are a dear friend, and if there's anything I can do to repay your kindness, I will do so gladly!"

"Well, Samuel, I could certainly do with a new well-tailored vest. For free!" He half-joked.

Abruptly, he stood and motioned farewell, on his way to receive two gentlemen entering the dining room, summer residents from Philadelphia. He knew where his bread was buttered; those industrialists owned the world. Many a deal was struck, or overheard, at the dining tables overseen by my friend. Many an opportunity, a reference, an investment, a private peccadillo, was whispered and eavesdropped. Ah, yes. It was the jungle habitat of the lions of commerce, The American Hotel. Predators and prey stepped about in a careful choreography, all the while dining on sauerbraten or wild boar.

It was fascinating to watch the caste system at work, those eager toadies in starched collar and borrowed fob and chain, attempting to impress some of the wealthiest men in America.

I observed the peacocks at table in full fan. The obsequious waiters tripping over one another to fawn attention upon them. Personally, I saw no stair to success in the cozying up to these men. I was just their summer-season tailor. Of course, it was in my best interest to keep them in sartorial splendor; at summer's end, many rewarded me handsomely for my service and technique. Looking at those Main Line men, America's elite, I laughed to myself. They were my clients. I've seen them in their underwear! I've made their physiques manlier with a bit of shoulder padding. To hide a bill of large denomination or a bit of jewelry for a paramour, I stitched many a hidden pocket in a pair of undershorts, accessed through a slit in a trouser leg pocket! I've measured every angle of their bodies, seen them in the nude. They held no fascination for me.

Paying close attention to the oak-framed clock above the door, I hurriedly spooned my soup and took a bite of the crusty rye. Hailing the waiter, I found the meal had been complimentary, a gift from Lafayette. I left a dime for the waiter.

The time was moving so quickly these days. Only two weeks until Fannie and my sons would be here in Mauch Chunk, all of us under one roof!

The lease began on August 1st, a Tuesday. Oddly, I remembered a Jewish superstition, a caution against inviting bad fortune: Tuesday was a lucky day to move. I wasn't a believer in old wives' tales. But we surely didn't need any bad luck, so I didn't tempt fate!

I would come to rely upon Norah Doyle, the head seamstress at my employ, to guide me through the second-hand stores. Old enough to be my mother, she proved a strong taskmistress.

"Now, Samuel, you'll be quick to learn where the man's bottom price lays, won't you? Offer him a third less just to open the talk. Then, he'll "Ach, du Lieber Gott!' you a few times. Never you mind him, though. He'll know right off you're not a real German, with your Hungarian accent. He'll most likely take you for a dunce. You know those Prussians think right highly of themselves, don't you?"

"But, Norah, I..."

She interrupted, "Don't look at anythin' like you fancy it. He'll pick up on that in a second, and you'll be the weak lamb. And, don't start talkin' like he's a bit alright, either, 'cause, sure as God made green grass, he don't think of you as kin. You're a tall and handsome man, Samuel. Stand tall as you can. These German types respect big physiques. They're all about bullyin'.

"I don't mind tellin' ya, Samuel. 'Tis you who'll be up against it, dealin' with them."

I listened and learned the lessons she taught, but in the end, Norah did all the talking. She was a woman who knew her way around a business negotiation. On her family's farm in Ireland, she learned the power of money. Selling a few potatoes or carrots for one or two shillings was no small trifle. They added up to her steamer ticket in 1887.

For three successive days on our luncheon recess, Norah and I rode the tram across the Lehigh River to East Chunk to shop at the Gebrauchte second-hand shops run by German immigrants.

Kitchen utensils, tableware, a few towels, and linen, were all found in Koch's Haushaltsgegenstände, a household items shop. At the Gebrauchte Möbel, used furniture store, on West 8th street, I bought a wooden table and four chairs, a chifforobe for each bedroom, and two upholstered chairs for the parlor. This place was a store in name only. It was nothing more than a hastily erected wooden canopy in the rear yard of a neighbor's house. At week's end, I hired a drayman to transport the furnishings to our new home.

All was ready.

On Monday, as I came in the rear door, Mr. Burnhauser called out, "Samuel, please come to my office."

With the exception of four changing rooms and my small office at the rear, the sales floor occupied the street level space from Broadway to the back alley. Floors, walls, and cabinetry were fashioned of dark mahogany, the high, tinned ceiling painted a creamy white. A new innovation, electrified lighting, provided general illumination. Leather chairs faced platforms in mirrored alcoves at four locations on the floor. This is where tailors pinned, chalked, and discussed alterations and fabrics with clients. In general, it was a place of quiet elegance, with oriental rugs adding to the emporium's immaculate sense of style. And that was as it should be when catering to the upper class of Philadelphia.

I followed Mr. Burnhauser to his office on the second floor.

"I know you're overjoyed that your family will soon be here. I wish to say how I've admired your steadfastness and resolve during all the years apart. I've never seen you brood or sulk, although I know you must have despaired many times. I admire your optimism, Samuel."

"Thank you, G.F." I blushed.

"Your artistry with the needle has produced not only beautiful garments but a customer loyalty I never experienced prior to your employ. I'd like to show my appreciation by participating in the glorious reunion of your family." He pushed an envelope across the desk to where I stood. "Open it." There was a crisp ten dollar bill inside. I was taken aback.

"Thank you, thank you very much, G.F. This is extremely generous, and I'm so grateful. The only things I lack are beds and a few tables and lamps, which this will buy with change to spare. Thank you."

"You're welcome, my friend, and don't worry. Your family will find, as you did, that life in America is good." We shook hands, and I returned to work.

I spent the evening readying the flat for Fannie, polishing furniture, cleaning windows and floors. I placed dishes and utensils in the cabinets next to the sink, cleaned the icebox, and hung curtains sewn from remnants of cotton shirt fabric.

I sat in every chair, laid on every bed, lighted every light. I thought: *How full of joy I'll be when they are sitting here, on these very chairs.*

But, how are *they* going to feel? I wondered if my sons will learn to be at home here, or will they long to return to Budapest? I worried about Fannie's response to this new country, this little town, this flat; to me.

I was concerned about the recombination of our family. My sons don't know me. Will they forgive my absence? Was I a good enough man to be a good father, husband? Will she still smell of apricots?

Above all, I feared that, at the very first moment of contact, I would sense Fannie's love for me had withered.

9

In October 1888, Samuel arrived at Castle Garden, New York City's Immigration processing center, at Battery Park

The following month, Indiana's Senator, Benjamin Harrison, was the Republican nominee for President. Vast sums of money were used to buy votes in this highly corrupt election, especially in the swing states of Indiana and New York. Harrison didn't win the popular vote but carried the Electoral College.

Four years later, Democrat Grover Cleveland was swept into office by a wide margin. Twelve days prior to his inauguration, the overbuilt and debt-ridden Reading Railroad went into bankruptcy. The Northern Pacific, the Union Pacific, and the Atchison, Topeka & Santa Fe Railroads followed. Hundreds of rail-dependent banks and businesses failed. After a run on the gold supply, which was tied to the dollar's value, European investors withdrew from American financial markets. On May 5, 1893, the stock market crashed. The Panic, one of the worst depressions in American history, continued for four years.

In August of 1893, amid this dire economic situation, Fannie and her three sons arrived at the newly opened Immigration Center on Ellis Island.

Fannie

Friendships, promises, and plans, all fervent and necessary while on shipboard, become vague and dispensable at journey's end. Nearing North America, my mates withdrew into themselves, and camaraderie withered away. To survive the isolation from all we held dear and the hurricane's violent assault, a cohesive group had formed. Though, for all that, there had been no future in the alliances made.

Without pretense, Henriette and I accepted our parting, thankful to have shared the voyage as intimate strangers. Josephine, Henriette, and I surrounded the boys in a group embrace, a tender and loving moment. She and I remained embraced as the children ran off. "Dear Fannie, I will never forget you, what we shared. Good luck, dear friend." Tears stung my eyes; "Yes, Henriette, you will always be in my heart, too. Be well and happy." As we disengaged, it was as if a great gust of wind had cast us away, so sudden was the emotional transition from sister to stranger.

After dinner, under a canvas shelter topside, passengers waited to sight land. Storm clouds shrouded the New Jersey coast, but during lightning flashes, the terrain was visible. Albert, unimpressed, said, "You can't see the houses or the people, and I'm soaked. I'd rather see what's happening in the salon." Eager to leave the enclosure, the boy told me, "Mama, I'm not lying. After lunch today, a Russian lady drank beer and danced the Hoochie Coochie. All the children were sent away, but we peeked over the canvas from the top bunks and saw the lady show her knickers!"

After fidgeting for some moments, Morris asked, "Mama, can we go now?" "Me, too, Mama! Morris will take care of me." I couldn't deny Rudolf his independence on this special night, our last aboard ship. "Alright then, go on." In a flash, they disappeared into the hatchway.

Alone in the shelter, I greedily consumed a few moments of solitude. Focusing solely upon myself, I shaped a plan for the morning. *Tonight, I'll hang my brown waistcoat from the bunk to release the wrinkles. Samuel cannot fail to notice how the white collar flatters my face; the bodice clings to my breasts. In the morning, after sponge bathing and a dusting of scented body talc, I'll employ Mama's lovely tortoise-shell combs to arrange my hair in an upsweep, leaving a few wisps to fall upon the nape of my neck. Samuel will certainly see that seductive invitation. At least, I pray he will.*

Worrying about the first instant of our reunion, I whispered, "Will he love me, will he want me?" Years of chastity were, thankfully, ending.

Pressing my forearms against my abdomen, I closed my eyes. Aroused by a heat radiating from my pelvis, I recalled my beloved enveloping and entering me, satisfying the most intimate of hungers. Intense spasms of passion brought joyful relief, and I smiled.

Leaving my hiding place, I joined a handful of passengers at the port rail. The warm rain proved no disincentive to these travelers, their eyes scanning the shore with apprehension. At this sighting of America, there were no cheers, just a mesmerized silence. The scene lent itself to introspection and the unspoken question: "We survived the journey. Now, will we survive the life we came to find?" Few milled about: the hour late, the weather foul, the gathering fog veiling the murky shore to the east.

Yet, below decks, this night was jubilant, and with good reason: our ship was afloat in American waters. There was much carousing in the salon. Music, dancing, and singing went on nonstop, and no steward or crew could impose discipline on the rowdies. From the midnight mooring at Sandy Hook until the breakfast bell, a foghorn moaned its bass notes. The beacon from the Norton's Point Lighthouse entered our porthole, casting a red glow on the bunks as it crawled around the dormitory on its rotation.

At dawn, a crowd packed itself against the starboard rail, gazing curiously at Coney Island in the City of Brooklyn.

Houses were scrubbed with the light of day. Puddles of rainwater, liquid gold in the morning sun, collected on unpaved streets. Housewives emerged from kitchen doors, and two young girls in white pinafores waved to us.

By eight bells, customhouse officials cleared the ship for arrival, and she moved slowly through The Narrows. Taking a place on the port side, I scanned the deck for Henriette but didn't find her. Rudolf and Morris straddled my hips. Albert, standing in front of my skirts, focused on vessels passing Staten Island. So slow was her pace, the ship left almost no wake entering the Upper Bay.

Nearing the statue, a fiddler played Sousa's "The Liberty Bell" in tribute. Tears blurred my vision of America's symbol. I was unprepared for her somber countenance and its effect on me. Her lamp lighted the way to the golden shore, yet she wore no smile, her eyes vacant. A solemn bargain was being struck: the promise of individual freedom for loyalty and devotion to the new land. I nodded to her, mouthing the words: "I do so swear. Thank you."

"Mama, I see the Lady's toes!" "The harbor's filled with boats!" "Where is Papa waiting?" "How will he find us?" "Mama, look at the buildings. New York is bigger than Budapest!" "Did you hear that ferryboat's whistle?"

Many said prayers, and tears streamed down bedraggled, happy faces. We hugged and kissed each other and even some of our shipmates. The collective joy and relief were almost unbearable. In a hoarse whisper, I said to my sons: "My darlings...never forget this."

Ellis Island came into view. Barges were departing or waiting to approach, ferries moving steadily toward their slips. I craned my neck to follow the activity, thinking that Samuel might already be waiting for us somewhere on that soil.

At 9:00, the Maasdam made fast to its berth in Hoboken, New Jersey. Within an hour, U.S. citizens disembarked, passing through customs on the dock. For our class, ropes barred access to the gangway until eleven.

Steerage baggage was dumped upon the pier and customs house officers slowly worked their way through hundreds of parcels, examining and marking each and every one with chalk.

The Mate gave one last directive: "Display your vaccination certificate prominently. And do not lose your manifest card."

A white card with two numbers on it was pinned to my shawl and to the shirt of each child, indicating the page and line where each name and facts of origin had been recorded as we registered for passage in Rotterdam. Captain Pojher's signature on the document upon arrival in New York attested to its authenticity.

We waited to board tugboat-towed barges, the August sun ablaze. The crowd grew restless and rude, shouting complaints to the officers, who ignored them. Addressing the anxiety, stewards distributed water and sandwiches, avoiding a potential melee.

The barges were double decked. With the exception of handheld parcels, all baggage was loaded below. A little before noon, the boys and I boarded the second barge load. Passengers were crowded shoulder to shoulder on the upper deck. On my right, Albert carried the rucksack. On my left, my arm around their shoulders, Morris and Rudolf stood holding each other's hands. A stout marine rope kept the human cargo from falling overboard during the fifteen-minute cruise. Amongst my fellow passengers, there was no conversation, no unnecessary chitter-chatter. My thoughts were dark. *Could we be turned away, deported? How long will we queue? Is there access to toilets? Will Samuel come for us?*

Stepping off the gangway, we passed under a metal and glass canopy and entered the building. Baggage was loaded onto carts in the entrance hall, to be reclaimed later, on the structure's west side. Unencumbered, we moved toward the ascending stairway.

Immigrants walked a medical treadmill on the "Stairs of Separation." Standing at the top, doctors performed a six-second examination, quickly glancing at each person, chalk-marking those with shortness of breath, difficulty walking, pregnancy, coughing, skin rashes, inflamed eyes, or pronounced age. Those marked were sent to medical offices on the lower level. They would either be cleared to return to the queue or admitted to hospital or quarantine.

Communicable lung ailments and trachoma, an infectious eye disease, were responsible for the majority of deportations, which accounted for only two percent of the arrivals. Known criminals—dangerous aliens—and those exhibiting "mental differences" were given an opportunity to plead their case to a Board of Inquiry.

Deportation was the worst possible outcome for the immigrant. Those escaping brutal regimes begged for their lives. It was not uncommon for many to vow they would jump into the sea on the return voyage. Deportation was the worst outcome for the shipping line, too, as they were obligated to return the deportees, free of charge, to their original ports of entry.

The Great Hall, spanned by a 60 foot-high vaulted ceiling, was almost 200 feet long and 100 feet wide. Sunlight streamed through large, clerestory windows along the east and west walls. Occupying the length and width of the place, aisles separated by wire fencing kept order as the immigrants proceeded toward registry clerks and immigration officers for a legal examination.

The process was very efficient. An immigrant with no medical problems was usually processed through the registry in three hours.

Fannie

At the top of the stairway, the Great Hall's gaping maw came into view, its immensity stunning. Separated by wire fencing, ten rows with ten wooden benches extended toward the desks of registry clerks.

Reaching the bottom of the stair, we entered the center row. Inching toward the desk, two hours passed. All the while, medical and immigration personnel observed us from a gallery on the upper floor.

Shuffling in silence toward the clerk, the boys clutched at my skirts, absorbing the fear and insecurity they sensed all around. I stood tall, unafraid, comforting them with my strength. We hadn't come this far for naught.

Referring to our cards, the clerk located our names on the *Maasdam's* manifest.

He questioned me in English and in German, "Where is your husband? Wo ist ihr Ehemann?"

I responded in English, "Pennsylvania."

"Do you have any money? Hast du geld?"

"Twenty-six dollars, Sir, American."

"Speak your names, please." " Sprich bitte deine Namen."

"I am Fannie Freed, and these are my sons, Albert, Morris, and Rudolf."

Albert stepped forward. "I am Albert Freed." Following his example and speaking clearly, in English, they said: "I am Morris Freed." "I am Rudolf Freed."

The clerk smiled, patting Albert on the head. "Willkommen. Welcome to America!" With those lovely words, our papers were stamped, and we left the Hall through an archway behind the registrar.

Descending the west staircase, we stepped into an area called "the kissing post," a lobby where relatives and friends waited to greet the newcomers. I saw no familiar face and moved forward with the crowd. Shuffling along, we passed a money exchange, baggage rooms, and an information bureau. Through the far door, I could see a covered walkway leading to the ferries.

There were lavatories for men and women, but there were no objections to sons and mothers remaining together. The large room was tiled in white: floor, walls, and ceiling. A half-wall separated the flush toilets from the single metal wash basin, which reminded me of a horse trough with spigots installed above the vessel every meter or so. Twenty people washed at the basin at once. A mirror ran its length, and it disturbed me to find I looked worn-out, pale. I combed my hair, smoothed my waistcoat, and applied a bit of lip rouge to my cheeks; the boys washed their faces.

The journey had been difficult and life-threatening, the test of Ellis Island harrowing and uncertain. I felt no joy, nor did my exhausted sons. My mind was weary, too weary to contemplate the risks I had taken, the courage of my children, what lay ahead.

We had arrived, yet our trial was not yet complete. The next hours would determine the course of my life, my children's lives. I straightened my shoulders, kissed the boys, and smiled. They needn't know I was terrified lest Samuel not come for us.

The lunchroom's din gained in volume as we approached the entryway. Yet, taking into account the hard surfaces of the space and the number of persons occupying it, the noise level was remarkably low. I suppose the sounds were absorbed by the humanity itself, whose conversations produced little more than a constant hum peppered by an occasional baby's cry. Those milling about scanned the place for kin or simply a place to rest. There were long tables with benches, enough seating for what seemed a thousand people. Places were set with plates, forks, spoons, cups, and napkins. After observing the scene, I relaxed, understanding the procedure was simple: find a seat and have something to eat. You will be found. Locating vacancies at a table close to the west wall, we stowed our hand luggage underneath. From that location, I had a clear view of the door and felt Samuel could not fail to see us as he entered.

Once we were seated, servers brought platters of boiled potatoes, cold meat sandwiches, bananas, and apples. Others filled cups with coffee or milk. A young man at our table said in Yiddish, "Vas iz das?" The server replied, "A banana." He shrugged his shoulders. Raising her voice, as if he were deaf, she spoke slowly, "It. Is. Fruit." A woman behind me called out to the man, "Es frukht. Frukht." "Ah, frukht," he said, bewildered. The server took the banana from his hand and peeled it, exposing the pale-yellow flesh. "Don't. Eat. The. Peel." "Ton nit essen de sholekhts," the woman called out. "Ah, adank." "You are welcome," the woman said loudly in English. Albert whispered, "Mama, he doesn't know what a banana is!" He rolled his eyes in disbelief, his brothers responding with uncontrolled laughter. Of course, always playing to the crowd, Rudolf fell off the bench and rolled about on the floor.

This food, provided at no cost to the aliens, was an incredible demonstration of American generosity. Perhaps it was the smell of hot coffee that brought attention to my empty stomach. But, more likely, my appetite was a response to the charitable sharing of America's bounty, gratitude for her affirmation that I was welcome and protected. Suddenly, I was famished and delighted in the taste of smoked ham and cheese on my tongue.

It was almost 3:00. Rudolf was tired and uncooperative. Rummaging through my tapestry bag, I found a stub of a pencil and a bit of brown paper with which to distract the child. He began to sketch a bearded old man asleep on the floor against the wall. Albert's patience with the confinement had run its course, too; his natural energy needed an outlet. I said, "Please, Albert, don't run into anyone. Be careful." For the next twenty minutes, he trotted around the perimeter of the room, before collapsing into a heap at my feet. Morris, lying on the bench, dozed.

I felt his presence before seeing him at the doorway. Not one of our sons pointed him out, called in greeting, or ran to embrace him. They simply didn't know who he was. I watched his eyes scan the room, brightening, then tearing, when they met mine. Samuel had matured, his face thinner, his small moustache gone. He strode into the lunchroom with casual assurance, so tall and handsome, a real American! My voice trembled, "My darlings, here is your Papa." Without a word, they stood to look at the man approaching us.

In one motion, he scooped all three boys into his arms and twirled around and around. He nuzzled them, smothering their faces with kisses. Albert craned his neck to look at Samuel's face. Morris, wide-eyed with suspense, adopted a mantle of stoic happiness, managing a frozen, insincere grin. Frightened to the verge of tears, Rudolf arched his back to break his Papa's hold but could not do so. His eyes sent mine a silent plea: *Save me*. All startled little fledglings in an unfamiliar nest.

Samuel sat on the floor, the boys standing in front of him. Looking carefully at each face, he said, "Albert, turn around so I can see how big you are." Albert turned slowly, drawing himself up as tall as he could. "Papa, I took care of Mama, like you asked." Samuel tousled his hair, "And I thank you for that, Albert, from my heart. I rely on your experience to teach me how to be a Papa." Albert laughed.

"Ah, Morris, the last time I saw you, you were a baby, one year old." He held the little one's hand between his. "Now, you're six but appear so much older. You're tall and strong, blessed with muscles like your Grandpapá Bruder!" Morris shyly looked at his shoes. He said, "I never called anyone 'Papa' before." Samuel smiled. "Do you love me, Papa?" Dear Morris looked to me for approval, and I smiled. Wrapping his arms around the child, Samuel wept. In a hoarse whisper, he said, "Yes, my dear boy, I love you very much." Morris, embarrassed, squirmed to escape his father's embrace.

Then, Rudolf stood alone. Our baby looked at his father. He had no idea what was expected of him. Without a word, Samuel scrutinized the little boy's face. Rudolf spoke to the stranger. "We came on a ship, and there was a big storm, and I never got seasick. I think I'll be a sailor when I'm grown!" Hesitating, he continued, "Are you really my Papa?" Samuel laughed. "I want to hear all about your trip and the storm. I *am* your Papa, and I love you. I promise we'll never be separated again, my dearest son."

He hugged all three, all the while rocking back and forth and kissing their faces. Respectfully, they allowed it for a while, but when they began to fidget, Samuel released them. Removing a piece of folded craft paper from his waistcoat pocket, he spread it open on the table. "Boys, these are licorice ropes, and there are two for each of you. Most luncheon shops in America sell candy. Isn't that a good idea? We have a long trip ahead, so try to save one of your ropes for later.

Albert and Rudolf held each other, laughing and jumping up and down in place; they could not contain their joy. Morris studied his licorice and asked, "Papa, are we rich like all Americans? Can we have candy every day?" "We're not rich, Morris, but we are Americans now. As soon as we leave this island, you'll see the way people live here, and we'll start speaking English. In a few months, you won't be greenhorns, ignorant foreigners, anymore."

"Now, it's time for Mama and me to have time together. Then, we'll collect your baggage and ride the ferry to the trains. You'll sleep in your own beds, in Pennsylvania, tonight!"

We turned toward each other. Although public displays of affection were frowned upon, he opened his arms to receive me. I moved into his embrace. We pressed our bodies together and kissed. Swaying in place, we tasted one another's breath, lips, cheeks, eyelids. In that beautiful moment of rediscovery, the lonely time of separation and sacrifice became a memory. The magnetic energy between us was undiminished, even after five, long years.

We were, once again, a man and woman in love. And a family.

Samuel

Waking from a restless night, I eagerly greeted the August sun, vowing to live that Saturday to its fullest.

G.F. insisted I not return to work for three days, so as to help Fannie and the boys become familiar with their new neighborhood.

Riding the first tram of the morning from East to Chunk, I allowed almost an hour for a fried eggs, ham and coffee breakfast at A Bite of Alright on Susquehanna Street.

Alfie Bradshaw was one of a handful of Londoners living in Chunk and a hale fellow, too. Monday through Saturday, from five in the morning until three in the afternoon, he served breakfast and lunch in the small restaurant across from the depot. A dozen backless stools were bolted to the floor in front of a metal counter that ran the length of the place. Behind the counter, a narrow aisle was controlled by Alfie's wife, Brenda. The couple had no children. "The Bite" was their baby. Through an opening in the wall, Alfie passed the ordered food to Brenda.

A tiny woman, Brenda wore a hair net, plenty of lip rouge, and a dark blue chemise protected by a starched white cotton apron with a red rose embroidered on its bib. She brooked no disrespect but had a ready smile and quick wit. She made the coffee, passed the orders to her husband, served the customers, and kept up a snappy patter. Her sister, Beverly, a shy and homely woman, washed dishes and floors, greeting diners with a nod. For the first two years I patronized The Bite, I thought Beverly a mute. When she finally spoke, it was a moment I'd not forget. A motorman on the Easton run had stopped in for a coffee while his stoker loaded coal for the return. Playfully, he pinched Beverly's chin and said, "Good morning, Sunshine!" Beverly turned, red-faced. "Well, aren't you the cheeky bastard! Keep your filthy hands to yourself, or I'll box your ears!" All eyes were on the motorman, who made an awkward apology. Beverly went back to her dishwater without another word.

Alfie looked out the pass-through as I sat down. "Hullo, Samuel! Well, today's the day, eh what?"

"I'll be catching the seven-ten to New York, my friend." Brenda interrupted. "Don't you worry, Samuel. Your wifey will be as luvly as you recall."

"Brenda's right about that, my friend. It's going to be a grand reunion; I'd bet a shilling on it. Now, I'd better be getting back to my pans, or Brenda will be on me for slacking! You need me to fix you something for the train ride?"

"One of the scones just out of your oven would be a treat for later in the morning, Alfie. Thank you. Travelers on a Saturday excursion may crowd the dining car, so I'm planning to have lunch at the Jersey City terminal. There'll be plenty of time, I think."

Brenda filled my cup with black coffee, adding three large spoonfuls of sugar, just as I liked it. "You're looking a bit uneasy, Samuel. Don't be down-in-the-mouth; this is the day you've been waiting for. Your Mum's not around, so tell Brenda what's troubling you."

"I'm worried I'll not find them. There's no way to know when their ship arrived at the quay nor when they'll arrive at Ellis. And then, if there's a queue of incoming ships, it could be many hours before they get through the registry."

She patted my hand. "Samuel, calm down. You'll find out all about these things."

I shrugged at her comment. "And what if one of them is unwell, quarantined at the hospital? Would I be permitted to stay with them, even *see* them? I'm girding myself for a day full of stress and strain.

"Fannie's counting on me to be there. But how will I find them? Will I need some kind of papers to prove I'm the Papa and they're my family? Which ferry takes me to Ellis? Where are the arrivals met? When I came to Castle Garden, we walked off the boat, showed our papers, said we were healthy, and that was it. We were in New York City, and anyone meeting someone just off the boat simply went to Castle Garden and milled around until they found their kin. The new immigration center is enormous, and I'm certain there must be strict rules about wandering about, mingling with the newcomers. I hope that America set up a system to help me find my family!"

Brenda was losing patience with me. "Of course, there's a system, Samuel. Don't you think they've attended to a little detail like people finding their kin? You're settin' yerself up for a nervous collapse! Calm down, Luv. Relax."

"If all goes well, and I find them in time to board the last train to Mauch Chunk, I'll breathe a sigh of relief. But, if we don't get to the Jersey City Terminal in time to make the last train, we'll have to sleep on benches in the depot!"

She tried not to laugh at my exaggeration. "Samuel, you'll figure it all out. I'm sure there are information desks with people to answer all those questions. You're not bashful, Samuel, and you speak perfect English. Go right up to the first officer you see and ask how the whole thing works. They didn't build that big place without thinking about all this! And you've told me about Fannie. Five years she's been taking care of everything. She's strong and resourceful. She'll get them all through just fine, you'll see. When all your worries are proven false, *I'll* be the one to say, 'I told you so!' Now, for the important question, Samuel: Are you bringing your lovey a little gift to show how you've been pining all this time?"

"Thanks, Brenda; I needed some mothering! I've been skimping all these years, so there's really no savings, but since G.F. gave me a few dollars to help getting the family settled, I did buy a gift for Fannie to remember her first night in America, a cameo pendant on a gold chain."

"You're a romantic, all right, and she's a lucky woman." Raising her voice, she called to Alfie, "You hear that, you cheap Brit? You might learn a bit of charm from the Hungarian if you paid him some attention!"

"I've got to go. The train is boarding."

"Don't worry about a thing, my friend," Alfie called out.

I left a nickel on the counter and moved quickly to the door. "Goodbye, all!" Crossing the street, I heard Beverly's voice. "Samuel, you forgot your scones!"

Running back to get the bag she held, I said, "Thank you, Beverly."

"Goodbye, and good luck, Samuel!

About a dozen passengers were at the station, a few climbing on board, others passing boxes to the baggage handler. I approached the ticket agent's wire mesh window; Joseph Schmidt was a neighbor from East Chunk. "Hello, Joseph. I'm meeting my family at Ellis Island today!"

"Good morning, Samuel. That's good news. It's been a very long time, hasn't it?"

"Five years since I've seen them. We'll be on the last train from Jersey City tonight. I need a round trip for me and four one-ways for my wife and sons, all three of them less than ten- years-old."

"Good for you, my friend. It's a grand morning for your trip. The last return is the 7:10 local, arriving around midnight. That's $4.00 for the round trip, $2.15 for your wife, and $3.00 for the children, $9.15 in total."

I counted out the bills and coin, putting the tickets in my inside jacket pocket. One couldn't be too careful when planning to pass through the always crowded Jersey City terminal, where pickpockets loitered about. I bought a copy of *The Mauch Chunk Daily Times* for three cents and got on board, finding a comfortable window seat. The Conductor punched a hole in the top half of my ticket, validating the eastbound trip. Leaning out of the car, he boomed, "All aboard!" The whistle tooted, and the train slowly left the station, exactly on schedule, 7:10.

Five hours later, I approached the terminal's information desk. "I need assistance, sir. My family is arriving at Ellis Island today. How can I find them?"

The young man said, "Follow the signage to the ferry slip. Take the one to Ellis, not to The Battery or Liberty Street. You'll disembark on the New Jersey side of the Island, where those cleared through the registry will be waiting. Check in the dining room or at the information desk near the currency exchange. If they've not been detained at the hospital, you'll find them."

"Thank you. I thought perhaps I'd be interrogated before being allowed on the Island."

"No, sir. Once the immigrants are cleared by registry, they are free to travel. And they stay free. That means you, too. You're free to travel anywhere, even if it's to return to Ellis Island! I'm sure you'll find them, sir. Good luck."

At the café, I ordered a bowl of vegetable soup and a pumpernickel roll, then made my way to the ferry. I bought a five cent, one-way ticket for the 2:30 boat; there was no fare collected from those leaving Ellis. My thoughts were racing. Were they on the island? Were they through the registry?

The ferry trip was not a voyage. In ten minutes, I disembarked.

Facing me was a queue of at least one hundred immigrants waiting to board the vessel I had vacated. An immigration officer was stationed at the door.

"Officer, can you tell me where I will find information about my family?"

"Go to the 'kissing post' information desk. If they're not there, try the lunchroom. There is no registry journal accessible for public use. There is, however, a list of ships whose manifests have been accessed today. It doesn't provide a list of passengers who have been examined, nor does it imply that all persons on that ship have passed through. But it will confirm if their ship is among those processed today."

"Thank you, Officer. Thank you very much."

The queue for the ferry extended through the doorway and into the building for at least fifty feet. I began to calculate how much time I had to find Fannie. Our train for Mauch Chunk departed at seven. We'd need at least an hour to queue and ride the ferry, then walk to the terminal and find the track. At the latest, we should board the 5:30 boat.

Walking quickly to the "kissing post," I found the *Maasdam* on the list. Looking around, Fannie was not in that throng. If she were here, she waited in the lunchroom. I paused in the doorway. The place was gigantic. Hundreds of people were eating or sitting on the floor, their backs against the walls. As when entering a maze, I began following the perimeter of the room, beginning with the wall to my left. I knew she was there, she *had* to be. We deserved a little good luck, didn't we? Five years of solitude and regret. Aren't we entitled to some happiness after all that sacrifice?

And there she was. As it had all those years ago in Debrecen, her gaze met mine directly. Those beautiful, deep brown eyes filled with love. Overcome, tears filled my eyes and ran down my cheeks. She was wonderful. She had survived. No, she had *conquered* every obstacle and threat: loneliness, raising the children alone, poverty, the campaign of her father to end our marriage. Always, she had been optimistic. Always, she supported and comforted me. I kept walking steadily toward her, my own dearest love. My wife.

My sons stood up, their faces turned to me. This man, their Papa. Weeping with joy, I lifted them all together, spinning around and around. I nuzzled their necks, kissed their heads, their faces. I sat on the floor and introduced myself to each one. They were so handsome and eager to please me, to love me. Then, distributing the licorice ropes I had brought for them, I turned to Fannie.

Opening my arms, she moved into my embrace. I cared nothing about violating standards of gentility. Swaying in place, I tasted her breath, felt the softness of her lips, her cheeks. Locking my hands around her waist, I pressed her breasts and pelvis tightly against my torso. Our bodies fit perfectly together. I could barely breathe, feeling the want of her. Our deepest bond, the sacred, passionate place we shared, was undeniable and everlasting.

10

In the early part of nineteenth century America, a man-made canal system connecting inland rivers was constructed. Wooden barges laded with agricultural produce, lumber, minerals, even livestock, were towed by horses along an adjacent path. The Canal Era opened markets and populated new areas in the Midwest.

In 1818, a group of businessmen established The Lehigh Coal and Navigation Company in rural Carbon County, seventy miles to the north and west of Philadelphia. The Commonwealth of Pennsylvania sold them ten thousand acres of coal lands and allowed them rights to navigate the Lehigh River. To transport anthracite coal from Mauch Chunk to Easton, a forty-six-mile series of dams and locks was constructed, the Lehigh Canal.

In 1827, a nine-mile-long train track was laid, descending nine hundred feet from the mines at Summit Hill to the wharves on the Lehigh River. The Mauch Chunk Gravity railroad replaced the wagons and tow road with coal-filled freight cars. It was the first railed road in Pennsylvania, and the United States.

By the 1860s, the efficiency of steam locomotion ended the Canal Era. The Gilded Age expanded American territory, and business opportunities brought explosive economic growth.

High wages for skilled workers lured millions of European immigrants to America. Yet, even with higher wages, the unskilled population was impoverished. The robber barons, two dozen titans, like the feudal lords, held the American economy in a stranglehold. Their monopolies, setting prices and wages, controlled all the economic sectors:

finance, banking, railroads, lumber, steel, coal, insurance, fur, real estate, tobacco, sugar, oil, and aluminum.

When the bankruptcy of the debt-ridden Reading Railroad precipitated the economic Panic of 1893, the overbuilding of American railroads came to its conclusion.

People in industrial cities and mill towns were starving. At its height, over fifteen thousand companies and five hundred banks failed; nineteen percent of the workforce was unemployed.

After blaming the Democrats, Republicans won landslide state and congressional victories in 1894. Two years later, Republican William McKinley won the Presidency.

The Depression was one of the worst in American history. There were violent strikes across the country, put down by state militias, events that gave birth to the American Labor Movement. All industries suffered, but Mauch Chunk's coal, an essential commodity, continued to profit. The area's seven grand hotels and Victorian mansions, home to thirteen millionaires, still afforded the wealthy a respite from the calamities of business and Philadelphia's summer heat.

Wages declined for local workers competing with migrants for mining, lumbering, and railroad jobs. Child labor, valued at only a few pennies a day, flourished.

With his work and pay dependent upon tailoring suits for industry management and vacationing robber barons, Samuel's livelihood was secure.

Fannie

The ferry delivered us to the Jersey City terminal. At the Lehigh Valley Line's platform, a Black porter loaded our bags onto a hand truck. "When you reach Mauch Chunk, ye'll have to go to the baggage car; the clerk will not look for you. Here's yer three claim tickets." Samuel gave him a dime for his attention; he tipped his hat in farewell and went off with our belongings.

Impatiently, I urged the boys to mount the steps to the second-class car. "Albert, find seats for us!" We had learned by hard experience how miserable a rail trip could be if seats were not secured. I needn't have fretted; with fewer than a dozen passengers, this was not the overnight train to Cologne!

In black thread, red horsehair cushions bore the line's monogram, LVRR. A bench installed against a window wall provided seating for twenty. Opposite and perpendicular to the bench, rows of high-backed double seats were mounted to the floor. The arrangement was comfortable and pleasing to the eye. Seat backs could be reversed, adjusting to the direction of travel, and Samuel did so to create a private area for us. How very convenient and comfortable for the family, a kind of personal parlor car.

The conductor bellowed, "All aboard!" followed by the clamor of metal wheel against rail. A steam whistle shouted a noisy farewell to the environs of New York City. At exactly ten minutes after seven, the engine began to move directly into the rays of the setting sun; thirty-three stops would be made between Jersey City and Mauch Chunk, arriving at midnight.

In spite of their exhausting day, the boys remained alert to their new surroundings, both inside the car and the landscape visible through the window.

"Papa," Morris whispered to Samuel, "so far New Jersey looks like a place of factories surrounded by falling-down houses, all jammed together."

"This part is industrial, Morris. Keep your eyes on the countryside; you'll soon see farms, hills, and forests. Why, New Jersey's mostly farmland!"

"Papa," Albert said, "I'm worried about school. I hardly speak English at all. The boys will laugh at me."

Samuel patted the boy's shoulder. "Albert, everything will be fine; try to relax, son. You'll be surprised to find many of the boys in your school speak very poor English. That's because their parents don't use it; they still speak German in the house. At first. everything will seem foreign to you, but in a few months, you'll not see it that way; you'll belong. I know it's your nature, but try not to fret. You'll make friends, and your teachers will love you and your brothers; of that I'm certain." Leaning over, he kissed the boy's forehead. "Don't be afraid. Everyone is in the same boat, Albert; everyone's fears are the same."

"Alright, Papa. I'll try." He turned his attention to the window's darkening landscape.

I could see Rudolf fighting to stay awake, his head leaning against the armrest, eyelids drooping. Samuel gently nudged Rudolf awake. "Come, boys, it's half past seven. We'd best eat dinner now."

We followed Samuel down the center aisle. With Rudolf in his arms, he slid the heavy door open. The cool evening air rushed at my face, carrying fine soot blown from the engine's chimney. In the gap between cars, the full moon lit the small, iron-fenced platform. I could see the dining car just ahead, the lamplight reflecting upon white table linen and gleaming steel flatware.

As the door closed behind us, the train whistle blew, its shrieking noise piercing the air. Startled, I gripped Morris's hand. "Mama, stop squeezing me so hard," he whined.

"I'm sorry, dear."

It would take just a second or two, one long stride, to cross the gap, but the train was moving, rocking from side to side. I held Morris and Albert's hands tightly. Samuel's grace and sure-footedness did not desert him. With one quick step, and still carrying Rudolf, he stood on the dining car side of the balcony.

Distorted by the sound of the wind, his voice reverberated, "It's not really dangerous. The fence will not allow you to fall. Just hold the connecting chain as a handrail and simply walk across. It's less than a meter, for goodness sake. Don't think about it, just go! And, don't look down!" But it was too late, I was already looking down. I could see the tracks and the gravel between the ties. They appeared to be slipping under our feet at breakneck speed as the train raced forward. Through the darkness, I could make out the wheels under the dining car, could hear the squealing of metal upon metal.

"Come ahead, Fannie. it will be alright. Here is my hand. Take it and come to me. Trust me."

Albert laughed at my anxiety. "Mama, don't be a baby. We survived a hurricane! Surely, you can make this little jump." He moved quickly to join his father, leaving me and Morris behind.

"Alright," I said to Morris "Here we go."

Having leaned over the gap, one of Samuel's hands reached my forearm, the other, Morris' shoulder. Urging me on, he called, "Egy, két, es három; one, two, and three!" Holding fast to his hands, Morris and I made the small jump. In the blink of an eye, we stood next to Albert.

I laughed. "For a woman who managed a trek across a continent, I am a fake, my dears! I suppose an empty belly and lack of proper sleep have taken their toll. So, let's eat!

Tabletop candles and wall-mounted electric lamps cast a warm light upon the dark paneled walls, and red velvet upholstery. Vases fixed to the tabletops held bright yellow daisies. Napkins, flatware, and dishes, all bore the black and red LVRR monogram. At capacity, twenty-five diners could be seated, Stewards wearing collarless white shirts and black trousers moved about the cabin filling water glasses and coffee cups or serving plated food.

Identified by a metal badge, Alex Morton, Steward, tall and red haired, motioned us forward. "Good evening, sir. There's available seating at the far end of the car. Your party will need two tables, as the larger ones only seat four."

Samuel, Rudolf, and I sat at the larger table, Albert and Morris took the one for two across the narrow aisle. Handing me a menu, Alex turned to Samuel. "The beef sandwiches are very good. They're served open-faced with gravy and slaw and roasted potatoes. The chicken potpie with accompanying salad is also recommended. For the children, there is fried chicken or macaroni with butter and cheese."

"Thank you," Samuel responded. "My wife and I will have the beef, and the macaroni will be a treat for the boys. Also, coffee for my wife and me and milk for the children. Thank you."

Alex brought warm biscuits with a small tub of sweet butter, and we devoured them all. In less than ten minutes, the meals were served, well prepared, hot, and flavorful. The coffee was dark and rich, poured from shiny stainless steel carafes into china cups. For dessert, the boys enjoyed vanilla ice cream with chocolate sauce. Samuel and I shared a slice of Nesselrode pie. Named for a Russian Count, a sweet pastry crust filled with a creamy pudding blended with chopped chestnuts, maraschino cherries, and candied fruits. Decadent, the menu claimed!

Luckily, the train was stopped at the Somerville station when we returned to our car, saving me the anxiety of jumping the gap again. It was near nine.

By this time, only seven passengers remained in our cabin, some sleeping, others reading. None objected when I removed the boy's shoes before they lay down on the unoccupied benches. Rudolf rolled over, faced the rear cushion, and was asleep in an instant. I covered him with Mama's shawl, her voice rushing into my consciousness. *When you wrap this around your shoulders, it will be as the embrace of my arms...*

To search for blankets to cover the children, Samuel left the car.

On a double seat in the row behind ours, a woman of a certain age, perhaps fifty, with an enormous bosom and equally enormous grey straw hat, smiled at me. I nodded in greeting. "Good evening, Mother," she whispered. "My name is Florence Britton. Are you just arrived from Europe?"

Replying in halting English, "Yes, this afternoon, from Hungary. I am Fannie Freed, and these are my sons, Albert, Morris, and Rudolf. My husband, Samuel, will soon return."

Florence smiled. "Well, bravo, dear, and welcome to America."

"Thank you. We're going to Mauch Chunk. Do you live in Pennsylvania, too?

"No, I live in New York City. I'm traveling to Rochester, to visit with my sister. Thirty minutes north of Mauch Chunk, at Wilkes-Barre, I'll transfer to an express train on the Asa Packer Niagara Falls line, and I'll be ready to stretch out in a berth on the Pullman sleeper; that I can tell you! I get the best night's rest on a train; all your cares float to some other world while you ride inside a silver bullet!"

"Sleeping in a horizontal compartment sounds very thrilling, Florence."

She seemed amused and said, "Well, I would argue how thrilling it is. Barely enough space for anyone of more than average size; not much room to be thrilled in any way. Also, once you pull the heavy curtain closed, little air circulates; it's a coffin, or maybe a baby's cradle! But, no matter, as I said, I get the best night's rest on a train; I'll be fast asleep by the time we cross back into New York State. Next morning, most likely near Ithaca, two hours from my destination, the porter will sound the chimes announcing breakfast is served."

I was thinking how extraordinary it was that twenty-four hours of travel were necessary for this woman to reach her destination at the opposite end of the state in which she began. It made me realize that New York had a greater land mass than all of Hungary.

Samuel returned with blankets, and I covered the boys, Morris already snoring loudly. "Thank you, Mama," Albert whispered, through a yawn.

"I love you, my darling. Go to sleep. I'll wake you when we arrive."

"Samuel, meet Florence Britton. She's traveling, overnight, all the way to Rochester; that's near Canada."

He greeted her with a nod. "Hello, Florence. It's nice to make your acquaintance."

"I'm happy to meet you, too. Well, I'm off to the dining car and probably will remain there drinking coffee until we reach Wilkes-Barre, so I'll say goodbye and good luck to you and your sweet family."

Holding my hand, she added, "Fannie, good luck and stay happy. You will love the life here."

"Goodbye, Florence. Have a safe journey and a lovely visit with your sister."

The children slept, and Samuel and I sat opposite one another.

Suddenly, the train lurched and rocked forcefully, nearly pitching me off the seat. In an instant, Samuel knelt before me, his strong hands holding my waist, steadying me.

Unaccustomed to this stranger's touch, my body tensed, recoiled. Not a word escaped my lips, yet my body shouted, *Who are you? I don't know you. Don't touch me.*

For the last hours, we had been performing the tasks of travel, attending to details and the children's needs, engaging in required, superficial discourse. There had been only the few moments at Ellis Island where the connection I yearned to feel, as man and wife, had been made.

His eyes widened in wounded surprise, and, remaining on his knees, his grip upon my midriff relaxed. Looking straight into my eyes, he said, "My dearest, we will find a way back to each other, I promise you that. I love you as I did at the first, and I feel the want of you as desperately as I did then."

As a dam bursting, without warning, I began to weep. I couldn't control the racking of my chest nor speak without sobbing. He pulled me to my feet, drew my body close, his arms sheltering me. Although I cried with gratitude when he declared his love, my tears also begged for absolution of guilt at the rejection of his touch. I felt myself collapsing. Had I, at long last, reached the end of the loneliness? Was I in safe haven, in the arms of my beloved, or in the end, would five years of neglect render our goal unattainable?

He wiped my face with his handkerchief and kissed me. Embarrassed at my loss of control, I stammered, "I must look a mess, all puffy and red faced!" and then, "Oh, Samuel, will we ever be the same as we were?"

"Fannie, we are not the same young lovers who said goodbye in Budapest. We've matured in separate worlds, but the place shared only between us will be ours again, it must.

He continued, "I've worked hard, and kept to myself, finding spiritual sustenance only in your letters. This last week, I've thought of nothing other than making love to you. I need you, Fannie, only you. We must never, ever be parted again."

Uncertain how to respond, I nodded. He pressed my hand to his lips. I closed my eyes.

The lights flickered, the train slowing to stop at Easton. Our fellow passengers departed, nodding silent goodbyes, so as not to disturb the sleeping children. After a few minutes, the Conductor called, "All aboard!" The whistle blew, and the engine began its working song with a screeching burst of steam, waking Albert.

"Mama, are we there yet?"

"No, my darling. It will be another two hours. Go back to sleep." He blinked, then closed his eyes.

Mama's shawl had dropped to the floor. I picked it up and covered Rudolf's sleeping form; he did not stir. Morris continued to dream, breathing deeply,

Samuel, his head leaning against the window, watched me as I ministered to the boys. He patted the seat beside him, inviting me to sit, which I did. I was keenly aware of, and distracted by, his thigh touching mine.

"Just think about it, Fannie. We've been on this train for hours and have still not left New Jersey. In Hungary, we'd be halfway across the country by now! America is enormous. There's space for every man to find his own place. That's the secret; there are no limits, like our family's future."

Nodding, I didn't belabor the point. It was lovely to hear the optimism in his voice, his pride of country. He had no way of knowing I had come to that same conclusion only a few hours earlier.

"Papa and I discussed the Panic; he said there may not be enough work to support us. Samuel, we're poor already. With a little luck, these events may not affect us. We can't fall too much further down, can we?"

"There's no arguing we've learned how to get by, except there's more to the problem than you realize.

"There's trouble in every mill, mine, and factory. The working man is held in little regard. Bravely, they walk off the job, rallying against the boss's power. When they do that, go on strike, they're replaced by scabs. Unions are organizing for better conditions, but the bosses own everything, including politicians. It's a struggle between the upper and lower classes. The upheaval in America is frightening."

It was time to change the conversation. These large events were not our affair; there was nothing we could do about them. Why waste our anger, energy, and hope? Our life centers on coping with each day, one at a time.

"I understand, but think of this: the bosses in Europe also had no regard for the poor. I crossed an ocean with three children, participating in a kind of strike for a better life. The truth is the worker and bosses are partners in keeping things going. The coal will not dig itself, nor will the steel spring up from the furnace. It seems to me both sides must cooperate, compromise. If not, there'll be no business or commerce at all, and thousands will starve. The government can't let that happen, so I'm optimistic America will figure it out."

He smiled, then laughed. "You're here for less than a day and already have the answers to America's predicament! What a fantastic woman you are! Oh, how I need you, my darling. Of course, I agree with you, especially regarding our own welfare as the main focus. The demand for coal remains strong and will not falter. As long as the mine bosses and the wealthy summer in Chunk, we're alright, I'll have work."

Conversation was disrupted as the train slowed at another small station, lights flickering on and off.

"Samuel, in Hungary, I had the nearness of friends and family. There were moments in which melancholy threatened to smother me, but I did not, could not, allow it. How could I? I was responsible, day and night, for the children. I worried about you, so alone here. How did you bear the loneliness?"

There was a small silence; then, he said, "Let's close the book on our exile. There's no point dwelling upon those times. You're here now, and our life begins anew. I pray you will love the man I am now, the American Samuel."

I felt the hair on my arms rise. My breath stilled, pulse slowed, a fine perspiration gathered on my upper lip. The phrase repeated in my mind, *Let's close the book on our exile.* Is it possible never to speak of those years? Had there been a breach of trust from which our love could not recover? Was Papa correct; is there an American family sired by Samuel Freed?

Alarmed, I shrank from confrontation. What could be gained, pressing him for disclosure? Logic told me life lived can never be relived. Logic told me our exile was not a part of our life together. Logic told me if I loved him still, then he's right; the book must close.

Apparently, while in my reverie, he had continued a discourse about life in Mauch Chunk. His voice, at first barely perceptible, gradually gained timbre as my comprehension and engagement returned.

"...It's not Budapest, my darling. Were it not for the wealthiest residents and tourists, there would be no cultural diversion at all. For a long time, I didn't allow myself to acknowledge how stifling small-town life is, how ignorant my fellow-settlers are, how slavishly they adhere to religion, how content they are for their children to follow them into the railyard, coal mine, or the floor of the dangerous iron foundry."

He paused, waiting for any kind of response from me, for an exchange of dialogue.

At that point, for the good of our future and for our love, I closed the book and joined the conversation.

"I'm sure there are *some* families who value education. You can't be so narrow-minded as to believe that none of them harbor ambitious expectations for their children? At least *some* must be blessed with intelligence, a sense of the opportunity America offers. I fear you've only met the fathers. I tend to think the mothers are urging their sons to surpass their Papas."

"I know I sound harsh, Fannie, but I've lived with them for five years now. The parents are resistant to assimilation; they keep the old ways. Hopefully, you're right; the new generation will liberate themselves."

I yawned. My body was so tired; there was no part of me that didn't ache. Could it be this was still the same day as our arrival at the Hoboken quay? The events at Ellis seemed part of a past life, lived ages ago.

He was telling me about his life, his voice natural, no tension. It became obvious to me he was completely unaware of my distress. We are two strangers; I was convinced of that.

My concentration waned as he droned on. "...I walk to work and enjoy the exercise." "...Trolley tracks are being laid to connect both Chunks, replacing a horse-drawn tram currently running from six in the morning to nine at night.

I yawned again; he stopped talking.

I managed a smile. "What about our apartment and the boys' school?"

"Four rooms at street level in a two-family house. And, Fannie, there's a front porch! I did my best to furnish the necessities, secondhand, but you'll make it a home.

Animated, he continued, "The school's on North Street, only two blocks from our flat. It's a new structure, of simple design; the very opposite of Budapest's schools, with their ornate, carved frontages.

Lessons are designed with minimum expectation. They teach rudimentary mathematics, reading, and writing; few attend secondary school. By their eleventh birthday, almost all the lads leave to earn a few pennies. Tomorrow, we'll begin learning English using the primers I bought. Our boys will be expected to keep up with the others on their very first day of instruction, and classes begin in three weeks."

The train began to slow, approaching Mauch Chunk station. The clock on the platform read a quarter past twelve.

The stop would allow ten minutes to detrain and claim our parcels from the baggage car. I stood up and smoothed my shirtwaist.

He reached for my arm as I passed in front of him on the way to wake the boys.

"Sit for just another minute. I meant to say this earlier but lost the thought. Even though I've made advancements, I have bigger dreams, a plan. I don't want us trapped in a place with no opportunity. Now that you're here, we'll start saving for a move to New York, where I plan to establish my own tailor shop!"

Forcing a happy smile, I said, "Samuel! How wonderful and exciting. New York City!"

Was my enthusiasm believable? I busied myself gathering our belongings, rousing the boys.

I felt no connection to Samuel. How could he not sense how confused and terrified I was at the thought of his having lived a secret American life, one in which I had played no part? For the last hour, he had been relaxed but unaware of the fear disconnecting me from him. Once, he would have known. Once, we were one. Once, he resided inside of me, and I in him. Our happiness was a private affair; ours alone.

As it had been on the tender in Hoek van Holland. What options did I have? There was no turning back. Would I find a way to accept a life lived together but not as one?

The weight of uncertainty manifested in extreme exhaustion of body, spirit, and mind. Were the queasiness in my belly, the leaden extremities, the slight headache, all consequences of the day's exertions?

Or were these symptoms caused by the likelihood that my life with Samuel would be a charade?

The 1890 census counted four thousand one hundred souls residing in the Lehigh River Gap's incorporated borough of Mauch Chunk.

Parallel to the river, Susquehanna Street ran north-south, making a steep descent into the valley and ending at Market Square and the train station.

At the square, Broadway advances uphill in a westerly direction, its tenancies impressive: the Carbon County courthouse, The American Hotel, the Dimmick Library, the Opera house, and the high school. The Scotch-Irish neighborhood claimed the pinnacle of Broadway's elevation.

In the neighborhoods, Irish and German pubs served beer and old-country dishes to their particular clientele, offering a nostalgic escape for the laborers, especially on payday.

Baseball leagues competed between townships, with games always well attended. On summer weekends, the town band played classical, popular, and martial music at the Market Square Bandstand.

In winter, on many days, commerce was impossible, the street blocked with snow or slick with ice. Keeping rail lines clear was a priority from November through April.

At 2:00 Sunday morning, August 13th, 1893, Samuel and Fannie, with their young sons, arrived in Pennsylvania, America.

Samuel

What a day! My family was here, in my sight, in my life. Proudly, I led them to the east end of the LVRR's platform and whistled for the baggage porter. The boys watched my every move, observing how a man takes care of his family's arrangements.

Dining on the train was an experience to treasure. Our first meal together in five years, Fannie and I talked and talked. I went on at length about life here and rediscovered her quick mind. She was aware of the political and economic situation threatening America and had thought how our family would be affected. She is so beautiful and intelligent, much smarter than I. I have to admit, I did, for the most part, dominate the conversation, but she was weary from her travels, so that was understandable.

There were a few times when she became quite emotional. At those moments, I got a glimpse into the incredible strain she had borne, raising the boys alone. I reassured her I loved her as ever I did. Most importantly, I urged her to close the book on our exile, not to dwell upon those sad and difficult years. I'm not certain—but I sensed she wasn't able to put the past behind her, at least not at that moment. I thought it best to keep the discussion informative for the remainder of the trip, to focus on the practicalities of everyday life, not on the emotional side. She needs time to adjust to the new place, just as I need time to adjust to married life again. I believe it will take a while for all of us to acclimate, and that is only natural.

Around midnight, we reached Mauch Chunk. At the depot's livery stand, hackies sat on their driver's boxes, yawning and nodding. The occasional snort and stamp of hoof indicated the horse's readiness to return to the stable and feed bag. Travel weary, we longed to retire as well.

In front of the station, standing on Susquehanna Street's brick pavers, Fannie studied the night sky. "I'm standing in a crater,

Samuel." I smiled at her remark. She lifted her face, raised her arms above her head, and made a slow rotation. "It's curious. There is no horizon, only a bowl of stars, the bowl formed by the mountains encircling this place."

"Papa, if we're in the west, where are the cowboys and Indians?"

"Albert, this was a place where the Indians lived, but they're long gone now. Cowboys drive cattle from the western territory to the railroads now, but they never did that here in these mountains."

"Papa, how much longer until we get home? I'm very, very sleepy."

I stroked his cheek. "I know, Morris. We're all tired. See those hacks there by the streetlamp? One of them will take us the rest of the way."

Rudolf, refreshed from his long nap on the train, had run across the street to the bandstand gazebo. Sitting on the painted railing, he called to his brothers. "Come over here, Albert, Morris! We can walk along the top of the railing! Wouldn't it be nice if there were carousel horses here? I can see the river, and it looks like black ink!"

Fannie called to the children, "Come now, boys, the coach is waiting. Don't be difficult; it's time to go home."

The baggage clerk approached, rolling the trolley laden with our bags. I motioned toward the livery stand. "Please bring them to the hackie."

"Where are we heading, sir?" "East Chunk, 46 West Sixth. Will the bags fit, or will I need another hack?" "No, sir, there's plenty of space in the rear box. The carriage can only seat three in comfort, so two boys will have to sit on laps. Fare is thirty cents."

He secured the bags with rope while we climbed onto the coach.

Brick pavers and streetlamps in Chunk gave way to gravel and darkness once we crossed the river into East. For the ten-minute ride, no conversation transpired; we were all just too tired.

As we turned onto Sixth Street, I said, "Fannie, darling, we're here."

"Thank God, Samuel."

In the stillness of that late hour, the clip-clop of hooves announced our arrival to the neighborhood. I felt a twinge of guilt when the colicky infant in the flat upstairs began to howl.

His parents, and the neighbors to the left and right, responded to the wailing. Lamps were lit, and people came to their windows to catch sight of what the commotion was all about.

The hackie helped me carry the bags into the parlor, and I paid the fare.

The boys ran inside and into every room, chattering to each other in Hungarian, which was comforting to my ear. It had been five years since I'd heard the music of my native tongue.

Fannie stood at the doorway, hesitant. "Step in, dear. Come see your house!" With my arm around her waist, I steered her past the bedrooms and through the parlor to the kitchen. She seemed relieved to step inside, to shut out the world, or perhaps she was simply reacting to my arm around her.

"Look, Fannie," I said, opening the door to the yard. "I can picture your vegetable garden right outside the door next summer!"

"It's all so wonderful, Samuel. I'm so proud of all you've arranged for us. Why don't you show the boys the sanitary and have them wash up at the sink? I'll get the bedroom ready."

She turned to ask, "Where will I find bed linen?

"I made up all the beds, dear. I knew we'd all be ready to drop by the time we arrived home!"

"Follow me, boys." They all used the sanitary and washed their hands and faces at the kitchen sink, as their Mama had instructed. Fannie was stacking the travel bags in the corner of the room. I heard her tell the boys, "Take off your clothes and lay them on the chair. Sleep in your underpants tonight. Tomorrow, I'll unpack everything. Now, off you go, boys, into bed."

It was a joy to watch the small commotion caused by a mundane activity. Oddly, I was sad and jubilant at once, for all the time missed and for the gift of renewal. "Goodnight, my sons. With you under my roof, I'm the happiest man on the planet. You'll find life in America exciting. Later, you'll understand how good is to be here, where you're free to accomplish whatever dream you wish to work for. Now, goodnight, lads. I love you."

Albert said, "Yes, Papa, I love you."

Morris, yawning, slurred, "I love you, too, Papa."

Rudolf, not to be outdone, piped up in a clear and wide-awake voice, "Yes, Papa, me too. I'm happy, too."

While Fannie attended to bedtime details in the boy's room, I stepped out into the yard, stealing a few moments for reflection.

What purpose would the truth serve? There had been many sacrifices already; compromising my honesty about one episode is only one more. A door must be closed here and never opened. I'm not a man given to deceit, but the lie is justified, to protect Fannie and our future.

I was only twenty-nine-years old. Full of pride and self-congratulation about the great adventure upon which I had embarked. I arrived with one suitcase and a few dollars in my pocket. At D.G. Bertsch, a good job was offered, but I had to prove myself.

Our clientele was not the upper crust. We suited school teachers, small businessmen, and the managing bosses from the mines, mills, and foundries. The shop was well appointed, salesmen knowledgeable and engaging. Cutting tables, sewing machines, fabric, thread, bobbins, buttons, linings, and sundries necessary to the fabrication of men's suits occupied the warren of rooms below ground level.

I had been hired on as Master Tailor on condition I demonstrate my craft satisfactorily. In all humility, it was obvious from the first day that my training in Debrecen put me heads above the employees at Bertsch.

The tailors and four seamstresses were eager to learn, and I had no shortage of time on my hands. I began a Wednesday evening class of instruction on Europe's needle craft. When it became clear the new techniques significantly improved work, Bertsch paid me an additional $1.50 each week to continue the lessons.

Annie was a diligent and quick-witted girl of nineteen. She lived with her husband, Timothy, in a rundown flat at the top of the hill, in Irish-town. Sponsored by a cousin in domestic service, she left Ireland to fill a charwoman's job at The American Hotel. On Sunday, Bertsch paid her to clean the retail floor at his establishment. When she asked him to look at her needlework samplers, he was impressed with the fine hand and offered her a seamstress apprenticeship.

I should have seen it coming, but I had my head in the clouds. For the first months, I was so weary at the end of each long week, the deprivation of my masculine needs was easily ignored. But you know what Alfred Tennyson wrote about spring and a young man's fancy!

Annie had the blackest hair I'd ever seen. Raven-haired, she was. With green eyes, alabaster skin, and a face dusted with freckles. She was no beauty, skin and bones, really. But, her need for me gave rise to a magnetic attraction I found unable to resist. One evening after class, we left the building and walked toward the train depot. Hidden from view, leaning against a sycamore, she pressed herself against me, and I didn't decline.

Desperate with guilt, I avoided conversation with her at work and feigned a stomach ailment, canceling that week's instruction. I was weak, a man isolated from all that was dear. It wasn't anyone's fault; my need answered her siren call. I found her note tucked into the pocket of my work apron, proposing an assignation at a ramshackle property just out of town, off Susquehanna Street. Her cousin, Siobhán, who cared for the old farmer, was off to New York for a niece's christening. Siobhán's bunk in an outbuilding was available and private.

The act was tender but without passion or artfulness, and was quickly climaxed. What I remember most about the experience was her fixation with my circumcised penis.

Our weekly encounters continued for almost two years. Timothy was a drunk who assaulted her regularly, but somehow, she considered it a normal Irish marriage. I suppose she was barren, as no pregnancy threatened the arrangement.

In 1891, Timothy was killed by a falling timber in the anthracite mine. Annie decided to leave for New York, and we said goodbye.

In truth, she had been a good friend, providing an outlet for my physical needs in exchange for a brief escape from her tedious life. It was an episode to be forgotten. Like a job that didn't lead to advancement. It happened, and now, it's over.

Returning to the house, I bolted the doors, turned out the lamps, and walked to our bedroom to resume life, and love, with Fannie.

Fannie

It was a relief to reach our new home, which was larger than our Budapest flat. The rooms had been freshly painted a soft green. Samuel's efforts to create a home were sweet, caring, and welcoming.

The children's bedroom was twelve feet from threshold to exterior wall, and nine on the longitude. The chifforobe, a tall cabinet of deep brown walnut, stood tight against the door frame, allowing space for an upholstered chair. A small table and iron bed frame filled the length of the window wall; the frame holding a firm mattress whose stains and worn places were covered by a muslin sheet. Two large feather pillows were wrapped in pieces of linen from Samuel's workplace. The boys scrambled over one another to lay claim to their spaces upon the bed. A Royal's ermine bed throw could be no more luxurious than the feather counterpane bought new on Susquehanna Street by their Papa. Ready for sleep, they settled happily into the new house.

Samuel kissed each one of his sons. "I'm the happiest man in the world tonight, all of us under one roof."

He left to lock doors, shut the lamps; to make night in the house.

Sitting on the edge of the bed, I gazed at their beautiful faces. "Goodnight, my darlings. Isn't it wonderful to be here, in Pennsylvania, resting in your own room? I'm proud of how you kept your spirits high all the way from Budapest to this night. At long last, we're a whole family again. Papa and I love you very much. Tomorrow, you'll wake up as Americans!"

I kissed each one, turned down the lamp, and closed the door.

Across the hall, Samuel waited. Waiting, too, was the answer I sought: had our love survived all those lonely years?

A warm August breeze caused the window covering above the bed frame to flutter. He lay naked under the sheet. "Fannie..." Putting my finger across his lips, I said, "Hush, my darling. Don't speak."

Removing the pins, my hair fell in waves around my shoulders. I undressed slowly, placing my clothes on the chair. Adjusting the lamp to its lowest setting assured that his complete attention would focus upon my movements. So many nights had passed; so much longing gone unsatisfied. For five years, I had envisioned this encounter, plotted its every move. The fantasy of measured tempo and motion intended to create a memory to relish through all the decades to come. Approaching the bed, shadows fell across my naked body. I heard Samuel's breath catch in his throat, took notice of his tear-filled eyes.

His smell was as I remembered, shaving soap and a unique musk. My fingers traced the muscles of his chest and shoulders, arousing us both. Our rediscovery was to be a serious coupling, unrushed, every motion savored. His outstretched arms welcomed me, and facing one another, we began caressing all the places of our remembered passion.

When he entered me, the release was immediate, excruciating, and intense. The treasured love I remembered had survived, had not yielded to the crush of time, we were one. The moment was full of magic; powerful. I whispered, "the essence of 'us' is here, Samuel. It still lives within us as before."

For a long while, he remained inside me, neither ready to draw apart. He whispered, "I love you, my dearest."

"And I, you," I answered.

The dreaded conversation about his life as a single man hadn't taken place. Our lives began anew in our Mauch Chunk bed that night. We tacitly agreed to leave the unchangeable past behind, not allow it to destroy our future.

11

In 1894, the second year of the economic depression, massive unemployment and extreme poverty gripped the country.

Businessman Jacob Coxey led a protest demanding the government create a roadbuilding, public works program. On March 25, 1894, with one hundred men, "Coxey's Army" began its march from Ohio to Washington, DC.

A militant faction of Coxey-ites formed their own army in Tacoma, Butte, Spokane, and Portland. Five hundred of their members commandeered a Northern Pacific Railway train for the trek to Washington. In Forsyth, Montana, Federal troops stopped the group, preventing them from reaching the capital.

In California, "Kelly's Army," named for its leader, made it past the Ohio River, where groups from all over the country joined for the final push to meet Coxey.

On April 30th, five hundred men reached Washington. The next morning, ten thousand supporters, including six thousand camped at a Maryland farm, lined the streets to cheer the assembly. Coxey and other leaders were arrested the moment they stepped onto the grass of the United States Capitol. Although no public policy was instigated by the march, it inspired the use of popular protest.

George Pullman designed the railroad sleeping car and founded Pullman, Illinois, a company town of twelve thousand workers. Following the Panic of 1893, he cut wages and jobs.

A group of workers asked to meet with Pullman to discuss low wages and poor living conditions and to propose a sixteen-hour workday. Pullman refused the meeting and fired the committee. Voting to strike, the men walked off the job on May 11, 1894. Pullman closed the yard gates.

The Pullman workers didn't actually work for the railroads, but members of the American Railway Union refused to work on trains carrying Pullman cars. It was a Union boycott in sympathy with workers, common men and women abused by their employer.

Arbitration was offered, with a deadline of June 26, 1894. Committees went to the company but were turned away.

The Union knew if their men went along with the boycott, they would be fired and replaced with scabs. Once scabs were hired, Union solidarity demanded all Union workers walk off the job.

On June 27th, five thousand workers walked out, tying up fifteen railroads. By the next day, forty thousand joined the action, affecting all lines west of Chicago. Three days later, one hundred twenty-five thousand workers on twenty-nine railroads had quit work. Buildings were set afire, and a locomotive attached to a U.S. Mail train was derailed. The disruption of the Federal mail service brought a reaction from President Grover Cleveland.

Claiming a violation of the Sherman Antitrust and Interstate Commerce Acts, the government obtained a court order requiring all actions be stopped. The strike was now a federal issue, and the President ordered troops into Chicago on July 3rd.

Three days later, six thousand rioters destroyed hundreds of railcars in the South Chicago Panhandle yards.

Six thousand Federal and state troops, thirty-one thousand police, and five thousand deputy marshals could not contain the rage. Illinois National Guardsmen fired into the mob, killing thirty people and wounding others.

The Union tried to call off the strike, but the Federation of Railroads refused and hired scabs.

The court order injunction, broke the strike. Trains began to move, and Federal troops were recalled. The Pullman Company reopened, rehiring those striking workers who would agree to sign a pledge never to join a union. These were known as yellow dog contracts.

The strike cost the railroads millions in lost revenue and property. More than a million in wages were lost to the strikers. Disorders in twenty-seven states included rioting, interrupted rail and mail services, a break in the availability of goods, and loss of revenue for farmers.

Congress and the mainstream press supported the use of troops, turning public opinion against unions and workers. As a conciliatory gesture, President Cleveland and Congress created the Labor Day national holiday.

Amid the civil disorder, Mauch Chunk's rail business was, for the most part, unaffected. Trains carrying coal to New York and Philadelphia markets had no Pullman cars.

Unaffected, too, Fannie and Samuel adjusted to life in small town America.

Fannie

Always an early riser, at 5:30, I padded, barefoot, to the kitchen, where I adjusted the burner to a simmer under the kettle. Two wall shelves next to the sink stored our hygienic necessaries. The lower one held a blue enamel bowl and Samuel's shaving kit. A boar-bristle brush and clamshell razor stood upright in a green-striped ceramic mug. On the upper shelf, two folded towels stacked next to a small basket contained a goat-bristled hairbrush, tortoise-shell comb, my hair pins. A small mirror was propped against the wall. I placed the shaving tools and enamel bowl on the sink's drainboard in readiness for Samuel's morning toilette.

Four heaping spoons of roasted, shiny-black coffee beans were measured into the grinder. Turning the handle a dozen times or so released the intoxicating oily essence. The bittersweet aroma of the grinds caused saliva to jump from under my tongue and wash over it. Emptying the grounds from the catch box into a small, water-filled *fendel*—saucepan—I set it to simmer on the burner.

It was the second week of September, I'd been in the house for only a fortnight. Waiting for the water to reach a low boil, I stood in the calf-high weeds of the yard, visualizing the vegetable garden of next year's summer, the one I'd plant just like Mama had done in Hungary. The air was cool, a sign that summer had left the valley. Leaves on the mountains were a dull, dead green; no longer vibrant. I loved autumn best of all. A time to prepare the nest for the harsh months to come, create a place to hold values and loved ones close, safe. Taking in a long breath of fresh mountain air, I returned to the kitchen.

I stirred the fendel coffee, strained the frothing liquid through a piece of cheesecloth into a large, earless cup. Three heaping spoons of sugar and cream poured carefully to remain afloat. That was how he liked his coffee, and I loved catering to him. Carrying the cup to the bedroom, I placed it on the table, the aroma filling the room. He began to wake, stretching and smiling before his eyes opened. "Good morning, darling," he said.

"Good morning."

Before he could sit up, I was lying next to him, kissing his face. How I loved this man. His long arms encircled me.

I giggled, "Samuel, your coffee will get cold."

"Yes, kedvesem, my darling, but it will not lose its flavor." The only Hungarian spoken in the house were whispered words of passion. This was our morning ritual, secret moments shared while the children slept.

"You'd better get out of bed if you are to catch the 7:00 tram."

I watched him walk, naked, to the kitchen sink, where he poured water from the kettle into the bowl and a few drops onto the soap in the bottom of the mug. Expertly using the shaving brush, he whisked the soap into a thick foam. I watched him lather his cheeks and chin, his neck; move his nose from side to side to cream his upper lip. Giving himself a long look in the mirror, satisfied all was ready, he paused to let the foam soften his skin. It is a singular, male endeavor, the shaving ritual. It is both a testament to the essence of manhood, hirsuteness, and the sensual primate ritual, grooming. This moment was what had been missing in Budapest. My man, mine. I knew every inch of his body, had caressed and tasted it.

He dressed quickly and took me in his arms.

"School begins at nine. Take the children to the principal's office to register them. Bring their birth certificates and the stamped papers from Ellis Island. I'll see you all this evening, by 7:30. I love you, dearest. Have a good day. Don't worry, everything will be alright."

An hour later, I set out with the boys for school.

Mr. Whitney, the principal, welcomed me into his office. "Guten Morgen!" " Bitte komm in, Frau."

Thank heaven, we were to speak in German; my English was not up to conversing with academics.

"My name is Fannie Freed. We arrived a few weeks ago. Albert is eight; Morris, six."

"What is their native tongue? Do they speak any English? Do they speak any other languages?

"We're Hungarian. Of course, they speak German, too. They've a good English vocabulary already; we've been working with primers and story books for months to prepare them. And we speak only English in the house; my husband insists on that. If there is any extra help or tutoring offered, we'd be most grateful."

"There are few Hungarian speakers in the school or in the neighborhood, for that matter. German is spoken and understood by most of the faculty and almost all the students. If there's any problem with communication, German will be the alternative. That's not to say a foreign tongue will be tolerated during instruction, Mrs. Freed. German is resorted to only in an emergency situation. Our teachers assign extra reading assignments to assist. My advice is to take them to the new Dimmick Library on Broadway. The children's section is well stocked with easy readers.

"Try not to fret; in less than three months, your sons will be English speakers. I've seen it time and again. Albert is assigned to Mrs. Abbott's first grade, Morris in Miss Crenshaw's kindergarten. As soon as they've been evaluated and deemed worthy by their teachers, they'll be moved ahead in grade. Mostly, their placement will depend upon their English language skills. Albert and Morris will have no trouble at all. They'll acclimate according to their individual intellects."

Mr. Whitney looked at the boys, standing side by side in front of his desk. Both wore starched white shirts, grey wool knee pants with black knee socks and ankle-high, laced shoes. They looked so grownup, their hair parted in the middle and slicked back with Macassar oil, lending them an aroma of flowers, palm, and coconut.

"Thank you, Mr. Whitney. Will they go to their classrooms now?

"Mr. Haas, my assistant principal, will take them to their rooms. Lunch is noon to 12:45. Be sure they are not tardy for afternoon instruction.

"Every effort will be made to help them assimilate into the student body. Good day and welcome to Mauch Chunk, Mrs. Freed." I kissed the boys, and Rudolf and I left to catch the tram to Susquehanna Street. Samuel suggested I visit the butcher, greengrocer, and bakery in town; he said East didn't offer the same variety.

In East, horse-drawn carts trolled the streets each morning. A few were local farmers selling milk, eggs, butter, and produce. Others called out, "Pots and Pans," or "Ice, blocks and chips. Ice." On Monday, Wednesday and Friday afternoons, Patrick Laughlin parked his metal cart on the corner of North and Eighth. His five brothers fished the Lehigh River, which was full of trout, carp, catfish, bass, and pickerel. Patrick was the salesman of the family, ringing his bell to alert the housewives within range. "Fresh fish," he shouted, "Fish!" For the first month, I shopped in East. Today, Rudolf and I were off on an adventure, to explore the Susquehanna Street marketplace!

Too young for school, Rudolf accompanied me everywhere, relishing my undivided attention. I thought of Albert, who had been about Rudolf's age when he appointed himself Samuel's replacement. Albert was always so mature, needed to take control of things; it was his nature. Rudolf was my baby, didn't act my equal or wish to be in charge. He craved recognition of his quick wit and charm, needed everyone's eyes to be always upon him. That was *his* nature.

At Holter's Butcher Shop, I purchased two pounds of ground beef chuck for our dinner's meatloaf. Then, to the M.C. Bakery for pumpernickel, and flour, apples, and green beans at Harold's Grocery.

On the return tram, Rudolf was so happy with the outing, he couldn't sit still on the bench. Standing, he did a little shuffle step, ending with a bow.

"Mama, you spoke English all morning to everyone! You're wonderful!"

I smiled, then pleaded with him, "Rudolf, please sit down. Everyone is staring at you."

"That's alright, Mama. Let them stare. I'm happy, and I don't care who knows it!"

I hugged him so tightly, he squealed. "Mama! I can't breathe." When I released him, he drew deep drafts of air into lungs, puffed out his chest, and rubbed his ribcage as if to ease a great pain. This child! Will he become a great stage actor?

Cocooned in that little house, we rewove the torn fabric of our life and love.

Surprisingly, adapting to a husband, father, breadwinner, and ultimate decision-maker took only a few weeks. It was an instinctive transition. When the Mama is happy, the husband and children are, too. And I was happy.

Barely a ripple disturbed Morris's demeanor. Perhaps it was his middle-child status. Content to observe and eager to please, he accepted Samuel's presence. Morris's goodness and trusting nature met a kindred spirit in his father.

Rudolf, always hungry for attention, instigated interaction at every possible opportunity. He ran to greet Samuel at the door, followed him to his chair, sat on his lap, conversing about the day's events.

Albert was another story. "Papa is always at work. He leaves before we're awake and returns after we've had our dinner. And on Sunday, attention is expected to be paid to *his* dinner, *his* coffee, and *his* suggestions for spending the day. I hate to say it, Mama, but he's treated as a king or something."

"My darling, you must try to end the responsibilities you shouldered. As the oldest, you set the example for your brothers; but you are their *brother*, not their father. I know you love Papa, and in your heart, you must feel how he loves you. Relax, do your job: be a good student and a good brother and a good son. Papa will take care of *you* now. Let yourself be loved; be a boy."

I busied myself keeping house and meeting the neighbors.

The whole of East, every street and block, was built with identical, two-story wooden houses butted one against the other. Each housed two rental flats with a porch. In the rear yard, every housewife hung laundry from clotheslines fastened near the kitchen door to a pole shared by four houses, eight families. The system ran like a beehive, I thought. Living on a street in a geometric grid, in identical houses. Men worked from sunrise to dusk, Monday through Saturday. Women's repetitive tasks described the week: Monday, washday. Tuesday, ironing. Wednesday, scrubbing floors and windows. Thursday, baking. Friday, greengrocer, butcher, and pot roast dinner. Saturday, bath day. Sunday, chicken and Church.

Every day of the week, except Sunday, women swept their floors, porches, even the dirt-and-gravel street in front of their houses. The mix of dust and soot from coal stoves, furnaces and the trains settled on windows and floors. It infiltrated every crevice; every pore of the body, the fibers of every fabric. White wash, a misnomer, hung a dingy grey on the clothesline. I waged war on the filth with bucket and mop, but it was like sweeping back the ocean with a broom, impossible.

One Sunday evening, Pastor Freundt, the Lutheran minister, knocked on the door.

Samuel greeted him, "Please come in, Pastor. This is my wife, Fannie."

"Would you care for a cup of coffee?"

"No, thank you, Mrs. Freed."

Samuel motioned for him to sit at the table. "I'm so happy your wife and children are finally here; thanks to Our Lord. When you boarded with the Pfennig's, we spoke once or twice about how lonely you were. Again, thanks to Our Lord and Savior, for your reunion."

After a pause, "I stopped by for two reasons. First, knowing what a gentleman you are, I'm certain you'd never want to insult your neighbors." He waited for Samuel's responding query; there was none. "Samuel, it's not respectful when, on their way to church, my flock pass your sons playing ball in the street. It's the Sabbath, Samuel; there is no play permitted on the Sabbath."

"Pastor, I fully understand, and will put an end to that. What is the second issue?"

"At first, I took you for a lapsed Catholic and made no attempt to bring you to our Lutheran brotherhood. Now that your family is here, may I invite you to St. John's? If you have declined from services all together, I understand and will wait until you find your way back to Our Lord. In the meantime, your sons are welcome in our sanctuary. Wouldn't it be a fine thing for them to be part of a community here in America?"

Again, Samuel made no direct response.

"Can you give me one reason why the boys can't come to service?"

"I have never given you an indication that I am interested in joining any congregation, Pastor. I don't want to be difficult, but it is a subject I consider private. I will, however, promise you that Fannie and I will discuss the matter. Thank you for your concern and invitation."

"Well, of course I respect your privacy and look forward to a positive decision. I'll be going now. God bless you and your family." He added, "Goodbye Fannie. Your husband is a good man."

"Thank you. Do drop in again."

Samuel saw the Pastor to the door, promising to consider his proposal.

"How would it hurt the boys to make this connection to the neighborhood and learn about the Lutherans? It's about America, Fannie, fitting into the local society."

I could find no argument to assimilation, so, on the following Sunday, our three sons walked to St. John's. They were none the worse for it and were accepted by the local children, which was the purpose of the whole exercise.

Residents of East were overwhelmingly German immigrants. On our street, there was one flat occupied by an American family. The children were accepted by their peers, but their parents were unable to bridge the culture and language divide. In less than a year, the family moved back to Allentown. East was a Teutonic ghetto.

The women managed German-speaking households, typical hausfraus in every respect. That's not to say they were all uneducated or unintelligent. Hani had arrived at Ellis in 1888, but like the others, she mastered only enough English for superficial interactions with outsiders. She had attended secondary school in Hamburg and recited poetry to her children. Hani's barely literate husband, Rolf, worked in the foundry from five in the morning until seven in the evening, earning less than a dollar a day wage. Hani was almost six feet tall and painfully thin. Bone thin, my Mama would say. She often did without so as to feed her husband and six children.

Guenther, the eldest, was ten; the youngest, Rosie, two. In spite of all the hardship, Hani had a wonderful sense of humor and taught me to play Skat, a German trick-taking card game. Almost every day, when the children left for school, we enjoyed an hour of conversation, a kaffeeklatsch, at my kitchen table, Rosie and Rudolf playing at our feet.

"I'm hoping Guenther will go to secondary school next year; his mind is too bright to be disregarded. But Rolf cares nothing for education, says it's a waste. He's already put Guenther's name on the foundry list for day workers. If his name moves up the list, I'm afraid he'll leave school." She sighed, "But, we do need every penny, Fannie."

"These are very hard times, Hani. I worry Samuel's wages will be cut. Winter is slow season, and who can say what will happen in spring? New suiting's not a necessity when a man can't even warm up a quarter for a decent meal."

"I'm eating dinner every other night now, Fannie. Rolf hasn't noticed it, but I've lost ten pounds since July. To prepare dinners for two nights, I dice the meat of one chicken and mix it with potatoes or noodles. Then, I use the bones and feet to make a broth to serve with spaetzel. Even eggs have become too dear, at twenty cents a dozen. And, to serve eight; I need two dozen to cook a decent omelet. Even served with potatoes, Rolf would be angry if I made an omelet for dinner. And, I can buy two pounds of beef for twenty-five cents, so eggs are a luxury."

"Large families are a blessing, Hani, but in times like these, it takes all your imagination to make the pennies stretch. I've been cooking cabbage dishes; they go a long way. A couple of pieces of flanken flavor it as a soup, or I'll make rolls stuffed mostly with rice and a bit of chicken. You know, a meal of noodles and one or two diced sausages can give bellies a filled-up feeling; I think it's the fat in the bratwurst. My boys are young, and we're only five at the table, so it's easier for me to stretch my budget." We sipped our coffee, and Hani spread some preserves on a slice of babka. I was aware this small meal might be all she'd have to sustain her until dinner.

"Hani, I think I'm pregnant." I blurted out. "My monthly should have come last week and didn't. It's very early, but I know the signs. My breasts are sore, and I sense a fullness in my pelvis."

She reached for my hand and squeezed it with affection. "Why, that's wonderful, Fannie! In these times, we need the luck a new baby brings more than ever" We were alone in the kitchen, yet she went on in a conspiratorial whisper. "Let's see. November conception will bring an August birth. You'll have to meet the midwife, Marta. She's Berlin-trained, excellent! If it weren't for her, I'd be dead. Does Samuel know?"

"I haven't said a word. Not until I'm certain."

"Best not to add worry to his burdens. The less the men know about women's business, the better. Making babies doesn't seem to concern men, except for the starting of them! They have enough on their plate, responsible for our wherewithal."

"Rudolf and Morris were both born in big city hospitals. The renovated house in Lansford they call a hospital is thirty miles from here. That could take two hours through mountain paths. I can't imagine making such a trip in labor, in a horse-drawn cart. And, if there were a real emergency, are they equipped for that?"

"Fannie, the local doctors do the best they can. There's only ten practicing in Chunk, and a few of them are drunks. Basically, they serve the working men. They had to graduate from college, I think, but the ones over fifty learned doctoring on Civil War battlefields, not in hospital centers. The younger ones, with medical training, rely on the midwives to do the birthing here. The doctors are called in only if, God forbid, there's trouble. It's your only option, Fannie. Having the child in the comfort and cleanliness of your own bed, with Marta attending, is the safest way. Far from a big city, we're lucky to have her." She paused, closing her eyes and sighing. "A woman walks in the valley of the shadow of death during childbirth. Take my advice: pray and read the Bible during the pregnancy so God will be with you when it's time for your confinement."

I didn't tell her I wasn't a praying woman; it wasn't the moment for a discussion of philosophy or religion.

"You know, Hani, I'm not afraid. Albert was delivered by a midwife, and he was my first. My body will perform as it has been designed to do *if* there are no complications. I know one thing for certain: I won't put my life in the hands of some country doctor with poor training."

Hani lowered her voice. "Two hours after I gave birth to Rosie, I started bleeding. Marta called Dr. Walters. They couldn't stop the bleeding. I said goodbye to Rolf; it was a sad moment. I was so tired and weak; I almost wished I'd die, God forgive me. Dr. Walters, with Marta assisting, removed my uterus. Right on my kitchen table! She insisted Dr. Walters wash his hands with carbolic soap before she put the ether rag to my nose. Well, as you can see, I survived. Marta lived in my house for the next week, feeding me pureed liver and green-leaf vegetables every night. She said it would thicken my blood. I prayed to God, and He answered me through Marta's hands."

"My God, Hani! That is a terrifying yet uplifting story. I'm so glad you're here, as I'm sure Rolf is, too."

"Ach, Rolf is the happiest man in East, Fannie. With me being fixed, he doesn't have to worry about making any more hungry mouths, if you know what I mean!"

We laughed and then were quiet. I wondered how all this would turn out in the end.

Life for the women in Mauch Chunk was limited, with no opportunity for cultural diversion. They were trapped in a life cycle of washing, cleaning, cooking, having babies, and caring for elderly or sick relatives. Still, the women were remarkable in their optimism. They prayed their children would escape the mine, foundry, and railyard, that education and ambition would lead them out of the mountains. When the economy collapsed, putting an end to their American dream, children as young as six were expected to add a few pennies to the table. The boys went into the mine, foundry, and railyards after all.

By fourteen, daughters married their brother's counterparts, to begin the cycle all over again.

> January 15, 1894
> Dearest Papa and Mama:
> I hope you are both well. I miss you both so much.
>
> We are all healthy and send love and wishes for a happy and healthy New Year.
>
> Albert and Morris are doing very well in school. Both have advanced two grades since their enrollment in class last September. All three speak English without an accent. At least to my ear they do! You would be so proud of them, Papa. Albert is very tall, almost reaching my shoulder. Morris is sweet, as always. I'm enclosing a picture of the railroad depot he drew for you. Rudolf is also growing so quickly, but still so thin. He has a healthy appetite, so don't worry, Mama.
>
> Samuel is well respected here and has established a new innovation at his employ. Every January, he oversees the inventory count of unsold bolts of fabric. Often, they are sold at a loss to remnant dealers. Papa, you'll be so proud of his idea: tailoring spring casual coats out of that fabric. His employer had to be convinced, which Samuel did. He met with the management of the Opera house, and they ordered eight coats for their ushers and ticket takers. Isn't that wonderful? The work will keep the tailors and seamstresses busy during the slowest months of the year! Also, they'll be clearing a two-year-old inventory. Aren't you so proud of my businessman-husband, Papa??
>
> I, too, am productive; your new grandchild will arrive in August. A new baby Mama could cook for, and Papa could spoil. IF you came to America. Won't you at least think about it? If you begin the journey in June, you could be here, with all of us, before the baby's birth.

Life is peaceful here, and I am happy, caring for the family. The only sadness in my life is that you are not here.

Write soon, and think of me,
Your loving daughter,
Fannie

February was brutally cold. Four feet of snow fell in less than two days. Businesses were closed, as were schools. The railroad dispatched messenger boys door-to-door, summoning all able-bodied men to clear the roads and, then, the rails. It was of vital import to the nation at large and our region, in particular, that coal transport is unhindered.

Washing the breakfast dishes, I felt a sudden twitch in my pelvis. No, it was not a gassy upset, it was quickening, the baby stirring in my womb. A memory to last a mother's lifetime; a fluttering of the fetus calling out, "I am here, Mother; I live." A memory to last a mother's lifetime...

"My dears, Papa and I have a special announcement. At the end of the summer, a new brother or sister will be born!"

Albert announced, "Mama, I'll carry the full washtub from today on."

Morris looked worried. "Can I hug you, Mama, or will it hurt the baby?"

Rudolf burst into tears and fell on the floor, writhing as if in agony. "Mama," he lamented, "Does this mean I won't be your baby anymore?"

We all laughed, and then applauded the performance. Rudolf stood up and took a bow, grinning broadly. "I was only joking, Mama. I'm happy. But I want a sister. Is it a girl, Mama?"

Samuel gathered us all in an embrace. Life in our little world was so good: happy and safe, loving, and warm.

March 19, 1894

Dearest Fannie:

I thought about how I'd tell you the sad news. How to gently write the hardest words I can ever write, but I can find no way around the sorrow.

Your Mama has died. For the last week, she was having trouble breathing and her legs were swollen. Even walking from the bed to the kitchen put great stress on breathing and caused her dizziness. The doctor said her heart was failing, and there was nothing to do for it.

Saturday night, as we've done for decades, I cradled her in my arms, and we fell asleep. The next morning, when I woke, her back was to me, and she didn't move as I sat up. At first, I thought she was asleep; but I knew something was wrong; there was a coolness in the bed, around her.

I left the bed, and coming around to the other side, saw her face, which was peaceful, at rest. There had been no agony or death rattle. She had just slipped away in the night with no word of goodbye; gone from me after a lifetime together.

She was buried Monday, in the Jewish Cemetery in Satu Mare, where her mother and father rest; and where I'll go when my time comes.

There is nothing you could, or should, have done, my dear child. Even if you lived in the house next door, your Mama would still have gone to the beyond. Do not feel guilty; it is no one's fault. We all come to the end of life; it's natural. She loved you very much; was happy that you are living your life as you wish it. She loved Samuel and your sons and never did a day pass without comment from her about all of you. She was content that you are happy, and that's the most important thing a mother can feel after raising a child.

Your loving Papa

Albert was the first grandson and born in Mama's bed. Her wholehearted love for him had forged a deep bond. He sat beside me on the settee, holding my hand.

"I remember how special she made me feel, Mama. Her cookies, her kitchen smells. She taught me how to mix paint colors, even though I couldn't draw."

"She loved you very much, Albert," I said, quietly.

He took my hand. "Mama, I know you're sad, but Grandmamá will always be near you, like an angel."

Morris was sullen for a few days. He asked Samuel, "Papa, I don't know what to say to Mama. How can I cheer her when I'm so sad? I thought I'd see Grandmamá again. That she'd come to America. But now, I *know* I won't, and that makes me cry. Will I cry every time I think about her, Papa?"

Samuel hugged him. "The pain will ease, my son, for your Mama and all of us. Life goes on for the living."

Rudolf, the actor, put himself in deep mourning, crying inconsolably for three days. "I know you think I'm playacting, Mama, but I really, truly, can't stop crying. I'm afraid I won't remember her face." I held him on my lap, rocking back and forth.

Samuel loved Mama deeply. "From the first, I knew she loved me. Were it not for her, our marriage might never have earned your father's blessing."

I sat Shiva in my own way, weeping in the quiet hours before dawn, lighting candles for thirty days, cooking Mama's paprikash and strudel. Papa loved Mama, but I wasn't worried he'd wither and die of heartbreak. No, not Papa. He would work and enjoy good health; that was his nature. Despite how much he loved me, I knew he would never come to America. For this, too, I wept.

On the first anniversary of our arrival at Ellis Island, we enjoyed a family dinner at The American Hotel, a rare treat.

Before sunrise the next day, a stream of fluid leaving my body awakened me. When I stood up, the wetness ran down my legs, pooling on the floor.

I nudged Samuel awake. "What do you want me to do, Fannie?" "Knock on Hani's door and send her for Marta. Tell her my water has broken." Quickly pulling on his trousers but still barefooted, he rushed from the room. "After I dress, I'll send Albert with a note to G.F. explaining my absence at work today."

Samuel helped me ready the bedroom, first cleaning the floor, then removing the bed linen and covering the mattress with an oilcloth sheet. The first pain of labor began in the small of my back, radiating to my abdomen. In two minutes, the spasm reached its height, then declined. A respite of twenty minutes followed. "Samuel, when Hani returns with Marta, see to the boys breakfast, help them dress, and go to Chunk, maybe lunch at the park. There's nothing you can do but pace and worry if you remain at home."

Labor seemed to stop for an hour. When it resumed, pains were still twenty minutes apart. At noontime, Marta examined me. "You're almost fully dilated, Fannie. I'd wager this baby will be delivered by 2:00."

I was confident there would be no complications with labor and delivery, and there were none. Contractions continued their rhythmic escalation, pushing the child down the birth canal. I relaxed between exertions. At 1:30 in the afternoon, August 13, 1894, Charles Freed, our first American-born child, made his arrival. It had been an easy confinement for Marta to attend; the baby small, my pelvis adequate. Her experienced hands cut the cord and cleaned the vernix from my son's little body. When the cheesy, white, natal skin protection was wiped away, Marta massaged him with mineral oil. The baby made few sounds, but his eyes were open, and he lifted his arms, perhaps reaching for me.

Relieved and pleased, Marta said, "Congratulations, Fannie. He is breathing well, and color is good. Although he's a lightweight, maybe five pounds, he's fine." She swaddled the child in a blanket and placed him in my arms.

Samuel and the boys returned close to five in the afternoon. Entering the room, Samuel wept with joy. "My love, my Fannie. Thank you. I love you."

Albert looked at the baby. "Another boy?"

Morris stared at the tiny face of his new brother. "He looks alright, Mama. Little, like a doll."

"His name is Charles, boys. Your brother's name is Charles."

Rudolf came close to the bed, touching the baby's forehead with his finger. "He's ugly, Mama. He looks like a wrinkled, tiny, old man."

Samuel and I laughed. He told the boys, "It's time for Mama and the baby to rest now. Let's make some dinner." He bent to kiss my lips. "I love you, and Charles, too!"

He proved to be a colicky baby who responded to the slightest noise with a jerking of his whole body, trembling. To calm him, I was obliged to hold him in my arms for most of the day and night. In constant attendance, I was unable to leave the house or garden for three months, when his digestive tract, maturing, ending the colic. To be fair, I wasn't missing anything in the social sphere. There was little stimulation outside the house; this wasn't Budapest. A new card at the concert hall was not enticing me; there was no concert hall. Spending an afternoon at the library or museum was not an option, as the Dimmick Library was not within walking distance and there was no museum.

I thought myself a cosmopolitan woman. Thought myself unable to live without the vibrancy of a big city electrifying the day and night. All the talk of a cultural wasteland and how impossible it would be to bear, was rubbish. With the pride of youth, I could not have foreseen this mountain-prison would, in reality, be a refuge. The very isolation and limited aspiration of the place blanketed us with a kind of protection, a peace. The pace of life acted as a salve, healing the scars of our struggle and the emotional uncertainty we brought with us from Budapest.

In the Lehigh Valley, we were marginally affected by the depression, eking out a living. The boys made friends and freely roamed Mauch Chunk. They no longer spoke Hungarian, and attendance at St. John's gradually ended. Pastor Freundt didn't come around again. I supposed he abandoned the wait for Samuel to find his way back to Our Lord and Savior.

Rudolf eagerly entered kindergarten in 1894, his charm casting a spell over his teacher, Miss Margaret McCloud, a recent graduate of Pennsylvania's Teacher's College.

A month after Charles's first birthday, I weaned him from the breast, and by Christmas, knew I was pregnant again, due the following summer.

Samuel

Millions were unemployed, some on the brink of starvation. There was violent protest against the government and violent response from the government. In our little valley, there were hard times, but even those who lost work were able to put bread on the table through the generosity of neighbors and the churches. At G.F Burnhauser, a few employees were let go, but the doors remained open.

G.F. went along with my recommendation to add a ready-to-wear line of casual jackets at a reasonable price. I had read about it in *Gentlemen's Magazine of Fashion*. It's impossible to tailor a coat for a universal body, but the idea of buying a ready-made garment was so modern. The *idea* sold the coat. A man could come in and leave with a new coat, right then and there! Custom tailoring was a process of many weeks. Choosing the style, the fabric, the lining, the buttons, cutting the pattern, basting, fitting, sewing, fitting, adjustments, and final fitting. With ready-to-wear, some tailoring would still be required: sleeves shortened, seams released to accommodate a paunch, perhaps additional shoulder padding—all at a small, extra charge. I reduced old inventory, kept the seamstresses and tailors busy during the winter months, and added to the profit column in the ledger. In spite of the recession, the coats sold out in the spring, and I received a commission on every one.

My world was stable, Life settled into a sweet routine. Order and a sense of purpose rejuvenated my spirit, my soul. Fannie and I were rich in the blessings of life: love had been renewed; our sons were healthy and generous of spirit; Fannie and baby Charles had survived the birth, hale and strong. She created a secure home, a base that allowed me a free mind to concentrate on earning a living and preparing a future plan.

Life unfolds in ways you cannot imagine. For five years, we had been thwarted at every turn, ill fortune pushing our dreams out of reach. Now, our future looked golden. "A new baby brings good luck," I've heard the women say. If that's true, then we have Charles to thank.

Indian summer of 1895 brought a visitor to the Hotel Wanetah, at the entrance to the Lehigh Gorge. I remember well, his visit to G.F. Burnhauser.

He asked to speak, in person, with the Master Tailor, and I was summoned. I handed him my card. "What can I assist you with today, sir?"

I guessed him to be sixty-five years of age and just shy of six feet tall; in a word, stylish. Removing his flat straw boater hat, a full head of short, white hair was revealed. A ready smile brought attention to his pointed beard and generous moustache, both well combed and trimmed. Taking him in from head to toe, he was the epitome of the well-born, well-connected, privileged, American man. He wore a three-button, single-breasted, pale blue Sack suit, distinguished by natural shoulder, soft vest, and cuffed, straight-leg trousers. To my practiced eye, the clean lines and precise tailoring had been fitted, cut, and sewn by a Master. A striped wing-collared shirt with pearl studs, floppy deep blue bow tie, and square-toed shoes with spats completed the costume.

Offering his business card, he said, "Mr. Freed, I am Elijah Brooks. I was in the neighborhood, as it were, lunching on a well-prepared smoked duck and shallots dish at The American Hotel. The proprietor, Herr Lentz, referred me to you, said I ought to see the fine woolens you offer, said I'd be impressed. So, here I am to have a look, spend a few moments on a busman's holiday, so to speak. You see, my family's in the garment business, too."

His card was unnecessary. I knew immediately who he was, having seen his photo many times in *Gentlemen's Magazine*. His grandfather had opened a tailor shop in downtown New York seventy-five years earlier. This gentleman, along with his brother and two cousins, was a managing partner of the premier men's clothier in America!

"Mr. Brooks, it's an honor to meet you. I'll be happy to show you our new wools, just arrived from England. Please follow me." He stopped at the table displaying ties, fingering the fabric. "The small-scale, repeated pattern has printed well, in spite of the characteristics of the silk. The foulards in our New York store may be of higher quality, but here in the hinterlands, I can't fault your replicas."

I said, "G.F., the proprietor, is visiting our New York suppliers this week, shopping for winter goods. He'll be disappointed to learn he missed your visit today. I expect he'd ask your direction in locating new sources for the foulards."

"I'd like to see your woolens, and if I may, the workroom. The tailoring process interests me. Even after seventy-five years, one may still find a better way of doing things. It was my grandfather's belief that innovation may be found in remote corners; who's to say where a fine craftsman may be working? Who can say where the next advance may be discovered? Perhaps right here in Pennsylvania!" His laugh was good-natured. I liked him.

We walked through to the cutting tables and machines. Garments in various stages of development were pinned to mannequins at every station. Mr. Brooks wandered the floor, sweeping his hand across the cutting table, checking for dust—he found none—looking in waste baskets, turning over a lapel to consider the facing's needlework. He asked seamstress Sharon if he might see the waistcoat she was working on. Using her tape, he measured the length and appraised the stitchery of her buttonholes.

"Very fine work, Miss."

Sharon nodded. "Thank you, sir."

Returning to the selling floor, I made introductions to the staff, who stood smartly at attention to shake the hand of one of the most successful tailors in the world.

"Mr. Freed, I congratulate you on your excellent shop. The place is clean. and goods are presented well. Your tailoring is first class, and I don't say that lightly. I see you're offering some ready-to-wear coats. You know that was an innovation of my Uncle Daniel."

"I am aware of the Brooks ready-to-wear; your uncle was a fashion pioneer." I quickly added, "And, thank you, Mr. Brooks. Your praise is appreciated. I'll be certain to share your comments with G.F. when he returns."

I escorted him to the door and shook his hand. He leaned toward me conspiratorially. "I return to New York City on Tuesday, Samuel. Will you join me for lunch at The American Hotel? Say, Sunday, at one?" Eagerly, I replied, "Yes, of course. I'll be there. Thank you again."

It was a bit early for Sunday dinner at The American, so we had the place, more or less, to ourselves. We ordered soup and salad. When our beers arrived, he wasted no time getting to the point of the meeting. "Samuel, if you decide to move to New York, you have a job waiting for you at my family's establishment."

I blushed, "The dream of my life is to move to New York, Mr. Brooks. This is most generous, thank you."

Our soup was served, but I found it difficult to swallow any of it. This moment was life changing. I had been struck by lightning! How could I maintain my composure, continue to dine, pretend this earthquake wasn't happening?

The waiter removed my soup. "Was there a problem, Mr. Freed?" he asked. "No, Rolf, thank you. I'm not very hungry. In fact, I think I'll skip the salad, too. Just a coffee will do."

Mr. Brooks had no trouble finishing either course and tactfully pretended he hadn't noticed my loss of appetite. Patting his mouth with the napkin, he looked at me. "Samuel, I know a well-trained professional when I see one. You'll earn a lot more money in the city. Contact me when you've made your decision; you have my card."

Guaranteed work in New York changed everything! I was on my way to my own shop.

That evening, Fannie and I began working out the details. Our savings were meager. If we skimped for a few months, maybe four, we might manage enough for the rail tickets, a month's rent, and food for a week.

Two days after Christmas, I wrote to Brooks, accepting his offer of employment. I received a reply from Edward Bachmann, foreman at the lower Broadway location. There was work for me, but not as a direct employee. Apparently, I would join other independent tailors, piece workers, who produced the ready-to-wear suits. If I chose to accept the employ, I was to wire Bachmann of my arrival date in New York.

Fannie asked, "This means you won't be a Master Tailor, suiting elite New Yorkers. Will you be happy doing that, Samuel?"

"The ready-to-wear line carries the same label; the clientele expect the same quality. It's not a step down. And, the pay reflects that: fifteen dollars for a six-day week, with a minimum of forty pieces, and add seventy-five cents for each piece above quota. We'll be on easy street, Fannie."

"Nearer to your own shop, my darling, that's what's important. Bless Mr. Brooks."

Mid-February, I met with Bachmann in New York. We agreed I'd begin work the following month, on Monday, April 6th. Before returning home, I signed a lease for a four-room apartment on the fifth floor at East 70th Street near Third Avenue. Rent was $15.00 a month, including heat and hot water. The kitchen was small, with a bathtub in the center, which served as a table when covered with a wooden plank. We would share a water closet in the hall with two other flats.

On the first of March, I asked G.F. for a few minutes of his time.

"Thank you so much for the opportunity to work for you, G.F. You took a chance on me, and it worked out well for both of us. After six years, it's time I established myself, built a future for my family. Brooks has offered me a job in New York, and I've accepted. With complete confidence, I recommend you advance Josef Schneider to Master Tailor. Or, if you desire another candidate, I'll stay for a month, to ease the changeover."

He was livid. "How dare you! I never thought you'd be disloyal. Brooks better not ever set foot in my store again, stealing my finest tailor! How underhanded! After all I've done for you, the excellent salary I've paid, how I've treated you as an equal, almost as a partner! How could you do this to me, just as we're buying goods for the summer season?"

"Please, G.F., this is not about gratitude or Brooks. It is what I want to do with my life. I don't want to remain in Mauch Chunk. I want my own place, and I want to live in New York so my sons may have advantages this town can never give them. I don't want our relationship to end badly. I respect you and am grateful for all you have made possible for me. Thank you, G.F., for everything. Now, let's keep our heads about us and organize my departure, so that G.F. Burnhauser will continue to provide quality clothing with good service, without interruption. What do you say?" In the end, with a handshake, Burnhauser agreed to promote Schneider and accept my departure with grace. It had nothing to do with him, personally, which he came to recognize when he gained control of his emotions and felt assured his business would continue as before.

At the end of March, my G.F. Burnhauser's work family gathered at The American Hotel for a farewell dinner in my honor. Burnhauser presented me with a fine black leather wallet containing a crisp twenty-dollar bill. "Good luck, Samuel. I'm going to miss you very much."

Although my appearance radiated confidence and contentment, I was unsure of what lay ahead. With a wife, four children, and a fifth on the way, I prayed the risk I was taking would turn out well. The underlying worry was I'd be in my own employ; there was no guaranteed paycheck. I hoped the machines would be in good working order and the foreman managed fairly. I worried a bit about, but did not dwell upon, the possibilities that I might be unhappy with the work, the equipment, the business climate at Brooks Brothers.

Fannie

Samuel was happy at work, recognized for his talent and training. The men of standing in Mauch Chunk insisted on his attention, and the men of millionaires' row relied on him for their appearance during summer's social season.

With his following, it was inevitable he would be offered employment opportunities in New York or Philadelphia. His talent and charm were apparent, his work perfect. So, it really came as no surprise to me when Mr. Brooks asked him to come to work for his family's famous company.

As Samuel's dream was closer to reality, my task was to prepare for the move.

Intending to buy new second-hand pieces in New York, we sold our furniture to the neighbors. The rest of our belongings were packed into a dozen boxes and crates. I received a letter from Papa with ten U.S. dollars to "help with the move." That gift was appreciated, as porters and drays added significantly to the expense of the venture.

On my thirty-fourth birthday, April 1, 1896, at 6:30 in the morning, the drayman loaded our packed property and left for the station. The livery cab arrived soon after, and our neighbors, including the Pastor, came out of their houses to bid us farewell and good luck. With hugs and handshakes all around, it was extraordinary that in a town where we'd not anticipated finding anyone with whom to converse, so many friendly connections had been made.

Hindsight may have smoothed over the roughness of the past, but I believe that our time in Pennsylvania was truly idyllic, the easiest of our years in America. Life seemed in our control; we were young, hopeful, and invincible. Yes, the dynamic nature of a big city was missing, but the lethargy of this place allowed us to heal and rest in the sanctuary of the valley.

We boarded the early express to New York, expecting to arrive in Jersey City at 12:30 in the afternoon. The boys were thrilled to be out of school and off on a new adventure. Even little Charles sang along when his brothers began a robust version of "The Sidewalks of New York."

I sat quietly, thinking about the hard work ahead and feeling insecure about everything. I could offer no help with finances, and with another child on the way, I was accountable for adding to our burdens. The train raced across the rural countryside, and new anxieties rushed in. But it was, as on the tender in Rotterdam, too late to turn back.

The boys dozed. Samuel and I leaned against each other and nodded off, he escaping his doubts, my pregnant body recovering some energy. Around ten in the morning, we ate hard-boiled eggs and bread with butter, all washed down with sugared tea.

A porter at Jersey City moved our possessions onto the Manhattan-bound ferry. Then we hired both a hack and a dray to get us from the Liberty Street quay to East 70th Street.

Six months pregnant and having carried Charles on my hip all the while, I was exhausted when, finally, we crossed the threshold of our second-floor flat. With no chairs, amid boxes and crates, we lay down on the parlor floor, happy to be off our feet, in spite of the unforgiving wooden surface. The next-door neighbors came by with a gift of ice for the kitchen box and sat with us on the floor chatting about vendors, shops, and the local school.

What a city! Samuel and I bought three mattresses, a kitchen set, and two chairs for the parlor from a second-hand store on Third Avenue, and it was all delivered by 8:00 that evening! Albert ran to the grocer on 71st Street, and that evening, we feasted on skillet-cooked chicken and red peppers, fresh rye bread and butter, coffee, and sliced apples.

"Come to bed, Fannie. It's almost midnight." I turned off the gas lamp and lay down with Samuel, my distress dissipating. His thoughts were fixed on the new job. "If it doesn't pan out, there's plenty of work in the city, my love. We're young, and we'll make a wonderful life here. Don't worry, dearest, I'm strong, smart, and have a valuable skill. I doubt I'll ever want for work. We'll be alright, trust in me."

The child in my womb stirred, a good omen; stretching, growing, as was the family, moving forward in America.

12

Structural steel, elevators, steam heat, plumbing systems, gas and electric lighting. These were innovations of the 1880s that gave rise to a unique and characteristic American architectural style, the skyscraper.

In 1883, Roebling's famous bridge spanned the East River, connecting Brooklyn, the third largest city in America, to New York City, which included parts of The Bronx. In 1898, the consolidation of New York, Brooklyn, Queens, and Staten Island created the City of Greater New York.

To allow pedestrian and horse-drawn traffic unimpeded access to the streets, an elevated roadway, the El, was constructed to provide for mass transit. The Els spanned major New York avenues from The Battery to The Bronx and downtown Brooklyn to the edge of Queens. By the fin de siècle, end of the century, the Manhattan Railway Company carried one hundred eighty-four million riders a year. Brooklyn Rapid Transit carried another fifty-eight million. These monopolies were granted ninety-nine-year charters by the State of New York, paying heavy tribute to the Democratic Pol and Tammany Hall boss, William Marcy Tweed.

Trains and trolleys were first powered by steam-powered cables, then steam locomotives, and, finally, electric cables. Trolleys crossed the Brooklyn Bridge to a hub for transfer to Els serving Brighton Beach, Bay Ridge, and Canarsie.

To promote orderly growth of middle-class neighborhoods, apartment buildings were constructed along the routes of the Els. These buildings provided professionals, businessmen, and white-collar workers all the technological advances of the day and superintendents, men on call for maintenance services.

An unprecedented influx of Eastern and Southern Europeans came to New York during the last decade of the century. The immigrants crowded into lower Manhattan's five-story tenement houses. The buildings offered four apartments on each floor and no elevators. Only street-facing rooms received light. All other ventilation was provided by a single air shaft. Few had running water and indoor toilets were not mandated until 1902.

Schools were overwhelmed, with more than eighty children per teacher in the elementary grades. Few children remained in school beyond age twelve. Although compulsory attendance was the law for many years, overcrowding denied entrance to many. Participation could not be enforced, causing children to shift for themselves. Tens of thousands became factory workers, shoeshines, newspaper sellers, beggars, and vagrants.

Cholera, diphtheria, typhus, and tuberculosis were rampant in the slums. Horse manure covered the streets. The city established a large street-cleaning force in 1894 to address that public health crisis.

By 1900, more than eighty thousand tenements had been built, and two thirds of the city's population, two million three hundred thousand people, occupied them. The lower East Side was the most densely populated district in the world.

In the spring of 1896, Fannie and Samuel moved into an apartment in a middle-class building on East 70th Street near Third Avenue.

Fannie

On Third Avenue, the elevated line ran from 125th Street to Water Street, near the Brooklyn Bridge, the fare one nickel. Every day,

Samuel rode the line from East 72nd Street to East 23rd. For another nickel, he rode the horse-drawn trolley to his workshop on East 22nd. Under the El, horse-drawn trams, hansom cabs, drays, and carts made crossing Third Avenue an adventure. With traffic moving in all directions and manure obstacles, one had to develop a keen sense of when it was safe to maneuver and where to place one's foot. And the noise! Day and night, there was never a quiet moment.

We were fortunate to occupy four large rooms in an apartment house, not a tenement. Sharing a toilet in the hall with three other families presented some problems in the morning, which were minimized by neighborly consideration.

In spite of scrubbing our apartment and the bathroom every day, barely a week passed without one of the boys being unwell with a sore throat or earache. Rudolf developed croup and the grippe. Several times, we brought him, burning with fever, to the German Hospital on East 77th in Lenox Hill. With care and cleanliness so poor, charity wards were generally regarded as places only for the dying. The doctor said, "Take him home. Administer cold-water enemas, keep him isolated, and force-feed sweetened tea and broth. There's no medicine I can offer, Madam. He has a better chance of recovery at home. Good luck." Rudolf did recover, and this scenario repeated several times.

Still, New York was a far cry from the medical wilderness of Mauch Chunk. There were fine private hospitals and free clinics and literally thousands of doctors' offices! Sloane Maternity, on Amsterdam and West 59th, was devoted to the care of women. A ten-day confinement cost ten dollars; for poor women, like me, care was free.

On July 27, 1896, Dr. Brodhead attended the birth of our fifth child, Rose. I was ecstatic. Finally, a daughter!

In September, Rudolf was denied entrance to second grade after visiting the school's doctor. "The boy is not admitted. His heart is too weak to survive the rigors of school. I recommend you keep him at home, strictly limiting his activities. I fear his life span will be short. If his strength allows, he may study at home with a private tutor. If you can manage it, I think it best he's sent to a milder climate, with cleaner air."

I begged, "Doctor, please check him again. Tutors are not possible; we're struggling to make ends meet as it is. I can't accept he's in such a desperate condition."

He snorted, "Mrs. Freed, are you questioning my medical judgment? The boy is very ill. There are few open seats in the schoolrooms as it is. In his place, a healthy child will have a chance at an education." He walked away, and I wept all the way home.

The thought of Rudolf's decline and demise devastated me. It was true he had always been susceptible to whatever ailment made the rounds in the household. Then, always, he rebounded. Painfully thin and lanky, he was agile and sure-footed and enjoyed a healthy appetite. Although it was unthinkable for him not to receive an education, there were no resources for a tutor. The dilemma: Rudolf's prognosis and providing him an education. I found a solution.

September 2, 1896
Legkedvesebb Rozsa:
I pray this letter finds you and István well. We are all fine and the new baby, Rose, is beautiful and robust. Your brother, Samuel, is healthy, working very hard and providing a good living.

I am writing about Rudolf. He was not admitted to school when the doctor discovered a heart condition. You can imagine how frightened I am at the prospect of losing him, but I do not accept the decision. With schoolrooms overcrowded in the city, I fear the doctors are searching for reasons to reject poor children.

I know the diagnosis is incorrect, Rozsa. The boy has suffered every childhood illness and survived them all. At first glance, he does not seem robust. He is skinny, but his muscles are strong and active. He was blessed by the quick wit and sharp reflexes of the Freeds, and also, by their pale complexion. I know Rudolf will grow and do well in school, if given the opportunity.

The authorities suggested the boy live away from the filthy streets and air of the city, and that is why I'm writing you.

Would you take the boy in for a while? We would pay you a few dollars a month for his board, and I'm sure he'll be a help to you in the house and to István on the river.

Please say yes, Rozsa. I'm begging you. You are my only hope. There is no other family to turn to.

Hálásan, your sógornő,

Fannie

So, it was decided Rudolf would live in Tarrytown, New York for a while, with Samuel's sister and her husband. A Danube River boatman in Budapest, István worked for the Nyack and Tarrytown Ferry Company, and he owned a fishing boat. On Sundays, his catch was offered as the plat du jour in the fine dining rooms of both The Phoenix and The Park Hotels.

The couple had no children and welcomed their nephew with open hearts, refusing any money for his board.

Samuel and Rudolf rode the New York Central, and the boy, for once justifiably melodramatic, sobbed all the way.

Twenty-eight miles north of the city, the mountains, river, and pace of life, very like that of Mauch Chunk, provided a familiar environment. The school required nothing beyond a certificate of smallpox vaccination for admittance, and Rudolf entered second grade.

October 15, 1896

Dear Mama and Papa:

I'm sorry for not writing more. I miss you all so much. Sometimes I cry when I think about how I'm so far away.

But I'm also having a great time with Uncle István and Aunt Rozsa! Being an only child is good. I am learning so much about the river, which is the main important thing about Tarrytown. Nyack is the town across the river *from here. Did you know the Nyack Indians moved up here from Coney Island?*

Auntie is a great cook and baker, and I help with everything. When I come home, I'll make you the best strudel in the world.

School is good, too. I've been skipped two grades because most of these kids are country bumpkins. Any City kid knows more stuff without even going to school. I'm reading a lot of Edgar Allan Poe. I can recite "Annabelle Lee" by heart. Also, I will relate "The Legend of Sleepy Hollow" to the family when I come home in December. The story takes place in the town north of here, and in one part, a man is chased by a headless horseman! It's very exciting, and I've read the story three times over.

I'll write again next week.
    Your loving son,
    Rudolf Freed

I wrote to Rozsa, letting her know I'd be coming to bring Rudolf home for Samuel's birthday, Christmas day. The boy did, faithfully, write to me every week, but after almost three months, I missed his enthusiasm and animation. Also, worry about his health never left me.

Samuel raised his voice, "Fannie, I forbid it. You are still nursing, considered still in confinement. It's not safe for you to travel."

I smiled at his judicial tone. "Darling, I am going. What danger is there? I'm a healthy woman, and Rose is a healthy infant. Wherever I am, everything she requires resides. I am fit, very fit, and do not agree to be confined in any respect. On Saturday, I'll take the Central and spend a night with Rozsa. It'll be a nice change of scene for me. I'll bring Charles, so he's not underfoot."

Samuel's tone began to soften. "What if it's bad weather? You might be stranded up there for days."

"And wouldn't an extended visit be a lovely treat for me and your sister? The boys are capable of taking care of themselves, and so are you. I'll make a pan of stuffed cabbage before I leave. If I'm stranded in Tarrytown, you'll go to the Deli on Third Avenue. You'll all survive without me. You're living in New York, for goodness' sake!"

Samuel looked at me. He sighed, then laughed out loud. "I guess I should know better than to forbid you to do anything."

"Yes, you should know better, my darling." We both laughed, and he reached for me. I looked over at Rose, sleeping in the cradle next to my bed.

"Shh, the children are in the next room."

"Yes, Fannie, and our door is closed." When we embraced, the pressure on my breasts caused milk to leak through my nursing corset and nightgown. "I'm sorry, Fannie. Is it uncomfortable?"

"Not at all. Ignore the dampness, Samuel."

While I was nursing, there would be no menses, and best of all, there would be no conception, either; thankful for that, we made love.

Saturday morning, the weather was bright and very cold. From the window of a New York Central car, I watched the brown-gray waters of the Hudson. Rushing southward toward the sea, it filled a three-mile-wide gap between the steep cliffs of the New Jersey Palisades on the west and the New York lowlands on the eastern shore. Cradled in my arms, Rose slept soundly, swaddled in a wool blanket. Charles pointed out boats on the river as the train made its way north. After an hour and twenty minutes, a ferry on its way to Nyack came into view. The Conductor came through the car, announcing, "The Tarrytowns, next stop!" At the brand-new depot, no hansoms were available.

The station was a stone's throw from the shopping district, busy with people out and about, no doubt preparing for Christmas. We stood on the street side of the station, and after a while, a ride came around. During the winter, with local fields lying fallow, many farmers make use of a one-horse shay, meeting arriving trains to earn a few coins.

The driver jumped from his perch. He was a stout fellow wearing a long, black woolen coat. A black hat sat on top of a brown knitted scarf coiled round his head, neck, and chin. "Hello, Madam. Welcome to the Tarrytowns."

He motioned to accept Rose from my arms, allowing Charles and me to step up into the rig. Once the blanket was arranged over our legs, he handed the baby to me. "Thank you, driver. I worried we might not find a ride. We're going to 26 Hudson Street, please. I believe that's in North Tarrytown, although as a stranger, I wouldn't know where the dividing line would be. Looks like just one Tarrytown should suffice."

He laughed, "You're right about that, missus. The two Tarries have no wall or streets or farms or any land separatin' 'em. Only the townies know where one begins and t'other lets off! So, you'll be visitin' a relative, missus? No worries, missus; it's very close by, on the river side of the train tracks, a block from the water. Not that you could have walked with the wee ones, though. And, with mostly every house in walkin' distance to the stores, cabbies are few and far between at the depot; they're mostly at the ferry landin'."

With no protection, or covering at the shay's front, we faced an icy breeze for the duration of the trip. Bouncing along the frozen dirt roads was uncomfortable, to say the least. I can tell you it was a relief when the ride to Hudson Street turned out to take less than ten minutes.

One block from the river, with a view of Nyack's distant hills, the horse came to a stop in front of a wooden house painted a pale yellow, with blue trim. To the side, Rozsa's vegetable garden slept under a blanket of snow.

The sky looked full of snow; however, the air felt almost too cold for it. I shivered as the blanket was removed from my lap and held the baby closer to my bosom. Climbing down from the shay, I paid the cabbie a nickel. From behind me, I heard the sound of a door being thrown open, slamming against the jamb. The driver tapped his hat with a gloved hand. "Thank you, missus; may your visit be a pleasant one; and a blessed Christmas to you and yours." I nodded to him and turned to greet Rozsa, who, wrapped in a shawl, ran to me, squealing, "My darling. I'm so happy to see you!"

I kissed both her cheeks. "Rozsa! I can't believe I'm here, at last!" Taking the baby from my arms, she held Charles's hand, guiding him to the door. Over her shoulder, she called to me, "Hurry my lamb; come in out of the cold!"

She laid the baby on the settee as I crossed the room to sit by the fire. "I didn't see a boat in the yard for the winter. Is István still fishing in December?"

Rozsa poured a cup of tea and brought it to me. "A few friends are coming over with a team of horses to tow it out of the water on the morning of Christmas eve. November was mild, and river ice is just beginning to form. The kind weather allowed him to fish all the way through the month. The extra money from the hotel chefs provides a nice rainy-day fund, Fannie, gives me peace of mind. You know what a penny pincher I've always been. I guess growing up poor does that." She refilled my cup and gave Charles another cookie. "Last week, the Ferry Company gave István a raise in pay and a promotion to machine room chief on The Rockland.

Fannie, he's moving up in the company."

"Why, that's wonderful Rozsa. I'm so happy for him, for both of you. I remember you bemoaning his terribly long work week. Now, with Rudolf here, providing company, the house is no longer lonely. Am I right, dear?"

A shadow of worry crossed her face. "Rudolf's a Godsend to me, Fannie; he's a wonderful boy. That aside, you are correct, I still worry about the long hours István is working. He's making continuous round trips from Tarrytown to Nyack starting at seven-thirty in the morning until seven at night. In all weather, Fannie. It's too many hours to remain alert. Working on the water can be dangerous; you can't be tired or distracted. On the bright side, the ferry slip is in walking distance from the house, which is nice. Most days, he's home for lunch."

She poured a cup of cocoa for Charles, who had been amusing himself on the floor, playing with Rudolf's tin soldiers. Rose was fussing to be nursed, so I began unbuttoning my weskit.

Rozsa went on, "You know, Fannie, Rudolf follows István around like a little puppy. He loves the fishing and tinkering with the small boat engine. All the boatmen and ferry workers know him; he can't stay away from the water. On many days, after school, he'll ride the ferry just for fun, making himself useful to the crew. One of the neighbors building a small skiff has asked for István's help this winter; even invited Rudolf. He'll learn boat carpentry and earn a few dollars in the bargain, too. So, Fannie, dear. We're happy and life is good, especially with Rudolf here. He's so like a son to us." She sipped her tea.

"Rozsa, your little house is lovely."

"Four rooms are enough for the two of us. Even with Rudolf, we're not crowded. We set him up in the room István used for fishing gear. The boy, with a deadpan face, told me he smells like a bluefish and the cats follow him home from school! At first, I was embarrassed and then told him he absolutely DID NOT smell like fish. I was really upset about that, sniffing all around his clothes and hair. I didn't smell anything. Then, he started laughing at me. Finally, I got the joke. We both laughed, but he really can be a prankster. I assure you, István painted that room and I scrubbed the floors with strong soap before the boy moved in."

"Of course, Rozsa, I'm sure Rudolf wasn't insulting you. He always sees humor and drama in everyday things. It's his nature." I moved the baby to the other breast. "Tell me how Rudolf is faring here. I worry constantly he'll succumb to melancholy, being so far from the family. You know he's over-dramatic, Rozsa."

"I'm so glad you're here, Fannie. I assure you the boy is healthy, and we're thrilled he's with us. The program of instruction at the new Union Free District School is rigorous; nevertheless, our lad was immediately skipped to the third-grade classroom. His reading and arithmetic amazed the teachers. You'll be pleased to learn there are only sixteen children in his classroom, a far cry from the city."

I buttoned my weskit and propped Rose, sleeping soundly, against my bosom, her head upon my shoulder. I asked Rozsa, "Are they on the ferry today, Saturday, knowing I was coming? I'm a bit surprised Rudolf wasn't here to greet us. Is this cause for concern? Could he be punishing me, Rozsa?"

She seemed surprised at my assessment. "Fannie, Rudolf is obsessed with the water and the boats. I don't think he'd miss a day out there if God himself was coming! He and István will be home by dinnertime; their last crossing from Nyack is at four. My dear Fannie, he's a marvel, brilliant. And, he knows how to get along with people, all kinds of people. That's a trait to cherish and will open doors for him. István tells me stories about Rudolf on the ferry. He entertains the customers with song or recitation and earns tips when they disembark. He has a knack for charming those around him, a real Hungarian, this one!"

I laughed, thinking about Rudolf on the boat. "Rozsa, there are no words to thank you. Has he been ill? How's his appetite?"

"In October, he was in bed for three days with a sore throat. Since then, he's been healthy. He's a skinny child with strong muscles, thanks to the work on the boat. He's always hungry, and he's grown a few inches since he's been here. Fannie, he's no burden; he's a pleasure; he's the son we never had." Her eyes filled with tears.

At 5:00, Rudolf and István came through the door. My brother-in-law was a rosy-cheeked, broad-shouldered man, with muscular arms. He strode across the floor enfolding me in his powerful grip. "Üdvözöljük, Fannie, welcome, welcome, welcome!"

Out of breath, I hugged him and turned to find my son. Rudolf stood in front of the settee, looking at the baby. "Hello, Rose. Do you remember me? I'm Rudolf, your big brother." The baby looked intently at him, and he did a little dance step, a large smile on his face.

"Mama, do *you* remember me? I'm your son, Rudolf, the sickly one!" He came to my open arms, his head against my bosom. We stood for a moment, swaying back and forth.

Rozsa and István left the room; she to the kitchen, he to the bedroom to change from his work clothes. Rudolf and I sat on the settee.

"My darling, how I've missed you. You've grown and have a good color, I'm so relieved. Your brothers can hardly wait for your return. Papa, too.

"I'm well, Mama. The New York doctors are dummies. I'm tip top. You should see me walk along the edge of the ferry's deck railing! No invalid could do that. And, at school, life is wonderful. My teacher loves me; all the lower grade teachers love me. I was cast as an elf in the Christmas play. You should've seen me, Mama. I was so great, stole the show from Santa!"

I laughed, "Still the actor, eh, Rudolf?" Then, on a more serious note, "Papa is counting the minutes until you come home. He's working very hard, though, causing me to worry he'll get sick. Lucky for all of us that his birthday is on Christmas; otherwise, he might not have had the day off to celebrate."

"Don't worry so much, Mama. Papa's strong. You worry too much." Then, "What train will we take tomorrow? Captain Lyon, the Rockland's skipper, told me to expect snow, lots of it. We'd better leave very early in the morning. I don't want to give up a single day with the family; I miss them all."

"I was planning to take the eight-fifteen, to be home at lunchtime. We'll have to hope for clear weather, but if not, a few days with your aunt and uncle will give me a little vacation."

"Mama, what better vacation could you have then being amused by me for ten days?" We laughed together, and then he stood to recite his elf part, interrupted by Rozsa's call to the dinner table.

Quick-witted and self-reliant, Rose's language and social development far outpaced what I remembered of Charles's babyhood. Within a few weeks of her first birthday, I weaned her. Three months later, I was with child again.

We decided to move downtown. Our four-room flat was just too small for Samuel, me, and soon to be six children. North of Houston Street, Greenwich Village apartments offered amenities comparable to those uptown but at lower rents. The nearer to the Lower East Side tenements, the cheaper the leases. Another benefit: Brooks' workroom on 22nd and Broadway would be a very short trolley ride for Samuel.

Louis Arnold Freed was born on March 3, 1898, at Sloan Maternity. At the end of my ten-day confinement, Samuel brought me and the baby home to a fifth-floor walkup on West 10th Street near the Hudson River. I was happy with the new place: five rooms with heat, hotwater, electric lights, a gas stove, and our own bathroom, all for $13.00 a month, with the first month free.

Albert earned two dollars a week as a carpenter's helper in a shop on Duane Street. I expected he'd be hired as a full-time apprentice when he finished eighth grade in the spring of 1898.

Morris, at twelve years, was a capable, yet distracted student. He found immense pleasure dawdling at a 14th Street music store, listening to gramophone cylinders and records. Some evenings, he delighted us with renditions of "I Don't Want to Play in Your Yard" and "After the Ball," songs of the Irish tenor, George Gaskin.

Four-year-old Charles rarely strayed from my side. A bit dull, he always appeared lost. His brothers ignored him, falling into Hungarian phrases to exclude him.

Albert confided to me, "He's a bother. Who wants to be with a four-year-old? We're different from him; as if we're from another family. We lived in Budapest, and he didn't. We lived without Papa, and he didn't. We aren't real Americans, and he is. *And*, he's a baby while we're already working or in the upper grades at school." I was disturbed by this household undercurrent and could only hope that as they matured, they would learn to love Charles.

For three years, the Tarrytown arrangement worked very well. Then, in 1898, István died of a cerebral hemorrhage. Rozsa, with no means of support, came to live with us. Rudolf's transfer papers were accepted by the neighborhood school, and he entered sixth grade.

Living down the street from the Hudson River, Rudolf became a dock rat, hanging about the piers at every opportunity. An experienced deckhand, fisherman, and swimmer, skills learned in Tarrytown, it wasn't long before he was earning a few pennies running errands for the longshoremen. They nicknamed him Rube, a gentle joke alluding to his life in the sticks of Pennsylvania and Tarrytown. Eager and willing, he proved a reliable, intelligent mate on the small boats ferrying passengers and goods along the Manhattan waterfront. Adopted as a mascot by the mariners, Rube learned phrases in languages from around the world, many of them unacceptable in good company.

Rozsa found work as a cleaning woman at the Victoria Theater on 42nd Street. She earned nine dollars a week for six ten-hour days, fifteen cents an hour. Contributing half her earnings to our kitty made a world of difference in our circumstance. During the last year of the century, we were not only making ends meet, we were putting some money aside for Samuel's establishment.

January 10, 1900
My dearest Fannie:
I am well, so don't worry. Aside from stiffness in my hands and feet on these cold mornings, I work every day, as always. I'm sure you remember Erno Weisz, the baker. His son, Csaba, has begun to work with me. I'm teaching him butchering, and he's learning quickly. He and Etti Grunwald are planning a wedding, and if all goes well, Erno will help them buy me out in a few years. I'm hoping to last another two years, when I'll be 70.

So, that's my exciting news. I can't imagine a time when I won't get up every day and go to the shop. To be honest, I never thought I'd live this long. If I didn't have the shop, what would I do? Play cards with the old men in the park? Find religion and become a 'Macher' in the Synagogue? I'm too set in my ways to change now. I read, prepare my meals; plant a few vegetables in the yard. Oh, and I write to you.

I loved the photographs of you, Samuel, and the whole family in front of the New York Public Library! I always knew Samuel would be a success. I may not have told you that, but I secretly believed it. After all, you wouldn't have chosen him if he wasn't special, right?

Your letters are very important to me. I live through them. I know my grandchildren through them. Rose looks like my mother. Did I tell you that already?

I miss you very much, and every day I think of you there, so far away. I think about all the joys I missed because of my stubbornness. Mama and I should have gone with you. Remember how you begged? I was wrong to choose a place over a person, the person dearest in the world to me. There's nothing I can do to change that now. Now, it's too late.

Remember me, my dearest child. Remember Hungary. Remember your childhood here in Nagy Karolyi. Remember your Mama and me.

Your loving Papa

I yearned to see my homeland and Papa again. I lived between two cultures: not an American citizen, but not Hungarian either. In my everyday life, what did a piece of paper from a government mean? It would change nothing. I lived here, alien or not. Why dwell on the negative?

Samuel and I had little uninterrupted time together, given his long workdays and the crowded household; still, our love remained the source of the family's strength.

Things were moving in a positive direction in America, in New York, and in our lives. On April 1, 1900, we stood on the sidewalk at 45th Street and 11th Avenue watching gilt letters being applied to the large storefront window: S. Freed, Custom Tailoring. Samuel, Albert, Morris, Rudolf, Charles, Rose, Louis, Rozsa, and I cheered, "Hip-hip hurrah!"

Samuel was so proud of all he had accomplished: bringing us to America, being recognized by Mr. Brooks as a fine tailor, coming to New York, providing for, and loving us all. All these milestones had been achieved by hard work, God-given talent, and vision. How pleased I was for Samuel's happiness. How I loved this man: more than life itself.

Although he continued at the carpentry, Albert bought a fiddle, determined to become a musician. Morris, working at the music store, received free cello lessons. The sounds of strings filled our apartment. In the seventh grade, Rudolf was a brilliant student, even though he spent every moment out of school fishing and working on the river. Charles barely mastered the most rudimentary first grade schoolwork. I reasoned *the world needs all kinds of people;* Charles will find a niche, somewhere.

Rose, vigorous and articulate, took charge of Louis, whose quiet personality was given to observing the scene.

Running your own business didn't guarantee a customer would walk through the door, and for a few weeks, none did. While there was a dearth of clientele, Samuel worked long hours to earn as much as he could from Brooks. Those first two months, he exceeded the minimum every week, and Rozsa contributed all her wages to help out. A co-worker from Brooks, returning to Europe to marry, sent a note asking Samuel if we'd be interested in taking over his lease on a six-room apartment, with bath, on East 13th Street.

"What do you think, Fannie? The rent's cheaper by five dollars. We'll have a little extra money at the end of the month. And, the landlord will paint the place if we move in by the fifteenth."

"Samuel, this will be the third move in four years. After each baby, we've moved closer to the Lower East Side, chasing the cheaper rooms. And, it's farther from the shop, way over on the East Side."

"I can take the crosstown trolley at 42nd Street, then the Second Avenue El, be home in no time, Fannie. You heard me say we'll save five dollars a month, didn't you? And, its SIX rooms!"

What could I say? Samuel was the earner; he alone bore the burden of feeding us all. Of course, I couldn't argue against moving into six rooms, with bath, now, could I?

I was at the end of another pregnancy. Our good luck baby was waiting to be born, with a future as limitless as the brand-new century!

May 18, 1900. Labor began on Friday afternoon, an uncomfortable pressure in the small of my back. After about an hour, Rozsa helped me to a cab, returning to care for the children, and sent Rube to tell Samuel.

At the Sloane admitting desk, my personal information was recorded, and the senior resident was called. In an anteroom, he asked about my labor and history of previous births, then recorded my temperature and pulse and did an internal examination. Free of infectious disease and lice, I was approved for admittance to the ward. The Resident doctor would follow my case and deliver the baby. Dr. Voorhees, the attending doctor on call, would be consulted in case of complication. Coincidentally, two years earlier, Dr. Voorhees, the Resident at the time, had delivered Louis.

The labor ward, a large room with windows along two walls, housed twelve beds separated by fabric privacy screens. With the exception of dark green floor tiles, everything was white: walls, window blinds, supply cabinets, bed frames, tables, linen, even enameled water pitchers and bedpans. All areas were well lit, and calm prevailed throughout the place, with whispered voices in the corridors.

Seven women labored. A few walked about or sat in white metal chairs. None were at rest. In bed, women lay, flopping every few moments from side to back. For those who walked, perhaps leaning against the wall, or squatting near the floor gave them ease for a few moments. In the chairs, first a seat cushion, then a soft pillow at the small of the back gave them temporary relief. Several thanked God for any small respite, and more than a few cursed their husbands.

My contractions were rhythmic and gaining in intensity, causing me to stand perfectly still while each cycle completed. I was assigned a bed, exchanged my clothing for a cotton gown, and sat down on the immaculate linen. The ward clerk made a list of my belongings and assigned a closet number for them. She told me there would be no food or drink for the duration and absolutely no visitors were permitted in the ward. Samuel would wait in the visitors' lounge.

Two years since Louis's birth had brought new hospital procedures: first, I was given an enema and then my pubic area was shaved. The nurse explained these were measures to prevent childbed fever.

My contractions began in earnest, and I endured them quietly as they peaked and abated. I knew the baby would be born within an hour or maybe two and relaxed as much as possible so as not to impede progress. I believed an intimate mental focus with my body and the child was very important, tranquility enabling the normal process. The waters broke, and the Resident was called; he placed a stethoscope on my abdomen. Asking if I might listen, too, I heard the fluttering sound of my baby's heart, beating as fast as a hummingbird's wings.

An hour later, I was moved, by gurney, to the delivery room.

Both doctor and nurse wore cotton caps, masks, and long-sleeved, loose-fitting robes over their clothing. At first, I thought perhaps I had some disease they wished to avoid. Later, I was told they were protecting *me* from contagion.

The assistant Resident came into the room and began to cover my mouth and nose with a sieve like, metal, mask. "The mask will be infused with chloroform, and you will fall asleep. The baby will be born at that time, painlessly, Madam." At that moment, although in the middle of a strong spasm, I managed to express, adamantly, my refusal to receive the medication.

In clear tone, I said, "Doctor, the thought of being unconscious terrifies me; it's akin to death. I absolutely do not want the drug."

I was not to be intimidated in labor. I'd been here too many times to feign ignorance. Clearly annoyed, the doctor left the room, taking the mask and anesthetic with him.

In the labor ward, the nurse had explained that the Resident routinely made a surgical cut to control tearing of the tissue as the baby's head and shoulders make the final exit from the birth canal.

I was having none of that, either, and spoke up. "Doctor, this is my seventh child. My body can pass it from the womb without the need to enlarge the opening. Please do not use your scalpel." He appeared amused, though his voice conveyed annoyance. "Madam, it is not for the ward patients to instruct the medical staff." At that moment, I grunted, bearing down, pushing the baby forward. He observed my experienced grit, and said with a chuckle, "However, I'll forego the procedure unless absolutely necessary."

"Thank you, Doctor," I said.

As the baby's head pushed to the end of the canal, I focused my mind singularly upon my anatomy. Lubricated by my secretions, the baby moved in a continuous motion, forced downward by uterine and pelvic muscle spasms. I felt myself opening up to expel the child.

It is hard to describe the immense gratification a woman feels during the moments when her child's head enters the outside world, its body still within her. There's a feeling of exhilaration so deep it cannot be likened to any other. Without distraction, the entirety of my body was engaged: my breath was held, diaphragm creating downward pressure, assisting the boa-like contractive waves. The little body slithered out with one final push, an exquisite bliss.

Just before midnight, Anna howled vigorously, announcing herself to be in this world, demanding attention to the presence of her unique soul. The umbilical cord was cut, and my seventh child was placed upon my breast. That joyous moment of isolation shared with her precluded all pain. Her aroma, which was my own, cemented our primordial bond. The placenta was delivered, I was cleansed, and Anna taken to the nursery. My gurney ride ended in the postpartum ward, where six women slept soundly, exhausted by their ordeals.

Samuel was permitted to visit with me for fifteen minutes. He covered my face with kisses, and we shared tears of happiness and relief. Before leaving for home, he stopped at the window of the nursery. Anna, swaddled tightly in a cotton blanket, was presented, viewed through a window, to her father by one of the nurses.

The next day, I felt strong and had a ravenous appetite. Anna was healthy, nursed with gusto, and my milk came in fully in three days. In a circumstance of pure luxury, I was coddled at Sloan Maternity. With no responsibility for my other life: children, husband, or household, I slept deeply, my body recovering, restoring itself, rebounding from the transformation it had undergone for nine months.

Every four hours, the baby was brought to me to nurse. When undisturbed by meals, breast feeding, nursing care, or doctor's visits, I slept.

Each morning, I received a sponge bath. Four times a day, the nurses administered perineal care, a warm water wash. Hearty food, carefully selected by a nutritionist, was served on an overbed table. Five days after delivery, sitting upright, I was permitted to dangle my feet over the side of the bed. On the seventh day, allowed to walk the length of the corridor, I looked at Anna's beautiful, serene, face through the nursery's glass; three days later, we were discharged. Sanitary and safe for mothers and babies, this excellent hospital had provided exactly the same treatment the richest woman in New York would have received.

Samuel and I wondered what the future held for Anna; would she be an artist, musician, teacher, doctor? Anything was possible for this child, blessed to be born in America in the new century.

Samuel

Thousands cheered. Singing and carousing in the streets of New York City welcomed "The Wonderful Century; The Scientific Century; A Titanic Century!"

The economy had recovered, factories were hiring. A period of great prosperity was predicted.

A lineup of bands, speakers, and blazing electric lights welcomed the century at the stroke of midnight, January, 1900!

Tailoring at Brooks was to rigorous standards, costing time in the details, and I rarely earned more than the piecework minimum. In four years, we had managed to put aside $38.00 for my shop, enough to buy a good, secondhand machine, a dressmaker's mirror, fabric, and supplies, and pay the first month's rent.

In February I found the place, an 11th Avenue storefront with a large window, two rooms, and toilet. The rent was $9.00, including heat and electric. The former tenant left sturdy wall shelves and a wide counter, perfect for cutting patterns. The landlord accepted my $5.00 deposit, and I signed a lease for an April 1st move-in.

The next day, I spoke with Bachmann. He wasn't surprised; he knew from the start I'd leave for my own shop when I could.

"I've signed a lease on 11th Avenue, beginning in April, but I'll continue doing the piece work."

He said, "We'll miss seeing you in the workroom, Samuel, but it makes no difference to me where the sewing is done, as long as it's done.

I was relieved and shook his hand. "As they did when I came from Pennsylvania, Brooks is making my move possible. Thank you, Bachmann."

"Listen to me, Samuel. I know you'll need a line of credit with vendors. We do a lot of business with the Merchant Bank on 28th Street, and my wife's cousin is one of the managers there. You'll go in and talk with him, and I'll vouch for you. Don't worry, my friend, you'll learn to owe people and sleep at night, like the rest of us!"

I met with Bill Stark, from the pattern house and Dan Abrams from United American Thread, and they wished me well. Dan's brother-in-law, Joseph Wells, a remnant broker and one of the organizers of the Garment Center Association, introduced me around to other suppliers in the trade. These industry 'Reps' offered me a net 30 account, with a forty-five-dollar open-to-buy. That meant I could place orders, on credit, up to $45.00, and pay thirty days after receiving the goods. I was on my way!

I shared all the news with Fannie. She had one reservation. "I worry about open credit. Buy what you can afford and pay cash up front. If you do that, I'll bet you'll get a special discount. Owing people is dangerous. Talk to the Reps."

With some brusqueness, I replied. "I know what I'm doing, Fannie. There's no way I can start my shop without some debt. Using the credit lines, I'll be able to stock patterns, fabric, thread, lining material, and buttons immediately. And, best of all: Bachmann already contracted to replace half their machines this year. Because of my good relations with him, he agreed to sell me one of the old machines for $7.00, practically a gift."

In a serious tone, Fannie said, "Right now, I don't have a lot of energy. After the birth, I'll help out with whatever I can. Rozsa's off on Mondays when the theater is dark; she can watch Rose and Louis. I'll bring the new baby with me to the shop."

I told her, "As the business grows, we'll be less dependent on the piece work. Before we know it, my own customers will sustain us. You learning to run the shop will give me a chance to work without interruption. I'll teach you blind stitching for the Brooks Coat linings. That handwork pays very well. I can scarcely believe we've reached this milestone, Fannie. my own business! This means Charles, Rose, and Louis will go to high school. Our money worries are over; I can feel it."

"With the shop on 45th Street and Eleventh Avenue and our apartment on East 13th Street, I can see another move coming. It's too inconvenient." She was right, and I promised to look for an apartment nearer the shop.

On April 1st, we opened for business. Across the large window, gilt lettering announced *S. Freed, Custom Tailoring*. Our carpenter son, Albert, presented me with a fine gift from his own hands: an oak platform for customers to stand on while I pinned and fitted their garments.

I believed uncertainty was behind us; I had reached the middle of my life, the stable part. At 41, I was healthy, loved my wife and children, and had my own business. The future was bright. Life was good.

I was hopeful the shop would provide enough income to allow Albert, Morris, and Rudolf to remain in school. In the meantime, all three found opportunities to earn a few pennies after school and on weekends. The extra money paid for luxuries: attending the occasional variety show or a few sweets for all to enjoy on a Saturday evening in our apartment whilst listening to the children's musical offerings and recitations.

The family was thriving, and in May, Fannie was delivered of a beautiful daughter, Anna. I was the proudest husband and father in New York City! A new business, a new baby, a new century; prosperity was in the very air I breathed!

Clients were referred by salesmen and workroom friends at Brooks. The customers they sent were up-and-coming men, those who knew a Brooks Brothers man was instantly recognized in the highest offices. The problem: that suit was very dear, costing a month's salary. Coming to my shop was the answer. If imported fabrics are surrendered, fine tailoring fashions a silk purse from a sow's ear, at downtown prices! From the very beginning, these young pretenders paid on time, and in full.

Neighborhood gents, office workers, were aware that apparel was important to their advancement, too. My pricing tailored a suit, with vest, for a week's wages. I earned a fair profit, and we were doing alright, thanks to the still available Brooks' piecework. After a while, there was no life outside the shop. I was the machine. The work of my hands, alone, produced the garment, and there were only so many hours in a day those hands could work. In the shop from seven in the morning until sometimes eight in the evening, I was overworked and fatigued.

New customer orders remained constant, a sure sign of growth. Then again, if I discovered an irregularity in a fabric while pattern cutting or a supplier's buttons or thread didn't arrive on time, I had to deal with every mishap. That was time away from the machine. Those delays reduced my efficiency and damaged relations with customers. Without Fannie's managing things one day a week, I don't know how I'd have managed.

Living on the East Side with a shop on the West, was inconvenient. Fannie prepared a pot of dinner for me to carry to the shop a few days a week. Not having to travel for the evening meal allowed me to work until nine or ten. Once or twice, I slept on the floor.

I couldn't justify the expense of hiring another tailor. Rudolf showed artistic promise and curiosity. He turned out a neat seam, paid close attention to my instruction, and enjoyed engineering pattern placement to maximize the use of our fabrics, but he was not a tailor. Along with Morris, he was selling newspapers to bring in a few pennies. I couldn't ask him to work with me full time, at least not yet; he was only eleven years old. Albert had never shown an interest in my work and earned a few dollars at the carpenters, dollars we needed. He longed to be a fiddle player, not a tailor.

It was a great disappointment to me that the boys couldn't continue to high school. Like all other immigrant children, we needed whatever they were able to earn.

I prayed good health would continue to bless me in spite of my overextended work schedule.

13

Fannie

I have observed, firsthand, how a new life stirs a deep response in humans. I believe the attraction to an infant is instinctive, primitive behavior. All ages, from the very young to the elderly, will quietly observe the perfectly miniaturized body, compelled to touch it, smell it.

With all our scientific advances, no invention induces the awestruck reaction to the complexity and mystery of the human species like that of a newborn infant.

Anna cast her spell upon the family. The serenity of her sleeping face, the movements of her tiny hands, a random smile, all so endearing, drew everyone to her. Even two-year-old Louis peeked curiously into the cradle once or twice before running off to play with Charles.

Then, there was our force of nature, Rose. Her maternal drive took control of my bedside after Anna's birth. She assisted me with every chore: folding rag diapers, bringing talcum to the kitchen sink at bath time, gently rocking the cradle, scolding her brothers when they became too noisy.

The eldest boys were spellbound by the brilliance of the human machine. Albert, at fifteen, was mature enough to recognize the immaculate order of nature. "Mama, there seems to be a schedule Anna's mind and body are following. Every day, she becomes more aware of her surroundings, and her body grows. It's amazing, isn't it, Mama?"

How delighted the children were as she began to recognize every family member, greeting them with a smile. Anna was healthy, nursed energetically, and, by ten months, in a language of her own design, identified "Muumm," "Popp," and each sibling.

Her first birthday was celebrated with song and a dessert of cooked fruits topped with heavy cream. Two months later, she refused the breast, began to cough, and ran a high temperature.

I sent Morris for Dr. Golding. "Mrs. Freed, the baby has pneumonia."

"Is there a poultice or medicine to relieve her, Doctor? She hardly sleeps, with the constant coughing. We're both exhausted. I try to spoon-feed broth, but she won't take enough to nourish her. The fever persists, and she's producing very little urine. I know she's lost weight. I'm terribly worried."

"The baby must be isolated, Mrs. Freed. The disease is virulent, easily transmitted. Special care must be taken that Louis and Rose do not touch or make any physical contact, not even step into the same room with her. I don't want to frighten you, but you must be aware that pneumonia is running rampant in New York; the papers say one third of the deaths are children under five years."

I began to cry. "Doctor Golding, is Anna going to die?

"I'm not saying that, but you need to know what you're up against. There are things you must do: scrub your hands with strong soap for three minutes before and after holding or attending to the baby. Linen, clothing, and diapers must be washed with lye soap and boiled for at least thirty minutes. If you follow these instructions and keep the baby behind a closed door, away from the rest of the family, there's a good chance no one else will fall ill." He paused for a moment, reaching for my hand. "Mrs. Freed, there is no pill or poultice I can prescribe; there's no medicine. In Boston, a few doctors have written of some success after packing the patient's chest with ice, claiming the cold kills the infection. Others administer small amounts of rum or other liquor. I'm not convinced these treatments are effective. Try to feed her broth or tea; keep her comfortable."

"So, you *are* saying Anna is going to die, Doctor?"

"I'm not God, Mrs. Freed. Anna's own defenses may be able to fight off the disease; only time will tell. Baltimore's Dr. Osler calls pneumonia *the captain of the men of death*. He says *it's overwhelmingly a disease of poverty*, which is obvious to me, practicing here. The fight for you, Fannie, is not only for Anna but to save the others in the house."

In a few days' time, her breathing became more rapid. She winced and cried, "Mama!" with each spasm. Within a few days, exhausted, she stopped speaking and was ghostly pale.

The order to keep Anna isolated meant my isolation, too. I was no longer able to prepare meals or attend to the others. Thank heaven for Rozsa. During that terrible fortnight, she kept the house and cared for Anna in the afternoons, allowing me a few hours of sleep.

As if there weren't enough difficulties to deal with, I began to run a slight fever myself, my breasts becoming heavy and firm, results of the baby's inability to nurse. To keep the engorgement from progressing to infection, I expressed my milk several times a day, which was uncomfortable.

The only help I could offer my child was to reduce her fever with cool baths, pat her back to break up accumulated mucous, and offer a few spoons of tea or broth. To soothe her, I sang lullabies while cradling her in my arms. Nothing was known to stop the onslaught. As the days passed, I had no choice but to acknowledge the inevitable outcome.

Coughing feebly, she lay against my bosom, too weak to cry. She looked deeply into my eyes, conveying her love and trust, anticipating my help in return. Powerless, I cried, my tears dropping onto her face. I thought of the months I had carried her in my womb, of her first movements.

At one in the afternoon on Sunday, July 28, 1901, despondent and fatigued, I surrendered Anna to the "Captain." *Gently take her spirit*, I pleaded; *spare her the labor to draw one more breath...*

Her little body shivered slightly as she succumbed, the muscles of her face calming as she entered her repose. At the actual moment of her death, defeat drained my soul; I thought how easy it would be to die with her, there, at that moment. In some abstract way, it was as if I *had* died. My mind and body were numb, and oddly, during the first moments, there were no tears.

Morris went to fetch Dr. Golding. Within half an hour, he arrived to record the death on Health Department forms. Although secular, we believed a traditional burial appropriate. There was no time to waste: Jewish law dictates interment within twenty-four hours.

As soon as the doctor left, Samuel wound cotton fabric tightly around my rib cage, binding my breasts to stop the flow of milk. An hour later, he took the trolley downtown to the Austrian-Hungarian Free Burial Association on Delancey Street. Just before midnight, I wrapped Anna in a white bunting and surrendered her body to Simon Theiman, the undertaker.

In the late morning, two coaches began the journey to Brooklyn's Washington Cemetery. They followed two black horses pulling Theiman's hearse, in which Anna's pine coffin lay.

For an hour and twenty minutes, the noise of hooves clattering on cobblestones prevented conversation, which was a blessing. The cortege came to a stop near the gate, where a short, full-bearded man wearing a black suit and hat waited, a Rabbi the undertaker had engaged. After placing Anna's casket on a small cart, Theiman's assistant began to push it.

We heard Albert call out, "NO." He ran to the undertaker, "I'll carry Anna, Mr. Theiman." Without a word, the boy rested his baby sister's coffin upon his forearms and stepped forward.

Theiman said, "Follow the Rabbi, Albert. He will lead you to the place."

Two men waited in front of a pit. Behind them, shovels stood upright in a pile of dirt. The gravediggers took Anna's coffin from Albert. Using a rope sling, they lowered it until the little box rested on the earthen floor of the chamber.

The Rabbi swayed back and forth, intoning the ancient prayer praising God's name. We all said, "Amen." Our family had little knowledge of this ritual; we understood no Hebrew. The Rabbi nodded to us. "Now, I'll recite the mourner's prayer, *Kaddish*. The father and mother will repeat each part after me." We nodded. "Yit-gadal v'yit-kadash sh'may raba," he began.

In unison, Samuel and I echoed his words. "Yit-gadal v'yit-kadash sh'may raba. Amen."

"Now," the Rabbi said, "Father and mother must tear a piece of clothing that will be worn for the duration of the Shiva period. It's an expression of pain over the passing." Samuel looked at me before tearing his shirt pocket. "Fannie, I'll tear the collar of your bodice. We can repair it later." I nodded.

Each of us scattered a handful of dirt gently upon the casket, and it was over. I was led quickly back to the coach.

Suffering from nervous shock, I moved through the day insulated from reality. Sadly, I was not able to comfort my family, nor could they, me.

Dr. Golding had advised every treatment known to him; I had done all I could during those twelve terrible days, but the reality was that once he took hold, there was no way to save my baby from the relentless, murdering, "Captain." Somehow, I would have to adjust and go on. I wanted to regain my strength, resume my activities but was unable to be *present* and moved about in a stupor for weeks.

Rozsa had taken leave for a few days but had to return to work or lose her position. After that, the boys pitched in to keep the house going.

When a child dies, a mother's intense sorrow cannot be fathomed by a man. From the moment of quickening until your own life ends, you, and the child to whom you gave life are one inseparable element. For the rest of my life, I lit a candle on May 18th in remembrance of the day shared only by Anna and me, her birthday.

A seven-day Shiva followed, with sheet-covered mirrors and little wooden stools upon which Samuel and I sat, both customs intended to prevent the mourner's distraction from prayer.

For a week, neighbors brought food and visited. In my deep melancholy, I received no comfort from the company.

Rose, Louis, and I made the trip from East 13th to Brooklyn every day for a month. The children did grow cranky, but I was compelled to go to the plot. Brooklyn's Fifth Avenue El terminated twenty blocks from the cemetery. From there, a horse tram brought us the rest of the way for a three-cent fare.

Anna dominated my thoughts, and Samuel's patience with my obsession diminished. He insisted I return to the family; I was needed. He was right, of course, but could not mandate my behavior. Gradually, over the next weeks, I began to emerge from the grief. Her face no longer appeared in my mind's eye every moment of the day; nights were less frequently disturbed by imagined cries for the breast. I combed my hair in the morning, without one of the children hinting at how disheveled I appeared. The melancholy eased its grip as the passage of time renewed my spirit.

On Sunday, May 18, 1902, Samuel, Rozsa, and the children went to Central Park Zoo's new primate house. I went to the cemetery to be with Anna on what would have been her second birthday.

It was a mild spring day; the sycamores along Bay Parkway were in full leaf, forsythia at the end of their bloom. We had been putting pennies aside, but there was still not enough saved to order the marble marker. Kneeling to clear the grave of winter's debris, I pressed my fingers into the soil, extending them toward my buried child. I fell forward, covering the little patch with my body, resting my cheek on the damp earth.

McDonald Avenue was a busy commercial thoroughfare. From the windows, passengers on streetcars may have looked out upon the cemetery, but lying prone upon the ground, I doubt I was seen. And that was as it should be, for here, in this place; I was invisible, in the grave with Anna. There was no solace to be found in all the world for this loss. I sobbed without restraint.

People said the pain would ease as time went by. I knew they were wrong. People said the child I birthed to welcome the new millennium was fated to have a short life. It's God's will. I knew they were wrong. People told me after a time I would get over the shock and grief, be my normal self again. I knew they were wrong. Pneumonia took my baby, not God, and I would never again be my normal self.

Later, at the corner of Bay Parkway and McDonald Avenue, I boarded a westbound streetcar and returned to my life.

My eighth child, expected in November, made it unlikely I'd return for another year.

Nora was born on November 18, 1902, perfectly healthy and beautiful. I rediscovered my sunny nature, and the family reflected my mood. That's not to say there weren't problems.

Charles kept to himself most of the time, ignored by his brothers. In particular, he avoided Rose, "Mistress Boss," as he called her, who dominated his every move. Under his bed, I found a cigar box filled with coins, stamps, a few hatpins, and a gold ring. They might have been found, but I feared the items stolen. His slyness worried me, but there was nothing I could do to change what was born in the bones.

Even with little time to enjoy quiet conversation, the love between Samuel and me was secure, comfortable. On Sundays, I cooked specialties from the old country or fish Rudolf had caught in the Hudson. Our apartment became a gathering place for neighbors and friends of the children, a place of happy times, stimulation, and music.

After dinner, a game of poker or craps might engage six or eight people, or a group would begin singing popular songs, accompanied by Albert's fiddle, Morris's cello, and Rube's new mandolin. A wager on a race at one of the New York tracks might be the topic of heated debate for an entire evening.

Rozsa began "keeping company," taking long evening walks with a Russian man, Leonid Denkovich, who lived in the next building. They married in the summer of 1903 and moved to Grand Street on the Lower East Side. Most Sundays, they came crosstown to have dinner with us.

The boys bought Nora a stuffed Teddy bear for her first birthday. Manufactured in Brooklyn, it was the most popular toy of the day, honoring President Roosevelt.

On the first of March, we moved to an apartment one flight above the shop on Eleventh Avenue. It saved Samuel crosstown travel after working late and allowed the children to say hello to him anytime. He cut back on Brooks' piece work to concentrate on his own customers. That was a good business decision, I thought.

A few weeks later, certain I was pregnant again, I told Samuel. Both of us resigned ourselves to the news without discussion. At almost forty-two, I had hoped by now my body would no longer bear children, Yet, here I was, with a ninth baby on the way. When would menopause begin?

I prayed for a healthy child, another safe delivery, and for this to be our last.

Samuel

When Anna became ill, work prevented me from helping. Nursing a sick infant is not part of a man's instinct, I'm sorry to say. I tried to soothe the baby but only got in the way. Finally, I left it to the women.

Losing Anna shocked everyone. We learned how fragile life is, how the loss of a dear one changes us forever.

Fannie was beyond consolation, frozen with grief.

A month after the burial, I had it out with her. "You must reclaim your life and responsibilities. I know you're suffering, but our children need you. I need you. Your attention and guidance carry our ship forward. Without you, we're at loose ends. You must stop the daily treks to Brooklyn. I'm not asking you, Fannie; I'm insisting on this."

In the softest of tone, I said, "I need you, dearest. We *all* need you to come back from that dark place. Please, Fannie, you must say goodbye to Anna. Please, come home to us."

I held her as she cried, then made love to her, the first time since the baby had become ill.

By the time autumn arrived, our household was restored to normal, more or less.

My business was good, adding new customers every week. At first, I was full of self-congratulation, then the reality set in. The new sales I was making had to be produced. To keep up with sales and alterations, my life became the shop. For months, at the machine from early morning on, I never saw the sunset. Fannie served me dinner at nine o'clock. "I'm almost too tired to eat, Fannie."

"Samuel, a telegram arrived a few hours ago."

October 16, 1901
Samuel Freed…647 East 13 St, New York City
Max died Sunday of dilatation of the heart. Buried Tuesday morning Mount Sinai cemetery.
Sarah Better…823 North 25 St, Philadelphia, Pennsylvania

Pushing my plate aside, covering my face with my hands, I wept. Fannie embraced me. In a quiet voice, she said, "Sweetheart, I am at a loss to find words of consolation. Max was as a brother to you, to both of us. Losing him, and Anna, in what was to be a joyous year, gives me concern about the new century. The opening of your shop bodes well, but these deaths were unnatural, not of old age. These tragedies test my optimism, Samuel; where are the sunny days of 'The Wonderful Century'?"

I read the telegram again. "In five years, Max visited us in New York one time, and I never went to Philadelphia, not once. I was too busy, working all the time. If I had it to do again, I'd have made more of an effort; I'm so ashamed to have taken him for granted. In my mind's eye, I see him as a boy, running with me through the vineyards in Tolcsva, then sharing the small bedroom in Debrecen. I remember how he derided me for my poor grades in mathematics, which came so easily to him. How he encouraged me to win your father's approval. I hear him making the argument that I must leave Budapest to give us a future, the night he convinced me to join him on the journey to America. And, after five years, when I failed to earn enough to bring you here, his unselfish brotherly love gave us the money for passage. Max dead? I am never to see him again, hear his voice...?"

She brought a bottle of schnapps to the table. She poured two glassfuls, and we drank a toast. "To our Max."

At first, the children didn't bother with Nora too much. That's not to say the baby was ignored or dismissed; no, that wasn't true. They observed her from a safe distance away, priming themselves for her loss, perhaps? Of course, Fannie was as attentive as she had been with all our babies.

Rose was even more obsessed with her new sister than she had been with Anna. "Papa," she told me, "Don't worry about Mama and Nora. I will absolutely never let anything happen to them." "Thank you, Drágám, my dearest; with you on the job, I don't worry when I'm at the shop."

By the time Nora was a little over a year old, outgoing, and good-natured, she was endeared to every member of the family. She sang along with the gramophone records Morris borrowed from the music store. Nora, so the boys told me, had a "perfect ear," musically speaking. That meant she was always right on key!

I kept the grueling hours for another year, though I knew I couldn't continue spending twelve hours a day working and another three making the trip to and from our flat. It was time to take steps to improve my workday, my life.

Leon Stein, the landlord, told me there was a vacant six-room flat with bath on the second floor above my shop. Because I was already a tenant, he offered me a discounted price on the apartment: $12.00 a month, including electric!

We moved in at the beginning of March 1904. I gave up most of Brooks' piece work, devoting that time to serving my own clientele exclusively. Walking upstairs for dinner made life so much easier; my mood was positive, ready to take on the world. I was satisfied with life, my wife, my family, my work, my shop, my customers.

At the end of the month, a few days before her forty-second birthday, Fannie told me she was pregnant again. Kissing her, I said, "Wonderful news, my darling!"

There were times I thought of the miners in Mauch Chunk, how their lives ground them down. Constant toil for a subsistence wage robbed them of youth and health, fixing them in a spiral of want, barely able to feed their children, whose numbers grew every year. The difference between that miner and me was I loved my work, and my earnings were, more or less, in my control. What I did share with the miner was the responsibility of an ever-expanding family, both a blessing and a burden.

It was possible for Fannie to bear another child every two years for another decade. I tried to take care, using rubber condoms most of the time. Fannie tried the Dutch cap, but Anna had been the result of its failure, so she discarded it. Whilst nursing, conception is suspended. Fannie and I proved that over and over, as she breast-fed each child for at least a year and became pregnant immediately upon weaning.

We understood, more or less, how the reproductive cycle worked and made an effort to abstain from intercourse during Mittelschmerz, the middle of the monthly cycle, when the egg, supposedly, is most ready for conception. Needless to say, our calculations never worked out. I guessed Fannie produced eggs on every day of the month!

In my heart of hearts, I prayed her "change" would come soon. Of course, I kept that prayer to myself.

By this time, I was reliably earning eighteen to twenty dollars a week. Our economic situation was further enhanced by help from the boys. Albert, at seventeen, was still at the carpentry, part-time. Happily, although not steadily, he was being hired as a fiddler at the variety theaters. Morris and Rube were selling newspapers. The three were almost grown men, tall, handsome, engaging, charming. Fannie and I were so proud of them. Most evenings, their friends joined us for dinner or to play music, cards, or charades. Our apartment was a gathering place, which made Fannie very happy; me, too.

I closed the shop half an hour early to meet the boys at Willy Katz's Deli on Ludlow Street. It was a hot August evening, raining buckets. The cobblestone streets were slick with a gooey, watery, fetid mush of garbage and manure. New York in summer was disgusting. I made use of an umbrella, but by the time I arrived at Katz's from the trolley, my trousers were soaked.

The place was packed with people, and if your party wasn't present in full when you sat down, you might incur the wrath of a waiter for wasting his time. New York deli waiters were a breed of their own. They did you a favor, serving food you were paying for! They wore white shirts with black bow ties and suspendered black pants. A white apron stained with gravy, mustard, and pickle juice wrapped around their girth, covered them from waist to knee. To the right of the door, three cooks worked behind a half-wall.

Every few seconds, they hollered to the waiters, "TWENTY-TWO, READY FOR PICKUP, C'MON, C'MON, C'MON, SHLOMO, ARE YOU A WAITER, OR A YENTA? PICK UP ALREADY!"

A waiter yelled, "ARE YA GONNA JUST STAND THERE, KIBBITZING, MISTA? SIT DOWN ALREADY, OR I'LL GIVE THE TABLE TO SOMEONE WITH SECHEL." Ah, you just have to love Katz's!

After a minute or two in the frenzied environment, diners no longer heard the cooks and waiters bellowing. The aromas of brisket and pastrami wafted through, acting as an anesthetic, and patrons took their seats like little lambs, mouths watering.

Katz's could hold about thirty people, with tables of four or six in the majority.

"Over here, Papa." Albert called out from a table near the window. The other two were not with him. Morris, in particular, was always late.

"I hope your brothers will be here soon. It's already almost seven. With this rain, there'll be no leisurely stroll on Second Avenue to digest our meal. The Odeon's Vaudeville starts at eight-thirty. I don't want to miss the first act, Professor Leonida's troop of cats and dogs."

Albert was excited to report, "Papa, don't worry. We'll make it in plenty of time. Listen to this: I'm playing at the Crotona theater on East Tremont this weekend! I showed up cold, and the manager let me audition; he had just learned the second fiddle was ill. I guess my six-dollar pay will be light by a day, but I don't care. I hate milling chair legs day after day."

"Try not to jeopardize your place at the carpentry, Albert. I know at nineteen, you can make your own decisions; just be sure to protect what you've got until the next job is lined up."

He dismissed my advice. "Papa, I think I can get Morris in, too. The grippe is going around the pit, so the cello may also be out for a few days."

Morris and Rube came into the Deli, out of breath, rain dripping off their hat brims. "We had to run from the trolley stop with no umbrella—we're two drowned rats! One of the horses pulling the late edition's truck dropped dead from the heat this afternoon, so I had to help offload. Then, Rube didn't sell the last paper until late, not a lot of people out in this downpour. The 48th Street kiosk doesn't protect me from the rain when I'm working on the sidewalk; I'm soggy to my underwear!"

"I hope you boys didn't let the nickels slip through wet fingers into the sewer," I joked.

The waiter, who had been hovering over my shoulder, tapped his foot to show his annoyance at our late arrivals and the sin of small talking on his time. Referring to us in a stage whisper, I heard, "A regular bunch of shmendriks, these guys, schmoozing on my time!" But we were New Yorkers, too; we weren't perturbed, just ignored him.

Rube hung his hat on a wall hook behind Albert. "I can't believe we're going to see The Avon Comedy Four! That's Smith and Dale with two other singing comics. This is going to be so great!"

Rube tapped his glass with a spoon to get our attention. Facing me, he said, "So, Smith asks the waiter, Where's the manager?" He turned to face Morris. In a deeper voice, "And the waiter, Dale, says: He's not here, he went across the street to a good restaurant!"

Even the waiter laughed at Rube's impersonation. We ordered pastrami sandwiches on rye, sour pickles, potato knishes, coleslaw, and black coffee. I didn't have to ask him to rush the order; at Katz's, the waiters made it their business to turn over the table as quickly as possible, maximizing tips.

Rube said, "Getting back to selling papers, Papa, even if the coins fell into the grate, Max Grossberg would make it up to me. I've been making him laugh since I was ten." He paused to take a bite of a pickled green tomato. "Papa, Grossberg had a long talk with me today, another reason I'm late. *Rube*, he says, *everyone reads the paper in New York. The greenhorns all read, and so can their kids. You're not too young to see there's no future in hawking papers on the street. Print is king! Get into the printing line. Hand set or operate the monotype; better yet, with your vocabulary, work as a proofreader. These are careers for a lifetime.* Believe me, Papa, I was very touched by him, caring about my future."

"That's good advice, Rube. You want to get into an office if you want to get ahead, like Grossberg said."

We walked the four blocks to the Odeon in rain driven by wind so strong, I had to chase the umbrella blown from my grip. Albert pushed his way to the box office, motioning to us when he had the tickets in hand. Pressed shoulder to shoulder in the crowded lobby, we shuffled through the doors into the auditorium. Musicians in the pit were playing a lively introduction for the animal act's stage entrance, while the audience milled about in search of vacant seats. It was customary to open with the animals, not a singer or dramatic piece, because the house didn't settle down for the first twenty minutes!

Albert ran up to the mezzanine. We made our way up the stairs, following the sound of the 'Freed whistle," a seven-note signature melody Morris had composed for us to communicate. Once seated, our attention was drawn to the second skit.

Three cats sitting in a neat line watch Professor Leonidas set a bowl of food in front of a black dog. When the Professor turns his back, one cat starts meowing, another rears up on its hind legs, baring its claws, the last one, with ears flattened, leaps at the dog, who runs away yelping. A drum roll sets the mood for the finale: all three cats sashay toward the bowl. When they sit down, holding their swaying tails high, they calmly eat the dog's dinner!

Meantime, the dog reenters the scene. Realizing he's been had; he lies flat on the floor crying pitifully before covering his snout with his paws. The audience went wild with laughter, whistles, clapping and foot stomping. The animals lined up with the Professor for a bow before exiting the stage.

The remainder of the evening's card included The Avon Comedy Four, Karina, a French chanteuse; and Princess Rajah, performing a sanitized rendition of Little Egypt's Hoochie Coochie belly dance.

I looked at my sons, sitting to my left and right. They were almost men, establishing their life's paths, each so different from one another, so intelligent and eager to conquer the world. I tried to remember my youth, life before Fannie. It was hard to recall. I was a boy, and then there was Fannie. Before her, I knew nothing of the world, or of love. Then I saw and loved her from the very first moment. Her honesty and exuberance for life prompted me to be a better person, a better man. My work, aside from paying the bills, satisfied a creative urge, but Fannie gave me purpose, joy. Her love provided the base from which our descendants will advance into the future. How beautiful life is, I thought. As my father had told me so many years ago: *Love a woman; she will make you a life.*

Relieved to find the rain had stopped, we moved from the theater into a humid New York summer night. I linked arms with Albert and Morris on the walk home. Rube skipped ahead of us, turning every so often to repeat a line from the comics or sing out at the top of his voice, "You're the flower of my heart, Sweet Adeline." or "Good-bye, my lady love, farewell, my turtle dove." With this entertainment, we reached 45th and Eleventh in no time. New York is a walker's city, the grid easy to manage, even with slippery cobblestoned streets.

Three days later, I felt unwell, feverish. Perhaps I had contracted la grippe while in the crowded Odeon lobby. Closing the shop at midday, I took to bed, exhausted. Icy chills racked my body, although I burned with fever. The next day, coughing uncontrollably, I brought up a bloody mucous.

Dr. Henry Hollings from West 43rd, made a home visit. After listening to my chest, he asked me to cough into a small jar. "This sputum sample will be analyzed by the Department of Health. I believe you may have pulmonary tuberculosis, Samuel. The treatment is rest and good nutrition, which offers the best chance for your natural defenses to wall off pockets of the infection."

The next afternoon, a health inspector visited. The sputum test was positive and showed the disease to be virulent. The inspector toured our apartment. He strongly suggested, insisted, I be quarantined away from the children and from Fannie in the last weeks of her pregnancy.

It was philanthropy, but also in his best interest, when the landlord offered us—no fee—a vacant apartment for my isolation. The boys carried a mattress, a small table, a kerosene lamp, a kitchen chair, and a few enamel utensils up the three flights of stairs. There was no electricity or gas available in the flat, but the electric wall fixture on the landing shed enough light for the boys to read the newspapers or play cards during the vigil.

My four sons never left that landing unattended, nor did they enter my room without a handkerchief covering their mouths and noses.

On Sunday, Dr. Hollings came again. Inserting a syringe needle between my ribs, he extracted fluid from my lung cavity. The procedure was uncomfortable but not really painful.

The Doctor said, "Samuel, this is a treatment of last resort. It'll do nothing to stop the disease but will ease your breathing." He pleaded with me, "You must force yourself to eat, take fluids. You're literally starving to death, my friend. I am very sorry there is no magic pill, but I beg you not to give up. Try to muster your strength."

The boys took turns coaxing liquids, reading aloud from the newspapers, begging me to fight on. Albert washed my body and kept the linen clean. He made small talk, to which I barely responded. He was frightened. I could tell by his attention to my care, hoping to save me by facing down the Reaper, not giving me up without a fight. So many years before, I had asked him, "Take care of Mama and the baby." I managed to whisper those words once again. He cried, laying his head on my shoulder, ignoring my contagion. "I will, Papa. But, please, don't go."

I lifted my head a bit and looked into his eyes. "Yes, Papa? You want to tell me something?"

My head fell back upon the pillow, my neck muscles too weak to support it. He dared not bring his mouth near mine, but he leaned his ear against it. I realized the extent of my body's dehydration when my voice emerged as a throaty, croaking, whisper. My lips and tongue were so dry; to form each syllable took a monumental effort. "Mama...love her..." was all I could manage.

Albert pressed his cheek to mine, his lips at my earlobe. In a gush of words and flowing tears, he said, "Dearest Papa, I understand and will tell Mama you love her." I nodded as he whispered, "Papa, my dearest Papa; how will we go on if you leave us?" I wanted to convey my confidence in their love for one another, their collective character and strength, that I was certain they would survive and prosper. Yet, all I could muster was a weak smile and then to purse my lips in a feeble attempt at a kiss.

Rube read Edgar Allan Poe stories to me; Morris played his cello. Even Charles took his turn wiping my brow. I heard Fannie speaking with the boys a few times, but she never entered the room. It was unbearable knowing I'd likely never see her face again, and I wept, tearlessly.

The coughing, though less forceful, was unabated in frequency. Two days later, with all my energy depleted, I closed my eyes and lay in silence upon the sheet. Too tired to think or soul-search, ponder regrets, or rail in anger at my bad luck, I gave in to the peace and calm.

I could hear the boy's voices on the landing, aware of the light cast from the kerosene lamp. I watched myself, as if from afar, rise from the mattress and move across the room to the doorway.

By the early 1880s, the science of microbiology established disease to be the onset of infectious agents, germs. A decade later, those pathogens were being studied and researched in a new discipline, immunology, how the body resists disease.

In 1892, Dr. William Osler famously wrote of pneumonia, "It is a self-limited disease, and has its course uninfluenced by medicine." Laboratory research of antiserums and antitoxins were being pursued but had yet to be successful. A year before Osler declared the body's own defenses sufficient to overcome disease, the first attempt to treat pneumococcal pneumonia with rabbit serum had taken place in Germany, to mixed results.

In 1900, forty of the forty-five American states established health departments to improve sanitation and hygiene, establishing Public Health as a responsibility of government. Microbiology was an infant science, but tests were developed to diagnose pneumonia, tuberculosis, and influenza, the leading causes of death in U.S. urban populations.

The most densely populated place in the world, New York's Lower East Side, was a breeding ground for these modern-day plagues.

Physicians were required to report all cases of tuberculosis to the Department of Health, but they opposed providing information, claiming intrusion on their independence and patient confidentiality. This resistance from the medical community prompted the agency to hire medical inspectors, who made home visits to patients and instructed families on containing the disease.

In 1904, Ernst Lederle, New York City's Health Commissioner, established laboratories for the inspection of water, food, and milk. Inspectors visited not only stores selling milk, but also the five thousand dairy farms supplying the city. Arrests were made, and fines levied for violations of stable ventilation, unclean milk pails, and unwell cows or milkers.

Inspectors called upon public baths and barbershops, educating workers and customers in basic measures to prevent the spread of disease: hand washing, soaking instruments in disinfectant solutions, scrubbing tile and toilets with strong soap, removal of garbage, not sharing drinking containers, and disposing of soiled handkerchiefs in closed receptacles.

That same year, Lederle opened community-based free clinics run by nurses to provide nutritional support and public education directly to New York tenement families, those most targeted by the disease.

One of those clinics was on 46th Street, three blocks from the Freed family's apartment.

Fannie

I waited on the sidewalk at the door to the Health Clinic on 46th Street, but the matron would not allow me entrance. "Please, Madam, it's best, in your condition, to stay out of the clinic. If you will wait here, an aide will bring the printed instructions for care of the consumptive to you."

Through the open doorway, I heard people coughing. "Sister, I understand your concern and thank you for that. The Inspector who directed me to visit here should have told me to send another family member; he said it was mandatory that I come. My husband has been diagnosed and is isolated. Four years ago, I lost a child to pneumonia. Our doctor explained tubercular care is similar." I went on, "Isolation, force fluids, dispose of sputum-contaminated rags, boil all items after sickroom use."

"Wash your hands frequently, Missus. The most basic of all, wash your hands after any contact with the patient. And keep the children away. You, in particular, must stay away. When is the baby due?" "By the end of next month." A young woman brought an envelope to the matron's desk and handed it to me. "Good luck. We're here if we can be of any help."

I climbed the stairs a few times a day, carrying soup, tea, or lemon water. I peered into, but never entered, the room; the boys took turns coaxing their Papa to take a few spoonfuls. For seven days, Samuel was unable to eat anything. His pain was evident with each gasping, wheezing, inhalation. The mucous he managed to dislodge into scraps of linen was quickly burned in a metal bowl on the roof.

On Wednesday, Dr. Hollings visited. "Sadly, his lungs are bleeding, filled with tuberculosis. It's as bad a case and as rapid a decline as I've ever seen. There's nothing more any of us can do for Samuel. You ought to prepare yourselves for the inevitable."

Close to three in the morning, Charles came into my bedroom. The boy was pale, eyes full of tears, "Mama, Albert said to come upstairs."

"Alright, dear, I'm coming." I shifted in the bed, pulling myself up to sitting. "Come here, Charles. Give me your hand and help me get up."

After visiting the bathroom, I followed Charles to the hall. I was breathing heavily. The baby, two weeks from term, had not yet dropped to my lower pelvis. The fetus was wedged under my ribcage, restricting movement of my diaphragm and full expansion of my chest. My body, no longer young, had little energy reserve in this ninth pregnancy. My legs were swollen, sleeping through the night was a memory, and a dull lower backache was ever-present. Both body and soul were exhausted.

I used the banister to pull myself up the steps, stopping to catch my breath at each of the three landings.

Morris and Rudolf came down to help me climb the final flight.

I asked, "Where is Albert?"

"He's inside with Papa," Rube said.

"Is Papa still with us?"

"Yes, Mama, but Albert says it won't be long."

At the landing, in a slow motion, Rudolf released his grip on my arm and collapsed in a heap on the floor, sobbing. I could not minister to him, not then. "Please Rube, get hold of yourself. I know you're distraught, but don't make this more difficult for me than it already is." Cross-legged, he remained on the floor crying, his head on his knees.

Morris said, "Mama, please don't go in there. If you get sick, what will happen to you and the baby...to all of us?"

I touched his cheek. "I'll be alright, Morris. Everything will be alright, my darling."

Albert came to the door, his face contorted with grief, tears running down his cheeks.

"He's near the end, Mama."

I embraced him. "I know, my son. There is nothing we can do to keep Papa with us on this earth. It is his time, and we need to help him leave peacefully. Walk with me to the bedside; there's very little light, and I don't want to fall."

Albert offered his arm, which I reached out for. "Mama, listen to what happened: near midnight, Papa appeared in the doorway, leaning against the jamb. We were so surprised, we just stared at him, didn't even say 'hello.' How was it possible he found the strength to rise from the mattress and walk across the floor? None of us had heard sounds of any movement in the room, yet there he was, ashen, trembling, and speaking."

"In a hoarse whisper, Papa said, " *You boys can go downstairs now. Tell your Mama I'll be leaving in a little while.*" We helped him return to bed and then I sent Charles to get you."

"Albert, dear, it is not uncommon for the dying to experience a final surge of strength before the end. When I was a young girl, my Papa told me of the phenomenon. Your father was saying goodbye to you."

Morris handed me a piece of white linen. I tied it in place over my nose and mouth before entering the room.

Albert guided me to the chair near the mattress. I whispered, "It's so dark I can barely see him." The boy turned the lamp's wick higher, casting a yellow light on Samuel's face. "Thank you, son."

"I'll be in the hall if you need me, Mama."

Samuel appeared to be in a deep sleep, the mucous in his airway making a rattling sound with each breath. I touched his arm; he did not respond, not even to blink an eye.

I wasn't certain he knew I was at the bedside, but I held his hand and whispered, "My dearest, are you aware of my presence? Do you know I'm here? I believe, over the years, we've said all there is to say to one another, haven't we? Our story is a pure and simple one. I saw you; I loved you. In all the universe, the essence of *our* souls found mates; wasn't that miraculous?"

Ever so lightly, I felt his hand squeeze mine. "Darling, I know you hear me. Please, don't suffer anymore, Samuel. Steal off into the starry void. I will come to you in time. Wait for me. Until then, your essence will abide with me always."

Caring not for the contagion, I removed my mask. With my finger, I traced the features of his skeletal face, almost unrecognizable as to be my Samuel. Kissing the forehead of my soul mate, I murmured, "*Viszlát, Szeretett*; Farewell, beloved."

My loving husband, the youthful optimist seeking freedom and opportunity, whose vibrant personality and charm drew people to him, the determined man who followed his dream, the father of our beautiful children; the man I loved with all that I was or ever could be, was leaving me, dying.

At 4:30 in the morning, on Thursday, August 18, 1904, Samuel slipped from life. He was forty-four-years old.

Charles ran to 43rd Street, returning with Dr. Hollings, who signed the Health Department forms. Albert and Morris left immediately for the Austrian-Hungarian Free Burial Society.

At some point during the day, the Tahara committee of the Society arrived to prepare Samuel for interment. As a woman, I was not permitted to take part in the preparation of the body for Jewish burial. From the parlor chair, I watched through the doorway.

Albert and Morris carried the casket from the wagon to our parlor, where two kitchen chairs faced each other to provide support for the wooden box. After placing a long board on our bed, Samuel's body was laid upon it, his feet facing the door. The boys assisted in the warm water ritual washing of the body, considered a release of the soul's impurities and an act of kindness by those participating. Special prayers were chanted, asking God to lift Samuel's soul into the Heavens and eternal rest.

It is customary for the deceased to be wrapped in a simple muslin shroud before being laid in the unadorned pine casket. It may have been customary, but I was having none of that. Samuel was proud of his tailoring skills and didn't skimp on his own suits of clothes. I chose a fine pin-striped brown woolen suit and vest from our chifforobe. Fashioned by his artistic hands, it was an appropriate, although unorthodox, suit for his burial.

As a sign of respect for the life ended, Tahara committee members and our sons kept an uninterrupted vigil at the casket until the hearse arrived the next morning.

Under a cloudy August sky, he was buried at Washington Cemetery, just a few rows from Anna's grave.

Prompted by a rabbi arranged for by the Society, the boys and I parroted the *Kaddish*.

The casket was lowered. The Rabbi tore my collar. This custom, expressing pain and sorrow, also demonstrates that the body is the garment worn by one's soul; and the soul never dies. Albert, Morris, and Rudolf: nineteen, seventeen- and fifteen-years-old, were adult Jewish men. They also tore their lapels.

In Yiddish, the Rabbi asked Charles, "Vi alt zanier, zun?" Charles, in a panic, looked to me. "He asks how old you are, son." Charles turned to the Rabbi. "Yesterday was my tenth birthday, Rabbi." Without another word, the rabbi guided Charles to stand beside Rudolf. "Thirteen is the age of majority; you are not yet a Jewish man, so you cannot say the Kaddish and can't tear your clothes." Casting his eyes to the ground, Charles was extremely embarrassed. Rudolf did pat his shoulder and give him the thumbs-up sign to cheer him, but once again, Charles just didn't measure up; this time, he was too young. I wanted to comfort him but was already having trouble standing for so long with a full-term baby in my belly.

"Put a shovelful of dirt on the casket," the rabbi said to Albert. He did as he was asked before passing the spade to Morris and Rudolf. I scattered a handful of dirt, unable to maneuver the shovel. Then, Charles and Rozsa—who carried Nora in her arms—and Rose and Louis followed my example. "Goodbye, Papa."

For the week of Shiva, neighbors brought food and visited from morning until evening. Then, it was time for the boys to return to work. Charles, Rose, and Lou to school.

I endeavored to make sense of the events overtaking my life but was not yet able to tackle its realities. Our means of support was gone, a dire prospect for the future. In less than a month's time, our ninth child would be born, fatherless.

If there was ever a time to set a strong example, this was it, so that first evening after Shiva, I called the children to the parlor to tell them where we stood. I sat on the settee with Nora in my lap, and Rose, Louis, and Charles squeezed in beside me. The boys brought kitchen chairs into the parlor, except for Albert, who leaned against the wall.

"My darlings, we all miss Papa. He will always be in our hearts. It may feel as if our shattered world will never be alright again, but it will be." I had their full attention now.

"I am captain of our ship now, and we're going to move ahead. With Rube's help, the shop will remain open, and Albert and Morris are earning. There is an insurance policy, which will pay our expenses for several months. We're alright with money."

My big belly left little room for Nora to sit comfortably, so she moved to Rose's lap.

"I am healthy. When the baby comes, I'll give birth in my own bed, with Dr. Hollings' help. Everything will be alright."

Albert stood away from the wall, addressing the group. "I promised Papa I'd take care of things, step into his shoes. I did it when I was a boy and certainly can meet the challenge today. Mama and I will make all the decisions together, so don't worry."

The response to his declaration was immediate: I should have expected it yet was taken aback, since we had had no prior discussion about his responsibilities. The little ones smiled, their mood brightening. Morris and Rudolf laughed hard at Albert's self-importance. Rube, as expected, fell off his chair to the floor. After several minutes of convulsive laughter, and a quick visit to the bathroom, Morris and

Rudolf stood at military attention, saluting Albert as "Cully," the Colonel! Albert laughed, too, and the sadness left the room. Life was already moving on; we'd be alright.

The next day, Albert and I met with the landlord and Cully took control of the conversation. "Mr. Stein, I posted a note on the door announcing fewer hours until after the baby is born, as we plan to keep the shop open, make a go of it. Papa's life insurance policy will pay the bills for a few months. My brothers and I are working, so we have things in hand. There's no way to say for certain how things will work out, but the rent will be paid on both the apartment and the shop."

Albert offered an envelope containing September's rent to Mr. Stein, who said, "Thank you, Albert." Then, to me, "Mrs. Freed, I am so very sorry about Samuel's death. He was so young, so vibrant. A man of his word, a true artist at his work, and I had a great deal of respect for him. I'll miss him."

Bachmann paid us a condolence call. He brought a few dozen Brooks' coat linings for me to work on to help keep things going. Out of respect for Samuel, I was assured they'd pay for whatever I could manage, with no weekly minimum. Mr. Brooks, himself, sent a note of condolence, praising Samuel's talent and his character. There was a twenty-dollar bill enclosed to help with expenses. What a gentleman.

Charles, by now a habitual school truant, was learning the ways of the street. With the new fraternal regime at home, he felt more estranged than ever before. I tried to console him, to diffuse his anger, yet he was glum and withdrawn. I believed at ten, he was too young to be included in discussions of finance. Only in later years did I realize how deeply he had been affected and offended by the exclusion.

Rose never let me out of her sight during the Shiva. She grieved deeply for her Papa; the way he would say, "Drágám, my dearest." She needed constant reassurance that I wouldn't leave or die, that I'd be with her forever.

Louis understood that Papa was gone, never to return, but keeping to himself, he asked no questions. Nora sensed the sadness all around and lifted our spirits with a smile and a song.

A lumbering she-bear, I moved my swollen body down the flight of stairs to the shop with great difficulty.

On Friday, September 23, 1904, my labor began just before sunrise, with moderate contractions five minutes apart. I prepared the bed with a rubber sheet, placed a metal bowl on the bedside table, and stacked remnants of white cotton at the foot of the bed. At 7:00, Rudolf went for the doctor, and Rose prepared breakfast for the family. She shooed Charles and Louis off to school, her brothers to work. To be of help, she stayed at home to care for Nora.

Dr. Hollings and his nurse arrived at nine; I was almost fully dilated. Giving birth was always an event fraught with the possibilities of unexpected complication. But not this one. This was to be the easiest and least traumatic of all; a blessing I felt the family deserved, given the situation. At 10:30 in the morning, I delivered my ninth child, and sixth son, into the hands of Dr. Hollings. With a firm grip on his ankles, the doctor hung the baby upside down, massaging his throat and gently slapping his back. After a moment or two, my child's first breath and cry were met with a joyless silence. The baby was placed on my belly. After cutting the umbilical cord, the nurse bathed and swaddled the little one in a blanket and placed him at my side.

"What is his name?" the doctor asked.

"Samuel, in his father's memory," I replied quietly.

I began to cry. Only a few months earlier, I had hoped for this to be our last baby. Eerily, fate had fulfilled my wish.

"There, there, Fannie. things have a way of working out. You and the baby are both strong and healthy. You have a wonderful family. Life goes on, my dear; life goes on."

Melancholy filled the house like a gas, displacing pleasure in every crevice. As soon as the detritus of the birthing bed had been removed, I dressed in a clean gown.

At my call, the children filed into the bedroom. It was a heartrending welcome indeed, each child kissing my cheek and staring at the baby. None of them greeted him by name, their Papa's name. Only Nora offered the baby a welcome. With quiet awe, she smiled, kissed his tiny hand, and said, "Hello, Sam."

Dr. Hollings said goodbye, reminding me, "All babies bring good luck."

Taking to the breast with energy and strength, Sam's tiny spirit, so eager to live, compelled me forward. The world is reborn in a new baby, hope for the future renewed.

At forty-two, having given birth nine times, it took many weeks before my body regained its stamina. Convalescence at The Sloane was a sweet memory. How grand those ten days of pampering had been: tender nursing care, food prepared for me, hours of undisturbed sleep, sheets changed every day.

Home birthing brought sleep deprivation, exhaustion, and worry. From my bed or the parlor chair, I planned meals, dispatched children to the grocer, directed the washing, checked that schoolwork was done, prodded the older boys to get to work, and nursed the baby on demand.

The apartment was quiet during the day, allowing time alone with Nora. She was easily diverted with a song, a story, or a picture book, and happily napped with the baby and me.

Thank God for Rozsa, who helped with the laundry or cooking every day. Her visits were to be short-lived, as she and Leon were leaving New York. She had quit working at the theater and was moving to Chicago at the end of October to care for her aging father-in-law. It was very sad to say goodbye to Rozsa. I had lost Anna, then Samuel. This felt like another death. We promised to write, but there was little quiet time in my life, little time to reflect and correspond. A few letters were exchanged over the years, but after many address changes, we lost contact.

Rudolf went to the shop every day, determined to make a go of it, doing the best he could. Two weeks after the birth, I made my way to the waiting piecework pile. Sam was a placid baby and slept most of the day in a blanket-lined box. Nora played with a ragdoll Rudolf had sewn from fabric scraps. Although there was ample time to do the hand sewing, I procrastinated, finishing only seven pieces in six weeks. Rudolf did much better than I, both in the quality of his stitch and in the pieces turned out. Thank God for Brooks!

There were few customers, mostly needing repairs, as Rudolf was not a tailor. Those folks lingered, enthralled by his animated discussion. It was remarkable that at fifteen, he was so aware of the world, so enjoyed sharing ideas with people. He could go on at length about many things: the Russo-Japanese War, a better way to wind a bobbin, the latest ship to dock in the Hudson, or a new tailoring detail he had learned since their last visit. Self-taught, his skills produced satisfactory work, but it was his charm that brought referrals from the neighborhood.

What would become of us here in America?

It is not natural for youth to dwell upon thoughts of death; youth must just live with no fear. So, it was not unusual that I had never focused on such matters. Anna's death had been a tragedy; but it had not threatened the family's welfare. Samuel's death was more than a tubercular statistic. He was our bedrock. Without him, how would I provide the necessities of life?

A sea change had occurred; the generations had to advance. My job was still to be the Mama: guide, cook, clean, run the household, and maybe add a few dollars to the kitty. But, from now on, my sons had to step into Samuel's shoes and support us.

PART TWO

14

During the first decade of the Twentieth Century, the second Industrial Revolution went into high gear. Improved factory techniques spurred production, and innovations in steam and electric power reduced costs and increased mechanization, urbanizing the working class.

Wilbur and Orville Wright's airship made the first man-powered flight. Henry Ford established his Motor Car Company. Electric washing machines and vacuum cleaners introduced the idea that household drudgery kept people from enjoying life. The first Major League Baseball World Series game was played between the Boston Red Sox and the Pittsburgh Pirates legitimizing sport as a leisure activity to be enjoyed by the common man. Boston won.

On September 14, 1901, when William McKinley was assassinated, Vice-President Theodore Roosevelt took the Presidential oath. At forty-two years old, he remains, to this day, the youngest person to hold that office.

A native New Yorker, Roosevelt won the Medal of Honor for service as an Army Colonel during the Spanish-American War. He had served in the New York State Assembly, was President of the New York City Board of Police Commissioners, Assistant Secretary of the Navy, and Governor of New York State.

A driving force for the Progressive Era, Roosevelt's face is carved on Mount Rushmore alongside George Washington, Thomas Jefferson, and Abraham Lincoln.

Roosevelt was an explorer and historian. He created the Conservation movement to preserve the natural world for posterity. Brokering the end of the Russo-Japanese War, he won the Nobel Peace Prize in 1906. During his second term in office, he began construction on the Panama Canal. Born to wealth, he championed a Square Deal policy, promising fairness for the average citizen by "busting the Trusts" of the robber barons, regulating railroads, and guaranteeing pure food and drugs.

His personal story was inspirational: born with severe asthma, he overcame a weak constitution through exercise and the sheer force of his will!

There wasn't an American boy alive during that decade who didn't aspire to Roosevelt's personal strength of character, his vision for America's leadership, democracy, and the endless progress he represented.

One might say Roosevelt was the very embodiment of New York: Both Progressive American stars on the ascendancy!

By 1910, the population of New York City reached four million, seven hundred sixty-six thousand, a twenty-five percent increase in a decade, and almost forty percent were foreign born.

The child growing up at the Century's turn enjoyed the expectation of opportunity and success in every conceivable and in never-before conceived ways.

Technology, science, architecture, transportation systems, medical advances, new industries, labor movement, social reforms, public-sponsored trade schools, specialty secondary schools, and free colleges benefited all New Yorkers regardless of economic station. To immigrant parents, still struggling to learn a new language, these developments and innovations must have seemed a fiction.

Indoor plumbing was required in all new construction and retrofitted in older tenements. The Williamsburg, Manhattan, and Queensborough Bridges opened. The Flatiron Building's architecture stunningly changed Manhattan's landscape.

Movies and phonographs ushered in an era where, for even the poorest citizen, leisure time was celebrated as a given, a concept unheard of in the European villages from which the foreign born had come.

In 1903, Edison's first action film, "The Great Train Robbery," a twelve-minute-long silent film, accompanied by a piano, was shown at New York's Huber's Museum, ticket price a nickel. A building used to present musical shows in ancient times was called an Odeon. With a ticket price of a nickel, the new activity was coined "nickelodeon."

In 1904, the first subway line was opened to serve the new tenement district of the South Bronx. Long Acre Square was renamed Times Square, where in 1907, a ball was dropped to welcome in the New Year!

In 1906, Governor Charles Evans Hughes created the New York State Public Service Commission, whose mandate included the planning of rapid transit lines for New York City. His Reformers developed a program of planned growth, aimed at providing an infrastructure to relieve the population density and dire social conditions of the slums.

The network of subway and elevated systems was designed as a public/private collaboration. Called the Dual System of Rapid Transit, the new lines would, simultaneously, open up large tracts of land in the Bronx, Brooklyn, and Queens to house working families, thus alleviating Manhattan's congested slums.

A profit-sharing agreement between the City of New York and both the Brooklyn Rapid Transit and the Independent Rapid Transit companies was struck. The transit companies would build, equip, and operate the subway for the term of ninety-nine years at a guaranteed, fixed five-cent fare. In return, the city would finance the venture with Rapid Transit bonds. By the end of the second decade, six hundred and twenty-one miles of track were in operation.

In the global scheme of things, America had entered the age of the machine and economic invention. Scientific insight and discovery benefited even the lowest classes. The new century began with a promise of limitless individual freedom.

For a family newly rendered fatherless, the struggle to survive was a daily grind.

Few options were open to Fannie, yet, somehow, she and her eldest sons must rise every day and find the wherewithal to provide.

When Samuel died, the three eldest boys, each with only an eighth-grade education, were nineteen, seventeen, and fifteen. Employed full-time, they weren't earning enough to feed, house, and clothe a family of nine.

Early on, a child understands his father's primary role: to earn a living, to provide. It is the sense of security and moral guidance a father's love bestows. After losing their provider, Albert, Morris, and Rudolf began to understand who their father was: each in his own way.

Albert

I suppose it was being first-born that shaped our bond from the start. There were no intermediaries, not even Papa. She loved me and took delight in the intoxicating truth that she had created a human being who possessed, at birth, everything necessary to live a long life. She had birthed an offspring, but I was not an extension of her; I was an ally, an equal.

It was my birth that made her a Mama, her girlhood drowning in my first breath and cry. To me, she was the perfect woman, and to her, I was the perfect son.

I recall nothing of my babyhood or of Morris's birth two years later, but I do remember the train station when Papa left for America. I was three. Papa said, "Albert, take care of Mama and the baby." I doubt that I remember his words, but having heard the story so many times, I have come to believe I recollect those exact words being said.

By the time Rudolf was born, I was four and not happy about the attention Mama gave him. But I was the eldest and, with Papa gone, Mama's partner. I helped her take care of my brothers, always reliable and serious.

Five years without Papa were wonderful. I read his letters and sent him greetings, too; but in reality, I quickly became accustomed to his absence. It was up to me and Mama, together, to keep us all happy and safe, clean, and fed. Before entering school, I learned to sweep floors and to cook simple things, like boiled eggs and potatoes. Yes, by the time I was seven, I considered myself to *be* Papa.

When I was six, Mama's cousin, Abe, took me to the Hungarian Royal Opera House on Andrássy Út. While waiting to present our tickets to the attendant, Cousin Abe said, "Albert, the year before you were born, Emperor and King Franz Joseph attended opening night in this magnificent house! You'll walk the same carpeted aisle as he; just picture yourself in the company of the Crown!"

All these years later, I still remember gilt figures carved into the walls, the formal attire worn by the audience, women in feathered chapeau, men in black beaver top hats, angels and clouds painted on the vaulted ceiling, and the seats upholstered in deep red. Budapest's wealthy and powerful occupied private boxes on the second tier. Through lorgnettes, eyeglasses with a handle, they viewed the stage, orchestra pit, and others of their station in boxes across the orchestra level seats.

Musicians were tuning up in the pit, and there was an air of excitement in the hall as we were ushered to our seats. I leafed through the libretto but couldn't read French. Cousin Abe noticed. "Albert, Don José is a Spanish soldier who falls in love with a beautiful gypsy, Carmen. He abandons his sweetheart and deserts his military post to pursue her. Unfortunately, she leaves him for Escamillo, a famous matador."

I paid very close attention to the story, my eyes wide with interest. "Does he die of heartbreak, Cousin?"

With a great effort, he hid a smile, a stricken look on his face. "No, dear boy, it's opera; there must be tragedy and high drama along with the high notes! In a jealous rage, Don José kills Carmen."

I was shocked to hear a man would kill a woman, no matter how angry he may be. "Cousin, is it possible to kill the woman you love? Why wouldn't he just go back to his old sweetheart and leave Carmen?"

He laughed, "The story is universal, Albert: how love can drive men insane, how disastrous it can be. But, listen to the music of the French composer, Bizet. He's a genius. The story is told in the music, boy. Listen for the melodies and harmonies and the instruments."

The orchestra began the overture, and I was transfixed. My soul stirred with the strings. Then, the magic began; the curtain rose.

After the performance, Cousin Abe and I had dinner at the Csárdás, a small restaurant on Dobó Út, near our apartment.

"Albert, I thought a lot about this day. If your Papa were here, you would already have attended a concert and maybe the ballet. It's important to learn and appreciate art and music. Without it, a man is only a dry set of numbers, the sum of his forints. The arts are very important to Hungary, but in America, I don't know. I wanted to give you a gift you'd enjoy for the rest of your life, dear Albert, and today's opera was that gift. Never forget how the music made you feel, boy. Nurture that feeling by listening to music wherever you are. To feel the ecstasy music brings your heart; that is a treasure I hope you'll take with you to America, one that will last your whole life."

"Thank you, Cousin Abe. I promise I'll always remember this day and the music."

For the two years before we left for America, I spent many Saturday afternoons attending matinee performances at the Opera House or Vigadó Concert Hall. In truth, I only saw the second half of those performances, after mastering the appearance of belonging to one of the patrons returning from intermission. Once in the hall, I took an empty balcony seat or stood in the shadows at the back of the house, with no one the wiser. Only one time was I chased by a theater attendant, who I easily outran!

At the Academy of Music, I sat in on a performance of Franz Liszt's Hungarian Rhapsody played by one of the Academy's professors, a man who had actually been a student of Liszt's. It was thrilling!

I knew the voice of each instrument, but the violin's plaintive notes brought me to tears. I longed to have one of my own, but with Mama sacrificing every day to save a few coins, there was no money for that. She said, "Maybe, when we get to America, Albert; be patient."

I remember living without Papa for those years. Morris and Rudolf have little memory of that time and don't speak Hungarian anymore, but I do, and that's another place where Mama and I connect. Charles and the younger ones are English speakers, understanding only a few Hungarian words, the gist of a phrase.

Two weeks after my eighth birthday, I left all I had ever known.

I bore witness to the greatest achievement of Mama's life aside from giving birth to all of us: coming to America. Leaving her country, culture, and family behind, she gave herself completely to the idea of a better future. To me, Mama was heroic.

The trip to America and Pennsylvania are memories of adventure, with an undercurrent of resentment for Papa's assumption to the head of house after so long an absence. I didn't understand why my belly cramped, the back of my throat grew dry, and angry tears stabbed my eyes when Papa appeared at Ellis Island. He looked at Mama with intensity, a longing, and ownership I had never seen before. I pretended not to recognize him; but his face was known to me. I didn't want to give up Mama. At the time, I didn't know there was a name for what I was experiencing; it was jealousy.

My parents loved each other completely, and watching them, feeling the aura of their love, was a stone in my shoe at first. I could do nothing to change it, I knew it was beautiful and right, but somehow, I felt diminished, no longer needed. Papa didn't scold or engage in a clash of wills with me. I was unaware that he observed my anger, resentment, and bewilderment, that he noticed how I bristled when they embraced or laughed at some secret joke.

I would do nothing to make Mama unhappy; I loved her too completely to punish her in any way. So, I made myself scarce, didn't hang about. After meals, I withdrew to read or went outdoors. The less I saw Mama loving him, the better. I knew it was wrong to feel these things, but I had been pretending to be a grown man for so long, all my life, really, it was hard to change my responses. He was Papa, and I was a child. Losing love, with grace, to another man was a very grown-up lesson to learn. Finally, I understood what Don José felt when Carmen chose Escamillo.

While building friendships with my schoolmates and living a boy's life, I gradually lost the need to see if Mama was alright every minute.

One night, Papa asked me to sit with him at the table before going to bed.

"Albert," he said, "You took care of Mama as I asked. You were just three-years-old, a baby. I never thought you'd take that responsibility as seriously as you did, but that is how you see the world, my son, dependent upon you. You are a good boy, Albert, and will make a fine man, given your determination and love of others. Now, dear boy, it is time for me to be the responsible man in the house. It was unfair of me to place that burden on you, and I hope you'll forgive me for that. You have been, and are, wonderful, my son, never complaining, always giving of yourself. I cherish you, my dear boy. Please learn to enjoy your life now, Albert, every waking minute of it. There'll be plenty of time later on to put others first. Now, live and enjoy the freedom of childhood. You've earned it."

I sat on his lap, biting my quivering lip. He embraced me, rocking from side to side, comforting and strong. There was nothing I wouldn't do for my Papa, who understood my pain and didn't dismiss it as childish. "Thank you, Papa," I said between whimpers, "Always, for all my life, I'll make you proud of me."

True to my nature, I saw my new place in the family. I would forge the trail for my brothers in this new country. I would always be Mama's helpmate, the big brother, and the responsible second-in-command to Papa.

Tall in stature and good at sports, I was accepted by the boys in East Chunk. Papa was well liked by the neighbors, a respected member of the business community, and tolerant of everyone. I was proud to be his son and aspired to be the man of principle I knew him to be.

Chunk was a backwater town with little culture. Their Opera House was a joke. Mostly gaudy vaudeville acts or variety shows played there, and it was hardly worth sneaking in the back door. Summer band concerts interested me, especially when they offered Schubert, Mendelssohn, or Bach, the composers so loved by the local German population.

In Hungary, our neighbors knew we were Jews who never attended synagogue. In Chunk, there was no synagogue, and no one knew we were Jewish. We attended the Lutheran Church on Sundays because Papa told us we would learn about American Christianity, our neighbors would be pleased to take notice of us there, and the pastor had asked Papa to send us. We didn't actually participate in any of the rituals, as we were ignorant of all religious dogma, and that went for Judaism, too.

Rube was fascinated by the massive organ and tried to figure out how it worked. He intently observed the keyboards, valves, stops, and pistons as they produced music with wind. Morris closed his eyes, humming along with the hymns and psalms, lost in the ancient songs of praise. I sat quietly until it was over, always Mama's good boy. I never felt comfortable attending church; we were deceiving the pastor, and I was glad when we moved to New York, where we didn't have to hide our religion, whether we practiced it or not.

I discovered any decision Papa made always benefitted the family first and sending us to church was no different. He confided his philosophy to me, "One must learn to adapt and live with all kinds of people. It's good to walk down a new road if the family benefits from it. Protecting the family is the most important thing in life, and I'm not going to let you boys be ostracized because of a religious label. We are good people and do not harm others. That's my religion. I came to America to live my own way, free."

Then, Charles was born, the little brat. He was the beginning of a new family, the American one. Maybe I was jealous, but I ignored him the first time I abandoned the role I had so carefully constructed as Papa's assistant. I did feel guilty about it, knowing it hurt Mama's feelings, but Morris and Rudolf were my real brothers. It was petty and childish, and I never anticipated the animosity toward him would carry forward through our lives. I am sorry for my part in isolating Charles, but the past cannot be changed. And, he was only two-years-old when we moved to New York City, so Mama couldn't really expect us to be attentive to a baby, could she?

NEW YORK CITY!

Mama spoke with the neighbors to find out about the local schools. She said, "I haven't come all this way to enroll my children in some overcrowded classroom. We live in a middle-class neighborhood and my sons will attend the best public school I can find."

So, I entered sixth grade at Public School, P.S.6, which had only opened its doors on 85th Street in 1894, two years earlier. The principal, Mistress Blake, was the daughter of the school's namesake, Lillie Devereaux Blake, a feminist author and reformer. The academics were strict, and classes included writing and science and art and even music, where I held a violin for the first time. I learned the history of string instruments. I learned that the violin's four catgut cords were not made from cats, but fibers of the intestines of sheep and goats. I learned to apply rosin, an oil of the pine tree, to the bow's horsehair to render it sticky, so the string and hair vibrate when the bow is drawn across. Still, Mama told me to be patient, "Maybe after the baby is born." Yet, even after Rose was born and Papa had steady work at Brooks, there was no money for un-necessaries.

I looked forward to when, at thirteen, I'd graduate from eighth grade and get a job. "Then," I told myself, "Then, I'll buy my own fiddle!"

As is my nature, I applied myself, studied hard. Stoically, I kept at my books, never wasting time, and was among the top students, looking forward to graduation in June of 1898. It turned out I never did graduate, didn't finish the last three months.

Mama gave birth to Louis in March of 1898, and we moved downtown to West 10th Street near the Hudson River. It was not only closer for Papa to get to work but had more rooms for less money.

So, I said goodbye to Mistress Blake and school. High school was out of the question. The family needed another earner. I didn't mind; P.S. 6 had given me a very good start.

I became apprenticed to a carpenter who made chairs in a drafty workshop on Duane Street. There was a coal stove, but we had to be very careful about sawdust igniting when refilling the grate. Grunfeld, the boss, was very stingy with the heat, blaming his frugality on the need for safety. I didn't much care for him, but the work was steady, the location convenient, and the family needed the wages. I sandpapered chair legs from eight in the morning until six in the evening, with thirty minutes for lunch, Monday to Friday. For me, there was no creativity in the work. I didn't have it in me to create a new chair design, and I found the sawdust annoying, sticking to my skin, clogging my ears and nose, collecting under my fingernails. Inhaling the dust caused me to cough and gasp for breath, and although Mama thought I'd become a carpenter, I had neither the talent nor the interest for it. I did that work because it provided a daily income of one dollar. My longing was to make a sweet, high-pitched fiddle sing.

Rudolf came home from Tarrytown when Uncle István died, and Auntie Rozsa joined the family a few months later, which was a big help to Mama. That's when Rudolf discovered the Hudson River wharf, only a block from our apartment. He became a fixture on the docks, the longshoremen adopting him as a mascot. To his credit, it wasn't just his bubbling personality that endeared him; he really knew everything about fishing and about engines and was a fantastic swimmer, all skills he learned from Uncle István! Rudolf was a celebrity around the docks, he was. Known by men from all over the world, they nicknamed him "Rube," you know, like a hick, since he had come from up-river, the sticks. The joke was really on the mostly illiterate dockworkers because Rudolf was certainly no dumb farm boy. Even at his tender age, he had read classic literature and could recite poetry and Shakespearean soliloquies. Rudolf demanded we all call him Rube, and with the exception of Mama, we all did. He was Rube Elmer Freed from that time forward.

Finally, on my fourteenth birthday, I bought a violin, the only selfish expenditure I had ever made, and music became the center of my life. For a few pennies a week, I studied with a teacher and shared my zeal, and instrument, with Morris and Rube.

When Anna died, I was heartbroken. Many nights, I had carried her in my arms when she was making her baby teeth. I nuzzled her neck and nibbled at her belly, making her laugh. She had the most beautiful baby smell, so fresh and new. I didn't make a show of it, but for more than a year, just like Mama, I mourned that little girl every day. When Nora was born a few months later, I didn't know how to react. If I loved her, would that betray Anna's memory? Nora answered the question by being the most wonderful, happy, intelligent, and MUSICAL little girl in the world. Her big-mouthed smile was glorious, her warmth contagious; she was an honestly happy child.

Then, Papa got sick. He had come so far from his beginnings in the mountains of Hungary, accomplished so much, been so courageous, had loved without reservation, given us all life. It seemed a dream, those three weeks of his illness. His suffering, added to the insult of quarantine from the ones he loved so deeply, was an unnecessary cruelty inflicted upon him. I watched my beloved father starve to death, lying on a mattress in a borrowed apartment. During those days in which I attended to his needs day and night, my youthful optimism drained away.

At the last instant of his life, all he had experienced in this world went dark...an electrical connection severed, as if the spark had never existed. Where there had been light, a black void descended upon those he loved.

I was nineteen, a man now.

Once more, I was the one to "take care of Mama." Even though Papa had asked that of me, no one had to tell me. As the eldest, the responsibility for keeping a roof over our heads fell to me. The Hungarian brothers declared their readiness to support the family. Morris and Rube were bringing in a couple of dollars hawking papers, but it wasn't enough. I couldn't blame Morris for quitting working for Grossberg. Morris wanted to play cello, and he couldn't become a real musician part-time. Rube quit the papers for Papa's shop. He had no choice, really. He was the only one who knew anything about clothing repair and working the sewing machine. Although playing fiddle on weekends, I was still at the carpentry. With this full-blown tragedy, my plans to quit the sawdust had to wait for a while.

Mama decided she and I would manage the family's finances together. Papa's books were easily deciphered, with $50.00 owed to vendors and suppliers. I called upon each creditor, who settled for twenty-five cents on the dollar. Any uncut fabric or thread was conceded by the creditors, kind of a good will gesture to help Mama and Rube continue the business. There were only a few customers with garments in construction, whose small deposits I refunded.

Mama had thought Papa's spending on an insurance policy a foolish waste. Now, we blessed Papa's foresight. I hoped the $450.00 would hold out long enough for Mama to feel secure and for me to figure out how to support a family of nine.

Morris

Albert was the practical one, Rudolf had the gift of gab, and I was the dreamer. We were the three Hungarian sons, Mama's men, a glorious triumvirate who had shared the excitement of her incredible migration to a new world. I felt she loved us in a special, more intense way than our American siblings.

Mama said the second born is the audience. Albert did it all first; I just followed along, Act II. He told me things about my babyhood: when I said his name for the first time, when I started walking. I don't remember anything, but I don't have to; he does it for me.

There is one memory of Hungary that is very clear. We visited our grandparents to say goodbye. I don't remember the house very well, but I do remember how Grandpapá made me feel. He paid me absolutely no attention and seemed angry at us. I let him hug me when we left but felt no love from him, and I didn't like that he made me feel guilty.

I have only one recollection of Budapest's train station when we left for Holland. Mama's cousin, Abe, came to say goodbye and gave each of us a book written in English. "Morris, this one is for you. I believe you're an old soul, full of love. This is the greatest love poem ever written as nonsense, "The Owl and the Pussycat." I know you'll read it over and over and never tire of its beauty. Now, Morris, be a good boy and help your Mama on the journey. Don't cause her any worry. Oh, and say hello to your Papa for me." The book was easy to read, with a little translation help from Albert and Mama. It remained one of my favorite love poems. Even when Rudolf recited it in an over-dramatic voice, I still loved it.

I remember the trip across the Atlantic Ocean and the terror I felt during the hurricane. I vomited and the boat rocked, and Mama told me to lie down with Albert on the cot and not to stand up, for fear of falling and breaking a leg. She tied a rope around the bed we were in so we wouldn't fall on the floor. I was so frightened, but Albert kept his arms around me and told me, "Don't worry, Morris. I'm a very good swimmer, and I'll save you if the boat sinks." For some reason, that made me feel better.

By the time we reached Ellis Island, I was so tired all I wanted to do was go to sleep. I'm pretty sure I was grumpy and didn't talk much to anyone. Then, Papa appeared, and I was happy. He wore a suit with narrow lapels, a starched-collared shirt, and a derby hat tilted to one side. He was tall and handsome, with a certain walk, not like the snobby Budapest men with their frock coats and exaggerated moustaches. Papa was clean-shaven. And he wasn't embarrassed to kiss and hug us in front of all those strangers! His smile made my face tingle; it was contagious. When he left Hungary, I was 5-months-old, and so had no recollection of him. At Ellis Island, at six-years-old, I saw his face for the first time and knew I loved him. Knew he was the best father in America, maybe all the world.

Life in Mauch Chunk is clear in my mind. I was happy to be left to read or daydream. Miss Crenshaw was impressed that a student with only limited English had a card from the new Dimmick Lending Library on Broadway. On the first day of school, I brought "The Owl and the Pussycat" to show her, and she read it to the class. That day, I met Erich, my best friend in Chunk. He, too, was a reader, but his father, a foundry worker who couldn't read, belittled Erich's love of books. We spent a lot of time at my house, reading. Papa bought me an English dictionary so Erich and I could learn words we encountered in books way too mature for us. In particular, I loved the adventures of Sherlock Holmes stories by Arthur Conan Doyle.

When Papa announced my brothers and I would attend the Lutheran Church on Sundays, I was confused but kept quiet. I had never been in a church before and found the atmosphere very pleasing. The wooden pews weren't comfortable, but the discomfort kept me from dozing, most of the time. I never expected to find myself looking forward to Sundays, yet the organ and harmonies of the choir stirred something deep inside me. It connected me to the power of the note, and my small voice rose earnestly to join the congregation. Albert poked me with his elbow when I stood to sing. He whispered, "Sit down, Morris, and lower your voice. Don't draw attention to yourself. We're just guests here. We don't belong."

I whispered back, "But I like it; it makes me feel good inside. Why can't I sing, Albert? The only one bothered about it is you."

Albert stuck his tongue out at me and pinched my arm. I sat down. He was the older brother and knew best about these things. I didn't tell Mama about it, but the next Sunday, when I stood up and sang, Albert ignored me.

He was the best brother, Albert. He took me everywhere he went, showed me the robin's nest under the train trestle, the eel rack on the river bend. One Saturday, we walked into town and around the back of the Opera House.

He said, "You see this door, Morris? This is the musician's entrance. You wait here until I open it. You understand?" I nodded. He explained. "I have a nickel for the show. When I'm in, I'll go round backstage and say hello to Mr. Elster, the Lutheran organist. He plays piano here on Saturday. After that, I'll sneak you in. It'll be a grand adventure, but you have to keep it secret, kind of like Sherlock and Watson."

"Alright, Albert, I'll wait here. Just don't forget about me." I got in without a hitch and followed him around the maze like backstage hallways. We sat down in the Children's Section while a matron dressed in a white uniform shot us a terrifying glance. Her job was to patrol the aisle looking for rowdy boys to eject. Albert stared right back at her. He had paid for a ticket and wasn't afraid. He always thought he was a grown up, knew everything; I didn't argue, just took it as his right, being the eldest.

The gaslights were dimmed, and two colored men played ragtime music on piano and banjo. I had never heard anything like it before. The syncopated rhythms made you want to get up and dance! A tenor followed with Stephen Foster songs: "Jeanie with the Light Brown

Hair," "Oh, Susanna," and "Beautiful Dreamer!" The audience was encouraged to sing along to "My Old Kentucky Home," and I became so excited, I stood up and joined in with no shyness!

I loved the smell of the Opera House, the red velvet seats and curtain, the dramatic lighting. The pit musicians were intent on the sheet music, and the conductor was masterful Then, there were the performers and their stage makeup. It was all magic. I fell for the theater and all who had the stuff to tread the boards.

Everyday life in Chunk was hardly remarkable, except for Charles's birth. At seven, I didn't really care about babies. Albert and I ignored him altogether.

I was obsessed with a library book, "The Story of the Solar System." One night, after dinner, Papa and I sat in the yard. He listened as I pointed out the constellations.

"Look, Papa, can you see Orion, the hunter, with his bow? See stars of his belt, the Three Sisters?" Oh, what a blow-hard I must have seemed to my father, playing professor with so little background. But Papa understood a nine-year-old's need to be respected, and that's how he made me feel. He said, "Thank you, Morris, for teaching me about the stars. It's natural for a father to learn from a son; that's how the world progresses."

One morning, I found an article cut from the newspaper on the kitchen table. In Papa's hand, across the top of the page, my name was written. It was about Edouard Roche, a French scientist who described the rings of Saturn as debris of a moon destroyed by the planet's own gravity. Proudly, I brought it to school to share with my mates. The message wasn't about the gravitational pull; it was that I had a Papa who respected my intelligence. That was a testimony to his love.

Mama said, "Morris, I think you could be a scientist when you're grown. Anyone can reach their dreams in America, so aim high."

It was a nice thought, but even I knew about the Panic, that men on our street were out of work, and their families were being fed by church charities. I said, "Even if there was enough work and poor children didn't have to earn a few pennies, school is over for us by sixth or eighth grade. Mama, I don't think a poor boy, like me, can stay in school for fifteen years to become a scientist."

She replied thoughtfully, "Dear son, just keep reading books, and be a good student. You'll go as far as your potential will take you. This is America, Morris. The Panic will not last forever, and school is free and open to all. Even a poor boy can aspire to a college education."

Mama didn't know that, although I was keen on science, it could not compete with the music in my mind. The Lutheran Church's organ was not my first exposure to beautiful music. I had already heard some of the world's greatest melodies in my own home, from Mama. For as long as I could remember, she'd hummed the musical themes of Schubert or Liszt while cooking or cleaning. I suppose I heard them when she carried me in her womb.

Three months after we moved to New York, Rose was born, and Rudolf was sent to live with Auntie Rozsa. The noise and commotion of the city kept a steady beat to the music of the street, where boys harmonized to popular tunes or played instruments together in small groups on building stoops.

At P.S. 6, I learned that music was related to mathematics, its number and set theories, note pitch and tempos measured geometrically. While learning the cello, it appealed to me that mathematical science and the artistry of music were interwoven.

Albert and I walked to P.S. 6 under the Third Avenue El with two other boys from our building. Technically, we didn't live in Yorkville, "Little Germany," where the school was located, and the residents of Yorkville didn't like us walking through their streets. Many mornings, we'd hear chanting from boys walking on the other side of Third Avenue: "Jüdisches schweine!" Jewish pigs. I was a pudgy child, with no athletic bent at all, a very slow runner. The bullies never actually started a fight, but they taunted us. On the very first morning, Albert taught me how city people walk. "Morris, walk a little faster, but don't run. Stand up as tall as you can, strut with purpose, like you're on your way to an important meeting! Don't look directly at them; just keep your eyes straight ahead. Learn to use your peripheral vision. You'll find that you'll see plenty, believe me. After a while, you'll practically see in back of your own head!" He laughed and clapped me on the back. I walked the "city walk" from that day on, moving ahead briskly and making no eye contact with others.

Two years later, we moved downtown to West 10th Street. Louis was born, and because Uncle István died, Rudolf returned to the family. Auntie Rozsa came to live with us a few months later.

Rudolf was different after being away from us for so long. He still was the family entertainer, always acting a part, but he was very sad about Uncle's death. He told me, "Morris, I learned so much, and he loved me so much." I said, "I'm sorry you're so sad, Rudolf, but it's not like losing Papa; you'll get over it. And, with Auntie coming to live with us, you'll have another mother in your audience. That'll be nice, right?"

Our new apartment on West 10th was across from the piers, and he spent most of his time there, kind of adopted by the rivermen. They called him Rube, and because he refused to answer to Rudolf, all of us did the same. "Rudolf is too German anyway; Rube suits me. My name is now and forever Rube Elmer Freed!" Who was I to argue? I didn't care what name he used. If Rube made him happy, I was happy, too.

Albert quit school and found a job in a carpentry shop. He hated it, but he was earning. I figured if he was working, I should, too.

The first pennies I ever earned in my life, twenty-five cents a day, was for an after-school job keeping song sheets stocked and playing gramophone cylinders for customers in a shop on West 28th between Fifth and Sixth Avenues. Music publishers and agents populated the neighborhood. You knew you were in the music district by the sounds of songwriters peddling their tunes on cheap, tinny pianos. That was how the area got its moniker, Tin Pan Alley. I was twelve.

Anna was born the next year, Papa opened his shop, and I graduated from the eighth grade. I left the music shop on Tin Pan Alley for a chance to earn some real money.

One of Papa's customers, Max Grossberg, owned a newspaper kiosk on Broadway and 49th and offered me a job. Blessed with a strong constitution and stout body, I had no trouble slinging bundles of fifty papers tied with rope. After a few months, the muscles of my arms and chest were as developed as an eighteen-year-old; even Albert admired my physique.

There were more than a dozen daily papers published in the city, most with early and late editions, and that didn't count foreign-language papers sold to the city's immigrants.

Although I only sold in the afternoon, I had to be at Grossberg's kiosk by six in the morning, to unload trucks delivering the morning editions: *The New York Times, The New York Post, The Press, The Herald, The Tribune, The Telegram,* and *The Mail and Express.* By mid-afternoon, the trucks arrived with *The World, The Sun, The Mail and Express, The Journal,* and *The Telegram.* Grossberg also carried a small run of *The Brooklyn Daily Eagle.*

Grossberg liked me; I did my work without complaint. Once the evening papers were stacked in and around the kiosk, I paid $1.20 for a hundred papers and filled my canvas sling with twenty-five to start the day's work. Papers sold for two cents, so when the one hundred stack was sold out, I ended the day with eighty cents in my pocket. If I didn't sell out, Grossberg refunded the difference to me. That was a hard-won concession of the Newsies strike, the publishers taking back unsold papers. Selling out was hard with all the competition. There were kids as young as seven who made a few pennies scrounging already read papers and reselling them at half price.

My steady customers were taverns around Times Square. Some had piano players or small musical trios creating an atmosphere for the rummies. I'd hang around if a good combo was playing in a back corner of the place, listening to jazz, ragtime, or the New Orleans sound called the blues.

When Rube turned twelve and done with school, I brought him along to help me sell, and it was great fun working with him, he was so amusing. Once, on the corner of Broadway and 42nd, he shouted, "Come and get yer papers and listen to the greatest poem ever writ!" A born showman, he stood on an upended waste bin and, in a very loud voice, began to recite "The Boy Stood on the Burning Deck." He began acting out the story while I circulated around the gathering crowd, selling our papers. The fiery death scene was fantastic, with him falling to the sidewalk in agony as the imaginary flames consumed him! A few out-of-towners tipped me a nickel for the show, and others threw pennies at Rube. What a great day! We laughed all the way back to Grossberg's by 6:30, having sold out our papers in short order!

At home, Rube reenacted the death scene and Mama laughed and applauded.

On Mama's kitchen table, we counted out $1.27 for Mama, keeping a dime for Rube and me.

Anna's death shocked and saddened me, truly it did, except at fourteen, my world was mostly about myself and learning to play the cello. After selling papers for a year and saving every penny possible, I finally bought my first instrument, second-hand, in a store on 14th Street.

Although Albert's tutoring on the fiddle helped me with the basics, I needed to learn from a real music teacher. There was no money for that, but one day I got lucky. I told the owner of McDermott's Tavern on Eighth Avenue, where I sold papers, about my cello. Mr. McDermott introduced me to the bass player in a trio that played every weekend.

Big James had started out on cello, then picked up the big bass when he fell for jazz. He was a colored man with huge hands and splayed-out finger pads, a physical distortion peculiar to string musicians after years of pressing the filaments against the neck and fretboard. On Friday nights, around midnight, I'd meet Big James at McDermott's, and he gave me an hour of his time. In spite of the poor quality of my cheap cello, Big James taught me everything he knew about how to coax a honey-dripping voice from my instrument.

I asked Papa what to do, how to find work with some security for the future. Should I stay working for Grossberg and play cello as a hobby? Was it possible to earn a steady living as a musician? He said, "Son, you must never give up your dream. If music is your love, then pursue it. There will come a time when you will have to choose a direction, and that may take you away from the responsibilities you feel you owe the family. Don't be afraid. While you're young, you must plan for yourself, alone."

"Morris," he continued, "At fifteen, I left my family home in the mountains for Debrecen. I wanted to get an education and find my true calling. I told my Papa; *I pray I'll find my path.* He said: *Praying for a better life is all well and good, but you must make yourself ready to find prosperity.* He was right, Morris. Get yourself ready with cello lessons and practice. You must be prepared when the opportunity comes."

As I said, I had the best father in America. He was a good man, committed to his family's welfare. Even burdened with the support of all of us, he maintained an even temperament, and I cannot recall him ever raising his voice or striking any of us. We all wanted to please him, to fulfill his dreams for us. We wanted him to live a long life, surrounded in his old age by adoring grandchildren.

When Papa died, not even Mama's embrace penetrated my gloomy confusion. Only alone with my cello did I find comfort. Mama said I was like Grandmamá, too sensitive to cope with the misfortunes of life.

I was seventeen. Five years unloading trucks and selling papers for Grossberg were ended. Rube and I bid Grossberg goodbye. Rube was needed at Papa's tailor shop, and it was time for me to move on with my music. If I was to be a musician, it was time to get going with it, to establish myself in the New York music world.

The good news was Albert was already playing fiddle at the Bronx theater on weekends, so I figured I had an in.

Rube

Papa died on August 18, 1904. I was fifteen. During the Shiva, Mama told stories of how she and Papa met, their quest to gain Grandpapá Bruder's approval, and their deep love for one another. She sang songs of her childhood, songs her mother taught her. I watched her face closely and listened carefully as she described how she read great books in her little room above the kitchen, the glory in the giant tree that grew outside her window; the one under which she and Papa were married.

I heard, not for the first time, of life in Budapest without Papa, how she found work to help earn money for the passage. Albert, Morris, and I joined in the storytelling when it came to the trip to America and the reunion with Papa at Ellis Island.

"Your Papa was the best man I've ever known. He loved without shame or fear; he didn't hide behind a false manhood. He respected people's opinions, even those of little children, who he believed gained insight and intellect by observing the world around them."

She went on, "You all inherited his good traits and would do well in life if you follow his thinking. Respect others, follow your kindest instincts, and love fully, without reservation." The combination of her honest words and expression captured Mama's personality: warm, intelligent, and brave. In spite of suffering the loss of her one great love, she was optimistic and hopeful, calming all of us with her strength.

"Everything will be alright, gyermekek, children; together, we'll go forward."

Shiva is a time of remembrance, and I concentrated my thoughts on how having Samuel Freed for a father had molded me.

Born the year after he left for America, I didn't set eyes on my father until I was four-years-old. Although I still remembered bits of the trip across the ocean, especially the hurricane, I certainly do remember feeling totally confused when I met Papa at Ellis Island.

Life in Chunk was no different for me than for any very young child living anywhere. I was mostly unaware of life outside the confines of my own family. Papa worked long hours and for much of the year, seven days a week; so, I saw little of him. I learned to respect him, love him, but mostly because Mama did; I learned by her example.

When my weak heart barred me from admission to New York's schools, Mama was sure I would outgrow the condition if I lived away from the filth and stress of city life, so I went to live with Papa's sister, Auntie Rozsa, and Uncle István in Tarrytown.

Miserable, I threatened to hop a freight home as soon as I could if I were sent away. It was no use; my parents were unmoved by my pathetic countenance and dramatic warnings of escape. Papa held my hand tightly on the train ride, lest I make a break from the car at one of the stations along the route.

What began as an exile became a two-year, life-changing journey. My aunt and uncle spoke very broken English, forcing me to rediscover Hungarian. Receiving undivided attention, I enjoyed the indulgence of being an only child, a sharp contrast to the crowded field I competed with for attention on monthly visits home.

We lived in a little house one block from a weathered Hudson River pier on Division Street, where Uncle's twenty-two-foot wooden boat was moored. Moving nets, rods, reels, hooks, lines, sinkers, gaffs, fillet knives, and creel baskets to a rear-yard shed from a small storeroom next to the kitchen, he made me a bedroom. Auntie told me she scrubbed the floor, walls, and ceiling with lye soap before Uncle painted the walls a beautiful Danube blue, but the faint odor of fish still lingered!

The first thing I did each morning was look out the window above my bed to see if Uncle's vessel, The Flag of Hungary, was still afloat. It was easy to spot, the hull painted with three horizontal stripes of red, white, and green, the colors of the flag Uncle saluted. He had been a riverman all his life; first in the waters of the Danube north of Budapest, then the Hudson.

With no children of their own, I was the answer to a prayer, and the very first day, Auntie told me, "Rudolf, István and I are blessed to have you here and will do anything to make you happy. I know you'll be heartsick so far from your loving mother and father, but we are not strangers. We're blood relations. You'll be loved and provided for as if you were our own child."

I went to her, putting my arms around her shoulders. "Auntie Rozsa, I behaved so badly on the train, and now Papa's gone back and won't know I'm sorry. My nastiness was not meant to insult you, Auntie; it was to punish Mama and Papa. That was wrong." I blubbered, unable to finish my thought. She said, "You know, dear, they didn't want to send you away, but you must go to school. It was a very wonderful idea, sending you to me. I'm honored to have their trust and welcome you under our roof."

"I suppose it was because they love me," I mumbled, unconvinced. She nodded in agreement, and I cried for a few minutes, stopping only when I heard Uncle call my name. "Rudolf, come out to the yard. I want to show you how to scale and fillet the pike I caught this morning." Kissing Auntie, I ran out the door.

I entered first grade with the hicks. After a few days, I was placed with the third graders because my reading was so advanced. I was tall, but very thin, a city slicker with an immense vocabulary and a knack for telling jokes and stories. The locals gradually accepted me as a sophisticated curiosity. The neighborhood girls came around, asking me to show them how to roll strudel dough, help them with their numbers, or recite poetry. The local boys found me amusing, but in this town, a boy was judged by his proficiency in all things related to the river.

I may have been Auntie's dearest nephew, but in Uncle's heart, I was his *son*.

Arriving in Tarrytown, I viewed the Hudson River as a watery road for boats, nothing more. Uncle opened my eyes to the unseen river-world, and its complexities. He had lived on the water since he was a boy and sought to give me a great gift: his experience and knowledge.

First, he taught me to read the moving water's map: the cycle of the tides flowing upriver from its southern mouth at lower New York Bay. Then, I learned to *see* what rocks or obstructions lay on the riverbed by watching surface currents move or eddy around them. General weather conditions, like rain, snow, and wind direction, caused us to alter our course to find where the fish were hiding. Then, there were the practicalities of his self-discovered mechanical engineering principles. He was a master of improvisation, using a bit of wire to keep a motor humming or a bit of cloth to seal a fractured engine housing. I learned to tie knots, fix and maintain the engine, tar, paint, and repair damages to the hull.

I learned the tricks of casting from a rod or trolling with a dropline, baiting, and setting the hook, choosing the weight, playing the fish, gaffing, scaling, and filleting.

"Fishing is a sport between prey and predator, Rudolf. That fish knows where to hide, where my line can be cut by swimming along the jagged outcropping of an underwater rock. I know that fish wants my bait, and I'm going to make it move like it's alive. In the end, I understand the fish on the line by the way he moves; the quick jerking motion tells me of his desperation to outswim the hook or a smooth pull as he plays out the line to determine its fullest length. In the end, if the hook is well set, that fish is mine, no matter how long we dance the dance." It was like listening to poetry, he was so passionate.

He worked for the Nyack and Tarrytown Ferry Company, managing their machine shop. After school, I'd run to the wharf to ride the ferry until his shift was over. Many times, the conductor, a friend of Uncle's, let me collect fares, and sometimes tips, after entertaining passengers with stories or whistling popular songs.

Fishing with Uncle in The Flag of Hungary early one Sunday morning, a mist clung to the water and obscured the Palisades on the western shore. Our lines were set, and he was quiet. My imagination conjured up how, in an earlier time, the Tappan Indians might have canoed through the mist to confront our intrusion in their Nyack, the Tappan word for fishing place.

Uncle István broke the silence of the morning to share what he had been mulling over. "Rudolf, I am a Hungarian man. No matter how many years I live in America, I will be a Hungarian man until I die. The Hudson is a great river but not as great as the Danube. I am a Danube Riverman, Rudolf. This life, on this river, provides for us, but I will be a stranger to this place no matter how many days of life I have in store. We are who we are born to be, my boy. You may not have been born here, boy, but you will live your life as an American. I will never feel that, never really belong here."

I was only a child, but I understood he expected no response from me. Sharing the deep loss he felt leaving his homeland cemented our bond. I had been privileged to learn what was in Uncle's heart, the doubts he carried, haunting regret about choices he had made that could never be undone. The lingering doubt of an immigrant. I wondered, *did my Mama and Papa feel the same?*

During the two years I lived there, Auntie shared things with me, too. She taught me to draw in charcoal, whittle a replica of Uncle's boat from a stick, sculpt a horse head from a piece of soapstone. I sewed an apron, crocheted a doily, baked bread, cooked rabbit stew, planted and pruned rose bushes.

I was happy in Tarrytown; the pace of life was slow, and my hyperactive personality calmed in response. There was so much time to read, and I read a lot. During those two years, I read: *Don Quixote, Les Misérables, Robinson Crusoe, Gulliver's Travels, Pride and Prejudice, Frankenstein, The Three Musketeers, David Copperfield, The Scarlet Letter, Anna Karenina*, and everything *Shakespeare*, which I read aloud to Auntie.

I visited the family on the last weekend of each month and never once brought a book with me, knowing there'd be no quiet place to read in our New York apartment!

There was no concern for my welfare, a seven-year-old, self-sufficient city kid traveling alone on the New York Central. Straight from school, I walked to the station and boarded the 4:00 to Grand Central Terminal. From there, an uptown tram on the Third Avenue El to East 70th Street got me to Mama's in plenty of time for dinner at 7:30, when Papa got home from work.

A far cry from the quiet orderliness of Auntie's, Mama's household was loud and full of activity. The tap-tap-tapping sound made when Mama chopped onions on the wooden board, whose warped curvature caused it to teeter and bang against the tabletop with every cut of the knife, added to the din. Underfoot, there was Rose banging a pot with a wooden spoon or crying for attention, Charles playing make-believe under the kitchen table, Albert and Morris going in and out with friends, water running at the sink. I'd wake to the sound of diapers being scrubbed noisily on a washboard in the bathtub or late in the evening, neighbors and friends dropping in. It all was fun, but there was no place to hide.

Papa worked until six on Saturday and slept until late morning on Sunday. I can remember visits home when I never said more than, "I'm a four-star student, Papa!" when he had a moment to ask how I was doing in school.

My return to Tarrytown on Sunday's 6:00 train left little time for me to spend with Papa. The hours passed so quickly, with several conversations going on at once around the lunch table, competing for his attention. But there were times, in good weather, when we went for a walk to the East River Promenade and watched the seagulls. I'd tell him all about the Hudson and how Uncle was an expert on the waterway. "It makes me happy to know you are well, and learning so much from István, son. Keep up your schoolwork and be a good boy for my sister."

"I will, Papa. Living there is pretty good, but I'd still rather be home. When can I come home, Papa?"

"Mama and I miss you, but we're grateful to them for taking you in. I'm not going to lie; you may have to stay until you finish eighth grade. There's a possibility that you can be admitted to school if a doctor certifies your health. We'll look into it. Be patient, Rudolf." The little time with Papa each month was in stark contrast to the time spent with Uncle every single day.

At the time, I thought I had outgrown being the family clown and actor because the commotion exhausted me! Returning on Sunday evening to the calm of Auntie's house was very satisfying. I felt safe, and lucky, to return to my very own, fish-smelling room in the little house near the river.

Then, everything changed. As I did every day, I walked from school to the ferry, expecting to do whatever work was needed: sweeping the waiting area, collecting tickets. The tasks filled in a few hours, until it was time for Uncle's workday to end, Auntie's dinner waiting for us.

The boat left Tarrytown for Nyack, and I headed for the machine shop to say hello. When I opened the door, I found Uncle on the floor between the workbenches, eyes staring up at the ceiling. He was not breathing, his face a pale, blue-white. I ran for the conductor, who told me, "Rudolf, you wait at the off ramp. We'll be docking in five minutes. Open the gate to let passengers off. I'll be right back." I was in shock, too stunned to cry.

The ferry employees on the Nyack side came on board to help move Uncle to a bench. They covered him with an oilskin tarp stored in the lifeboat. Then, the ferry started its return run. Uncle's body was carried to the storage shed at the dock to await the undertaker. Fred,

Uncle's best friend, took me home and broke the news to Auntie, who collapsed on the floor.

Fred sent a Western Union to my parents. Fred's wife, Eva, and a few other women brought pots of food, loaves of bread. Eva stayed with Auntie that night.

I still had not shed a tear. When Papa arrived the next morning, the floodgates of my mind opened. The kindest man, who taught me so much, had loved me so much, was dead. I felt like I'd been stabbed in the heart with a knife.

Papa stayed for two nights, when Mama came to join him and to bring me home. I captained The Flag of Hungary to the water near the Tarrytown lighthouse, and Auntie opened the urn containing Uncle István's cremated ashes. Observing his wishes, she scattered his remains in the lesser Danube, the Hudson. Reading the mourner's Kaddish from a prayer book for English speakers, Papa's voice rang out over the choppy waters of the river that morning. Auntie and Mama cried softly, and I sobbed, sniffling noisily, my snot dripping onto the little motor.

I listened that evening while Auntie and Papa planned what was to follow. "Rozsa, you must come to live with us. There is nothing here for you, no means of support or family. As your only kin in America, I love you, and feel this is the best option." Auntie said, "Fred has offered me $500.00 for the house and boat. I told him I'd let him know."

"Everything will be alright, dear sister," my Mama said, "Leave everything in the house, just take your clothes and keepsakes and come to us; live with us."

On the way home, I stared out the train's window at the green waters of the Hudson. Would I ever see this place again? I had been so happy living with Auntie and Uncle. Papa moved to sit next to me as the train lurched, its screeching wheels negotiating the dangerous piece of curved track in the Bronx, Spuyten Duyvil. "Rudolf," Papa said, "I know you're mourning the loss of István. He was a good man and a loving uncle. You'll have the knowledge of all the things he taught you for the rest of your life. Isn't that a gift to treasure?"

"Yes, Papa," I said, "I just want to cry. Why did he have to die; he wasn't an old man?" I wiped my nose on my sleeve. Papa handed me his handkerchief. Starting to blubber, I squeaked out, "Everything can disappear in a minute."

"It's true, Rudolf, nothing is permanent. You will find a way to celebrate the life of your uncle, to be thankful for the gifts he gave you. I promise you will feel happy again, in particular, you'll be happy remembering the times you spent with István."

When I first returned to the fold, after two years away, it was strange to share a bed with my brothers again. They were glad to see me, but they were different, older. They weren't really interested in my experiences upstate, and although they said how sorry they were about Uncle, they shed no tears.

The tumult of our household was jarring, and I became very quiet, wondering if I'd ever fit in again, if anyone even cared that I had come back home. My usual sunny nature and sense of humor had been left in Tarrytown.

"Come here, gloomy Gus," Mama called to me, patting her lap. I sat down, my eyes on the floor. "Don't you think I haven't noticed your melancholy, Rudolf? Even nursing Louis and housekeeping, I see you; you're not lost in the busyness."

I squirmed in her lap; she held me close, turned my chin up to look into my eyes. "You were sent away of necessity, for your own good. Now, you've returned to us in good health, and for that I am thankful to my sister and brother-in-law for the care and love they gave you. This is the first time someone you know has died. Uncle István was a good man and loved you very much. Why, you were the son he never had, so you must take comfort knowing you made him very happy, dear boy."

Whimpering, I decided to confide my guilty secret; it was too big to hold in anymore. "Mama, I think I loved Uncle more than I love

Papa. In the five years since we came to America, Papa's been my everyday father for only three of them. For two years now, Uncle has been my everyday father, treated me with kindness, taught me so much, changed my life. I feel Papa knows I've betrayed him, and I'm frightened he won't love me anymore. Uncle was as much a father to me as Papa is; can I be forgiven for that?"

"It's alright; Papa understands. He loves you and will always love you; you are his own flesh and blood. This will all sort itself out, I promise you. Time will heal your hurt, my darling. The world will still spin around, no matter what happens in our daily life. Now, dry your eyes and find your brothers, or go to the river and say hello to the ferrymen. Tell them about all the things you learned from your uncle. You'll feel better, I know you will."

I hugged Mama for helping me recapture my place in the family, where I belonged.

Charles, at four, wasn't much of a talker and still hid behind Mama. Rose, although already showing a strong personality by bossing Charles around like a little lamb, was only two, and Louis was a newborn. After two years in exile, Albert and Morris were still my real brothers, the American-born children; another family.

I entered school with no medical exam. I guess that doctor was right, living away from the city's filth had cured my heart.

Our new apartment was one block from the Hudson, a perfect location for this river rat.

I hung about the docks at every opportunity. With stringy sinews, useless for loading cargo, I could navigate, deal with passengers' needs, hose down decks, or lubricate an engine. I soon became known on the waterfront as an experienced hand, ready to earn tips for odd jobs.

One day, a deckhand dropped a wrench overboard at pier 24. I heard, "Hey, ain't you dat skinny rube from upstate? How about you dive in and find my wrench? I'll give ya a dime if you do!" I did, and he did.

From that day on, I was called Rube. The melodramatic part of me loved that name. I could play dumb like a rube and get away with it, pretend I didn't know something, saying, "I'm just a rube from the sticks."

In all weather, men came in small crafts or on foot to fish around the piers. While living upstate, I had become a very strong swimmer; even underwater, where I could hold my breath for three minutes. So, when a fisherman's hook and line tangled or a pair of spectacles had to be retrieved, you'd hear the regulars call out, "Hey, Rube, c'mon ova heah!" I worked out the tangles for tips.

For laughs and the attention, I'd "accidently" fall off the pier and stay submerged near the pilings, causing some bumpkin mark to panic, screaming, "A boy is drowning here! Somebody help!" A crowd would gather, peering into the green-gray, dirty Hudson. I'd swim underwater out to pier's end, climb up the spikes in the piling, and stroll back toward the scene. Looking into the water, I'd say, "What's the problem?" Everyone laughed and applauded the hilarity, except the out-of-towner who had tried to save my life!

Also, there was always a coin to be earned teaching a novice to fish around the pilings or working on a Jersey-bound ferry for the afternoon. I learned bits of many languages and helped the longshoremen read English newspapers and pamphlets.

My life was tied to the river, and I daydreamed about signing onto a steamer and traveling the world. When we moved to East 14th Street, just before Anna was born, I watched the turn-of-the-century fireworks from pier 17 on the East River, and it was grand!

Then, Papa opened his shop, and I was so proud. He was an entrepreneur who had moved the family up a rung on the social ladder. My friends' fathers worked in garment center sweatshops or did manual labor.

Overwrought by Anna's death, Mama scolded me for being melodramatic, but this time, I wasn't hamming it up. That could have been me, the baby who died. I, too, was a child whose life had hung in the balance. Also, I understood the sad truth that there wasn't a family we knew who hadn't lost a child during birth or to disease.

I made friends easily, and so did my brothers. Our apartment was the gathering place on Sundays. Albert brought a fiddle home and taught me and Morris the basics. Albert told me, "Rube, I didn't expect an eleven-year-old to have a good musical ear, but you do; as good as mine, maybe better!" A year later, when Morris bought his cello, I learned to play it and preferred that string to violin forevermore. We couldn't share the instruments and play together, so I bartered with an Italian boatman: four day's work got me his beat-up mandolin.

At twelve, finished with school, I was working with Morris, hawking newspapers. Life was fun, I had no responsibilities, and the world was exciting! Baby Nora was born, and I adored her. She had such a big smile, was so smart. She knew all our names by her first birthday and sang "Yankee Doodle Dandy" in perfect pitch before she was two!

Just before Papa got sick, Grossberg talked to me about finding work in the printing line, maybe becoming a monotype operator or copy holder. I talked to Papa about it the night we went to the vaudeville show, the night he first became infected. Papa's death was gruesome.

Watching his agonies for three weeks put me into melancholy. The night he died, I collapsed on the floor outside his room. The family's world had ended. Forever more, we'd speak of our life as "before" or "after" Papa.

Grossberg paid a Shiva call. Morris told him, "Rube's got to run the tailor shop now, and I've got a few nights' work at the Crotona Theater in the Bronx, playing cello. If I'm going to make playing music my life, I'd better start doing it now. Thanks for everything, Mr. Grossberg, but we both have to quit working for you."

He said, "I understand, Morris. I'm at the kiosk if you need to come back for a while, but I do believe you'd better start right now if you're going to earn a living in music. I'm so very sorry for the death of your father and hate to lose you and Rube. You've been good Newsies, and I'll miss you."

"Mr. Grossberg, thanks for taking a chance on me. You were a good boss."

"Rube, if you decide to take my advice and set your sights on the printing line, come and see me. I've got connections."

Mama's mood was unpredictable, and I stayed out of her way so I wouldn't utter some careless word to provoke a crying jag or a sad, stony silence. I was of no use to anyone, walking around in a daze of depression. I was confused, couldn't sort out my feelings. It wasn't like the death of Uncle, which had taken away the presence of a man who talked with only me, without distraction, every single day. In truth, I hadn't spoken very much with Papa, had lived in the same house with him for only eight of the fifteen years of my life. I felt I didn't know who he was. I loved Papa and knew he loved me, too, but the loss was less personal than Uncle's had been, more about the family.

A few days after the funeral, we all gathered in the parlor. Mama explained the situation and how we were to carry on.

She and Albert took up matters of family finance. Morris and I were happy not to be burdened with this financial business, as we both were impractical, unreliable, and immature when it came to money. Mama and Albert met with Papa's suppliers and customers, who all expressed what a gentleman Papa had been, what an honorable man.

I hoped to learn custom tailoring by trial and error, which would take time. So, in the beginning, I saw myself only helping out until Albert and Morris got themselves good paying jobs. No matter how optimistic I was about the abilities I had inherited from Papa, no one could count on me being the main earner.

I reasoned I enjoyed being creative, so the idea of bringing a bolt of fabric to life as a finished suit was a challenge. Couple that with the electric machine's quality seam, and I believed I could keep the doors open, run the business in spite of my lack of training.

Six weeks after Papa died, Mama came downstairs to the shop. She brought two-week-old baby Sam, who slept soundly in a blanket-lined box under the counter.

Mama, baby Sam, and I spent the days together in that one room. She encouraged my attempts to learn the trade, and customers came in for repairs, but no orders for suiting were taken. In the end, there was no tailor in the shop. Thankfully, it didn't take long before I figured out how to do the hand-sewn blind stitching for the Brooks Brothers' piecework. After a week, I turned out twice as many as Mama did, and, if I do say so myself, my stitches were perfect.

Even Papa would have said that.

15

New York City's first publicly supported House of Correction, Workhouse, and Poorhouse opened in 1736, and the first general hospital providing medical aid to the poor in 1791.

In the 19th Century, both private and religious-affiliated organizations responded to the squalid living conditions of the city's poor. The Charity Organization of Society, The Home for the Friendless, The Children's Aid Society, The Randall's Island Orphan Asylum, the Orphan Asylum Society, and the Society for the Reformation of Juvenile Delinquents established refuges for the orphans and half-orphans, those with a single living parent unable to provide for their welfare. The New York City Lunatic Asylum on Blackwell's Island (now called Roosevelt Island) opened in 1839. It was the first municipal mental hospital in the United States.

In 1847, New York State established The Commissioners of Emigration, an agency to oversee and address the care of needy immigrants. Fifty years later, The State Board of Charities supervised and inspected all public and private facilities receiving state aid, except those overseen by the Commissions in Lunacy and the Prisons.

Aside from religious institutions, there were societies or brotherhoods representing every immigrant's country of origin. These organizations served as a bridge between the old and new worlds, where native tongue was understood, a burial place could be arranged, advice and camaraderie were offered, and referral to municipal and state agencies was facilitated.

For babies and children from newborn to five years of age, the primary places of shelter were The New York Infant Asylum, The Hebrew

Infant Asylum, and the Catholic Sisters of Charity's Foundling Hospital. The facilities received public funds and were overseen by the State Bureau of Dependent Children. At the end of each month, the asylums submitted census reports to collect their subsidies from the city: thirty-eight cents per day for each child less than two years of age, and two dollars a week for those between two and five.

The Hebrew Benevolent Society was organized in 1822 to ease conditions for the destitute among the eighty thousand Jewish souls living in New York City. In 1853, the group opened the Jews' Hospital, later renamed Mount Sinai. An orphan asylum didn't become a reality until seven years later, when the state legislature authorized the Common Council of the City of New York to grant public funds for the purchase of a parcel of land at East 77th Street near Third Avenue, upon which the first shelter for Jewish orphans and half-orphans between the ages of five and sixteen was constructed. Another facility was built in Brooklyn in 1878.

The Hebrew Benevolent Society paid an Irish farmer $138,465.00 for his land at what would become Amsterdam Avenue between 136th and 138th Streets. The facility built on this parcel, The Hebrew Orphan's Asylum, was originally designed to hold six hundred inmates. Eventually, it would accommodate one thousand seven hundred.

The institution was completely independent. It produced its own electricity, provided central heating and indoor plumbing, and maintained a laundry, bakery, and kitchen. There were six dormitories, two dining halls, numerous storerooms, an assembly hall, reception areas, administrative offices, classrooms, a library, two swimming pools, and a synagogue.

Opening in August 1884, with three hundred seventy children, the Amsterdam Avenue HOA closed its doors in 1941.

From its beginning in 1860, on East 77th Street, The Hebrew Orphan Asylum fulfilled its mission for eighty-one years, providing shelter for more than thirty thousand children.

Fannie

Grieving or collapsing into the depths of melancholia were indulgences unavailable to a widow with eight children. When Shiva ended, I gathered my strength to present a strong and competent mother, fully in control of her world. The children were deep in shock and desperately needed to be both comforted and *called upon* to participate in the family's survival. I was alright: we were alright. We would stand up and carry on, with the help of the eldest sons, there would be food on the table and a roof over our heads.

The older ones, Albert, Morris, Rudolf, and even ten-year-old Charles, were mature enough to understand that with the shop rudderless, we had no means of support, no money to rely upon. Albert and Morris were working and would continue to do so. Rube agreed to keep the shop open, with my help, of course. "We'll make a go of it, Mama. How hard can it be to use the machine to sew a straight line?"

Charles, still in school, would need to find a way to add something to the table. Rose, in third grade, offered to take care of the laundry and help with meal preparation and caring for the younger children. Louis, six, and four-year-old Nora, were only peripherally aware that something very important had happened, that Papa was gone from us, but they were in no panic, showed no anxiety. The simple truth is: the Mama is the center of little children's lives, and I was clearly still with them. Of course, baby Sam needed only my breast to remain blissfully unaware of the catastrophe into which he had been born.

I had never been a woman whose attention was drawn to fashion's whims and trends. I am an ordinary woman, blessed with a personality and intellect well suited for the responsibilities of my gender: birthing and nurturing, maintaining a nest, and teaching life's lessons to my offspring.

There had been no income for the weeks prior to Samuel's death. When removing his clothes, I discovered $20.00 in a box in his underwear drawer, a precious gift from the beyond, I called it. That $20.00 tided me over until the first of October, when the New York Life Insurance agent came to hand-deliver the $450.00 settlement.

The sum kept the rent paid on our flat and the shop for the next eighteen months. Surely, the four of us could earn $15.00 a week among us to buy groceries and pay the electric bill.

Before Thanksgiving, Brooks Brothers terminated our relationship. I couldn't blame them. In almost three months, Rudolf and I had completed only thirty linings.

The winter was brutal, with temperatures remaining below freezing for the first three months of 1905. By the end of February, almost fifty inches of snow had fallen, making Eleventh Avenue barely passable, the dirty snow piled high at the curb and against the building.

Carrying the blanket-wrapped Sam under my shawl, I made my way to the shop door. Nora straddled Rudolf's hip, and he held my waist to steady me. His sure-footed grace reminded me of the agility he'd demonstrated climbing down from the top bunk during the hurricane on the Atlantic so long ago.

"Mama, I'm thinking of having a sale on the wool suiting fabric. There's no point in having it collect dust on the shelf, right? I wrote to Stark and Son to see if they're interested in buying it back for $20.00. If not, I'll cut it up into three-yard lengths and offer it to our customers. What do you think?"

"Rudolf, my darling, you want to have some fabric on hand, just in case. But, maybe see if Malik, the tailor on 45th Street, is interested. Take a walk over there today. Couldn't hurt to have an extra $20.00." He went that day; Malik wasn't interested. It was winter, slow season.

Rube sewed a rag doll for Nora from scraps. "Nora, baby girl, isn't she beautiful? How about we use two black buttons for her eyes and call her Little Nora?" Like his father, he respected children's intelligence; he liked them, and they loved him.

Rudolf was not a tailor; he couldn't design, fit, or sew a suit of clothes. Repairs and hems brought in about $4.00 a week, so on Sunday and Monday, when the tailor shop was closed, Rube went back to Grossberg and earned $3.00.

Albert was bringing home about $6.00 from both jobs: the carpentry and the Crotona. Morris played cello there, too, but the position was not steady. He went back to lugging newspapers for Grossberg, too. All told, he earned $5.00 a week, most weeks. I insisted the boys keep a dollar or two for carfare and have some spending money in their pocket. After all, they were young men, entitled to a little independence, weren't they?

In total, our income was about $60.00 a month. Rents were $28.00, which left less than $10.00 a week for food.

Then, there was Charles. Occasionally, he added a dollar or two, telling me he delivered messages for a "guy in a club" on the lower East Side. I worried he had fallen in with Russian-Jewish gangs from First Avenue, the money ill-gotten.

"What do they want with you, Charles? How do you know them? What do you do for them? Why don't they hire their own kind? You're a native-born American, not a greenhorn Slav!"

Charles curled his lip. "Mama don't be such a snob. The Russians are smart businessmen, and they like that I'm not related to any of their kin or competitors. They trust me because I don't speak or understand Russian, and I know how to keep my mouth shut, stay out of trouble. I just deliver envelopes once a week to a guy on Pier 15."

I asked, "But, Charles, what business are they in?"

"Never mind, Mama, their money is green, and we need it."

I stopped arguing. What was the point? I was grateful he was still in school and prayed he'd stay there until he was twelve, at least finishing eighth grade.

I was exhausted, nursing little Sam, helping Rudolf in the shop, caring for the house, and worrying about money. The winter season dragged by with hardly a ray of sunshine penetrating the grey skies.

Midafternoon, I'd make my way upstairs to prepare dinner. Rudolf kept the shop open until 6:30, Tuesday through Saturday, although for many days, the little bell on the shop door never tinkled, not once. There were a few weeks when our income was only two dollars!

But I will say there were good days, too. Spending time in the shop kept me engaged with the outside world, gave me an opportunity to converse with customers and neighbors. Some, with no tailoring needs, dropped by just to say hello, and that kept my spirits up. A piece of strudel, a well wish, sharing a laugh or bringing a jar of homemade soup; these kindnesses sustained my hopes for better days. I almost convinced myself it was possible to make things work, to support the family this way.

In April 1906, almost two years after Samuel died, when the insurance money ran out, I began receiving $17.00 a month relief from the Hebrew Benevolent Society.

Falling behind on the rents, the landlord came to see me.

"Mrs. Freed, I'm so sorry for your trouble. I haven't given you an increase since Samuel died; I know you're struggling to make ends meet. I can't continue extending credit on the rent. I have expenses to pay, too. I have another tenant ready to move in, a shoemaker, who wants both the shop and the apartment. But here's what I'll do: if you can pay half the rent on both the apartment and the shop, $14.00, I'll let you stay for another three months. Then, if you can't afford it, the leases are up. And you've got to pay by the fifth of the month. You understand, Mrs. Freed, $14.00 a month for May, June, and July. I can't do more than that. I'm so very sorry."

I understood he wasn't running a charity. I nodded and kept from crying. "Thank you for everything, Mr. Stein. Rudolf and I can't make a go of the shop. Tell your shoemaker he can open his business right away. If you can give me until the end of the month to find a place, I'd be grateful.

"To be honest, we don't need six rooms anymore. Beginning this week, I'll be getting relief from the Benevolent Society, and I'm only eligible if there are no earners at home, so the three eldest boys are moving elsewhere. Albert and Morris are already renting out a bedroom on Mott Avenue up in the Bronx. They're working part time at the theater and the carpentry and music store. Rudolf's boss, Grossberg, from the newspaper kiosk, is letting him sleep in the kiosk. It's small, but there's even a toilet and sink in there. He has no place to keep his clothing there, so that's still here, and he comes home to bathe, but Rudolf is making do with it for now! Oh, and Mr. Stein, I'm also applying for relief from the Bureau of Dependent Children. If I get that, then I'll be alright."

Rudolf said, "Grossberg really went out on a limb for me with Hymie Bloom, his cousin's husband. Hymie is the foreman of McCauley's Publishing on Worth Street. Anyway, he talked up how good I am with boat engines and sewing machines and begged Hymie to take a chance on a really smart kid who needs a break. So, Mama, for $5.00 a week, I'm a maintenance man, but after I prove myself, maybe I'll start operating the type machines. Sleeping in the kiosk is pretty comfortable and doesn't cost a penny! I'll do it until I can afford better, making enough to rent a bedroom someplace. You can count on $2.00 every week, Mama. When I make more, I'll give you more. Isn't it wonderful?"

Two weeks later, I moved to a second-floor, two-room, apartment on 102nd Street and Second Avenue. It was a small place, with only room for the necessities. Mr. Stein let me store our belongings in his basement.

The parlor faced Second Avenue, and there was cross-ventilation from the air shaft window in the kitchen. The toilet was down the hall, shared with two other families. A chest of drawers served as an end table near the upholstered chair that had been Samuel's most comfortable place in happier times. Our kitchen table and chairs crowded the floor next to a bathtub with a board covering the top. There was a small icebox and gas stove. Two mattresses leaned upright against the wall in the parlor, to be laid flat on the floor at bedtime. Charles, Rose, Louis, Nora, Sam, and I shared those mattresses.

The "Society" sent an evaluator to review my situation. When she saw the mattresses and my five children, it wasn't difficult to approve assistance. They granted me relief of $10.00 a month which covered the rent with $1.00 to spare. In total, my monthly income was $27.00.

Albert and Morris, clearing $8.00 a week, brought me half of that each Sunday. Add Rudolf's $3.00. and, all told, after rent, I squeaked by on about $46.00 a month, $11.50 a week to pay for food, electric, gas, and sundries for six of us. We were as low as we could get, or so I thought.

I had no choice but to register Charles, Rose, Louis, and Nora at the Benevolent Society's Hebrew Orphan Asylum. I wanted to be ready when the day came that I could no longer provide for them, poor darlings. They knew nothing of my trip to the Asylum. I didn't believe that information would serve any useful purpose until the action was necessary. Why cause the children worry?

The Asylum was on Amsterdam Avenue and 136th Street. If need be, the children could remain there until they were sixteen, but I would never let that happen. NEVER!

Sam was only two, so he would have to go to the Infant Asylum on East 61st Street. If things hadn't turned around by the time he was five, God forbid, he'd become eligible to join his siblings uptown.

Although I registered Charles and Rose, in my heart of hearts, I felt that at twelve and ten, they could remain with me, no matter what. I signed them up in case something happened where they'd be out on the streets…in case I died. As long as I was healthy, they were perfectly capable of taking care of themselves while I worked if I could find work.

The littlest ones, well, that was where the heartbreak was. Louis and Nora occupied their own small-child world, unconnected to our daily difficulties. Sam was sweet and, as expected, trusted me, just like Anna had in her last days. I will never forget how she looked into my eyes, pleading with me to keep her alive. Never, if I live to be one hundred, will I ever forget the look of betrayal I received from that doomed child. I am the Mama, all-knowing, all-giving, the kiss-and-make-it-better Mama. Is it possible for a child to survive a mother's abandonment? My Sam was so little, only two. He was oblivious to the dire circumstances of the family and his imminent separation from me.

In January 1907, I slipped on a cobblestone while crossing Second Avenue, and was hit and dragged along by a streetcar. An ambulance from the German Hospital on 77th Street responded.

I never lost consciousness, in spite of having struck my head hard on the pavement. There were abrasions and scrapes all along my left side, but, fortunately, no bones were broken. Released with instructions to rest and cleanse the wounds, I made my way home. My head throbbed, and a hot, stabbing pain radiated from left hip to shin with each step. There was no money for a cab, so the thirty-block walk was terribly difficult, stumbling on piles of dirty snow and ice along the way.

For several days, I took to my bed, dosed with aspirin tablets given me at the hospital dispensary, and relied on Rose to run the house.

For three days under the covers, I was very low, waking each morning to a bleak sameness, with only one thought: will I feed my children today? There was no one with whom to talk or share the crushing responsibilities of my life. I missed Samuel: his touch, his gentle humor, his loving, his guidance. At forty-five, living on the dole, I was adrift and exhausted. My life had fallen apart. I was widowed, physically disabled (albeit temporarily) with neither trade nor skill, and the sole support for five children less than thirteen years of age.

I was convinced a broken bone had been overlooked by the doctors. My leg and hip pained me for many months, and a slight but permanent limp remained. Also, I was stone deaf in my right ear, an affliction I had noticed coming on.

On April 25th, I received an eviction notice. Near emotional collapse, the very next day, I surrendered Sam to the nurses at the Infant Asylum on 61st Street.

Two weeks later, we moved to two rooms on East 100th Street off Third Avenue. In exchange for rent, I mopped stairwells and hallways, kept trash from accumulating at the stoop, distributed rat poison around the basement and rear doors. Given my physical condition, it soon became obvious I was unable to perform the tasks. Evicted five months later, we moved to a building on East 102nd Street.

From September on, I received relief of $18.00 a month from the Bureau of Dependent Children. I took in washing at that location, earning about $2.00 a week.

Altogether, with relief, laundry earnings, and what the boys managed to spare, I was able to keep afloat until February 1908, when we were again evicted for nonpayment of rent.

In all honesty, during those months, I became inured to always being pennies from complete ruin.

When we had a few dollars, it seemed we were generous in a way only those always on the verge of insolvency can be, sharing our table with neighbors, even lending a few pennies to help them get through the week. After a while, you accept that day follows night without any of your help or design, and *somehow* you keep going for another day.

Every Sunday, when the boys visited, they brought whatever cash they could spare and groceries for dinner. Those gatherings reminded me of Samuel's family in Tolcsva, joyful and interesting, a welcome distraction from our situation.

You'd have thought we were living on easy street if you had been there. Meals were consumed with gusto, and everyone talked at once. Conversation might have been about the latest in fashion: wavy hair and broad-brimmed hats, or high-waisted, narrow, ankle-length skirts. At one point in the evening, Morris might sing out a popular tune, "Cuddle Up a Little Closer, Lovey Mine," his tenor voice still so pure and lovely. Then, the discussion turned to the Brooklyn racetracks at Gravesend, Sheepshead Bay, and Brighton Beach! The reformers and politicians, with Governor Hughes leading the fight, wanted to pass strict anti gambling laws. The boys argued that betting was good for the state, bringing in all that money. I was a bit perturbed, given our circumstance, to learn they were frequenting the tracks, gambling on the horses.

Albert brought me a few dollars each Monday. He was twenty-two. How I hoped he'd find a nice girl and begin his life; he had been preoccupied with my welfare for too long.

Having no sponsor or money to grease the right palms, Morris was down-in-the-dumps about how the New York musicians and industry policy kept a tight circle, a closed shop. Without telling anyone, I started saving a few pennies in a mason jar, earmarked for an Atlantic City train ticket for my dear Morris.

Rudolf let us know he had filled in for an absent copyholder, giving him hope for advancement from machine maintenance and typesetting to a steady white-collar position at a desk!

Charles came by on the weekend to bring a dollar or two but lived elsewhere, I didn't know with whom. Occasionally, he brought home a few groceries.

Rose, at eleven, was taller than all the boys in her class. She was of solid build, with strong hands and a regal carriage. At school and on the block, her forceful personality took center stage. Although she didn't take direction well, if so inclined, she was capable of excelling at school. Even so, she put forth little academic effort and intimidated the teachers with her sharp mind and tongue.

Louis's quiet demeanor obscured his strengths; he would not be unsettled by bullies and was a fine student and loving child.

Five-year-old Nora, outgoing and always singing, continued to amaze all the musicians in the family, who used her vocals to tune their instruments.

Saturdays with Sam were unbearable for both of us. He wrapped his arms around my neck and wouldn't let go for the whole of the two-hour visit. Farewells were moments of stark terror for the child. "Mama, Mama...please don't go. Mama, take me home." His cries haunted me, breaking my heart again and again.

This was not the life I had envisioned, and my disappointment and guilt were excruciating. For the most part, though, I managed a strong front for the children's sake. They suffered enough on their own and didn't need an hysterical mother burdening them with her inadequacies and helplessness. I smiled, hugged, and kissed them. I told them I loved them with all my heart and would always make sure they were safe and healthy and not hungry.

The times were hard, harder than I can retell. Living on the edge, uncertain of the next day's meal, was a cruel reality.

In January 1908, we lived on East 102nd Street for a few months before being dispossessed again; then Rose, Louis, Nora, and I moved to 106th Street. It was a one-room storefront with a storeroom and toilet in the rear, where I kept the mattresses during the day.

Equipped with a very small stove, sink, and icebox, the room was large enough for the kitchen set, Samuel's upholstered chair, and an end table and lamp. From the basement on Eleventh Avenue, Albert retrieved the oak stand he had constructed for the tailor shop so I could begin offering dressmaking services. On strong white paperboard, Rudolf lettered a sign for the window: "Mrs. Fannie Freed, Dressmaker." I was living in one room, four of us in one room.

Two years had passed since moving out of the building in which Samuel had died. During that time, I retrieved a few of the things stored in the basement. Mr. Stein had been very kind, but few of our possessions remained. Gone was a chifforobe filled with dresses, a cedar chest with sweaters and shirts, a box of shoes, a settee. Of course, I couldn't say who had stolen the worthless articles, but it was hurtful to think neighbors we knew would do that to us, have no compassion for our situation.

By this time, after being evicted five times, there were no belongings in the basement, and all I had in the apartment was Samuel's chair, two dressers, the kitchen set, two lamps, and a chairside table. In the flotsam of a lifetime, no matter how dire the circumstance, necessities moved with the tide: bed linen, pots and pans, some dinnerware, a winter coat, a broom, mop, and bucket. Particular sentimental attachments were never misplaced: photos, one of Mama's framed landscapes and a doily she had crocheted, a few books, a box of tin soldiers.

In the chaos of loading boxes onto carts and hand trucks when moving from one place to another, I did manage to add to our inventory: the two mattresses had been scrapped, replaced with three folding cots and a small settee salvaged from curbside discards set out by a family being dispossessed next door. Always with me, even in the one-room flat, were Samuel's sewing machine, a pair of scissors, needles, thread, and remnants of fabric. Deep in my heart, I still believed these legacies might save my family, provide the means to bring my baby home. They were not items with which to be careless.

Yes, 1908 was a very trying year.

Albert, with chronic lung problems since his days in the carpentry shop, was out of work for most of the winter. Morris, although a working cellist in Atlantic City, was just barely paying his own bills and couldn't send anything. The print shops, in fierce competition, were engaged in a price war, causing Rudolf to be laid off for lack of work.

In June, at rock bottom, I met with an administrator at the Hebrew Orphan Asylum.

"I am compelled to break up my home, no longer able to manage. Even with the relief grant, I can't keep the family alive."

The woman, Mrs. Sattler, said, "Mrs. Freed, I understand. We'll take care of Louis and Nora, give you a chance to get back on your feet."

She went on, "You cannot go on this way, with barely any food in the house and constant worry. I wish I could persuade you to admit Rose as well."

"Thank you, but there's no need for that; she's self-sufficient, and I need to have her with me."

"It's alright, Mrs. Freed. If you change your mind, she is always eligible until she's sixteen! Visiting is from noon to three on the first Sunday of January, April, July, and September."

"Please Madam, can't I visit every week as I do at the Infant Asylum? It's cruel to separate the children from me for three months!"

She touched my forearm kindly, "With over eight hundred children in residence, we simply can't have visiting every week; it just gets too unmanageable. Ninety percent, like your children, are half-orphans, with at least one, sometimes two, parents. Where would we put two thousand people on a Sunday afternoon? For that reason, only one visitor per inmate is permitted; and please don't bring sweets. The diet is carefully prepared; we don't want the children getting upset stomachs. I'm sure you understand. Visiting is very disruptive to the routine; a once every three months, one-visitor policy will have to suffice."

I was very unhappy to hear that. "But Nora is only six. She needs to know she's not been abandoned. She needs her mother." I began to cry. The weight of the commitment bore down on me, defeating my spirit. "At least she'll see Louis..."

"I'm sorry, Mrs. Freed. There are rules. Boys and girls don't interact in the building. There's just too big a population here, impossible to control if everyone could roam all over the place. You understand, don't you? The safety and well-being of the children is our main concern. This is not a prison, but it *is* an institution, run by rules in place for good reason."

I wept with tears of shame and grief, but also with thanks for the respite these charitable people were offering me.

"Your children will be safe, secure, and well-fed, Mrs. Freed. Although your heart will be aching, you will not have to worry about putting bread on the table."

There was no other way; I signed the commitment papers.

"Tomorrow, around noon, a social worker will come for the children. They don't have to pack anything, as we'll provide everything they'll need, even toothbrushes."

I waited for a streetcar on the opposite corner. The enormous Renaissance structure that was the Asylum dwarfed the neighborhood buildings and blocked the sky. An iron fence girded the complex, keeping the world out and almost a thousand children in. The place was as far from home as a child could be, but I had no choice. I was destitute, and this place rescued my children from the streets.

In the morning, I prepared a breakfast of oatmeal with raisins and warm milk. I watched Louis and Nora closely, to imprint in my mind their every expression, freckle, and eyelash. I washed the dishes; the children ran off to play on the building's stoop.

Later, I called, "Come inside, Louis."

The boy gave his ball to Rose and made his way down the stairs to the storefront entrance. Nora, playing with her rag doll, remained on the stoop with Rose.

"Come sit on my lap, dear."

"Yes, Mama."

"I know you understand that we're in a bad way, with very little money to pay our bills."

"Yes, Mama."

"It was the hardest thing I've ever done, bringing Sam to the Asylum, but I couldn't care for him and find work. He's safe and fed there for the time being."

"I know it was hard, Mama." The boy leaned his head on my bosom, whimpering quietly, tears beginning to run down his cheeks.

I continued, "My darling, we've been receiving relief from the Hebrew Asylum, and I visited their place yesterday. It's a big house where children like you and Nora live all together until their Mamas can bring them home again. I have no choice. Please try to understand I can't keep you and Nora with me right now."

"Yes, Mama," he wept. "Like it was with little Sam."

Wiping his nose with my hanky, then kissing his cheeks, I held him close to me, whispering, "I promise it will only be for a short while; until I have steady work and your brother's regular employ. It's for the good of the whole family."

My bodice was soaked with his tears. His words came in gasps. "I don't want to go, Mama. Please, I'll be good."

"You are a good boy, Louis, a very good boy. You've done nothing to make this happen. It's not your fault. With Papa gone, I can't care for the family. I love you so, Louis, my darling. If there was any other way, I wouldn't do this."

"Mama, please."

"I'll write to you every week and visit when it's allowed. I'll never miss the chance to see you, Louis. Don't forget I love you."

"Yes, Mama."

"Please bring Nora to me, so I can explain it to her."

"Mama, she's so little. She'll be so scared. Please, Mama. I'll go, but keep Nora home."

I shook my head slowly. "There's no other way, Louis."

He went to the stoop and led Nora inside.

Clutching her dolly, she sat to my right on the settee, Louis on my left. She looked up at me, like Anna had done, so trusting. Although I knew she wouldn't fully understand what my words meant; she listened, and I spoke.

"Nora, my darling, tomorrow, a nice lady is coming here. You and Louis will go with her on a trip to a house where many children live all together."

She was frightened, her eyes wide open, darting back and forth between my face and Louis's, her lips quivering.

"You'll go to school there, and I'll visit as much as I can. And, you'll come home soon."

She repeated, "We'll come home soon, right, Mama?"

I held her close. "Yes, my darling. I promise we'll celebrate with paprikash and strudel when you come home."

She reached for Louis' hand and started to cry. "And Louis will be with me, right, Mama?"

"Yes, my darling. Louis will be with you, and I'll visit as often as I can."

Louis said, "It's alright, Nora. It'll be fun. Lots of new friends. You'll play with so many new friends. And you can bring Little Nora. It'll be an adventure."

Nora smiled at Louis, then looked up at me. "Alright, Mama. Louis and I will be alright."

At noontime, on Wednesday, July 8, 1908, the social worker came to fetch my children. She was accompanied by a boy of about sixteen.

"My name is Ann Rubin, and this is Harry. He's a monitor in the administration office and helps me bring new admissions to Amsterdam Avenue. I was a resident at the HOA when I was your age, Nora, and I'll see you every day because I teach at the school you'll be going to!"

Nora smiled, "Do I call you Miss Rubin?"

"Ann is fine. Now, let's get your dolly and get ready for our big trip." She turned to Louis. "Are you all set, big man? It's a little confusing right now, but you'll settle in in no time at all. There's always a lot of things going on, and you'll make new friends."

Before they left, I called Rose to come in and say goodbye. She was despondent, crying so hard her face was red and puffy, hardly recognizable.

She hugged her brother and sister, unable to speak a word.

Nora and Louis just stared at Rose's face, and when they saw her devastation, they became frightened.

"Are you sure we have to go, Mama?"

"Yes, Louis, my darling, but it won't be for very long. I'll do my best to bring us all back together."

"But, Mama, will Rose be alright?"

I laughed, "She will be alright. She'll write to you very often. Right, Rose?"

To which Rose, still unable to speak, answered with a vigorous nodding of her head, tears streaming down her face.

1909 brought better days.

In the spring, Charles joined Rose, Sam, and me in a four-room apartment on Park Avenue near 112th Street; rent, $13.00.

United Hebrew Charities granted me relief of $11.00 a month, only $2.00 shy of my rent.

By the summer, most weeks I earned $4.00 working as a charwoman for the landlord and providing dressmaking services to the neighborhood women. The setup was ideal, as I was at home to care for Sam, who began Kindergarten in September. Rose was thirteen, attending high school on First Avenue and earning $2.00 working as a coat model in the garment center on Saturday.

Rudolf was a copyholder at Prendergast Printing on West 24th Street. He lived at a boarding house on East 12th and gave me $15.00 a month. Morris sent $5.00 by Western Union from Atlantic City. Albert was struggling to live on his own and couldn't spare anything. Charles contributed $3.00 a week, earned working at a grocery store. So he said. My total income: $58.00 a month. After rent, gas, and electric, that left almost $10.00 a week to buy food and sundries.

After a year, Louis and Nora returned home, and that first evening was one we all would remember, with kisses and squeals of delight. I prepared paprikash and strudel, as promised.

The disastrous decade ended with the family having survived every heartbreak and deprivation. In April 1910, the census taker recorded us—everyone but Morris—all together, living on East 119th Street.

And for all that, life was good. There was no point in dwelling on the hardships.

Louis

Beginning when Mama was hit by the streetcar, I was scared she would die. She worked hard to keep the building clean and also take care of Sam. In the end, it was just too hard, so he was sent to the Infant Asylum.

Four months later, put out by the landlord, we moved; and Mama took in washing. She tried to keep us and, finally, all worn out, one day she explained why Nora and I had to go away for a while. She said *it was in the best interests of the whole family.* There would be no worries about our having enough to eat, she would visit and write. It was only until she figured out how to improve our situation.

A woman and a teenage HOA inmate came to our apartment. and Mama hugged and kissed us goodbye. My brothers were out of the house, but Rose was home. She cried so hard, her face so swollen and red, I hardly recognized her. Neither Nora nor I really understood what had happened to cause us to be sent away. We had been happy and didn't know how bad things were. The worst part of that day was that we had no idea what was in store for us. I brought one thing with me, a photo of Mama. Nothing else, no clothing, books, or toys. All Nora brought, all she had, was the rag doll Rube had made for her after Papa died. She loved that dolly so much.

I'll never forget walking through the iron gate, holding tight to Nora's hand. We shuffled toward the heavy doors, passing from one world to another. The noises of the city and the hot air on Amsterdam Avenue gave way to the cool stillness of the high-ceilinged reception hall. Far-off voices and a few footfalls reverberated along the stone floor, adding to the other worldliness of the interior.

We sat on a wooden bench in the office; a woman wrote in a book. Nora's dark eyes searched the faces of everyone coming through the door, but there was no one familiar there.

After a while, a girl of fourteen or fifteen came for Nora. Always social, she stood up tall and smiled. The girl smiled back, "My name is Rachel. I'm going to take you to the dormitory and show you everything. Don't be afraid, Nora. I've been here since I was younger than you are, and I'm happy. You'll see; the HOA is a good place." After a minute, she said, "Say goodbye to your brother, and let's go."

I said, "Try not to worry, Nora. I'm living here, too. Everything will be alright." We hugged each other, but she only smiled at me; didn't speak. I think she was in some kind of shock. I couldn't help crying as she disappeared from view down the dark corridor.

Bernie introduced himself as a monitor and told me to follow him. There were two infirmary wards on the fourth floor of the main wing, one for boys, one for girls. Dr. Jacobi visited the institution every day.

In the infirmary, a nurse examined me. I was vaccinated and given an eye test. "Welcome to HOA, Louis. You're a healthy ten-year-old, and I expect you'll thrive here. The monitor will bring you to the dormitory now. Good luck."

First, Bernie showed me the bathroom. There were urinals and five toilet seats without any privacy surround, installed along one wall. You pulled down the toilet seat and sat on it; your body weight holding the seat in place while you had your movement. When you stood up, releasing the seat, it popped up against the wall, activating the flushing mechanism. I was amazed by the simple precision of the system yet wondered if I'd get used to crapping in plain sight of everyone. On the western wall, from one end to the other, wall mirrors hung over long, metal water troughs with many spigots. Toothbrushes were kept in wall-hung, numbered cubbies; mine was 4332. At the door to the dormitory, bewildered and frightened, I started to cry, and vomited on the floor.

"Ugh! You're disgusting, Louis. Now, you're gonna clean that up; I'll show you where the utility closet is. Follow me."

Embarrassed and sad, I followed silently.

"Take a mop and bucket." I did. "Go to the bathroom and fill the bucket with water, then come back to your puke spot."

"I can't carry the filled bucket, Bernie. It's too heavy. Can you help me?"

"You're a real baby, Freed. I hope you ain't gonna be a pain in the tuchas for the rest of the time you're here."

He groused at me but did carry the bucket to the spot, where I mopped up the puke. Rinsing the heavy mop was almost impossible, given my small hands, so I kind of pushed the glop around with it and asked Bernie to help me lift it into the water. He leaned against the wall and laughed at me. "Are ya kiddin'? That's disgusting." Lucky for me, at that moment, a janitor appeared from nowhere and said, "Get out of here, both of you. You should have called me right away; you made the mess worse. Now, beat it!"

I said, "Thanks, mister." He sent me a dirty look.

Running to catch up with Bernie in the dormitory, I was fascinated with the ingenuity. It was a large, open room with no decoration. Beds were arranged in rows, so that at one glance, every inmate could be seen by the monitors. The iron bedsteads had hooks on the head rail and a retractable shelf under the cot could be pulled out and used as a seat for dressing.

The cot I was assigned was unmade, but my inmate items were stacked up on the springs. A cup and toothbrush, two towels, two sheets, one pillowcase, two blankets, one pillow, two piles of clothes, and a pair of black ankle-length, laced boots.

"Hang your towel on one of the hooks on the bedstead." Gesturing to a stack of clothes, Bernie continued, "Put on this uniform; let's see if it fits."

I took off my clothes, folding them neatly. The school-day uniform was a single-breasted jacket made of slate-colored Kentucky jeans cloth, a white collarless shirt, knee pants, white stockings, and the black boots. There also was a large red, white, and blue handkerchief. I hated how I looked, hated how the coarse fabric felt against my skin.

I couldn't button the jacket; it was too tight across my belly, as were the pants. Luckily, the boots were only a little big.

"The pants and jacket are too small."

Bernie looked me up and down. "You're a fatty, Lou-Lou. I bet you're a really slow runner, too." I didn't answer him. "Don't worry about it; I'll tell the dorm counselor, Florence. She'll get you the right size or let out the seams. You're lucky. Girl dorm counselors are a new thing for the HOA. The big shots think girls are more 'mama-like,' so the softies, like you, won't be so homesick."

The second stack of clothes was for Sabbath, whatever that was. Another ill-fitting suit, this one blue with a double-breasted jacket, short pants, and a white, collared shirt. The finishing touch was black stockings held up by garters. So dumb looking. Well, I guessed it was like joining the army; you gotta wear a uniform.

"You can try on the Sabbath clothes later, Lou-Lou. Might as well do it for Florence, so she can figure out how to make it fit. For now, put all the clothes on the pull-out shelf and put one of the blankets over the springs. Then cover that with a sheet. Then a blanket and another sheet. Put the pillowcase on the pillow, and you're ready for tonight! Now, take off all your clothes, wrap the towel around you, and follow me."

Next, I had to take a tub bath with Bernie right there, which embarrassed me but didn't faze him one bit. "Don't forget to wash your tuchas and your petzel, Lou-Lou," he taunted.

Privacy of any kind was of no importance at the HOA. Everything was open and public, even toilet use. I dressed in the regular uniform, even though I couldn't button the pants or jacket. I felt a buffoon, certain I looked like a clown wearing ill-fitting clothes. It was humiliating. Mama would have been so angry, would have fixed it. I was so unhappy. I felt hot tears stabbing at my eyes but couldn't, wouldn't, give Bernie an opportunity to ridicule me again, so I got control of myself.

"Morning bell rings at 5:45; that gives you an hour to wash, dress, and prepare for breakfast." I was too cautious to ask any questions or speak at all. I finished the bath, put on my uniform, and Bernie and another boy marched me to dinner, one on either side, like a prisoner being led to the gallows.

Waiting in line, a boy standing next to me made a funny face to cheer me up. I laughed out loud and felt a most terrific slap on the side of my head. It had been delivered, purely at random, by a monitor who had happened along at that moment.

On the first floor, behind the synagogue, the dining hall had long tables with benches on either side. I was amazed at the number of inmates sitting down to the meal. The line moved steadily until reaching the serving tables, where an already filled metal pan was pushed across the counter. The day's menu: tuna fish and noodles with a portion of bread pudding plopped down next to it. The monitor said, "This is one of the best meals of the week, so don't leave anything over."

No matter how I tried, I was unable to swallow. In fact, for the first few days, I had no appetite at all. After that, although the menu was boring and tasteless, I ate what was given. No water was offered at the dinner meal to prevent bed-wetting, and no snacks were served, so I was always thirsty and hungry.

Resident girls cleaned up the dining room. They wore middy blouses and skirts made of the Kentucky cloth, with black stockings. On the Sabbath, they wore white dresses and white stockings. Kindergarten girls, like Nora, wore white dresses and stockings with an apron over their clothes to keep them from being soiled. The littlest boys wore a Buster Brown collar and a flowing knotted tie with their blue suits.

Nora attended P.S.192, an in-house primary school set up with city approval for the youngest children and taught by the governors.

All the older children attended Grammar School 43, at West 129th and Amsterdam Avenue. The monitors supervised as we walked the seven blocks to school in column formation. On many days, we were verbally assaulted by the neighborhood Irish kids, but we never broke ranks. I was a good student and enjoyed escaping to the public school classroom.

We received religious training, learning by rote, with no understanding of the commandments and prayers. I knew nothing but learned that the Sabbath was a day of quiet reverence observed by all the residents.

The library was well stocked, and every child was given a lending card. Physical training was compulsory, and once a week, I endured calisthenics in the basement gym. I know there were swimming pools on the ground floor, but during my stay, the boys' pool was closed, possibly owing to the overcrowding at that time.

On Thursday night, lectures on various topics were offered: "Ben Franklin," "City of Washington, D.C.," and "Life of the Esquimeaux." In mild weather, a huge white sheet was hung from windows of the central wing courtyard, providing a screen on which a motion picture was projected. We watched from our dormitory windows or the fire escapes. I loved sitting on the fire escape, my legs dangling.

Clubs were organized and run by the children: poetry, writing, book discussion, drawing, storytelling, even "Secrets of Magic" were offered. The HOA cadet corps had won first place in state competitions. The corps drilled on Sundays, and the Governor of New York, Charles Evans Hughes, reviewed them the summer I arrived. The HOA military band, the best boys' band in the City, was led by Philip Egner, who went on to be the bandmaster at West Point. I began lessons on the clarinet with Mr. Egner, who said I had a gift for music.

Corporal punishment was not permitted but was part of the fabric of the place. Lucky for me, the old order was changing when I was admitted. Prior to my time, the older boys reported to governors, former orphans who were now college students. The governors paid no attention to the discipline carried out by the monitors, who maintained absolute order by fear. Bullying was the order of the day, and if a boy was singled out, there was no way he could escape the "standing punishment," where you were forced to hold a pillow above your head for an hour. If you dropped your arms, the monitor rapped your melon with the stick from a toilet plunger. When I was admitted, girls replaced the male monitors, which improved boys' dormitory life immensely.

The female governors were not much more attentive, as their main ambition was to get married and leave, but Nora insists that she had never been mistreated or threatened in any way. In fact, Nora always spoke with warmth of her days at the HOA.

During the first week, I was blue, crying myself to sleep every night. Then, the letters began to arrive, and I knew I hadn't been forgotten.

Visiting day was the only time I saw Nora, as the boys and girls were strictly segregated. When I found out I wouldn't see Mama until the first Sunday in September, six weeks from my admission I was so sad, but there was nothing to be done about it. I kept track of the days with a daily pencil mark made on the headboard rail of my cot.

Mama brought something she cooked or baked, a magazine or book for me, and perhaps a paper doll for Nora. Sometimes, Rose or one of my brothers came because Nora and I were both entitled to one visitor, so Mama didn't get counted twice! Even so, the administration frowned upon too big a crowd visiting, so it was mostly just Mama. We sat on her lap for four hours, the length of time allowed for visits. I was happy she brought Sam home from the Asylum: he was so little and needed Mama more than any of us. She promised she would kiss him for me, and it wouldn't be too much longer until we'd be together again.

We were permitted to send and receive mail, but outgoing letters were reviewed before posting. Every week, I received mail from Mama and at least one other member of the family. Even Charles sent a note once in a while. Mostly just a: *Hello there, hope you're doing fine*, with a nickel wrapped in a scrap of newspaper. Best of all were the daily love notes from Rose, with whom I was closest to in age and sibling bond.

Master Louis Freed
H.O.A.
Bronx, New York
December 25, 1908

Dear Lou: I miss you so much I think I'm going to die! Is it terrible there? How is Nora doing? Do you see her every day? Mama is so down-in-the-mouth, but she never cries in front of me. I'm trying not to be such a big-mouth and boss to Charlie, because I know it hurts Mama's feelings (you know how hard it is to be nice to him, right?). Anyway, Lou, I'll see you on visiting day next week. Today is Papa's birthday. He would have been forty-nine. I cried thinking about it.

Well, little brother...Keep your chin up!

Your loving sister, Rose.

P.S. give Nora a kiss for me. Thanks.

Master Louis Freed
The Hebrew Orphan Asylum
Amsterdam and 136th Street
Bronx, New York
February 11, 1909

Hi, Brother:

I guess by now you've figured out all the in-and-outs of living in that prison. Just joking!

I miss you around the house, Lou. Even if your nose was always in a book.

Mama, Rose, and Sam moved again! They're in four rooms on Park Avenue near 112th Street now. She's also on relief, so that helps.

I'm sure you and Nora don't want to stay there, but we're all doing our part now, Lou. These are very hard times. We're all working hard to pay Mama's expenses and our own. I've taken more hours at the carpentry, even though I hate it. We need the money, and I can't earn a living with my violin alone. Rube's boarding downtown. He got promoted to copyholder at Prendergast, so I guess he's going to be in the printing line for the rest of his life.

Morris sends a few bucks a month by Western Union. He's not earning much, and expenses in Atlantic City are high.

You're a real soldier for not writing weepy letters to Mama. She's sad and worried enough. We have to be strong for her.

I'm hoping to get in to visit you next month, but the HOA is strict about the number of people allowed in, and Mama's presence is more important.

Be a good boy, and study hard in school. Getting an education is very important.

Give Nora a kiss from me. I promise we'll get you out of there as soon as we can.

Albert.

By my eleventh birthday, March 3, 1909, the HOA was providing shelter for more than a thousand children. To house them all, cots were set up in the corridors, and still there was a waiting list.

With so many more poor Jews coming to New York, I worried they might take all the jobs that Mama can do, leaving her without the means to take us home.

Eligible to stay at HOA until sixteen, I panicked at the thought. Four more years? I had to do something, so I started a letter campaign to free us. Every day, I wrote separately to Mama, Rube, Morris, and Albert; begging them to work harder to bring Nora and me home. Days dragged on; spring became summer.

And then, one day, it was over.

Florence came to my table in the dining room.

"Louis, your brother is waiting for you at administration. Come with me to the dormitory to collect your things."

"Which brother is here? Is it Albert? Is it Rube?"

"I don't know, Louis. Just do what you've been told."

"Is my mother dead, Florence?"

"Just come with me to get your things, Louis. You'll know soon enough."

"What about my sister, Nora? Has she been called too?"

"I don't know, Louis, just come on."

Twenty minutes later, I reached the administration office with my belongings. Tying the ends of my red, white, and blue handkerchief together, I had fashioned a pouch which held my belongings: two pairs of underwear, a toothbrush, a hairbrush, and Mama's photo.

Nora was waiting on the same bench we had occupied on the day we arrived a year earlier. "Hello, Louis. Are we going home?"

"I don't know anything, Nora."

At that moment, the door to the office opened, and Rube stepped into the entry.

Smiling broadly, he said, "Well, well, well! Who have we got here? Could these two castaways be my own dear brother and sister; waiting all this time for their very favorite brother to rescue them?'

We stared at Rube. *Was he joking?*

"I thought I'd give myself a birthday present of you two! Today, I am twenty-years-old! What do you think of that?" He about doubled over laughing. At that moment, I knew Mama was alive, that I was going home.

"Happy birthday, Rube!" Nora and I said in unison.

"Come here, you two." He kneeled, and Nora and I rushed to hug him. It was the happiest moment of my life; I thought my heart would burst through my chest!

"Are you ready to come home, or do you want to stay a while longer?" He laughed so hard, spittle landed on my face.

Nora said, "Does Mama know you're taking us out of here, Rube? Did she say it was alright?"

Rube stopped laughing, his voice very soft. "My dearest child, it's alright. It's better than alright. It's the only right thing in the world today!"

He put his arms around us, and we all started to cry…tears of happiness, they were.

It was July 12, 1909, and Rube brought us home.

At dinner, except for Morris, still in Atlantic City, we were all together, eating paprikash. When it came time for strudel, we wished Rudolf a happy, happy Birthday!

The mass emigration from Russia and Eastern Europe to America was at its height during the year Louis and Nora lived at the HOA. The Lower East Side was declared the most overcrowded community in the nation, the people living hand to mouth. Given this desperate condition, there were many abandoned, homeless, neglected, and delinquent Jewish children needing help.

In January of 1909, President Theodore Roosevelt called the first Conference on the Care of Dependent Children.

The President said, "Home life is the highest and finest product of civilization. Children should not be deprived of it except for urgent and compelling reasons. Dependent children should first be kept in their own homes whenever possible, with foster homes as a second choice and institutions as a last resort. In future, resources will be channeled directly to the parents, so as to keep children within their own family structure."

It was the death knell for orphan asylums all over the country.

16

More than fifteen million immigrants, most from southern and eastern Europe, arrived in the United States during the first two decades of the twentieth century, a number equal to the arrivals of the previous forty years.

With no knowledge of English or American customs, the immigrants filled unskilled jobs in hostile work environments at low wages. Most worked a ten or twelve-hour day, earning forty percent less than they needed. Income inequality was at the same level as it had been during the Gilded Age.

In reaction to political corruption, the Progressive Era Presidents Roosevelt, Taft, and Wilson, expanded the Interstate Commerce Commission, and created the Department of Labor, Federal Reserve System, and Federal Trade Commission. Four constitutional amendments were ratified: the 16th (federal income tax), the 17th (direct election of U.S. Senators), the 18th (prohibition of alcoholic beverages), and the 19th (women's vote).

Profound changes to the American dream gave rise to the middle class. After historically protecting business interests since the beginning, the federal government was breaking new ground, legislating social welfare programs and economic reforms, regulating big business, and promoting scientific research. Child labor laws, eight-hour workdays, and minimum wages for women working in industry were enacted. The Workmen's Compensation and Safety Act provided income after illness or job-related accident. In public education, mandatory kindergarten, a comprehensive curriculum, free textbooks, and teacher pensions raised the bar for all.

In New York City, construction of the subway system was underway. Residential and commercial development followed the train lines, and a five-cent fare enticed a huge migration from the densely populated Lower East Side of Manhattan to the farthest reaches of Brooklyn, Queens, and the Bronx. It could be argued that the vision and commitment of Governor Charles Evans Hughes and Mayor Seth Low not only saved Manhattan and New York City from a host of social ills and the inability of banking and business expansion, but also created a better life for millions in the exurbs of New York.

The New York Public Library opened on 42nd Street, motion pictures were talking, mail was delivered by airplane from New York to Washington, DC. People with telephones were able to dial numbers without operator assistance. Radio, projected to become a household utility, was available to homes reached by electric lines.

For our resilient immigrants, ten years had passed since Papa died. Life had stabilized, continuing its forward motion. A new, American-born generation had reached adulthood.

Fannie

March 1, 1913
To: Mrs. Fannie Freed
349 East 32 St, #2 rear New York City, NY United States of America
Cousin: it is with great sadness I notify you of your dear Papa's death. My uncle Samuel Bruder, aged eighty-one years, buried this morning Satu Mare Jewish Cemetery beside your Mama. He lived a good life, died in his sleep.
Abraham

From: Abraham Bruder

743 Orczy Út #36 District VIII Budapest, Hungary

March 3, 1913
Dearest Cousin:

I received your wire about Papa. Thank you, dear Abe. It is strange to think you are the only relation in Hungary with whom I still enjoy contact.

The last communication I received from Papa was at the end of December, assuring me he was well on his way to living forever!

I had not seen the face, nor heard the voice, of my Papa since leaving Hungary twenty-one years ago.

In spite of this, I always felt his presence, knew, though separated, we were in the world together. I learned to accept letters as a substitution for real life. In Nagy Karolyi, he lived and breathed, walked the familiar streets, greeted life-long neighbors. In New York, I gave birth to his grandchildren and lived my days in a different universe. Parallels do not meet at a crossroad; only through the written word did we observe one another's lives. Observed in isolation.

Was there pain in the absence? Yes, on occasion, my decision to leave the motherland and my parents caused pain but no regret. In my soul-searching, I cannot say I would have returned to Hungary had that been possible. Life's purpose is to protect my children, and they are Americans. Coming here was the most important decision ever made; and I never once thought of returning to Europe's pomp and hypocrisy. Even as a woman of small means, America's promise offers a future to all. That is not to be found in the monarchy.

Now, I speak of my Papa to my children, attempt to recreate their grandfather's personality, his spirit, but that is impossible. My eldest sons retain vague memories of his life force. Those remembrances are of singular moments during their farewell visit when they were little more than babies. I can keep his memory alive during my lifetime, but after another generation, well, Sándor Bruder's existence will vanish.

Abe, dear, I'm thinking absence has its benefits. When I look into the mirror, I don't recognize the fifty-one-year-old woman staring back. In my Papa's mind, and yours, I'm still the twenty-year-old Fannie you remember. And, in my mind's eye, <u>you</u> will never age, no paunch or sagging jowl, no bald pate; isn't that nice? To me, you'll always remain youthful and dashing, my loving cousin, the gay bon vivant, holding forth at a coveted window table in the coffeehouses of Budapest.

I can hear your mother's voice, may she rest in peace, asking me, "Why can't Abraham find a nice woman and raise a family?"

Since you haven't and didn't, and I expect your law practice has prospered, there doesn't appear a reason to withhold the pleasure of a trip to New York to visit me. Do think about it, Abe, we're not getting any younger, you know.

It has been almost ten years since Samuel died. For the first five, I lived in poverty and want, often uncertain as to where our next meal was coming from. Distanced from parents, cousins, or the familiars of childhood, I looked only to the immediate future; counted only on my own sense of order, purpose, and obligation, to protect and provide for my children.

With that said, I did not feel bereft of kin; no, I can't complain of loneliness, Abe. For all the hardship, I was never lonely because I had my children, who at times supported me and at other times, were supported <u>by</u> me. As they matured, the elder boys did not falter in their responsibility to provide for the family, for our survival. And they did it with the unfettered spirit of youth, regardless of our station, our circumstance.

So, relatively speaking, for the last three years, we are stabilized, and I am a truly happy woman.

I am living in a two-bedroom flat with Rudolf, Rose, Louis, Nora, and Sam, Jr. Louis and Nora are attending high school. Both are excellent students! Rose is modeling coats in a cloak factory showroom in New York's garment district. She's keeping company with a neighbor down the street, who works with Rudolf at the Prendergast Printing Company. I'm hoping they'll wait a year before marrying when Rose is eighteen.

I'm pleased to say Albert is <u>almost</u> earning a living as a violinist in a theater uptown, his passionate vocation surely influenced by the music you exposed him to at the Budapest Opera house when he was a boy. To make ends meet, he's a night watchman in a north Bronx factory. You remember how seriously he took his responsibilities, Abe? At twenty-eight, he's no different! He tells me he can't afford a sweetheart, that <u>I'm</u> his sweetheart. I worry he'll become a set-in-his-ways bachelor while taking care of his Mama. Morris plays cello in a hotel orchestra in Atlantic City, an oceanfront resort area in New Jersey, a five-hour train trip from here. He visits every few months.

Rudolf is living with me for the present but is keeping company with Gussie Geduldig, the daughter of an Austrian family from Ostrava. They'll marry in the fall. Gussie's family emigrated in 1896, and her father has had no reason to learn English, working as a deliveryman for a German-owned beer distillery in Brooklyn. It's odd he's made no attempt to assimilate because all their children have been educated here. Gussie and her sisters graduated from Hebrew Technical Institute (like Gymnasia); her brother, from Teacher's College.

Charles comes by once or twice a month to contribute to our overhead, but he lives downtown near the East River docks, where his Russian bosses have import businesses.

I'm earning a few dollars a week offering garment repair in my apartment, Samuel's sewing machine still providing bread for the family!

So, my dearest Abe, life is good! We're not flush, but we're not poor, either. There's still a coin or two to spend on a show ticket or a wager at the horse track!

I'm so grateful for my loving children. How I wish you could know them, Abe. Intelligent, witty and resilient.

With that sweet thought, I'll sign off on this dispatch.

I look forward to hearing from you, dearest Cousin.
    Fannie

The door swung open. Breathless after taking two flights of stairs on the run, Rudolf announced, "Mama, I'm leaving Prendergast!"

I rested the wooden spoon against the mixing bowl and looked up. He was so handsome, Rudolf. At a height of six feet, one inch, a suit of clothes hung from his spare frame in the most stylish way; I'd say an "elegant slouch." He had a theatrical air, and wit, that attracted women and charmed men. Adopting a British resonance to his conversation caught the ear, piquing a listener's interest to the viewpoint of this seemingly down-on-his-luck member of the peerage! Rudolf, the Anglophile, had even taken to wearing a monocle with a chain draped behind one ear.

Since childhood, he loved to play a part. He lectured or amused, but never, ever, was he a bore. Many times, I watched him delight a group visiting our flat, delivering a punchline, or recounting an ordinary incident with an unexpected ending.

So, here he was, striking a pose in the doorframe, one hand on his hip, the other on the brim of his hat. Ah, Rudolf knew how to deliver good news.

"Mama, I'm hired at Alverson Press. In six-month's time, I'll be joining the proofreaders and steady employment! That could mean twenty-five bucks, *if* there's work for a full week. And, with Gussie's nine bucks bookkeeping at the ribbon factory, we can feather our little nest."

I smiled and clapped my palms together. "Wonderful news, my darling. You're on the way up, son, on the way up. What's the position for the first six months?"

"I'm working the monotype, the most boring job in printing, and it's the lobster shift, midnight to eight in the morning. Also, although the work may not be steady, I'll have to show up every night. If they're slack, they'll send me home."

"The more you talk, the less secure this job seems."

"Mama, in the end, the printing line isn't much more reliable than the music business. Even a proofreader's salary is a maybe. If there's no work, there's no pay. Remember when Papa told Albert not to quit the carpentry for music, that it wasn't reliable? Well, look at Albert now: he's full-time fiddle at the Crotona, doing what he loves. Of course, he's not making much, because "full-time" is only four days a week in the business, but he's still a bachelor, so he can live on that take home.

"Me, I'm going to be a married man next week. I'll have to work two jobs, print and cello, to put food on the table. Gussie is behind me one hundred percent, though."

"If you're on the lobster shift, that'll leave the whole day free for you to continue cello lessons at the Settlement House. I only want you to be happy, Rudolf. Happy. You're young, and life is your oyster."

"Next weekend, I'm playing with the Beethoven Society at the Fourth Street School and getting paid $5.00! They play some pretty hard stuff, Mama, but I'll stick along with them. And, I'm going to audition with the chamber group at the Jennings Street School. My teacher at Settlement House thinks I can keep up with the others around town, so I'll give it a try. He might just be looking for the extra lesson fees, but it's keeping my dream alive. Now that I'm getting married, I need a steady job, and that's Alverson's. My first night is Tuesday, a week after the wedding."

Setting a cup of coffee on the table, I gestured for him to sit down.

"Yes, Mater, I'm a man on the move, accepting responsibility and building a real life! A new job and a *wife*! Maybe next year, Gussie will present you with your first grandchild! You'll be losing me, Mama, but only to my in-laws down the block. Gussie wants to move in with them for the first year so we can help them out, and that's alright with me."

Seriously, I ventured, "I wonder if wedded bliss will be possible living with the Geduldigs, Rudolf. I admire Sali's immaculate, organized household. I also admire that all her daughters graduated from high school and Max from college. That's a great source of pride for any immigrant family. That said, they seem to lack a sense of humor, but that might just be the *German* in them." I was quick to add, "Oh, I don't mean Gussie! She's a wonderful girl, smart, congenial, and with a great sense of humor!"

"She fell in love with all of us, Mama, not just me. Our open door to the neighborhood, the food from your stove, the laughter, and the music. We may not have money, but we know how to welcome and enjoy people. That's what Sali's house is missing. Maybe I'll teach them how to put some zest in their lives when I'm living there."

I opened the oven door. The babka was nicely browned. I stuck the wooden end of a safety match into the center; it came out clean. Setting the pan to cool on the stovetop, I returned to the table, where Rudolf was reading the racing form. I turned the burner under the last of the fendel coffee.

"I don't mean to dwell on the Geduldigs, Rudolf, but you may discover living under that roof, that Sam Geduldig is probably no cause for joy, and that's why Sali is so quiet and sad looking. He's a man who like his schnapps a bit too much."

He spooned four teaspoons of sugar into his cup and motioned for me to refill it. Nodding, he said, "They've all got an education, and that's a feather in their caps. Both Sali and the old man attended the Hebrew schools in Ostrava, yet he has no intellectual curiosity, no technical skill, no vocation. He came all the way here from Austria to drive a truck for a Brooklyn beer company? *She* was the student but, as a woman, had no opportunity; so, she saw to it that her children got an American education, *especially* the girls. Max, his wife, Bertha, and the new baby, Rhoda, moved to Paterson, New Jersey, last fall, where he teaches at the high school. He's an alright guy, a few years older than me, and not one to enjoy a card game or day at the track, although I keep trying to loosen him up. He's a smart guy, but you know the *Germans*. They think they're smarter than everybody else.

"I do like Gussie's sister, Rosepearl, and her sweetheart, Hermann. You know his family owns a hotel in the Catskills; he's a terrific guy. Big man, six feet six, I'd guess. Always ready to laugh and likes to dance. Also, he's a horse player and a crapshooter, so we have a lot in common.

I leaned toward him. With Rose at work and Louis, Nora, and Sam at school, there was no one home to hear our conversation; still, I lowered my voice. I was no gossip, preferring to accept people without judgment, as they presented themselves to me. Yet I wanted to know if Rudolf was aware of the family secrets Gussie had shared with me. When we were part of the family, wouldn't we be affected by Geduldig's problems? Quietly, I said, "Gussie and I spoke of her father's drinking, for which I sympathize. She also told me her sister, Nettie, suffered from extended periods of melancholy and threatening behavior. She also said Nettie's husband, Jack, is a bit of a dope, who caters to his wife and denies anything about her is "off." Do you know of these behaviors, Rudolf? Is Nettie unbalanced, or is Gussie exaggerating a high-strung personality? Gussie said she always felt passed over by her mother; that Nettie is the favored child. I'm pleased Gussie feels comfortable sharing her feelings with me, and I'd urge you, while you're living there, to always make your new wife feel loved. The thing about Nettie is she's blond and blue-eyed, the beautiful, Germanic baby of the family. She gets the attention, which Gussie resents. But every family has that, Rudolf. Look at Charles and all the rest of you. He's always been the odd man out from the time he was born. It must hurt Sali to see the girls' conflicts and jealousies."

He reached for the babka, and I pushed his hand away. "It's still too hot to cut. You'll have to wait!"

"Sure, every family's got the oddball. Charles has a lot of problems, Mama; you've got to admit that. When I got him that job at Sperry-Hutchinson last year, I pulled a lot of strings, and in the end, they let him go after three months. I didn't tell you then, but you should know the truth: the foreman caught him red-handed, stashing sheets of green stamps under his clothing. He was selling them to his Russian buddies. Believe me, Mama, I had to do some fancy talking and slip the foreman $6.00, to keep Charles from being arrested." He sipped his coffee, his face an angry scowl.

The revelation was stunning to me, although deep down, I always knew that's how Charles got by. I touched his hand. "Don't be upset, dear boy. I would have learned of this sooner or later. Thank you for protecting your brother, even though you felt betrayed. You did it for the family, for me. I pray he'll find his way in the world. He's so alone, feels so unloved."

I turned the babka out of the pan and onto a cutting board. The aroma of the sweet bread was distinctly sugar and chocolate, but edged with a sourness, to which the mucosa of my nostrils reacted, causing a current of saliva to envelop throat, tongue, and palate. The response of my taste buds was to the nuances in this flavorful Russian masterpiece. It was the first time I'd baked Frances Romoff's recipe. She and her son, Joe, Rose's sweetheart, lived over on 28th Street. After meeting him at the New York Monotype Organization, Rube invited Joe for dinner and poker one Saturday evening. He was captivated by Rose's wit, charm, and card sense.

She won 25 cents, taking the biggest pot of the evening. Like Gussie, Joe was drawn to the family. He was a good man, a hard worker, but his claim to fame, in our circle, was that he was not an immigrant. The child of an American father and his Russian bride, Joe was born in Beldz but arrived in America as a citizen.

Clearing the baking paraphernalia away, I sat facing Rudolf. Reaching into my apron pocket, I removed a few folded papers. "This came from Morris this morning, his travel plans. Listen to this: 'Mama, I'm still playing Thursday to Sunday at The Chelsea, making about $15.00 a week (I'm enclosing five). Since I can't take off work, I was glad to read in Rube's last letter that the wedding will be on Tuesday, the fourteenth. I'll catch the early Monday morning South Jersey line from Atlantic City to meet the Baltimore & Ohio's Royal Blue at

Philadelphia. It's scheduled to arrive at Whitehall station at the Battery at 1:00 in the afternoon. Here's the good news: I don't have to be back in Jersey until Friday, so I'll be looking for work in New York all week. Being alone out here in the hinterlands isn't a bed of roses. I have to admit, after four years traveling around the Baltimore/Philly/Atlantic City circuit, music is still not providing a steady income. But, Mama, it's the only work I want to do, so I'm not giving it up. If I'm going to eke out a living, I've decided I'd rather do it in New York, near my kin. I'm sick of being away from you and the family. I hope everyone can meet the train, Mama; I'm bringing a surprise!'

"So, what do you make of all that? Your brother is sad and lonely away from us. But, what's the 'surprise'?"

"Well, I think it's all good news, Mama, Morris coming back to New York! He'll get hooked up with a steady gig, and if not, there's plenty of places to earn a buck when he's not scratching that cello. I guess he'll take up the empty couch I'll be vacating. Well, well, what do you know, Morris back in New York!"

Ignoring work and school, the whole family, including Gussie, gathered at the Whitehall Ferry slip at the Battery. It was speculated the surprise would be a woman. What else could it be? Morris didn't make idle conversation, nor did he share his innermost feelings easily. Not antisocial, one would call him an engaged observer, reserved, a man who relished being immersed in his music. When he asked for us to meet him, well, that was akin to a royal command performance.

The mood was gay, expectant, one of waiting for the curtain to rise, I'd say.

The very next day, Rudolf and Gussie would be married, a milestone for the American Freeds, and wasn't our family deserving of a holiday, of a week of holidays?

It was a bright and unusually warm October day at the Battery. I wore my navy blue shirtwaist with the high collar and Mama's tortoise-shell combs in my hair. I was hatless and coatless, as the noonday temperatures reached nearly 80 degrees.

We milled about the area, where boats of all kinds, scows, ferries, tugs, sloops, cargo carriers, even some five-masted schooners, made their way about upper New York Bay, probably the busiest waterfront in the world.

Albert, Charles, Rose, Louis, and Nora congregated in a loose circle facing Rudolf and Gussie, whose backs were to the river. Gussie was telling them, "I was only six-years-old when the *Rotterdam* navigated past Lady Liberty. It was December and very cold, but my mother insisted we all go on deck to see America. Mother, with baby Nettie in her arms, was overcome with emotion and began to weep. My sister, Rosepearl, and I embraced each other and followed suit, blubbering all over our coats. Our mother scolded us, all the while using Nettie's blanket to clean our lapels of spittle and snot! My father said, 'Liberty isn't very pretty; she looks like a French scrubwoman'. Brother Max was writing in his journal, keeping the moment unforgotten. It was such an important moment, but I'm sorry to admit I haven't been back to see this harbor in twenty-one years." She stopped speaking. Awed by her own memories, dear Gussie burst into tears. Rube hurriedly handed her a linen handkerchief from his pocket and put his arm about her shoulder. She blew her nose, dabbed at her eyes, and looked out to the Statue. Rudolf cleared his throat and raised his voice a bit to capture the attention of his audience. "Now, let's remember that Mama, Albert, Morris, and I came across during one of the worst hurricanes ever recorded! And, I remember every single minute of it! Let me tell you, I didn't think we'd make landfall alive."

Sam and I didn't stay for the performance, although I expect it was even more thrilling than the reality! We made our way to the Baltimore and Ohio train kiosk near the Battery's rampart, to inquire whether the train was on schedule.

Sam stepped up to the ticket window.

"Excuse me, sir. My brother is arriving on the Royal Blue Line from Philadelphia. Can you tell me where we meet him?"

The Ticketmaster looked at him, then pointed across the waterway. "See that big, red brick building that looks like a castle, kid? That's the Pennsy Railroad's Communipaw Station. The B & O's Royal Blue ends its DC run right there. There's a tunnel for the Pennsy line into New York, but they won't let the B & O use it, so passengers get ferried over here. They'll teletype me when the train arrives, and I'll give you a wave. Then, watch for the ferry with Whitehall painted across it. That's the one your brother will be on."

"Thanks, mister," Sam said, smiling.

At almost 2:00, a shrill whistle caught Sam's attention. The Ticketmaster waved his arm and pointed toward the Jersey shoreline. Sam waved back, making the thumbs-up sign. "There's the Whitehall ferry, Mama. See it? It's coming straight for the Battery. Here he comes!"

Morris stepped off the ferry onto the cobblestones of the Battery. He wore a grey, vested suit, a high-collar white shirt, and navy-blue bowtie. Hatless, he carried his cello by a handle attached to its brown canvas case. At his side was a woman, wearing a wine-colored satin shirtwaist with a bodice of cream-colored lace. As tall as Morris, almost six feet tall, she walked with grace, like a dancer. Slender, auburn-haired, and dark-eyed, an Irish beauty with a milk-white complexion!

Rose, standing at my side, poked me with her elbow, whispering, "See, Mama? You thought he was so lonely and had only his cello to occupy him! Morris is a sly one, keeping her under wraps, and she's a beauty!"

I laughed and hugged her. "Oh, Rose, I'm so happy for him. You know how I worried about his social life, working when the rest of the world is at play. I should have taken into account there'd be others working odd hours in a resort city."

Everyone was laughing and waving at Morris, high spirits all around! Rube ran forward to embrace his brother, to be the first to meet Morris's woman. "You are a crafty one, Morris! Who is this vaudeville star?" Morris laughed. "Rube, everyone: May I present my

Nellie? Her full name is Ellen Carney Freed!" There was a collective gasp as all eyes focused on Morris. "Nellie and I were married in February by the Justice of the Peace in Atlantic City. So, Rube's not the first to tie the knot!" He turned his bride toward me. "Nellie, this is Mama." I smiled and said, "Welcome, my dear. You are most welcome."

She began to reach for my hand and thinking better of it, put her arms around me. Looking me straight in the eye, she said, "Mama, I luv Morris with all me 'art, and I do hope you'll all accept me inta the family."

She was lovely.

Speaking as the Papa, Albert announced, "I'm certain Papa is watching us today, his spirit embracing us all." Morris said, "Hear, hear!"

Nora came to stand with me, put her arms around Nellie's waist. "Hello, Nellie, I'm Nora." Nellie smiled. "Well, aren't you the sweet little cailín. That's Irish for girl, she explained. "And, I have a cousin with the very same name, so I know you and me'll be great pals, dear Nora."

Then, the couple was rushed by our crowd. Handshakes and embraces and kisses and, yes, tears. I wept for my Samuel's absence from Morris's joy and from his place at Rube's wedding on the morrow. I cried for the void left behind by his unnatural, youthful demise, happy moments stolen from that beautiful man and from all of us. Samuel's essence, his spark, still lived within my breast. Was it happenstance that the very place Morris presented his bride to us was the very spot Samuel stepped from the *Hammonia* twenty-five years earlier in October 1888?

The aura surrounding us was otherworldly. I looked around, aware of boat whistles and street vendors, horse-drawn carriages, and electric trolleys, the sounds of construction along the piers, dogs barking, and gulls screeching. We were enveloped in the sounds of New York, yet they didn't overtake our family's verbal exchange, buffered as we were in a tight clutch around Morris and Nellie.

Morris made the introductions to each one. She smiled and said sweet words carried on a lovely, lilting, brogue. "'Tis luvly to meet you." "'Tis grand to finally see you all." "'Tisn't it a fine day, then, to return to New York?" "Sure'n you're much taller than I had been told." "I'll not be tellin' a fib when I say bein' a secret is hard on the conscience, ya know." "I pray you'll all be forgivin' us for not comin' sooner. That's all on Morris, but, 'twas near impossible to get the days off, ya know. He thought the news too important to send in a post, so, please, my dears, please be forgivin'."

Growing serious, Morris said, "I didn't want to send the news in a letter, and then weeks kept going by. So, what do you all say? You still love me?"

Louis stepped forward. "I'm so happy you're back, Morris. And I know I speak for all when I say: We still love you, and why not? If this beautiful Nellie loves you, so can we! So, I say, three cheers for Morris and Nellie! Hip, hip, hooray!"

And right in front of all those New Yorkers passing by, we shouted, "Hi, Hip, Hooray. Hip, Hip, Hooray, Hip, Hip, Hooray!"

Morris hugged Louis and then declared he was starving for some New York pastrami on rye.

Nellie took a hanky from her purse. "Mama, dry those tears. 'Tis a grand day, all about weddin's and luv with kin all together."

And she was correct.

After hailing a few cabs, we were off to feast at the Second Avenue Deli. It was Monday afternoon, past lunch, too early for dinner. Surely, there'd be empty tables!

The waiter was more than six feet tall. A few greasy black hairs had been carefully combed, from ear to ear, across the bald hemisphere of his wrinkled scalp, bridging the space between the earpieces of his thick-lensed, black eyeglass frame. A filthy apron was wrapped twice around his skinny waist, held in place with a black sash. Sweating profusely, he greeted us at the door. "Awright, give us a couple minutes to set up, folks. No problem sitting eleven at this hour." A long table was covered with a white cloth, and two waiters worked quickly to lay dishes and cutlery, bottles of seltzer, and bowls filled with half-sour and sour pickles, sauerkraut, and hot and spicy green and red cherry tomatoes.

"Awright, youse've been heah befaw, so waddaya want? Startin wid you, lady."

Nellie stared at the waiter and whispered to Morris, "What language is he speaking?" Morris said, "Welcome back to *Nu-Yawk*, sweetheart!"

The newlyweds and the almost-wedded sat across from each other at the center of the arrangement. It was decided that Morris and Nellie would stay at a boarding house on Second Avenue and 23rd Street; my flat was just too small to accommodate all of us.

Reaching across to hold Gussie's hand, Nellie asked, "I'm over the moon to be here for your weddin', Gussie, dear. I've ne'er been to a Jewish marriage, and Morris doesn't know much about it. Tell me what to expect."

Eager to make friends with her new sister-in-law, Gussie took a deep breath and began a dissertation. "We're to be at the Austrian-American Association Hall on Ludlow Street at six in the evening. Rabbi Greenberg will read our marriage contract, the Ketubah, in Hebrew and English. Albert and my brother, Max, our witnesses, will sign the contract, and we're legally married. The Rabbi will chant a few prayers while Rube and I stand under a canopy, called a Chuppah, crocheted by my mother. That signifies the roof of our house. We take a sip of wine after certain prayers, and Rube will kiss me. Next, he'll step on, and break, a glass, which represents the destruction of the ancient temple. Everyone shouts, *Mazel Tov*, Yiddish for Congratulations. Finally, we'll be served dinner, while Albert's friends from the Crotona play dance music. I guess that's a Jewish wedding in a nutshell, Nellie!"

Rudolf began roaring with laughter, and we all watched, waiting for him to speak. "My little Swipes, that was an amazing reduction of the rite! If only the Rabbi would condense his prayers, too! Your version is brilliant, Swipsey! Nellie, if you believe we'll be having dinner any time before 10:00 tomorrow evening, you're being led down a path. Once a Rabbi has a congregation of more than three Jews, he can't help but drag out dozens of prayers to recite! I hope he prays for my brother's arm muscles, for strength to hold up the corners of the Chuppah, while the ceremony drags on. If not, the roof of our house might come crashing down!"

Nellie might have been a little shocked at Rube's blasphemy, given her Catholic upbringing, but she laughed along with the rest of the nonbelievers at the table. I needn't have worried; I should have expected any woman falling for one of my sons would not be a strict believer in any religion.

Gussie warned, "Please don't make it into a Freed spectacle tomorrow, boys. No laughing; be decorous, respectful of the Rabbi. It's only for an hour or so, I beg you. Save the jokes for dinnertime." She pouted a bit, but Rudolf hugged her shoulders and kissed her on the cheek. "Swipsey, the Chuppah bearers will be on their best behavior, I promise!" Everyone laughed and Gussie pressed her palms together, in prayer. "Please, boys, please be good for your new sister!"

Conversation lulled as sandwiches overstuffed with pastrami, corned beef, and salami, were distributed around the table. Morris leaned in my direction. "Mama, isn't my Nellie beautiful?" His wife blushed, embarrassed.

"You are certainly beautiful, Nellie; my son is right to say it. And, I'm so happy for both of you. While you're waiting for that matzo ball soup to cool, tell us about yourself. Do you have family in America?"

Rose said, "Tell us how you and Morris met. What were you doing in Atlantic City? Are you a musician too? Tell us everything, Nellie, the whole story of the love affair!"

Nora said, "Will you go back to Atlantic City, or are you here to stay?"

Albert put down his knish and called for order. "Hold on, everyone. Give Nellie a breath of air! Let the poor girl have her lunch." To which Nellie said, "'Tis alright, Albert. I'll come clean! Here's my story..."

Everyone fell silent, their eyes on Nellie, who looked directly at me with an honest gaze, eyes full of intelligence and kindness. "I come on the *Lucania* from Queenstown, England, on April the ninth, 1905. My brother, Kevin, livin' in Brooklyn, was my sponsor. I had $60.00 in my pocket, as the immigration demanded. I was eighteen, which makes me twenty-six today, so you don't have to do the addin'. I had already been workin' as a chambermaid in Castlebar, Ireland, that's County Mayo, for three years. Both my parents are gone, God rest 'em; taken by the pneumonia last winter. I had two younger brothers, both dead of scarlet fever before their fourth birthdays, God rest their wee souls. I have a sister, two years my senior, Mary Patricia. She came to the U.S. a year before me, stayin' with Kevin while waitin' for me to make passage." Nellie stopped for a few spoonfuls of soup, and we all went back to eating our own food. We were enthralled by the animated recounting of her story and the lovely Irish accent, which made every word seem a musical note.

When she was ready, she continued. "With all the immigrants comin' into New York, Mary Patricia and I could barely find work, and when we did, the wage was so low, only those fresh off the boat would take it. Kevin was workin' in a pub near the docks on the Gowanus Canal. The patrons were a rowdy bunch of lowlifes comin' off the cargo ships, most not speakin' a word of English. Kevin was beat up on a regular basis, just for bein' Irish, and the three of us decided to leave New York. 'Tis no secret my countrymen love horseracin', and the bookies in Sheepshead Bay knew my brother. One of them told Kevin if he wanted out of the city, he ought to think about going to the Atlantic City, over in Jersey. 'Twas a beautiful racecourse there, two, in fact, where Kevin might find employ as a groundskeeper or in the stables cleanin' up after the horses. For sure, there'd be chambermaid work for me and Mary Pat at one of the hotels along the boardwalk. So, it was off we went. On the very first day, The Hotel Chelsea hired my sister and me on the spot! We were clean and pretty, spoke English, and were experienced maids. 'Twas summer, and the place teemin' with guests; management was thrilled to be takin' us on. By the end of the season, I had watched Morris playin' in the salon so many times I knew the playlist by heart. I saw him at the employee lunchroom, and we made googly eyes at each other. We started meetin' and goin' to a revue or dancin' at a supper club once in a while. I fell for his beautiful smile and those warm brown eyes and his kind heart. In six months', time, we didn't want to be livin' apart, our need for each other become that great, so, we got married. Kevin and Joe Glover, Morris's bandmate, stood up for us on February the fourteenth, Saint Valentine's Day. Just two romantic lovebirds, my Morris and me. Sure'n that's the whole truth about me and us!"

She smiled broadly, showing perfectly straight, white, teeth! No Hungarian diet ever produced such teeth. I couldn't help but think how lucky my grandchildren were going to be, inheriting that dental trait from their Irish mother.

Rudolf and Gussie's wedding was a happy affair. The boys managed to behave themselves, but Sam Geduldig finished off an entire bottle of schnapps and fell asleep on a wooden chair, embarrassing poor Gussie.

The next morning, the newlyweds rode the Long Island Railroad's electric coach to Locust Valley, spending a three-day honeymoon in a hotel across from the Piping Rock Racetrack. Rudolf came home with $4.00 in winnings, a lucky omen to begin their married life. They moved in with Gussie's parents, as planned, and stayed a year.

Morris and Nellie leased an apartment on West 56th Street. He played cello for the Fox Theater on Broadway, earning twice his previous pay, but the rent and expenses were much dearer in New York, so the increase didn't amount to anything. On June 11, 1914, Nellie gave birth to my first grandchild, Robert Samuel Freed, named after my beloved.

Rose and Joe Romoff rode the subway to City Hall and were married on the fifth of August, the day after the European War was declared. They set up housekeeping in The Bronx, near Rudolf and Gussie, who gave birth to a beautiful little girl, Thelma Annette, on May 4, 1915.

For the next few years, I lived in the East 32nd Street apartment in relative comfort, thanks to the children. After graduating from high school in 1916, Louis was hired on as a credit and collection man at Lord & Taylor on Fifth Avenue. Since learning to play clarinet at the Hebrew Orphan Asylum, he wanted to earn a living with the instrument, but there was rarely money to pay for lessons, so it remained a hobby. Nora, the family scholar, worked in a bookstore on Second Avenue after school, and summers as a copyholder at Alverson Printing.

Well-liked, Sam was an easy-going, sociable boy with a real talent for the violin, which was developed at the free classes offered by the Settlement House's Music School. Before his fifteenth birthday, Sam was performing at private parties and musical recitals around town.

War in Europe was declared on August 4, 1914.

Painfully aware of their ancestry, German, Austrian, and Hungarian immigrants in the neighborhood were quick to point out to anyone who would listen how they had split from fathers, brothers, or friends fighting for the enemy. Many in the neighborhood changed their Teutonic names and hung American flags, bunting, or the photo of a son in uniform on windows facing the street.

In 1917, when America declared war on the Central Powers, my sons registered for the military draft. Neither Albert, Morris, nor Rube was eligible for service. Resident aliens for twenty-five years, none had become naturalized citizens. Albert was thirty-two, too old for induction. Morris, at thirty, and Rudolf, twenty-eight, were married with children.

No, I didn't forget Charles. A mother's guilt is a complicated matter, and to this day, I dwell upon the disturbing enigma that is my Charles. Was his personality born in the bones, or did I create the place that nurtured his unhappy tendencies?

When he was two, we moved to New York, where I was adapting to a new environment, hoping Samuel would make a living and giving birth to Rose. Charles rarely sought attention, and for that I was grateful.

Every two years, another baby came: Louis, Anna, Nora, and Sam. It was natural to meet the urgent cry of a new infant before tending to the older children's needs, though in the midst of all that, I see now, Charles was eclipsed.

The unexpected onset and swiftness of Samuel's disease put a halt to the normal rhythms of life in our little universe. For three terrifying weeks, the attention, efforts, and energy of the family were focused upon *him*, day, and night. I was nine months pregnant, exhausted, and at my wit's end. Charles's tenth birthday, four days prior to Samuel's death, was not celebrated, barely acknowledged. How sad for that little boy to have been forgotten by his mother. I apologized to him later, but I can't change the past. At the time, a child of ten years was not considered capable of processing adult situations; he was not included in discussions of our survival. In hindsight, I understand he was fully aware of the dire situation. Now, I regret my ignorance and neglect.

After Samuel, all pulled together, all but Charles. I believed Charles *wished* to contribute, though he's never learned to devote himself to a task, never saw things through. After a history of truancy, he quit school prior to finishing eighth grade. He was unskilled, unschooled, uncommunicative, a poor candidate for hire.

He volunteered no information as to how he spent his days, so I stopped inquiring. Occasionally, Charles was home for dinner and slept in the flat, but I knew nothing of his pals or love interests. We rarely shared a conversation; and when we did, there had been no depth. His interest in family matters was minimal. There were seven others to house, clothe, and feed. I couldn't cope with or respond to his behavior.

Charles was the worry of my life. I couldn't change his personality nor undo past injustices. I was only human, after all.

The United States Government came to my rescue. In 1917, Samuel Freed's American-born son was enlisted to save the world for democracy. Charles was drafted into the Army.

Rube Freed's Diary

Austria-Hungary occupied the former Ottoman territory of Bosnia and Herzegovina for thirty-six years. On June 29, 1914, in Sarajevo, Bosnia, a student and a member of Young Bosnia, a revolutionary group, assassinated Archduke Franz Ferdinand, the heir to the Austro-Hungarian throne. One month later, on July 28th, Austria declared war.

As deep-rooted European alliances arranged themselves to protect existing or promote ambitious goals, the Balkan crisis enlarged beyond the continent.

Military action engaged in territories of Europe, Africa, the Middle East, the Pacific Islands, China, Indian Ocean, and North and South Atlantic Oceans.

The Central Powers were Austria-Hungary, the German Empire, the Ottoman Empire, and Bulgaria.

The Allied Powers were France, the British Empire, Russia, Serbia, Belgium, Montenegro, and Japan. Italy joined the Allies in 1915. Romania, Portugal, and Hejaz in 1916; the United States, China, Greece, and Siam in 1917.

Armistice was declared on November 11, 1918. More than seventy million military troops, including sixty million Europeans, had been mobilized. Nine million combatants were killed.

Four years, three months, and two weeks of warfare precipitated the Russian Revolution and Civil War, after which the Soviet Union was formed; there was unrest and revolution in Asia. These events resulted in the creation of the League of Nations.

In 1919, at the Paris Peace Conference, the Big Four- Britain, France, the United States, and Italy- imposed the terms of a series of treaties upon the defeated Central Powers. Political, cultural, economic, and social realities across the continent were profoundly altered. The Treaty of Versailles, signed in the Grand Trianon Palace, virtually ended the existence of the Austro-Hungarian, German, Ottoman, and Russian Empires by partitioning and transferring their colonies and territories to neighboring Allied Power states.

The Treaty of Trianon, as it came to be known, sanctioned the dismemberment of the Hungarian State.

Fannie

In 1921, the League of Nations registered the Treaty of Trianon. With her land mass reduced by more than seventy percent, Hungary no longer had direct access to the sea, and although there was no actual trek, a forced migration of more than three million Hungarian speakers were exiled. As the map of Europe was redrawn, Nagy Karolyi became Carei, Romania.

It had been decades since I walked the soil, but Hungary's punishment affected me deeply. My children joked I was a displaced person, a citizen of neither America nor Hungary. I didn't find accentuating my national limbo amusing. With the city of my birth expunged from the country of my birth, vital records and history were lost.

As my parents are unknown to my grandchildren, so it will be with me, unknown in three generations.

Charles

It was September 1917; I was twenty-three and going to war. What difference did it make if I was the black sheep? Not one single iota of difference, it turns out. That Mama didn't protect me from the neglect and icy scorn of my elder brothers, that I was shut out when Papa died, that I was an idler, playing hooky from early childhood, that I had been a thief and found company amongst the street gangs. All that was swept under the carpet.

Mama and all my brothers, sisters, nieces, and nephews, gathered at Rube and Gussie's apartment in The Bronx to wish me well. After this gathering, this tribute, if I were killed in battle, they'd mourn with clear consciences; they'd made amends, hadn't they?

Two-year-old Thelma was straddling her hip when Gussie opened the door. "Dear Charlie! The man of the hour! Come in, come in."

The men were sitting around the parlor, except for Sam, still at fiddle lessons downtown. The women in the kitchen fussed with pots and pans and serving platters. I heard giggling and dishes clattering, smelled sweet and sour cabbage. Nellie poked her head from the kitchen. "Hi, Charlie! Will ya be a dear and tell little Bobby his gun is just like the one you'll be usin'?" My three-year-old nephew ran out from behind his mother to show me a wooden toy rifle, complete with a rubber bayonet. "Look, Uncle Charlie, I'm a doughboy!"

Albert, Morris, Rube, and Lou all stood up to shake my hand; Lou actually hugged me. Joe Romoff, holding one-year-old Alby on his lap sucking milk from a bottle, nodded but didn't rise. The atmosphere was as it always had been, a veneer of fellowship, a cool and distant undercurrent. No matter, we were all there, a charade to ease Mama's unrest at my leave taking. I did hope for that, did love my Mama. With all the terrible luck she had, with all those kids and being widowed, she kept her sanity and put food in our bellies. She deserves a better life now, and I forgive her, really. There was nothing she could have done to force them to love me, she had to ignore it in the end, but *she* loved me, I do know *that*.

Platters of food were spread across the kitchen table, and we all lined up to fill our plates. It sure was delicious, and, in spite of the forced affection, I enjoyed being the center of attention.

It gave me a warm feeling when Rube said, "Charlie, we're all so proud of you. You're going off to kick the Kaiser's arse, and I can't think of anyone in this family better prepared to do that. You've been fighting the world since you were a kid!" I couldn't help but laugh at that. "I just want to say I'm very fond of you, little brother, and won't rest until you're safely back in New York." Gussie started bawling, which she does often, a real romantic.

Albert had plenty to say. "Charlie, as head of the family, I can tell you we're all worried about your safety and pray for your safe return. From what I'm reading in the papers, training at Camp Upton will be no walk in the park. All draftees from counties in Connecticut and New Jersey will be there with the New York City men. You're going to see the real America, Charlie; every family is sending their boys. You'll be bunking with gangsters, laborers, lawyers, policemen, and even plumbers. Everybody's in on this."

"I wish I could go with you, Charlie," Lou said with a pout. "I don't understand why the registration was only for men between twenty-one and thirty-one. At nineteen, I'm just as fit as anybody and twice as smart as most."

I told him, "There'll be another call-up in a few months; it's all about how many are needed, Lou. If there's enough to fill the trenches without drafting men under twenty, they'll not be calling you up."

Mama was quick to scold. "Louis, don't talk nonsense. Boys are dying. This is not a game. I'm praying for Charles's safe return, and I'm also praying for an end to the madness. Why are young men being sacrificed all over the world? Why can't we just all live in peace?"

Well, that was it, Mama's take on it. Rube stood up, the others following his lead. Without a word, the Freed spectacle, as Gussie referred to it, began. Albert, Morris, Rube, me, and Lou, draped our arms about each other's shoulders and began to sing in plaintive voice:

I didn't raise my boy to be a soldier/ I brought him up to be my pride and joy./ Who dares to place a musket on his shoulder?/To shoot some other mother's darling boy?

All verses of the antiwar song were sung with sad faces and mock tears.

When they were done, Mama said, "Alright, alright, you've put on your show, but this is war, and boys are being gassed and losing limbs and being blown to bits. It's no joke and not a romance. I'll go down to that draft board myself if they try to take Louis next year. Nineteen or twenty, he's just a boy, for God's sake."

The doorbell rang and Sam came in. There were Hellos all around and a hug for me. Sam was the best of the lot, I thought. Such a good boy. At thirteen, he was almost as tall as me.

"Well, Charlie, though I wanted to play a few military marches on my fiddle tonight, the music doesn't fit. The strings just don't get the blood boiling like the brass section! By the time you beat the Huns and come back, I hope I'll be earning a living in a band somewhere."

Nora left the parlor to arrange a plate of food for Sam. Rose and Joe, with Alby asleep on Joe's shoulder, began making ready to leave. Nellie went into the bedroom to nurse Virginia, the baby born last July fourth.

I was ready to end the evening, too. Tomorrow, I'd be leaving for Long Island for sixteen weeks of training at Upton. Some of the family would be seeing me again at the 34th Street Ferry slip at nine in the morning; and that might be the last time I see any of them in this life. Who knows what's in store?

I registered on June 5th, was inducted three weeks later, and spent the summer waiting for orders. On August 30th, the big parade kicked off at 10:00 in the morning. Thousands of draftees joined those in uniform, marching up Fifth Avenue from Washington Square to 50th Street. It was a grand day for all New York, with thousands lined up to pay their respects to us, Liberty's finest!

Mayor Mitchel, Governor Whitman, and Teddy Roosevelt were on the reviewing stand, and they must have been shocked to see what a rabble we were. I couldn't believe we'd ever be a fighting force but was ready to do my part, eager to get into the action. I had no idea what it was going to take to whip us into shape.

A fine drizzle met us Thursday morning at the East River slip. There were probably thousands, but I don't wish to exaggerate. To my surprise, the whole family came, the little ones, too. They waved handkerchiefs and flags, like they were seeing me off on a pleasure outing.

After the crowd milled about for an hour, a ferryboat whistle signaled it was time to board and cross to Brooklyn.

Uniformed officers circulated among the crowd, calling to the men, "Make your way to the boats. Say your goodbyes. NOW."

The family stood in a circle around me. Mama never smiled or spoke. She was red-eyed, chin a-quiver, and scanned my face intensely as if to burn my image into her brain.

Rube wept, of course. "Charlie, my boy, I know I neglected my brotherly responsibilities and beg your forgiveness. I'll make up for it when you return, dear Charles." Overcome, he embraced me, then looked deeply into my eyes, patted my shoulder, and turned abruptly to leave. I had to smile; he loved a dramatic exit, Rube did. Gussie blew a kiss, Thelma waved bye-bye.

Albert and Morris shook my hand, both tearful. "Good luck, Charlie," Morris said. Albert gave me the Papa look, all serious and instructive. "Keep your head down, Charles. Keep a lookout at all times, just like you learned to do walking the streets of New York." He added, "Come home, Charles. Mother needs you. Write her when you can."

Lou and Sam hugged me. "Be careful, Charlie. Come home." "Yes, Charlie, come home safe."

Rose said, "Charles, I know I treated you like a dog when we were kids. I'm apologizing for that now. I promise to be a better sister when you return. Stay out of the line of fire."

Nora kept it simple: "Charlie, don't go getting yourself killed. Mama would die of a broken heart."

Nellie held Virginia in her arms, swaddled in a blanket. "'Tis goodbye then, Charlie, but only for a short time. I'm thinkin' this conflict will soon be endin'. Be careful and good luck."

I knelt to look Bobby in the eye, his toy rifle slung over his shoulder. "Be a good boy for your Mama, Bobby. When I come back, I'll bring you something from the war, maybe a flag or a medal. How about that?" I tousled his hair, and he saluted me. "YES, SIR!"

Mama stepped close to me, tears running down her cheeks. She leaned her head on my shoulder, arms clutching me tightly, as if her strength could tear me from departure.

"My dearest Charles. I love you. Have loved you always. Please, my darling, please, come home to me."

I kissed her wet cheek, held her close for a moment, but I had to go. "I love you, Mama. I know you always loved me, too. I promise I'll come home. Be well, Mama, take care of yourself."

A minute later, I was swept along with the men, all happy to be getting a hero's sendoff.

I kept Mother's red hat in sight almost to the Brooklyn side, where we marched down Flatbush Avenue to the Long Island Railroad depot and boarded special trains for the sixty-mile trip to Yaphank. A special spur had been constructed to bring troops and supplies directly to Camp Upton.

Rumor on the train was that we'd be shipped to the front in four months, when training ended. That was OK with all the boys in my car, who whooped and hollered; we were keen to "kick the Kaiser out of Europe." No one had any idea what we had to learn and why it would take four months.

After spending two hours crowded into cars in the end-of-summer heat, there was a near-riot as we pushed to get off the train. Uniformed officers shouted orders and blew whistles, trying to herd us into lines and move us to headquarters.

Interpreters among the draftees helped the sergeants pronounce foreign names as we were called to receive a uniform, two army blankets, two tin plates, a large agate cup, and a knife, fork, and spoon. Then we were directed to our barracks.

This was the 77th Division, National Army. I was assigned to the Seventh Company of the 152nd Depot Brigade, Field Artillery. "Depot" meant we would be used as replacements at the front. The next day, I was sent for a physical exam. The precision of the system was amazing; two thousand men were processed in a single day!

The mess hall served more than five hundred at one time. My first meal was beefsteak with brown gravy, baked potatoes, beans, coffee, and rice pudding with plums in it. Breakfast was bacon, scrambled eggs, two peaches, toast, and coffee. We were served meat three times a day to give us energy for hours of marching on the parade ground in full uniform.

Special rec centers for the soldiers were built in the nearby towns. Saloons were closed within a five-mile radius of camp, and no unescorted women were allowed in the area. There were three hostess houses in camp, where soldiers and women volunteers from local towns met for dancing.

A newspaper, organized and published by the YMCA, kept us informed, and entertainers like Mary Pickford and George M. Cohan performed.

There was plenty going on in the barracks: gambling, fights, swearing, and bullying, which I would guess was to be expected when thousands of men are confined. Slackers and objectors were publicly humiliated or sent to military prisons.

Rifles arrived after two weeks, and that's when our training began in earnest. Split into two groups, ally and enemy, we dug trenches. European officers, who had seen action at the front, taught us to go over the top to throw hand grenades, crawl through barbed-wire entanglements, and use machine guns and gas masks. A British officer led bayonet practice, and some boxers among the drafted men demonstrated defensive and aggressive moves in hand-to-hand combat. In December, we watched a tank navigate no-man's-land, a training area resembling the real thing.

Training heightened the dread about what was coming. In a few weeks, there would be no more games, I'd be facing the possibility of being killed or wounded.

I didn't think too much about dying, but getting wounded, being in pain, gave me night sweats. There was a lot of talk about laying your life down for your comrades. I didn't think I'd do that and couldn't imagine someone in a trench taking a bullet meant for me.

I hadn't spent much time brooding over my personality or how my hand was dealt in life. I accepted I wasn't born under a lucky star, and people seemed to dislike me on sight. I don't know why that was; I never snubbed anyone or thought I was better than the next guy. It was just my lot. I was kind of a sad sack, and that doesn't get you invited to parties. I remained a lone wolf in the barracks and later on, too. It's how my life always had been lived, who I was.

We were issued a sleeve insignia to identify the 77th as the Liberty Brigade: it bore a likeness of the Statue of Liberty embroidered in gold on a blue ground with the numeral 7.

Every six weeks, I had weekend leave. Mother prepared all my favorite foods, and I walked the neighborhood in uniform. Mother, Lou, and Nora visited camp twice during my training. Rose and Joe brought baby Alby on Thanksgiving and once again in February, on his second birthday.

On Christmas Day, the division paraded up Fifth Avenue, to cheering crowds. At the end of January, there was a celebration at Upton. After dinner, campfires were lit, and the camp band played popular tunes. We banged our tin plates and sang out, "Over there, over there, send the word, send the word to prepare. That the Yanks are coming, the Yanks are coming." Marching in long lines, we worked ourselves up to shouting the final line: "O'ver, we're coming o'ver, and we won't be back 'til it's over, over there!" It was quite a sight, thousands of young men hugging each other, many sobbing like babies. Four months' training was done; it was time to put our lives on the line.

Early the next morning, my company stood in formation to salute the first contingent of the 77th assembling at the train station, leaving for the front.

A week later, I shipped out on the SS *Vauban*, an English vessel lent to America as part of the British shipping program. Cramped quarters and poor weather added to my seasickness, making me too ill to think about the danger waiting in Europe. We disembarked in Liverpool, were deployed to a rest camp, and then sent on to Calais and Camp de Souge for three weeks of training before relieving the French artillery and participating in the occupation of the Baccarat sector of Lorraine. The division entered the line at Vesle, commencing an attack on the German positions.

I don't think I can really paint a full picture of the grotesque misery of warfare, but this may give you an idea: We were dug in behind barricades in the trenches. Trails were narrow, with crevices that filled with rainwater, keeping our boots wet. I was infected with lice. It was the height of summer, and I was in full uniform. That means I wore underwear, a long-sleeved tunic/shirt, tapered trousers, ankle-length socks, puttees—bandage-like fabric wrapped around my lower legs—knee-length boots with laces, a steel helmet, rifle, a holstered side arm, and a body strap supporting a bayonet, kit bag, and gas mask. The stench of dirty men, rotting boots, and stagnant water and the smell of burst grenades and ammo, manure, and dead horses made me gag. I had little appetite, which was good because there wasn't much food. Fires couldn't be lit at night because we were so close to the enemy, and the constant noise of artillery left me hard of hearing for months after.

I was sleeping with my back against the back of a kid from Brooklyn when a grenade exploded above our heads, in midair. It took a few seconds to stand up, dizzy and wobbling from the shock. All that remained in the hollow space where that kid had been, was a crushed torso with his head attached. His legs were gone, vanished. I was terrified, and ran to another part of the trench, where I crouched down to make myself as small as possible, pressing my body into the dirt wall, weeping in despair and fear, and praying there was a God who'd save me.

At the end of August, I began to fatigue, which I thought normal for a soldier at the front. It turned out to be the Spanish flu, which killed more than fifteen thousand American soldiers in France alone.

During the night, I ran a high fever and started vomiting. In a few hours, all my bones ached, and I had diarrhea. Sent to the sick tent, I watched boys in the beds around me gasping for breath, their faces turning blue from lack of oxygen. At the end, they were spitting up a bloody foam from their lungs. Many of these lads died in twenty-four hours or less, that's how fast the flu claimed them. I don't understand how, but my body's defenses overcame the illness.

The 77th moved on to the Argonne trenches and forest, but the war was over for me.

The lack of food at the front and dehydration from the flu resulted in a big weight loss. With only one hundred fifteen pounds on my almost six-foot frame, I was too weak to stand on my own legs without assistance, and I looked like a cadaver.

From the field hospital tent in France, I was sent by ambulance and train to a soldier's sanitarium. On November 11th, the war ended, but I still had a long fight to wellness.

On April 7, 1919, I was carried by stretcher onto the SS *Virginian*, a troop ship that left St. Nazaire, France, docking in Hoboken, New Jersey thirteen days later. From there, a hospital ship transported me to a Public Health Service hospital on Staten Island, where I rested for a month. No visitors were permitted, given that the pandemic still raged in the States.

A late-winter's chill hung over the city, blowing across the Battery. As my ferry neared the dock, I saw Mother and Sam immediately, waving and smiling; she held a small American flag. Noticing my discomfort facing the cold wind, Mother wrapped her shawl around my shoulders. It didn't help, really. The weather contributed, but the cold I felt was deep in my bones, death waiting within. Emaciated and weak, I presented a caricature of the man I was. A line drawing, not a portrait in full. "Let's get you home, dear. I've got soup cooking. All you need is Mama's care, healthy food, and rest. Oh, dear Charles, how I've prayed for this moment. You, come home again."

Sam put his arm about my waist, and I leaned on the boy, making our way slowly across the Battery toward the hack stand.

It was a relief to be set up in a bed at Mother's. Protected from the world, I was convinced I'd make a full recovery and gave myself completely to Mother's instructions and ministrations.

At the end of May, when I was strong enough to make the trip, I reported to Camp Upton to demobilize and collect $103.75 in pay.

The 77th distinguished itself, having made an advance of nearly forty-five miles, suffering almost two thousand battle deaths and ten thousand wounded. A total of one hundred forty-six Distinguished Service Crosses were awarded them.

New York proved herself in another way: there had been almost four million American soldiers in the fight, and four hundred thousand of them were New Yorkers, more than from any other state.

I was proud I had served, felt better about myself. Before the war, I was a nobody, had no trade, always a sourpuss, just another angry, sad, uneducated, and invisible man on the streets of New York. Going through training, not getting kicked out, learning to go along to get along, meeting other invisible men like me; well, I was not alone in the world. Seems like putting us invisibles together was how America won the war. I was as good as anyone. Proud.

Welcomed by all and being the center of attention was a new experience for me. Still, I was very sick; the pneumonia that lingered cut me down. I couldn't walk for more than a few minutes or climb a flight of stairs without sitting down to rest. The doctors had nothing to offer; my lungs were shot, and there was no telling how long they'd keep working.

Disabled vets were eligible for vocational training, and for men too bad off to work at all, special pay was available. The trouble was, the Bureau of War Risk's process was so tangled by red tape, after a few months, I gave up on any help from the government. Being dependent on Mother and my brothers kept my spirits low.

Mother said, "Try not to be so down in the dumps. You never know what life will bring. Remember all the trials we went through after Papa died? Everything worked out in the end; don't give up hope."

And she was proven correct; life *did* work out in the end. In spite of my dismal personality and my infirmities, at twenty-five, my life wasn't over.

I was invited to the Eastside Veterans group to talk about my experiences in Europe. That was where I met Regina Schwartz, a slender, pretty woman, who saw something worth loving in me, a broken-down failure of a man.

In 1911, two years after her parents left Hungary, Reggie immigrated, too. She and her sister, Pauline, were accomplished dressmakers and opened a shop on the Lower East Side.

Reggie was shy, wary of strangers, and spoke very poor English. She was also seven years older than me, which gave my brothers something to snicker about. Needless to say, she was uncomfortable in the company of the Freeds, who interpreted her introverted nature and poor English as a lack of intelligence, or was it just the continuation of their rejection of all things about Charles? Anyway, except for Mother, I didn't care about what the family thought of Reggie. I'd been the outcast all my life. Reggie and I would live our lives together; we needed only each other. She was wonderful, kind, and anticipated my every need. Also, given my condition, her steady income was a blessing.

We were married by Rabbi Abraham Goldman, on Monday, September 29, 1919, at the synagogue on 23rd Street. The families gathered for a meal at our apartment, a three-room, street-level flat on East 97th Street.

It was bittersweet to have gained self-worth and the love of a woman at the same time I lost my health and vigor.

Spanish flu, the 1918 influenza pandemic, lasted from February 1918 to April 1920, infecting five hundred million people, a third of the world's population. The death toll: between twenty and fifty, possibly one hundred, million. In particular, the stronger immune systems of young adults were ravaged by the disease, causing that age group to present the highest mortality rates. Overcrowded medical camps and hospitals in war zones created ideal breeding grounds for the disease.

17

The Roaring twenties was a time of contradictory expectation in America.

Many supported the prohibition of alcohol, urged government to curtail innovation, and keep foreigners and European influence out.

Others embraced new invention, the international exchange of art, letters, fashion, music, cinema, and individual freedom.

With weapons of war no longer needed, American manufacturing slowed down. The mood was basically "To hell with Europe. Let's take care of America." The United States didn't join the League of Nations, which was President Wilson's baby.

The Bolshevik Russian Revolution and the rise of the American Communist Party provoked national fear and hysteria, a red scare, resulting in a witch hunt to expose sympathizers and reinforce the postwar isolationist mood. Strict quotas were placed on immigration, and racial hatred intensified in the South, as the Ku Klux Klan terrorized and lynched Blacks with impunity. Prohibition created a violent underworld, controlled by gangsters whose exploits kept newspaper sales brisk.

On the bright side, by 1923, the economy had recovered, and an average working man's wage was $5.00 a day. Even *they* were investing in the stock market, which was rising at lightning speed, month after month.

Ready-made clothes were offered for sale at less than half those produced by the gentleman's tailor. In the new era, people had little time or patience for fittings. Buying on the installment plan put new fashion or invention within reach of ordinary people. Scarcely was debt satisfied when a new model or trend appeared. Buying on credit, often an unending cycle, was adopted as part of the American way of life. Referred to as "consumers," the working class was barraged with flyers, handouts, and coupons for everything from canned foods to newly discovered vitamins. It seemed there were no limits to the easy life; use your credit, why not have it now?

The availability of electricity drove the economic, cultural, and technological advancement of the era. In 1920, just thirty-five percent of households received power, less than five percent in rural communities. By the end of the decade, almost seventy percent were electrified.

Radio, the first mass medium, distributed news and entertainment to the nation, beginning with Pittsburgh's KDKA, the first commercially licensed station in the country. By mid-decade, there were two and a half million radio sets across the country.

Republican President, Warren G. Harding, won the first election in which women participated, following ratification of the 19th Amendment.

Albert Einstein was awarded the 1921 Nobel Prize for Physics for his explanation and discovery of the photoelectric effect; that light is both a wave and a particle.

Lighted signs using colorful neon gas replaced Broadway's paper adverts.

Fannie

Taking stock, I can say after weathering the darkest years as a widow, life had reached a comfortable plateau. How proud my dearest Samuel would have been to witness the beautiful people we produced!

Even Albert finally left his bachelor's life behind when a Hungarian beauty, Bertha Hollander, was hired at the Crotona Theater.

"Mama, I was late to work, didn't use the stage entrance, just ran to open the main door. I heard a buzzer and realized the ticket seller in that windowed kiosk under the marquee had alerted the guard to stop my unpaid admittance!

"I was startled, then amused, so, I walked back to explain I was an employee. And there was the most beautiful, hazel-eyed girl looking at me."

I was so happy for him. I was beginning to think that at thirty-eight, he'd never find the right girl. "Go on, my dearest; tell me more."

"She was born in Fekete, Mama; the same year as me, 1885. The city is now in Romania, like Nagy Karolyi. Seventeen years ago, she and her sister, Sidonia, came to their brother, Alex, in Brooklyn. Now, Bertha lives with Sidonia and her husband, Gustav. The sisters are dressmakers. In fact, Mama, they run a business out of their Bronx apartment."

"Isn't it an interesting coincidence that both you and Charles found Hungarian dressmakers?"

After keeping company for a few months, they were married in August 1919, by Rabbi Shmuel Grossman. After a buffet dinner at Sidonia's, the newlyweds departed on the midnight Pullman for a honeymoon in Syracuse. As for Albert: I worried about Bertha's first pregnancy at age forty, but Lucille was born, with no complication, on her parents' first anniversary.

As Christmas of 1922 approached, Louis, Nora, Sam, and I still lived in the two-bedroom apartment on East 32nd Street. Happily, for all of us, Rose and Joe and their three boys occupied the flat on the second floor, directly above me.

Removing my hat and coat to the wall hook, I leaned on my cane for support to cross the parlor's threshold and reach the easy chair. From the settee, her feet tucked under the cushion, Nora looked up quickly and smiled. She was reading, "The Curious Case of Benjamin

Button," the latest from Fitzgerald. I knew she didn't want to be disturbed, but I needed to talk, to express my frustration after the day's events.

"I visited the Hungarian Consulate today. I want to know if Abe is alive; I haven't had a letter from him in six months."

Shifting in the chair to a more comfortable position, I went on. "I've no other contacts in Budapest, and since the Freed's wouldn't have known my cousin, anyway, there's no reason to pursue that avenue." Quickly, I added, "I haven't heard from any of your father's family in Tolcsva in decades, not even after your Papa died, not that I'm blaming anyone for losing touch."

Nora placed a scrap of paper into the library book to mark the place of interruption and looked at me. "Alright, Mama, tell me."

"I know you only know of Cousin Abe through my description, but he's the last living relative I have in Hungary. He helped your Papa and me defy my father's opposition to our love. It's important you hear this, Nora. I want my grandchildren to know the story, where they came from, who their grandparents were, how they risked everything for love. It's important, Nora. Don't hide behind your books."

Her body relaxed. Nora's lips curled in a smile, ever so slightly. "Yes, Mama. I know, against your father, you followed the man you loved to a new world. I promise I will tell my children if I ever have any."

"Nora don't patronize me. When you fall in love, you'll understand. Love is the only thing a poor man can call his own in this world. Money can't buy it. Kings can't demand it. It cannot be arranged by clergy or ancestry. It knows no spoken language. Love is the purest form of human contact."

"Yes, Mama. I know you and Papa sacrificed for love. It's a story your grandchildren should be told at bedtime; I know, I know."

She laughed. "Okay, Mama. I promise to write your story so it will not be lost to the ages. Now, what happened at the Consulate? Were the furnishings all covered with velvet and gilt? Heavy drapes on the windows? Did you speak Hungarian? Did you see Count Szechenyi, the Minister?"

"It was terrible. The clerk was rude, typical Hungarian know-it-all. I remember his type well from the government workers in Budapest. If it wasn't for our travel broker, as a woman alone, I'd still be waiting for exit papers! Alright, alright, I know I've strayed from the point!

"I walked on East 52nd Street from Third to Fifth Avenue, and it was cold. You know it's the first Hungarian Embassy on American soil ever, and they spared no expense to impress, to show they aren't in tatters.

"It was so European, with ornate chairs and tables, gilded and lacquered. The walls hung with paintings of King István, the Parliament building, the Danube, and the Opera House. Even a tapestry with scenes of battles from centuries ago hung along the stairway. Everything is so boastful, their glorious past, their royalty, how sophisticated they are, as if they weren't the enemy, causing the slaughter of millions in the war!"

"Mama! Get on with it. Are they going to find out if your cousin Abe is alive or not?"

"Well, I don't really know if they will or *can* help me. The clerk instructed me to write a letter requesting a search of Budapest death notices. Of course, it must include Abe's particulars and explain how I am related, including proof of that, which I can't possibly do. There's no way to show blood between me and Abe. If I can prove I'm a Hungarian citizen, and show Abe's signature on my marriage contract, maybe they'll look into it.

"To prove my birth, without the actual paper, they want to see my exit papers and Ellis Island documents. If I were a Naturalized U.S. citizen, that paper would have my place of birth listed, but I am not legal here. I'd have to petition city hall in Nagy Karolyi to search for my birth record. "Here's the irony: Nagy Karolyi is in Romania now, so technically, I'm not Hungarian!" I began to cry, overwhelmed.

Nora sat on the arm of my chair, handing me her handkerchief. "Mama don't cry. I know you're worried about your cousin, but you've been here forty years next summer. Who cares about all that! And, do you have *any* of those papers?"

I sobbed. "I've only my marriage Ketubah with Abe's signature, my Ellis Island papers, and your Papa's death certificate. I suppose I'll have to accept there's no hope to learn if Abe is still alive."

Hearing myself say the words gave me a strange feeling of comfort, finality. "I believe he's gone, Nora. Remembering him for loving me as a sister; well, that will have to suffice."

After a pause, "Don't forget to include Abe in the story of Papa and me. He was our champion; if it weren't for him, we may never have married."

"I will, Mama. Now, how about getting out of your corset and getting comfortable? I'll start dinner. Louis is working late, but Sam should be home soon. I'm frying chopped steak with onions for him, pork chops for you and me. Lyonnaise potatoes and red cabbage on the side. Sound good? I'll bet you're hungry, too, after schlepping across town to that little bit of Hungary!"

In the bedroom, removing my shirtwaist, corset, slip, heavy stockings, and buttoned shoes, I reached for the pink chenille robe. The bottle of aspirin sat next to a water-filled decanter on the end table. I swallowed two pills, hoping to deaden the gnawing pain in my hip and knee, residual discomfort from the streetcar accident twenty years earlier.

Just making the trip to the Consulate was all I could do. There was no point in pursuing the inquiry. If he was dead, what would I do? Travel to a cemetery in Budapest to put a stone on his headstone? No, that's not possible. There's no money for such a trip, and I'm too old and infirm to travel. And with no American, Hungarian, *or* Romanian legal status, I'd be denied entry at all borders.

I live in national limbo, which doesn't impact my life unless I wish to travel. It seems ungenerous of America that I remain an alien after birthing six children for her, but officially, I am a widowed guest.

I looked at myself in the mirror, pushed a wisp of hair behind my ear and nodded, pleased with my image. At sixty-one, I still had almost all my teeth and only a few grey hairs. I wore the same dress size I'd worn forty years ago, when I stepped off the *Maasdam* onto the soil of this splendid place and into the arms of my beloved.

So, what's the difference if when I die in America, I'm not a citizen? The grave requires no papers. It's a place with no country, no government, no border. Still, I lived, and bits of me live into the future. A poor woman can love and reproduce. Those are her legacies. That endures. *That's* why I want Nora to write the story for my grandchildren.

I heard voices from the foyer. Sam was home from his weekday job at the New York Bank for Savings. I recognized Rudolf's voice and Morris's, too. Tying the sash of my robe, I went to join the family.

"Mama, my love!" Rudolf bellowed, wrapping his arms around my waist. Morris and his friend, Joe Glover, hung their coats on the wall hooks.

"Oh, what a wonderful surprise! Will you stay for dinner? Nora, run out for a few more pork chops."

Morris hugged me; Joe kissed my cheek. Sam smiled. "Hello, Mama. What a day!"

Nora left for the butcher, and the boys sat around the parlor, me on my chair, leg raised.

"Dears, you're all in high spirits! Did you meet Sam on the way?"

"No, Mama, I didn't work today. Neither did Rube. We all met for lunch at the Automat on Broadway."

Sam turned to me, an earnest look on his face. "Mama. Listen to what I have to say. I hate my job at the bank. I can't get into the musicians' union until I have the dues and initiation money. The pickup jobs playing fiddle on the weekends pay peanuts. The speakeasy circuit is too rough a crowd for me, and the dance emporia aren't hiring new guys; believe me, I've tried."

He stopped for a breath. I kept still. "Well, Joe offered to sponsor me for a traveling job, and I said 'yes.' It pays great, Mama."

I noticed beads of sweat forming on his upper lip. I thought, '*He said yes*'?

Nora swung the door open with a bang. Sam ran across the room to relieve her of the brown paper bag while she removed her coat.

Surprised, she said, "Gee, thanks, Sam. Can you put the chops on the cutting board in the kitchen? I'll be right there."

Rudolf jumped into the breach. "Mama, it's going to be great money, and the boy will travel, always a learning experience! For the last year, Joe's been a bandsman on the cruise ships out of New York. He says it's great. I know you're going to object because Sam's only nineteen, but he's not a baby anymore. Me, Albert, and Morris were supporting you by the time we were his age!"

Sam returned to the settee, watching my reaction, hoping I wouldn't put up a fuss.

Morris grumbled, "You're all making this out to be a bad idea that needs justifying. It's a good idea, Mama. The cruise bands are a very close-knit group, and it's only for two months at a time. You're sailing around the Caribbean and South America in January and February and then come back to the freezing New York City. You make good money and work only a few hours a day. What's bad about that? If I didn't have a wife and two kids, I'd go myself!"

Joe picked up the conversation. "Mrs. Freed, I just finished a two-month New York-Buenos Aires round trip. We docked at Rio, Trinidad, and Barbados; what beautiful ports. I earned $300.00 for the trip, with meals and bunk included. I'm booked but can't do the January voyage; my mother is in the hospital out on Long Island."

He paused for the punchline, "If I vouch for him, Sam can take my band seat. We play at lunch, tea, dinner, and in the lounge until ten.

Then, we're free to visit the ports in the mornings. All the kid needs is a tuxedo and his fiddle."

I looked from Joe to Sam, still keeping quiet. I smelled onions sauteing in butter. Nora called from the kitchen, "Speak up so I can hear you! And don't upset Mama; she had a bad day already!"

All eyes were on Sam. He took my hand. "Mama, you and Nora know how I hate clerking at the bank, how I can't make a nickel with my fiddle. I won't be able to earn that kind of money here for years, for God's sake. The *Vauban* leaves on January 11th, only two weeks from now. Joe's going to get in touch with Ernie Eagle, the bandmaster, and put in a good word for me. Joe says he *knows* I'll be hired."

There was a very heavy pause. Nora came in from the kitchen. "Dinner's ready. As soon as this world-shattering decision is made, I'll pan-fry Louis's chopped steak. Just say it's alright, Mama. He's a man now; it's time you stopped worrying about him. You didn't worry about me when I had to leave school at fifteen to start copy-holding, did you? It's time for Sam to grow up."

"Thank you, Nora, for pointing that out to me. Just to be clear, I always worry about you. I worry about all my children."

Facing Sam, I said, "Although you were raised in a big city, you know nothing of the likes of a low-life crew. Joe won't be there to look after you, and I will fret about the dangerous, criminal, and illiterate lot with whom you'll be living. Your ports of call are all primitive, lawless dockages, where an unworldly chap can be preyed upon." I looked him straight in the eye, waiting for his defense.

"Like Rube said, I'm almost nineteen, and we need the money. And, Mama, not to be harsh, but I don't need your permission. I've already told Joe I'd fill in for him, so I hope you'll be a good sport and say, good luck and bon voyage. What do you say, Mama?"

Nora went to the door, stepped out into the hallway, and yelled up the stairwell: "ROSE! ROSE!" Five-year-old Woodrow came to the second-floor landing. Leaning over the railing, he shouted, "What is it, Aunt Nora?" "Tell your Mama to come down right now. There's a show going on worth seeing!"

Rose entered the scene, carrying her newest infant, Richard.

"Dear God, what scheme are you cooking up now?"

Nora said, "Sam is going off to play fiddle on the bounding main! They're trying to find a way to get Mama to send him off into the sunset with her blessing!" There were giggles all around, not from me, of course.

I know when it's time to accept things out of my control and move on. This was one of them.

"Sam, without Joe to look after you, I'm against the plan. However, my advice is: In the end, it's your life. Be careful, my son, and do as you wish."

Morris asked, "Do I understand you to mean if Sam had a caretaker, you'd salute the idea, Mama? Albert can't quit the Crotona. He's a regular there; it just wouldn't make sense. And thinking about Bertha and little Lucille isolated in that apartment way out in Far Rockaway; well, he just wouldn't do it. Nellie would be alright taking care of the kids, but I'm not walking away from my cello seat; I worked too hard to get it. Charlie's got no kids but also no instrument, so forget him. Lou is out, too; they're not looking for a clarinet player."

"Well, that leaves me!" Rudolf jumped to standing. "Joe, do you think Eagle will hire my cello? You know I've been playing for years, mostly for free. What do you say, Joe?"

Joe laughed, "Rube, you're a real pal to help get Sam on that boat. If I don't fill the vacancy, they'll blackball me next time. I'll swear to the bandmaster *and* the ship's mate that you're as good as any cellist in New York. You think Gussie will let you go?"

There was silence in the room, then they all started laughing so hard, Rudolf rolled off the settee onto the floor, clutching his belly.

I couldn't believe my eyes and ears. Gussie was pregnant for the third time, the child due in April. She and Rudolf had just leased a four-room flat on East 184th Street, with a February 1st move-in; yet, my sons were cooking up a fantasy that would leave all care on her shoulders.

I wasn't amused. "That is the most irresponsible idea you've ever had, Rudolf! I'm sure Gussie won't go along with this."

Nora laughed even harder, gasping out, "You never know, Mama. Gussie loves him because he's so unpredictable and impractical. She knows how much he wants to be a musician; I'll bet a quarter she'll say it's OK."

I thought about that. "I won't take that wager; she can't refuse him anything. If Gussie agrees, I agree, too."

The baby began to whimper. Rose rocked back and forth on her heels to comfort him. True to her nature, she had a few caustic remarks to make. "Dickie needs his feed, so I'm going back upstairs now. Here's the truth as we all know it: Gussie's a pushover, so Rube will escape his responsibilities *and* New York's winter for two months. With her mother and sister living in the same apartment building, Gussie'll be fine. Even Nettie, the crazy sister, will help her out with the two girls. Pregnant or not, she'll be alright. So, bon voyage, Sam, and Rube. Think of us while you're enjoying the tropical breezes!" We could hear Rose laughing as she made her way up the stairs.

Rudolf was downright giddy. "I think we should have a drink to celebrate."

"And I think you should go home and talk to Gussie. You haven't left the dock yet," I added.

Morris boomed, "I think we should have a drink AND dinner; I'm starving."

Later, Rudolf related their conversation to me. Gussie said, "We have only five dollars in savings and I'm six months pregnant. I know how much you want this, so I'll go along, but maybe Fannie can stay with me to help with the girls until you come back." Then, he said, "You're a good sport, Swipsey. It's a once-in-a-lifetime opportunity, one that might change our lives forever. And $300.00 will set us up!"

At long last, Rube was a musician.

The Lamport and Holt vessels, SS *Vauban*, SS *Vestris*, and SS *Vandyck*, were three sister ships built in Belfast, Ireland, in 1912. They were chartered as military transports during World War I.

In the 1920s and 1930s, the company offered the traveling public a five-thousand nautical mile, twenty-three-day, voyage from New York to Buenos Aires, Argentina. All that, for four hundred fifty dollars.

The ships made two-night stops in Barbados and Trinidad and four nights in Rio De Janeiro. At the terminal, Buenos Aires, a week to re-provision gave the crew an opportunity to sightsee before making the return trip.

For four years, beginning January 1923, Sam Freed played violin with the band on all three of the Lamport and Holt sister ships. His brothers, Rube, Morris, Albert, and Louis, joined him on at least one voyage.

After WWI, when the Trianon Treaty redistributed European territories, America witnessed a massive influx of stateless people. Russians escaping the revolution, those expelled in ethnic cleansings, and those deprived of nationality by the new nation states petitioned for naturalization. Proof of nationality was, for the most part, unnecessary when traveling. It wasn't until December 15, 1915, that citizens leaving the United States were advised to obtain a passport in order to gain access to countries that required it.

The process toward citizenship by naturalization began with a visit to the most convenient court, called a court of record, to file a petition, an application.

Petitioning was an action taken by aliens to renounce their birthplace. The petitioner was required to declare the place of birth, date of arrival in America, description of physical attributes (age, height, skin color, eye color), names and ages of spouse and children, and place of residence. Affidavits were mandated to include the notarized signatures of two American citizen witnesses. After five years elapsed, a Certificate of Naturalization was issued. It wasn't until the outbreak of WWII that passports for United States citizens were required to reenter the country.

Sam

Albert and Morris volunteered to pay Gussie's bills until she received Rube's first month's wages by Western Union.

So, it was settled, and the next day, Rube told the foreman at Alverson's he would be taking a sabbatical, as he termed it, forced by a family crisis. Coincidentally, the firm was experiencing a slack time, which influenced the cordiality of Rube's boss, who put up no kick to this unpaid leave! The understanding was he'd be back on the job the last week of March. Gotta hand it to him, Rube could talk his way through anything. He said the foreman grasped his hand, wishing him luck, and pumped his arm up and down vigorously!

Departure was on a Thursday. Mama, Rube, Gussie, and I took the 2:00 Liberty Street ferry to the Lamport and Holt pier in Hoboken. A layer of thick black clouds enshrouded the city. A mix of freezing rain and snow, driven by a northerly wind, bit into my face.

The ferry tossed and lurched its way across the Hudson. Getting off, Rube wrestled with his cello and suitcase, almost falling on the slushy pier. He whispered to me, "Won't it be nice to feel the tropical sun, Sammy, my boy?"

Rube whistled for a porter, who stacked our belongings onto a hand truck and led the way.

Gussie walked in front of me, holding on to the tail of Rube's coat for balance. She looked so sad and apprehensive, like a sparrow with a broken wing. Mama held tight to her daughter-in-law, though I think it was as much to help her navigate the snowy mush as to give comfort to Gussie.

Of all the people I never expected to see—*Charlie* was at the dock! "Little brother, I couldn't let you and Rube sail off the edge of the horizon without saying goodbye, now, could I?" Looking pale and gaunt, he managed a weak smile; it had taken a big effort for him to be there.

I embraced him. "Charlie, thanks so much for coming. It means the world!"

"When I heard the name of the ship you boys were sailing on, I had to come. There was no way I'd miss it! The SS *Vauban*! Can you believe it? You may not know this, but she's the SAME *Vauban* that carried me off to the front six years ago!

"You see a shiny black hull, polished decks, and a striped funnel, but she's the same grey tub underneath.

"Can you believe the adverts? 'The finest in the world! An elite V-Class luxury ocean liner'! Who're they kidding? She's an old warhorse with a new set of knickers!"

I know it made Mama happy to have Charlie involved in a family event; he and Reggie never quite fit in, and I can't remember the last time I'd seen him out and about during cold weather, given his bum lungs. Reggie probably didn't know he was at the dock, or she might have advised against it, or, at the very least, would have been with him, making sure he had a scarf and layers of wool to keep him warm. He worked Monday, Wednesday, and Friday in the mailroom at The Bronx Veteran's Hospital, sitting on a stool for most of the day. The truth was, he only made a few dollars; she supported them with her sewing machine. From their Upper East Side flat on Kelly Avenue to the dock in New Jersey was a difficult trek for him. I worried he had overtaxed himself, and Reggie would be angry. So sad, Charlie's story. He was only twenty-nine years old. The war, or should I say, the flu, had cut him down in his prime.

Longshoremen were loading provisions and cargo into the hold, and passengers were dressed for a society event, in evening coats with fur collars. There was a newspaper reporter from *The World* taking photos of a couple I didn't recognize.

Joe Glover waved to us from under a tarp stretched across the rear deck. He was talking with a tall, stout man, about fifty, I'd say. Hatless, the man wore a plaid cape! His thinning, grey hair was combed across a balding pate, a pince-nez perched on his nose, under which a pencil-thin, jet-black moustache scrawled across his upper lip.

Rube motioned for the porter to bring our things to the place where Glover was waiting. Grumbling to himself all the way up the gangplank and across the snow-covered deck, he dumped our things into a pile. "Take care of the porter, Sammy," Rube said. I gave him a quarter, and he gave me a dirty look before leaving.

Rube clapped Joe's shoulder. "Joe, my friend! Well, here we are! Can someone remove our bags to the appropriate cabin?"

Joe beamed. "What did I tell you, Ernie? This is Rube Freed! He's the wittiest cello in New York, and your passengers will fall in love with him."

Rube grabbed Ernie's hand in a firm shake, conveying the strength of a man who knows what he's doing. "A pleasure, Ernie, a pleasure. I've heard so much about you and look forward to working for you. This is my brother, Sam. The finest fiddler you'll ever hear. His Schubert will bring tears to your eyes. He's been playing the city circuit since he was fifteen. You won't be sorry you've taken on the Freed boys; I can assure you."

Eagle stared, wide-eyed, at Rube. Was he thinking: *Is this guy British?* Or, more likely, maybe: *I'm already sorry I've taken on the Freed boys.*

Joe thought it an opportune moment to say goodbye. "Thanks, Rube, Sam. You're swell pals. I know you're gonna do great. Enjoy the tropics and don't drink the water!" He shook Eagles's hand, pulled his coat collar up to shield his face, and ran out into the dismal weather.

Eagle called after him, "Bye, Joe. See you on the next trip."

"Hello, Rube; Sam. A pleasure. Let's get on with it. The ship will sail at 9:00. We play in the dining room at 8:00. There'll be a rehearsal of the playlist at 6:30. My assistant, Sol, will fill you in. Got your tuxedos?" Rube and I nodded. "Get your things and follow me down the ladders, which is ship talk for stairs. It's three ladders down to D; the deck over the engines. We're in cabin D-8."

Picking up my fiddle case and valise, I followed Rube, who followed Ernie. All of us, even Mama with her cane, slowly worked our way down the narrow ladders to the band's quarters. "This reminds me of our crossing. Remember the narrow stairs, Rube?" "Yes, Mama, I do, it was exciting then; today, it's a nuisance and dangerous for you. Do be careful. If you're not able, later on, Sam and I will carry you up."

At the landing, Ernie told us, "Find a bunk and closet. Unpack your valises, then come to the crew's salon at the end of the passageway, starboard; that means the right side of the ship, for you newbies."

Belowships, everything was painted a dull grey, probably hadn't been refreshed since Charlie sailed to Europe! One hundred thirteen crewmen, segregated by job description, were housed in three cabins arranged with floor-to-ceiling steel cots. The dirty men- stokers, boiler-room workers, electricians, greasers, and general maintenance workers- kept to themselves, farthest aft, nearest the engine room. They even had their own bathroom. Dining room stewards, cooks, and provisions men lived next to us and shared our bathroom. Bandsmen and room stewards were in the smallest quarters on board.

Our mates had scribbled their names in black paint on the doors of the closets they claimed: Warfield, Ritchie, Brown, Jewell, Kinsington, Mitchell, Kybart, Warham, Eagle, Quirk, Rutherford, Bowyer.

A shoe or hat, perched on a cot let us know which were spoken for, leaving only three on the bottom row.

Rube declared it a disaster. "The worst place to be, the bottom bunk. If the guy above is seasick, you're going to catch the spray. If the toilet overflows, you're in the soup. If a guy is drunk, he'll step on your pillow or face, trying to climb up. The worst place."

Mama said, "Please, Rube. No dramatics. Just go along and make the best of it. The impression you make with the musicians today is important."

"How about these two? They look comfortable, and right next to each other." Gussie always tried to cheer things up. It only took a few minutes for her and Mama to stack our clothes in the closets and hang up our tuxedos.

"There! Now, you boys are both set." Rube gave her a kiss. "The best wife in New York! Thanks, Swipsey."

With his eyes closed, it looked as if Charlie had fallen asleep sitting up on one of the cots, but he was awake, waiting for his breathing to ease up after coming down the ladders.

"You alright, Charlie?" "Yeah, sure..."

In the salon, Eagle was ready to present us to the ensemble, who were drinking bootleg hootch out of cracked teacups in a room filled with cigarette smoke.

I looked over at Charlie. "You want to leave now, Charlie? I can help you up the stairs if you want." He rasped, "Nah, I'll wait for Mama and Gussie. I may need them to get me home. Reggie's gonna kill me for coming here today. Probably take a week in bed to recover."

"Gee, I'm sorry, but I'm glad you came." "Me, too," he croaked.

With hooded eyes, they watched us enter the salon. Eagle said, "Look lively, boys. These are the Freed strings. Sam on fiddle, Rube on cello. This is their mother and brother and Rube's wife. The boys've been vouched for by Joe; we're all set. C'mon, and show you have some class; say hello to your new chums."

Maynard Rutherford, the piano player, stood up and shook my hand, nodded to Mama, Gussie, and Charlie. Cigarette smoke from a stub held at the corner of his mouth curled up, obscuring one eye. "Nice ta meetcha."

Arthur Mitchell didn't bother to rise he waved his hand in a big arc. "I'm the standup bass. Welcome to the floating crap game!"

"Walther Bowyer here. Clarinet and sax."

Eagle pointed to a chap lying on a settee, fast asleep. "That's Herbert Quirk, from Connecticut. He starts every cruise drinking pretty heavy. Really great drummer, Herb, but he's seasick until we get past Cape Hatteras. He says the booze helps." Everyone laughed, Herb groaned.

Rube went round to shake each hand. "I'm so happy to be here with you fellows. I'm hoping you'll cut me some slack until I figure out the lay of the land. This is my wonderful wife, Gussie, who's got the biggest heart and most generous soul in New York." Gussie waved to all the men, and in unison, they said, "Hello, Gussie." Rube was just warming up. "That pale-faced guy is my brother, Charlie; he says this tub took him to the front in 1917. This guy here is my brother, Sam. The best fiddle player you'll ever hear, I guarantee it! And, this, this, is my dearest Mother, Fannie! She's worried about her boys traveling to exotic places, so please tell her we're in no danger." Everyone laughed.

She stood with her arms folded over her breasts, her purse dangling from one elbow. Mama had been paying close attention, studying each man's demeanor. I sensed she wasn't impressed with the band.

Maynard approached Mama. "Mrs. Freed. 'Ya know, I'll personally watch yer boys every minute. No harm'll come to 'em, I promise."

Mama responded in all seriousness. "Mr. Rutherford, I'll hold you to that promise. I'm a poor widow, whose wonderful sons put food in my mouth, a roof over my head. I'll be praying for their safe return every day and night."

Turning to his bandmates, he said, "Awww, ain't' that sweet? My own mother's gone now, but she never worried about me, not even for one single minute." Then, putting his hand over his heart, "Mrs. Freed, I solemnly swear to keep your boys safe."

At that moment, a dwarf, dressed in a full-length raccoon coat, his face barely visible under a hat of the same fur, made a grand entrance.

He appeared to be a talking version of the very animal whose skins he wore! Out of breath, and with a hint of a German accent, he managed to say, "Sorry I'm late, had to take care getting from the ferry! This damn weather scares the bejeebers out of me. If I fall, my bum hips will break like matchsticks!"

Ernie Eagle took the floor. "Alright now. Party's over. Rube, Sam, this is Sol Menschkeit, the band manager. He's not going with us, just here to make sure the Mate has all your papers. He's the guy who'll give you your pay on March 8th, so be nice to Sol."

The little man removed his gloves and put his hat on a table. Rummaging through a leather pouch, he extracted an envelope stuffed with documents. "Sam, you're OK; your birth certificate will be held in the first mate's safe. Rube, if anyone asks, you were born in Pennsylvania, a bona fide citizen of the United States of America! With no proof and no passport, I swore an affidavit for you in front of a judge friend of mine in Brooklyn, so relax. I hope I got your birthday right.

"Ernie has a $100.00 advance for each of you. Vunce you're out of the New York harbor, he'll giff you each fifty bucks. Then, another fifty in Buenos Aires the night the return trip starts. Zat'll leave two hundred dollars waiting ven you come home! Don't get in no fights. Just do your verk and stick togedder. Any kvestchuns?"

Rube raised his hand. Sol ignored him.

"OK, zen, that's all. Bon voyage, gutbye." He turned and disappeared into the stairwell.

Eagle clapped his hands for attention. "It was nice to meet the Freeds, but it's time to go. Mother, make your farewells; you'll see your lads in two months' time. Dinner for the crew is at six. We rehearse in the room next to the laundry at 6:30, showtime at 8. Go easy on the hootch."

The climb topside took fifteen minutes, with Charlie and Mama stopping to rest at each landing. Also, Gussie complained the upward trek strained her belly. Rube said, "C'mon, Swipes, you're doing fine. Just take your time; there's no rush."

Mama with her cane, pregnant Gussie, and Charlie gasping for breath didn't paint a picture of health, and I worried they'd not make it home without calling for an ambulance!

Coming out into the evening darkness, Mama adjusted her hat and scarf. "Thank heaven, the snow has ended, the wind, too. Sam, dear, I'm satisfied you'll be alright, so I'm happy for you, my darling. Still, do be careful. And, don't worry about me. Your job is to make sure Rube sends his pay immediately, and to write once a week. I'm looking forward to having a vacation with Gussie, once you men are out of our hair!" She laughed and kissed my cheek. "We better hurry to make the ferry. Now, go back to the ship. Sam; you should have had better sense than to come out without a coat."

"Mama, I love you. Thanks for being a good sport about all this. Once you're on the New York side and in the subway, you'll be in The Bronx in less than an hour. And Charlie's stop is much closer, so Reggie will have him dry and warm in no time."

My words were encouraging, though not convincing. I added, "I'll write, I promise; and I'll try to keep my big brother on the straight and narrow."

Rube was walking to the ferry slip, his arm around Gussie, drying her tears and kissing her. I embraced Mama and Charlie, then ran back to the gangway, shaking from the cold. Once on deck, I waited in the reception area, watching through the window for Rube's return. Coatless, he ran back, entering the room with a huge smile on his face. "Sammy, dear boy! We're free!"

There were still forty minutes before dinner, plenty of time to tour the boat. The dining room had vaulted ceilings and marbled columns in niches around its perimeter. Setting the tables, the staff looked smart in black trousers and vest, white shirts, and bow ties.

Wine storage had been built into the starboard wall. Above it, cantilevered from the wall, a stage jutted out fifteen feet from the floor. I could see five seats, music stands, and an upright piano. "Look at the footlights, Sammy. The uplighting will give us a dramatic shadow when we're playing, like angels on high!"

Sliding doors gave direct access from the dining room to the Salon, which had a stage large enough for cabaret acts, a white baby grand piano, and, I'd say, up to ten band seats. Round tables and gilt-framed chairs surrounded the dance floor.

A bartender was cleaning glassware and waved at us. "Hello, mates." Rube went to shake his hand. "We're with the band, Rube and Sam."

"Welcome aboard! You can call me 'Trini,' 'cause I'm from Trin-i-dad!" The huge black man threw back his head and laughed. "Good luck and keep your notes sweet."

We peeked down the first-class passageways but didn't go down. And there was a gym, where young swells could exercise and lift barbells; we peeked in there, too.

Barely audible through the static, we heard the mate's voice broadcast from speakers along the ceilings: "All ashore that's going ashore." Stewards in white uniforms scurried around delivering telegrams and fruit baskets.

"We'd better get down for dinner," Rube yelled over his shoulder as he bolted down the nearest ladder. We had no trouble finding the dining hall, the smell of stew our road map.

It was going to be great, just like Joe Glover said. Easy money.

Fannie

Poor Charles, so sick and robbed of his youth. I swear, he looked like a corpse by the time the subway slowed down at his 62nd Street stop. Then, he had a two-block walk to this apartment; too far, if you asked me.

Gussie rummaged through her purse, then scribbled something on the back of an envelope. "Charlie, give this to Reggie. It's the phone number of Mr. Daley, the pharmacist on Webster Avenue. He keeps a notepad on the wall to jot down emergency messages for his customers. I'll send Thelma down every thirty minutes to check, so please make sure Reggie calls to say you made it home."

Charles stood up, holding onto a ceiling strap for balance. After kissing me and Gussie, he stepped out the door. "Bye, bye, Mama, Gussie. Kiss the kids and be well."

Opening the apartment door, Gussie called, "Hello! We're home!" The radiators were hissing and banging, putting out heat, welcoming us. I handed my coat to Gussie, who hung it in the closet. She called in to the kitchen. "Yoohoo, we're here!" In the kitchen, Nettie was lowering the gas flame under a percolating coffee pot. "Gussie, Fannie! I'll bet you're glad to be out of that lousy weather. Georgie and the girls are in the bedroom, playing checkers. Stanley's just gone home with Mother, who'll put him to bed." Gussie embraced her sister and said, "Thanks, Nettie, for watching them all day. I'm so tired, but I *had* to go, *had* to see the boat and the men Rube's traveling with."

I always stared at Nettie; she was so beautiful, her blonde hair done in the latest fashion: bobbed to shoulder length, parted on one side, and set in those dramatic marcel waves. Her large, sky-blue eyes and long blonde, almost white, lashes drew your attention. Her skin was soft and shell pink, truly a beauty, in spite of her short stature. Like their mother, Sali, the sisters weren't even five feet tall. While Nettie inherited a lovely, petite figure, sadly for Gussie, she was the image of their father: dark eyes, dark hair, and dark complexion. And stout.

"You must be exhausted, dear. Put your feet up and take a rest. I made kraut sveckles and meatballs and already fed the children. I'll take some downstairs for us now. I'm sure Mother is hungry, and Hermann is likely back home, too.

I asked, "What about Jack?"

"Not until eight; the last packages are collected at six, then he has to take them to the main post office. He's got the grippe but went to work anyway. I think he's putting in all this time to earn a few extra dollars to celebrate our anniversary next week."

Nettie called to the children, "Girls, come say hello to your mother and grandmother! And Georgie, you come, too. Give your auntie a kiss and also Fannie; then, we're going downstairs."

"Aw, do I have to?" Seven-year-old boys don't like to be kissed and fussed over. Georgie was a handsome boy, and I thought, *how sad about his mother.*

Thelma and Leonore skipped into the room, holding hands. Although Thelma, the image of Rube, was three years older than Leonore, they were the same height. That was where the resemblance ended, though. Leonore had her Austrian grandmother's complexion and blonde hair. The girls kissed me and said goodnight. So did Aunt Nettie and her son, Georgie.

A house with children is alive, full of promise, making memories. I shared Gussie's bed while Rube was away. I didn't have the heart to tell her it disturbed my sleep when she threw her leg over me during the night. She had a generous nature, Gussie did. I observed her giving a nickel here, a dime there to children on the street, mostly, but also to a stranger who looked downtrodden. Maybe that was why she was always broke.

When they moved into the building, the family included Sam and Sali, and Gussie's sister, Rosepearl. Now, Sali, Nettie and husband Jack, Rosepearl and Hermann and their sons, Georgie and Stanley, lived together in a three-bedroom apartment on the building's second floor.

Rosepearl and Hermann Tiger had been introduced by a mutual friend at a social gathering in an apartment down the street. They married three months later. At Stanley's circumcision, Sam Geduldig served as Sondek, godfather. That evening, he started running a fever and, within a few days, died of pneumonia. It was a terrible loss, followed by an even worse tragedy.

Six weeks after Stanley's birth, the doctor visited. The new mother was ill, very ill. It wasn't the normal course of adjustment and recuperation after confinement. Rosepearl's general condition was declining. She had a sore throat and no appetite. Her breasts, feverish to the touch, were painful when the infant suckled. She discontinued nursing for a week or so, then resumed, but stopped again. Pus began to leak from her nipples.

Hermann wouldn't leave her side all the while Rosepearl was so sick. Then months after Stanley's birth, the poor woman finally succumbed to milk fever, an infection that had slowly taken over her body; she was twenty-nine.

Hermann took a job selling brushes door-to-door in Newark, New Jersey. He said it was the perfect job for him. "It gets me out of the house and keeps me from having to make any real conversation. It's a job for a lost person, no permanency. New customers every day, new territory every week. It suits me."

The Tiger family operated a hotel in the Catskill mountains in upstate New York, and Hermann was expected at the hotel in March, when the season opened to celebrate Passover.

Gussie said, "His family doesn't realize how changed he is. He hasn't worked at the hotel since before Rosepearl died; that's more than a year ago. He says he can't go back, too many memories and people up there who knew her.

"Also, the boys have to stay here with my mother and Nettie, who have been their mothers since Rosepearl died. There's no way they're going to live in the mountains with the Tiger family. They're my sister's children and should be with *our* family.

"You know Nettie is barren, been married for seven years and not even a miscarriage! She and Jack want to adopt the boys. For the time being, Hermann's not discussing it, but if he tries to take them away, there'll be a battle royal. I'll say this: Nettie's not one to be taken on.

She may be a little unhinged, but she's very, very intelligent and tenacious."

Nettie's husband, Jack, worked as a messenger for the New York Life Insurance Company. He wasn't a good provider, but he adored his gorgeous wife. On weekends, Nettie earned a few dollars as a salesclerk in Klein's "on the square" department store on 14th Street. That was a good idea, as holding down a full-time job was not possible, given her unpredictable mental state. Nettie was prone to depression and erratic behavior. A few days before I was to return home, I heard Nettie's shrill voice coming from the kitchen. "I'll kill you, you bastard. I know you think you're better than me. I hate your guts, you AND your kids, spoiled brats. AND Rube, too, that piece of shit."

As quickly as I could get there, I stepped between them, trying to protect Gussie. Nettie was too fast; she pushed with both hands and all her strength. Off balance, Gussie grabbed for the stove, burning her hand so severely, she howled in pain, which brought Nettie back to reality.

"Oh, no! I'm sorry, Gussie. I'm so, so sorry." With that remark, she ran out the door and back to her mother.

I chipped some ice from the block in the box under the windowsill and told Gussie to hold it in her burned palm. We left immediately for Dr. Steigman's office down the street. He applied black salve and covered the wound with an elastic bandage.

Later, Gussie told me, "Nettie responds to the voices in her head, who tell her people mean her harm. Maybe they said I was a threat of some kind.

"Fannie, these spells frighten the children, and me, too. When Rube is home, she knows to stay away if she's unwell; she's afraid of him. When Jack comes home tonight, he'll give her medicine for a few days, dope her up with a sedative. My mother will have her hands full, taking care of the boys and Nettie, too."

I was very upset but said what was on my mind. "You and Rube ought to think about moving away from here. She was all red-faced, and I thought she was going to kill you!"

"This happens maybe twice a year, so for the most part, she's able, with the help of my mother and me, to make meals, shop for groceries, and look after the children. Rube says she needs to go to a mental asylum. My mother says, *over my dead body*. When she says that, Rube usually whispers to me, *that may be the day your sister's finally put there, over your mother's dead body!*

The day before I returned to 32nd Street, I heard Nettie ranting in the stairwell. The girls were at school, Gussie out to the butcher. I slid the chain on the door bolt to prevent Nettie from coming in. I didn't tell Gussie. What was the point? The Geduldigs, acutely aware of Nettie's condition, did not speak of it, but her derangement was always an undercurrent. Every family has its undercurrents.

The boys returned home looking very handsome: healthy, and suntanned! For Rudolf, the trip had been a grand escapade and gave him time to think. In the end, he decided a musician's lot was not for him. Putting on a great show of remorse to the Alverson's foreman for having left the job, he pledged to commit himself to excellent work and attendance and was rehired.

For Sam, well, Joe Glover had told the truth: it had been easy money. Much more than my son could earn here in the city.

Louis, Nora, and I sat at the kitchen table watching Sam count it out. "THREE HUNDRED DOLLARS for two months' work! There's only two here, Mama, 'cause Rube and I spent a few bucks along the way. It was great. And, I've got to tell you about Rube. He rehearsed and practiced every spare minute, very serious about keeping up. By the time we got to Barbados, seven days at sea, no one on that ship could tell he wasn't a professional musician. I love the traveling life, and our bandmates, well they're the best!"

Louis was excited. "Sam, that's fantastic, what a payday! You think I could do a trip? I sure could use the money. If you and Joe could put in a good word, I'd love it."

Sam gave Nora twenty dollars. "I want you to buy something nice for yourself, Nora. I hear you've got a beau, some guy who runs a cigar store on Lexington Avenue. You want to look nice for him, don't you?

"You've been home a few hours, and Mama's already been gossiping! His name is Max Kaminsky, and he *owns* a tobacco store. He's a bookworm, like me. In fact, we met walking into each other on the steps of the library. Gee, thanks for the gift, Sam. I was thinking of getting a short bob, and this will help with my makeover."

Sam clapped his hands for attention. "Here's the big news. I've decided to stay with the ocean band as long as I can. I'm booked back on the *Vauban* with Joe, leaving on the twentieth. Mama, our money worries are over!"

I was not thrilled to hear he was going away again, but there was nothing I could do to stop it; he was a grown man, almost twenty.

"Well, dear, it looks like you've been launched!"

Several pillows kept me upright throughout the night, allowing full expansion of my lungs. My ankles were swollen, and the pains in my hip and knee were constant.

The doctor was concerned about my high blood pressure, advising me to avoid stressful thoughts and elevate my feet whenever possible.

I kept that to myself. Nothing would be gained by spreading bad news.

18

Sam

I booked onto the *Vauban* in March, with Joe Glover looking after me, then again in May, when he wasn't.

She hadn't been on the last three cruises. I'd remember if she had been.

The second night out of New York, halfway to Barbados, she walked into the dining room and directly to our table. Coming to a stop in front of my chair, her eyes met mine without a blink.

She actually put her hand on my shoulder, pressing down slightly. To hold me in place?

"Hello, y'all, I'm Myrtle. Ah'm the ship's manicurist. You'd be ah-mazed at the tips ah earn on this tub, massaging the hands of the swells." Her Tennessee drawl stretched out each syllable, tantalizing and seductive.

I was stunned by her entrance, the brazen yet intriguing way she carried herself. The persistence of her touch. I gulped and squeaked, "I'm Sam, from New York."

Pulling a chair from the next table very close to mine, she sat down, crossing her black stockinged legs. Maynard, Herb, and Walther started laughing and stood up to dispose of their trays. Maynard whispered, "Good luck, Sammy boy. You're in for it now."

Myrtle didn't look at them, didn't seem to hear them. "Ah was bawn in Tinnessee, but ah lived in Chicago foah a tahm, then a yeah or so in Pittsburgh. Ah guess, at nineteen, ah figger ah can look for adventure, so heah ah am!"

I fell hard for Myrtle. She was so worldly; I was born in the big city, but compared to her, I was still a boy. Her fashions were radical. She wore very short skirts and even a deco-inspired velvet pajama suit. One couldn't help but stare at how she carried off wearing a chemise, a knee-length, loose-fitting garment with no definition of her waistline, which was tiny, or her bosom, which was ample and gravity defying.

She always looked chic, especially when her bobbed hair was hidden under a cloche hat, one eye dramatically obscured by a floppy brim. She wore powder, lipstick, rouge, eyebrow pencil, and eye shadow every day, all day. Her nails were filed to long points, painted to match every outfit. It didn't matter who was around, she did it all just to please herself. Myrtle needed sex a few times a day, and we did it in every dead-end gangway and niche on deck.

"Let's get married, Sam, dahlin'. It'll be such fun, travlin' around, livin' footloose. That is, when we're not livin' the ha-life in New York City!"

I was such a babe in the woods, such a dumb bunny. "I'm so in love with you, Myrtle. Let's do it! How happy it'll make my mother, knowing I have a wife to look after me."

On the last night in Buenos Aires, the captain married us, even assigning us private honeymoon quarters for the trip home.

We made our way down the ladders to C-Deck. Before opening the door, I picked her up in my arms, to carry her over the threshold, a mandatory gesture on one's honeymoon. Feeling sentimental, I said, "I'm the proudest man in the world tonight, dearest. This is heaven, being with you."

When I stepped into the room, she craned her neck to take it all in. "Are y'all making a joke? This stinks. You laak this? That captain really made fools of us, Sam. Ah was sure he'd give us a first-class cabin, and *this* is what we get? Put. Me. Down."

She started to leave, but I barred the door with my body. "Where are you going, Myrtle? The boat's full, there are not top deck cabins to be had. The captain was doing the best he could. It's not that bad."

Giving me a withering look, she said, "Ah can't wait to be done with the phony Brits runnin' this tub."

I was happy with the bunk, even though there was barely enough room for a mattress; I'm sure it had once been used as a utility closet. I made love to her all night long, and that's all I wanted.

"Y'all are too naïve; need to harden up, become a man. But, don't y'all fret, honey; when we get to New York, we'll staht really livin'."

"For certain, Myrtle, darling. New York has everything. Life there will be exciting." I wanted to make love to her; that's all I thought about. I'd do anything to please her.

Back in New York, we moved in with Mama, Nora, and Lou. I said, "It's temporary, Myrtle. With my next pay, we'll find our own place."

Fannie

In July, Sam and his bride moved in with me on East 32nd Street. I welcomed Myrtle with open arms, never wanting to be interfering or judgmental. If this is the woman Sam wanted, I'd be the loving mother he wanted, too.

Before dinner, Sam announced, "Myrtle isn't going with me on the August sailing; Morris is. She needs a rest and wants to get to know all of you. So, Mama, she'll stay here till we get back in October. I know you girls will get along famously!"

Louis looked at Nora, then me, and rolled his eyes.

Louis was cordial and wasted no time with small talk. An hour later, he told me, "I'm going to stay with Ronald Klingman for a while, so Sam and Myrtle can have my bedroom for as long as they need it." He packed his things and left before the dinner dishes were cleared.

"Well, now, wasn't that so kahnd of Louis?" Myrtle chirped. "He's a dahlin'."

I kept still. Nora and I were already sharing a room, so we all made the best of it.

"Mama," Nora whispered to me in the darkened room. "Did you see the underwear she hung on the drying rack in the bathroom?"

"No, dear, but I rarely make it through the night without going, so I'll see it then."

"Mama, why did he marry her? Is she pregnant? What could she want with him? Did she think Sam has money? I think they're both in for a rude awakening."

"Shh, Nora, they'll hear you. How about we give her the benefit of the doubt. She's also very young; maybe she has a tragic story, a difficult childhood. Maybe she was orphaned. We don't know anything about her yet. Maybe she'll be the best thing that ever happened to Sam."

"That's my Mama, the world's greatest optimist and believer in love conquering all!"

"Goodnight, dear Nora. Let's get some rest. I'm exhausted."

At 3:30 in the morning, I went to the bathroom. The drying rack was suspended from the ceiling above the tub. Over one of the wooden rods, hung a bustier of cream-colored silk. Tiny black pussycats with pink tongues and white whiskers were embroidered along the cleavage edge.

Sam had been very enthusiastic about his wife. "She's the cat's meow." Now, I understood what he meant; there were the pussycats to prove it!

And, who was I to disparage, to judge? Hadn't I been passionate when I was their age? Can I forget the ardent demands of youth? No,

I'd never forget that part of my life; it's the best possible remembrance of who I was. I loved, I wanted, I needed, I gave it all for love. Recalling the heat of my body brought a smile, and though I knew it was a trick of the mind, I smelled my Samuel's body, still potent in memory.

A few days after Sam and Morris left on the SS *Vestris*, Myrtle found work as a Times Square hotel manicurist.

As it is my nature to treat those of small and great intellect with the same respect, I made friends of all kinds and learned much from those I encountered. I wouldn't say Myrtle was dumb. She had no education, could speak no foreign language, and had read none of the important books, but she had *smarts*, and her worldview was just so different and refreshing.

She never spoke of her parents, merely hinting that she had been on her own since she was very young. She followed every movement I made in the kitchen with curiosity; I supposed her own mother had not taught her to bake or cook. She asked about my life as a girl in Hungary. She was interested in everything, which, to my way of thinking, made her a very intelligent person. So, in the end, I would say that she and I definitely learned a thing or two from one another, and a fondness developed between us.

Nora made a small effort, barely concealing her contempt for Myrtle. "She's a whore, Mama. She tricked Sam into marrying her, and she'll break his heart in the end. I can't stand being in the same room with her."

Having dinner with Max Kaminsky every evening after work kept Nora out of the apartment, although she always came home to sleep. Myrtle worked on weekends, giving Nora private time, which she enjoyed.

To be fair, Myrtle was very flamboyant and charming, with her Southern accent giving a certain lilt to the tales of tropical islands and famous clients on the ship.

We watched, with awe, how she could move her body, dancing with abandon to the newest songs on the radio. Her favorites were the lindy hop and the Charleston, which had only just made its debut in the show "Running Wild." Both dance crazes had their roots in Black jazz music, and Myrtle said she knew a lot about the Blacks, coming from Tennessee. I had a feeling her admiration of Blacks was limited to what they could do for white folks but avoided that conversation. She had married a Jew, hadn't she? There had to be some history of tolerance in the forces that molded her.

Myrtle was expert at Charleston, moving to the quick rhythm and flapping her arms like a bird. There were nights she said she was working late, but I suspected she was at a dance hall or speakeasy. I kept mum, sensing she was bored and resented Sam's absence. The wired money was nice, but fifty dollars was not enough.

When Sam returned in October, they had a big row because Myrtle hadn't even begun to find an apartment, said she didn't want to be bothered with that, didn't have the time. It was decided she would join him on the next voyage. It turned out Albert and Louis also went on that cruise.

Sam was happy, "It's gonna be great, the four of us together, more a vacation than work! Gee, I wish you could come too, Mama!"

Sam

When I left Myrtle, she had promised to find an apartment for us in New York, set us up for a real life together.

When I got back, she hadn't done much of anything.

"Ah'm tired from all mah travels, y'all. Ah needed time to rest and have your de-ah Mama take care of me. She's a dahlin', by the way."

Mama and Nora kept quiet, just went about daily life without getting in between me and my wife, which was OK by me.

"Ah'm not stayin' here, sleepin' all alone on that lumpy mattress while y'all are gallivantin' all over the seas. Ah'm bored and always broke, and ah've decided to go back on the ship." She pouted, turning her face away from me.

I tried to soothe her, quickly agreeing, "It was unbearable being without you those months. You're right about booking on. I only want you to be happy."

She got her job back. Even the mate couldn't say no to her.

The winter cruise, November to January, is the busiest of the year, being Christmas and all, and they needed two more musicians, one of them clarinet, Lou's instrument! I went to see Glover, now the bandmaster, and talked him into hiring Lou and Albert! There was an extra hundred as a Christmas bonus, which made it all the sweeter.

Myrtle finished her last manicure at six o'clock. The sunset in Rio was spectacular, all purple and orange streaks across the sky. In full makeup and a very short chemise, she found me, with my brothers, in the dining room. Just above her left ear, a long, black feather fanned out, like a flag, held in place by a black velvet band circling her head. God, she was gorgeous; I reached for her hand, needing just to touch her skin.

She pulled away. "Tonight, is New Year's, and ah'm going to celebrate the staht of 1924 in Rio, Sam. Y'all are welcome ta join me, but if not, that's ahlright, too! It's a hot town, and ah'm gonna find some hot music and dancin'."

My brothers, uncomfortable, got up to leave, taking their trays to another table. I didn't stop them.

I pleaded, "But, Myrtle, you know me and the boys are playing until two in the morning. How about waiting for us? The joints in this city are open all night."

"This ship is too boring, and y'all are with ya brothers all the time. Ah hardly earn any money at all, and y'all don't get paid until the end. Ah hate this. Ah'm sick of the whole rat's nest of a ship. Ah want to go back to New York, and ah want y'all to get a really good, steady job, so ah don't have to work just to buy a cheap pair of hose."

What could I do? I loved her. We cooked up an escape.

We told Joe, Albert, Lou, and the captain. We said, *I* said, "Myrtle is pregnant. She's unwell, and we need to leave immediately for New York."

My brothers kept their mouths shut. This was their baby brother's problem. The captain had heard it all before. He said, "See the mate and sign off on the voyage. Your pay ends this moment."

At the adjacent slip, the *Vandyck* was on its northbound run to New York, so I talked to the bandmaster and the purser. To convince the fiddle player on the *Vandyck* to take my place on the *Vestris* cost me $100.00 out-of-pocket, but at least I'd be working his seat for the return and get some of my pay back. Myrtle mostly worked for tips, so she was totally bust, with no job on the return, AND, we had to pay for her lodging and food. Even with an employee discount, it cost me another fifty. I was a little upset, but it was what Myrtle wanted, and I was in love.

Fannie

With Louis, Sam, and Myrtle on the ship and Nora staying at Max's most of the time, I was alone, and for the first time, I felt vulnerable; old.

For that reason, I was not unhappy when Sam and Myrtle came back to New York early. To my surprise, they didn't stay with me. They rented a room in a boarding house on 43rd Street.

I was worried about Sam; he could only find work in the speakeasies downtown, which paid very poorly. His wife worked at a hotel in Times Square, also earning only a few dollars a week in tips. I couldn't afford to help out, and they never asked me, anyway. None of the family saw much of them, not even me. There was nothing I could do other than be ready if Sam needed me in some way.

When Louis came home from the ship, we had a heart-to-heart.

"What will you do now, Louis, look for work as a clarinet player?"

"No, Mama. I don't want that life. I didn't like living in a bunk with men who don't bathe and haven't read a book in their lives. It's a clique, and I've never been comfortable hanging around with "the guys." They think no one understands music but them. And women, well, women fall all over themselves to sleep with a musician, as if they're under some kind of spell. And the drinking and smoking, well, I guess I'm just a prude."

"Don't be so harsh on the musicians, Louis. The life they choose, tight with their own, is because they *are* kind of special, compelled to play the notes. Bathing, reading, even loving a woman can't compete with a true musician's calling. The chords they strike can inspire others to love, to weep, to go to war. That's a powerful gift, Louis. An obsession, maybe.

"So, back to Lord & Taylor?"

"No, Mama. Ronald Klingman and I are heading for Winston-Salem, North Carolina. His family has a department store there, and we're going to run the credit and collection department. That's why Ronald came to New York in the first place, to learn the business. Installment buying is a way of life now, and there's lots of money to be made for the men who collect pennies from the working stiffs every week."

He gave me five twenty-dollar bills. "Here, Mama. This will pay your bills for more than a month, till I leave in March."

"I know you'll be alright, Louis. Don't worry about me; the others are nearby, all in the city. If I need help, they're here."

"I love you, Mama."

"And I love you, my dearest." I added, "I'm happy you're going, Louis, I'll bet there's a lovely Southern girl who's waiting for you, destined for you."

He laughed, "You're such a romantic, Mama. If there is a girl waiting for me, she will have to be *very* special, to draw out this introvert. From your lips to God's ears, as they say, Mama."

Sam

For no good reason, other than Myrtle wanted her own place, we rented a room on West 43rd Street. It was the dead of winter; we were almost flat broke. Nora lent me twenty bucks. I was lucky to find work at the Venture Inn, a speakeasy down on 14th Street. Myrtle was hired back as manicurist at the tonsorial parlor in the Hotel Times Square, a real dive.

"Y'all better figyah out how y'all are going to dig out of this hole, Sam. Ah don't understand how ah married the only Jew in the world who doesn't know how to make money! Ah'm not going to stay with y'all in New York, livin' one step above a niggah."

My God, how did I get here, with this woman? Her cruelty knew no limit. I was so low already, I had to disregard what I heard her say or destroy the few shreds of self-respect I had left.

"Maybe it'll be best if I go back on the ship. I can wire you all my pay, so you won't have to work. What do you say, honey? I can't help it if I'm at sixes-and-sevens when it comes to my career. There's just no work. I'll make it big in the long run. Just stay with me. I need you."

She batted her lashes at me and, in a little-girl's voice, said, "If that's what mah Daddy thinks is best, then ah'll go along. Ah'll even see y'all off at the pier."

Then, she laughed and patted the cushion on the settee. "Now, honey, c'mon ovah and give me some of that beautiful Jewish salami." She was a cold, cold woman, playing me for a sucker. Yet, gratefully, I made love to her.

I had a bad feeling about her living alone in New York. I knew in my bones I couldn't trust her, but I loved her. What a sap I was.

I went back to the band for the next three trips, coming home between cruises. Each time I gave *her* all my pay, except for fifty dollars, and she gave *me* six days in bed, my reward for leaving her on her own, no questions asked.

Once again, Joe Glover came to the rescue. The *Vauban* steamed into New York Harbor ahead of a brisk October breeze. We stood on deck, admiring the cityscape.

"Sammy, I'm quitting cruise ships; this life is a real grind. We're never gonna get anywhere with our music, and the living conditions are horrible. I'm going home, back to Long Island."

I thought he was kidding. We were making four hundred a trip by then. As Bandmaster, he got an extra hundred. "You think you can get this kind of a payday in a shack on Dune Road? C'mon, Joe. There's not enough going on out there."

"Listen, Sam. I got a letter from my mother, telling me about the new country club they built out in Southampton. It's got a golf course and swimming pools and everything the richest stiffs in New York gotta have. Jimmy McLoughlin, the manager of the place, does the hiring. Ma told him she wants me to come back home; he should find an opening for me in the orchestra. Jimmy is Ma's first cousin; for fuck's sake, he'll do anything for her."

"Will he hire me, too?

"Why not? You and the Missus can live on the cheap in Ma's boarding house on Old Mill Road; we'll be one big, happy family!"

"I don't know if Myrtle will go way out there."

"C'mon, Sam. You'll love the Shinnecock Hills; real, authentic Indians live there. Won't Myrtle look sexy in a soft pair of moccasins?

And, hey, she can work at the club, too. They got a barber shop, a real fancy one. She'll make some big tips out there."

Joe winked, "Kidding aside, it may be far from the city, but it's beautiful, and the work is waiting, a steady gig. Trust me on this."

We had already missed the summer season, which ran from Memorial Day through Labor Day, but Jimmy hired us anyway for the Thanksgiving and winter season. This club made a big deal of Christmas, New Year's, Valentine's Day, and Easter, the Gentile membership demanding year-around activities.

Myrtle's cruise experience got her hired; at least I think her experience got her the job. McLoughlin surely liked the way she looked; I could see that.

The place was gorgeous, no expense spared in the design and furnishings. Aside from golf, tennis, and swimming, the main clubhouse offered fine dining, billiards, a card room, lounges, smoking rooms, an exercise gym, private party rooms, and a salon that seated five hundred. The bandstand had room for thirty.

Bandsmen's attire was supplied to us at no cost. For afternoon musicales, I wore a white linen suit with trousers widened to twenty-four inches at the bottom. A white shirt and brown bow tie and brown and white spectator shoes completed the costume. In the evening, a first-class black dinner jacket with peaked lapel and wide trousers were striking. Under the coat, a white waistcoat and black tie, copying the fashion trend set by the Prince of Wales. Black patent leather wing-tip shoes finished off the ensemble.

I was feeling my oats. I was a very fine musician and making a living doing what I loved. What more could a fellow ask of life?

Not to be immodest, I considered myself good-looking; six feet tall, with a slim build and wavy hair. I wouldn't think of straying from Myrtle, not even when the upper crust Grande Dames flirted with me at the Valentine's Day ball.

I thought: *Geez, I'm only twenty-one. Those old bats could have been as old as Mama! Were they kidding?* There were strict rules about fraternizing with members or guests, and I wasn't going to risk being fired. Besides, I had an exciting, beautiful wife.

Myrtle, exposed to the gentry, was even more unhappy with our station and with me. Iola Glover told me, "I spotted your wife strolling down Beach Road on the arm of a swell from the city. You better have a talk with her."

When I cautiously mentioned the rumor, Myrtle got mad. "Ah'm sick of y'all and with our life. There's never enough money to buy anything nice, and we nevah go out of an evening because y'all are always working."

Then she looked straight into my eyes, squared her shoulders, and spat out: "And for your information, ah'm twenty-seven, not twenty-one; what do y'all think about that?"

I didn't answer; no answer was needed. Then, working herself up, she screamed at me, "AND... I CAN'T STAND THE SIGHT OF Y'ALL!"

I was broken, knew this was the end. Tears fell, no, poured, from my eyes. "But, you're my wife, Myrtle; I love you. We'll patch things up. I'll work less hours."

Contorted with rage, her face darkened, though her voice was dead calm. "Y'all are a first-class fool. And, here's another flash for y'all: we were never legally married because ah already *had* a husband, Wilmer Reichart, a drunk ah left in Pittsburgh in 1922, without a note of goodbye!" She stormed out the door of our room, slamming it for emphasis.

Stunned, I couldn't speak, just stunned to silence.

Mama had worried my naiveté would make me a target for criminals on the high seas. It turned out this woman was the nightmare Mama never dreamed of.

She had gall, that much I'll give her. She didn't even move out of Iola's; just moved down the hall, sharing a room with another single woman. She put on a stony face if we passed in the hall or met at the breakfast table. Imagine snubbing *me* as if I had mistreated *her*!

Broken-hearted and angry at my own gullibility, I avoided making eye contact when in the same room with her. She planned to stay on at the club for the entire season. In search of her next quarry, I thought.

Fannie

Nora, Max, and I went upstairs to Rose and Joe's for Thanksgiving dinner. The aroma of roast turkey and baked sweet potatoes cooking in all the apartments mixed together to fill the stairwell and hallways, a keen reminder of the building's community.

Nora carried her contribution to the meal: two pies, an apple, and pumpkin. Max brought an assortment of bread and rolls and two bottles of French sauterne. I made chopped eggplant with onions and olives, sweet and sour meatballs, and apple strudel: my Mama's recipe.

Rube, Gussie, and the three girls were spending the holiday with the Geduldigs. Charles and Reggie couldn't make it; he was too weak to make the schlepp from downtown. Albert was working, Bertha and Lucille with her people in Far Rockaway. Morris was working, too, but Nellie, Bobby, and Virginia were at Rose's.

Only two of my children were out of the city that evening: Louis, who sent a telegram from North Carolina, wishing us all a happy day, and Sam, who sent no word at all.

I had a feeling things were not going well for him. I'd worry for the rest of my days about my baby, I supposed.

Rose's house was always full of noise. Alby was eight, Woody, six. They were equal in height, though Woody had a smaller frame and passive personality, which made him a target for abuse by his older brother's aggressive nature. When the two got started, it wasn't long before Woody would be crying and coming to Rose with a bruise or skinned knee. She wasn't a sympathetic mother, often ignoring them completely. Dickie, at two, seemed intent upon playing with his wooden blocks, yet he was very well aware of his surroundings. I noticed a muscle tic in his jaw when Alby taunted Woody. Little children are not off in their own world; they are seeing everything. Colin, just a month old, stayed asleep in his cradle in the bedroom throughout dinner.

Nellie, in her forties, was still so lovely. "Dear Fannie. 'Tis so good to be here tonight. You're lookin' fit, very fit! Ain't it beautiful seein' so many of yer grandbabies under one roof?

They're quite a bunch, and they luv bein' together! Have ya seen our Virginia? A real beauty, that one is, the spittin of me mother, God rest her soul."

At that moment, Bobby, Alby, Virginia, and Woody came out of the bedroom, little Dickie toddling behind. They were arguing over a rental property Virginia owned on "The Landlord's" game board. Having never played, I was of no help. Nora read the directions aloud, determining Virginia was owed three dollars by Alby. The children ran back to the bedroom, except for Bobby, who picked Dickie up in his arms and carried him inside to join the others. Bobby loved babies, a sweet trait for a boy of ten.

Rose had been born with a strong personality. The tallest girl in her class for all the school years, she was no bully but also not afraid to defend herself against anyone who tried to take advantage of her. Intelligent, but uninterested in books, she never was much of a student. She ran the roost in her house, and her husband loved it. He was mild-mannered, and thought Rose the smartest, funniest, bravest, and most interesting woman in the world. Wasn't that lucky for her?

Although Joe always had worked steady—still at the monotype machine—Rose was not a good manager, often running out of money before the next payday. She never asked me for a loan, and that kept me from having to tell her "No." As I was supported wholly by my sons, it would be unfair to give their money to Rose. It wasn't only a matter of principle, though. I lived frugally, with little cash to spare.

I suspected that Louis had been helping Rose out on a regular basis, but they were careful not to let Joe know about it. Those two had always been very close, Rose like a second mother to Louis when he was a little boy. For as long as I live, I'll never forget how she cried when the social worker came to take Louis and Nora to HOA. Her grief was beyond consolation, and she was only twelve at the time. She wrote him at the orphanage almost every day.

Cleaning up after dinner, I sat in the kitchen to dry the dishes, my leg aching. Nellie and the kids said their goodbyes, kissed me on the cheek. "Goodbye, Grandmama. I love you," Virginia told me. "I love you, too, my beautiful girl. Come to see me when you can."

Nora and Max left to bring our platters downstairs, and Joe began getting the boys ready for bed.

Rose and I, alone in the kitchen, enjoyed another cup of coffee.

"Dinner was delicious, Rose, thank you. The children are so wonderful. If you asked me to describe how much I love them, I doubt I could find the words."

"That brings me to what I want to tell you, Mama. I'm not going to dance around this: We're moving to a six-room apartment on Stebbins Avenue in The Bronx. With four kids, there's not enough room here.

"It's a brand-new building, Mama, with a full-time super and eighty-five apartments. The one-bedroom flats rent for only sixteen a month; wouldn't you like that, everything brand new?

I kept still, knew Rose was just warming up. "Mama. Is there any reason you shouldn't come with us? You've been here for fifteen years. Rube and Morris are both uptown, too, so you'll be closer to all your grandchildren.

"And, Nora won't be living with you much longer. Max told my Joe he wants to get married by next summer, going to pop the question New Year's Eve.

"Sam and his floozie won't be settling into a normal life ever, if I'm seeing the situation correctly, and, well, they're way out on the Island anyway. Then, Lou will probably find a wife down South, but if he does come back alone, he can live with you.

"I don't want to leave you, but moving uptown is best for my family. The Bronx is beautiful, with parks and wide boulevards, and the schools are the best in the city.

"We're moving on January 15th. Don't make me beg you, Mama; say you'll come."

Everything she said was true. Louis was gone, Sam was gone, and Nora would be, too. Rose's argument to move uptown was more than a suggestion; it was the only sensible action. I realized I had come to the time in my life where my children worried about *me* as much as I worried about *them*.

Rube and Gussie asked me to move in with them, and I was glad for the invite; why live alone? I could still help out a little in the kitchen, and it would be grand to be in the midst of a young, happy, family.

19

Fannie

Rudolf and Gussie's apartment had only two bedrooms, and the children's was filled with furniture: two beds, a crib, and two dressers.

"Perhaps I should rent my own place, like Rose said.

"No, Mama, we'll find a way to make room. You only have a small dresser and a single cot. At the end of the hall leading from the girls' bedroom to the bathroom, there's a niche where those things will fit nicely." He was right. That became my little space, and I was fine with it.

I overheard Thelma talking to Gussie. "Grandma can't stay there, Mama. It's only a hallway. There's no window, and we'll bother her when we brush our teeth in the morning. It's not fair. Let her take my bed; I'll sleep near the bathroom. Really, Mama, she's old; we should make her comfortable."

"Grandma's fine with that spot; she actually likes privacy. And she gets up to go to the bathroom at night, so it'll be convenient."

Nora moved uptown with me, sleeping on the settee for the month of January. She moved out on Sunday, February first, the day she became Mrs. Max Kaminsky. The ceremony, officiated by Rabbi Shmuelevitz, was performed in Rose's parlor, with all my children in attendance. Louis came from North Carolina. Even Sam came, alone, from Long Island.

That evening, twenty of us, including Max's only sister, Esther, filled a private dining room at the Concourse Steak House. The food was delicious, the conversation lively.

Rudolf began a rambling toast, "Here's to my baby sister, Nora, and the tobacconist whose pipe she ignited!" "SIT DOWN!" Morris and Albert yelled in unison. "YOU'RE DRUNK!" Everyone laughed, even Gussie, while helping her husband navigate to the door; it was time to put him to bed. After much wrangling back and forth between my sons and their new brother-in-law, Max paid the bill.

Rudolf still worked the lobster shift, sleeping all day. It was a schedule that taught Thelma, Leonore, and Pearl, to move about very quietly, not to disturb their Papa. They kept themselves busy reading or playing with paper dolls. The tranquil household was a far cry from Rose's, with those rambunctious boys!

At ten, Thelma was not shy but possessed a reserved quality, a quiet maturity. Where she resembled her lanky father in build and had her mother's dark eyes and hair, Leonore favored Gussie's mother, fair and blond. Luckily, both had the Freed height. Leonore, an energetic and inquisitive eight-year-old, was very bright, capable of reciting a poem from memory after only one reading. Pearl, the sweet-tempered baby, was almost two, her birthday in April, like mine.

Life was pleasant, and The Bronx *was* a beautiful place, as Rose said.

On Tuesday, April 1st, I turned sixty-three. Rube decorated the parlor with red ribbon bows and a "Happy Birthday, Grandma" poster designed and painted by Thelma. With Aunt Nettie's help, Leonore baked a pineapple upside-down cake in my honor. I received telegrams from Louis and Sam, cards from Morris and Nellie, and a box of chocolates from Bobby and Virginia. Albert dropped off a gift box with a lovely silk scarf and a jar of homemade apricot preserves from Reggie. Rose, Joe, and the boys took me to the deli on Fordham Road for dinner.

I was blessed, surrounded by so much love. Content that my children, except for Charles's poor constitution and Sam's sad love life, were secure and healthy.

Warm weather arrived early, as did Easter, with a big parade down the Grand Concourse on April 12th. I went along with Rube, Gussie, and the girls to watch the marchers, all dressed in their Easter finery and elaborate hats. I couldn't help but remark, "America is so democratic. Look at this: Jews marching and lined up to watch an Easter Parade. My Papa would have liked this mingling, celebrating each other's holidays."

Rudolf said, "Mama, don't get all teary-eyed about America's brotherly love. The Irish Catholics run New York politics and the police and fire departments. As long as the Jews stay in their own neighborhoods and don't aspire to top-level jobs, it's O.K. to show how tolerant New Yorkers are, with Jews marching in Easter Parades and buying Christmas trees."

Gussie didn't like that. "Don't be such a crab. We all have Gentile friends, and your own brothers married Christian women. You sound like a bigot right now, so unlike you. And, don't spoil all the fun for the girls." Gussie always protected the children.

I had seen her in action a few times. Once, outside the greengrocer, a woman slapped her child, maybe a three-year-old, across the face, then dragged him by his wrist down the sidewalk. Gussie reached for the woman's arm, bringing her to a stop. In a gentle voice, she said, "Don't hit him. You'll be sorry later. He's only a baby; teach him to be good. Beating him will only harden his heart. Please, Mother, don't hit him anymore." The woman was shocked at this petite stranger's plea and burst into tears. "I'm sorry, Missus. You're right." That was a remarkable show of character from my daughter-in-law. I loved Gussie; she was a truly good person.

Trees were in full leaf, and banks of wild, golden forsythia covered the discarded trash in vacant lots. In the springtime seasons of my youth, the scent of lilies of the valley and lilac enlivened me, put a zip in my step.

This year, I was feeling so listless, I had little energy to respond to the natural flowering; even Rube's cooking didn't tempt me.

At the onset of fever, chills, coughing, and stabbing chest pains, Dr. Lippman was called. He thought I had the grippe and advised bed rest, plenty of tea, broth, and aspirin.

My bed was moved near the parlor window to protect the girls from infection as well as allow them to sleep undisturbed by my coughing.

By the third week of May, Lippman feared I had pneumonia, and although there was a promising new serum vaccine being tested in the wards and laboratories at Bellevue Hospital, it was not yet available for general use. I coughed into a jar, and Dr. Lippman had it analyzed. Pneumonia, Incurable. There was always hope my body would cure itself, but given my high blood pressure and age, the doctor was not optimistic.

Pneumonia's Captain of the Men of Death had taken Anna twenty-three years earlier and had returned for me. In my mind's eye, I saw Anna's face, felt her little body against my bosom, heard, again, each labored, shallow breath. Now, I understood the fatigue, the body's final, exhausted surrender.

I was at the last place of transit reached by all. The end-riddle revealed; pneumonia would carry me, unafraid, into the everlasting darkness. How much time was left, a few days, a week? I felt no panic or anxiety. I was content with my life and how I had lived it.

Windows were opened during the day to allow sunshine and fresh air into the room, and there was music on the radio to cheer things up. Gussie and Thelma fussed over me. Leonore brought me a water glass filled with pansies she had picked from a flowerpot on a stoop down the street. Rose cooked a pot of chicken soup. With little appetite, I managed a few spoonfuls to show my appreciation.

While their mother bathed me, brushed my hair, and changed my gown, Rose's boys ran down the stairs to play on the stoop.

Five-year-old Lucille proudly presented me a plate with a piece of her Mama's famous strudel. "Thank you, Lucille, for bringing this to me. Your Mama is the best strudel baker in New York!" She smiled, and Bertha lifted her to kiss my cheek.

Reggie sewed a lovely silk bed jacket to keep my shoulders covered. Nellie, Bobby, and Virginia brought a potted plant and sat with me for a while.

Nora, Albert, Morris, and Joe Romoff stopped by at the end of their workday, every day.

Rube wired Sam and Louis. I was shown a telegram, letting us know Louis would be catching the train to New York from Winston-Salem early Wednesday morning.

On Tuesday, Sam came from the Island, without Myrtle. I scolded him for leaving the County Club just days before the holiday weekend. He brushed off my concern about the job, held my hand, and cried softly. He had to return to Southampton on Thursday, so we had only the next day to be together.

I fell into a perspiring sleep several times; still, Sam did not leave my bedside.

Animated, he regaled me with the goings on at the swanky club, and life on Long Island. "That's wonderful, Sam. I know you love it out there. Now, tell me, how is Myrtle?"

His demeanor changed, lips quivering, eyes watering. "Mama, she never loved me. She was so cruel. How dumb I was; why didn't anyone tell me? Oh, Mama, this is the worst part: we were never really husband and wife. Oh, yes, I believed we were, but when she walked out

on me, she told me she was married to some guy in Pittsburgh and had never divorced him. She was a bigamist, Mama! A bigamist!"

"You were too young, my dearest, a gullible boy in love. It wasn't your fault. You're in pain, Sam, but it will ease. The love you grip so tightly today will fade away. The true love of your life is still unmet. Be patient, and don't lose faith in love."

The Myrtle story came to an end as evening shadows fell across the windowsill. I was very, very tired.

The plan was for Sam to have dinner and spend the night with Nora and Max, who lived closest to Pennsylvania Station. He needed to board the train to Southampton at 5:00 in the morning to be at work for the lunch crowd.

Embracing, we both understood that it could probably be for the last time.

I whispered, "My baby, I love you."

Leaning on my breast, he sobbed and said, as he had at the Infant Asylum so long ago, "Please Mama, don't go."

It took all my strength to offer him comfort. I laid my hand on his head, stroking his hair. Haltingly, I whispered, "Sam, love is everything. In the end, it is the people you loved that gave your life meaning. Give it freely; give all you can."

"I will, Mama. I will."

"Goodbye, my dearest. Remember me."

"Yes, Mama. Always."

Standing to leave, he kissed my cheek.

Rose brought two aspirin tablets. Her baby brother kissed her goodbye, and I watched him leave the room.

After a while, the aspirin began easing the pain in my chest.

I thought I heard my beloved Samuel's voice and opened my eyes.

"Fannie, my dearest, my love."

Wearing the blue sweater my Mama had knitted for him, he stood at the bedside, close to my shoulder. His hand reached out to touch me, the sun glinting on his wedding band.

Rube

On Saturday morning, Rose sponged Mother's body with a solution of cold water and alcohol, bringing her temperature back to normal in less than fifteen minutes. By afternoon, she felt improved, having taken in some fluids, and eaten a bit of soft-boiled egg.

We were all on edge, and there was not much conversation. The radio played softly to distract us. I was sure my siblings and I wrestled with the same doubts: could we keep her comfortable? Could all of us stay positive, knowing this had only one possible outcome? Everyone wanted to be with Mother, but we had to work, and the children needed to go to school, to be out from underfoot. We needed to support one another, yet we also craved privacy so each family could deal with their own grief. How do we balance the attention Mother has to have with the needs of our young families? How much should the children be told; should they be shielded, kept from Mother's bedside? This was not the time to withdraw into oneself; we had to pull together. Mother had lived through worse. So could we.

A telegram arrived from Sam, expressing his profound sadness, being so far away, and I wept for his frantic need to be with the family.

Charlie and Reggie came by for an hour. Poor Charlie, so weak and out of breath that Albert and Morris had to sit him in a kitchen chair and carry him up the stairs to our apartment. Reggie had fabricated a mask to shield Charlie's mouth and nose, so fearful were they of possible contagion, his lungs already compromised. Although it seemed a hilarious costume at first, none of us had the heart to kid him about it, even though the comic relief might have been good for us.

Dr. Lippman came by after six and spoke with us in the kitchen after examining Mother.

"You're taking tender care of your dear Mother, yet you must understand there's nothing you can do to stave off the inevitable."

There was also nothing more *he* could do.

"It's best you say your goodbyes and do all you can to keep Fannie comfortable now."

Rose stepped forward. "I'll be responsible for my mother's nursing care, Doctor, whatever is required."

"You may offer tea, broth, or water but don't force any food. Over the next days, she'll most likely have a profound loss of appetite.

"Your mother's body is in the process of dying. As it shuts down, she'll become immobile and unable to communicate. That is not to say she won't hear your voices and movement in the room, so continue to speak to her and with one another. I believe the sounds of familiar voices are a comfort to the dying, although I don't know for sure."

Albert asked, "Is Mama in pain? If she can't speak, how will we know?"

"There is discomfort from respiratory congestion, but pain is dependent upon one's particular threshold for it. I'll leave opium drops for relief, if needed." He turned to Rose: "Only three drops of the liquid on her tongue. Be very careful not to overdose." Rose nodded.

"I must mention that, although unlikely, Fannie may become agitated or delirious, which can be very disturbing to watch, especially for the grandchildren; don't allow them to witness that.

"Finally, deep pulmonary secretions will produce a rattling sound with each breath. When the respiratory system is overwhelmed with fluid, breathing will cease."

Gussie began to cry and leaned against me for support. She knew only too well how the next days would unfold, remembering her own father's death from lobar pneumonia two years earlier.

Lou arrived as the doctor left and went directly to the parlor. When he saw Mother abed in the dimly lit room, he was heartbroken. With the exception of Sam, we were all at hand.

In soft voices, we talked about what a remarkable woman Mother was and how much we loved her. By her example, we had learned the value of strength of character, of humor, of tolerance. She encouraged our love of music and learning and kept a sunny outlook, so her life, and ours, were not wasted in bitterness.

Eyes closed, she listened to our tribute to her, occasionally nodding her head or managing a fleeting smile, but not a word left her lips.

Morris, Albert, and I set up chairs and music stands near the sickbed and played some of Mother's favorite melodies: Liszt's Liebesträume, a few of Schubert's string pieces, and Bartok's folk music.

The strings had their effect on the children. Bobby, Thelma, Virginia, and Dickie slept like puppies, intertwined on the parlor floor. Pearl and Leonore had long since found their way to bed. Woody and Alby managed to stay awake, in rapt attention to the music and the stories we were telling about their grandmother's life.

No one wanted to leave. It was as if we believed our collective energies would help Mother hang on. Around midnight, with Colin cradled in his father's arms and Lucille's sleeping head bobbing about on Albert's shoulder, those not staying the night made their way downstairs. Lou insisted on staying with us, even though Max and Nora begged him to come home with them. It was decided he would be the night nurse, allowing Rose to leave her post until morning.

Sunday, the house was so filled with people, there was barely room to fit the extra chairs borrowed from neighbors. Contrary to how others might have behaved, we enjoyed the gathering, finding in our communion a way to accept the looming tragedy.

Bertha's sister, Sidonia, and husband, Gustav, came for a few hours. All my in-laws visited for the day: Sali, Nettie and Jack, and Hermann Tiger with Georgie and Stanley. Even my brother-in-law, Max, and Bertha with their three daughters, took the train in from Paterson. Every family brought food, baked goods, or schnapps.

It was a day to embrace one another, relating stories uniquely ours. It was a time of farewell, but not of sorrow. All the grandchildren were together, part of the ritual of passage for their grandmother. In many ways, it was a happy day, one they would remember.

Midafternoon, I took a walk to get some air and check on the children.

On the stoop, Leonore, Virginia, Woody, Dickie, Lucille, and Stanley were engaged with an elaborate puppet theater they had built from junk found near the garbage cans.

I saw Bobby, Thelma, Alby, George, and the three sisters from Paterson in a huddle at the far end of the vacant lot next door. As I approached, I couldn't help but smile.

Georgie was teaching his cousins a game. Craps!

Standing at one end of a rectangular space smoothed out in the dirt, he held a pair of dice, no doubt borrowed from the Tiger Lodge, his grandfather's upstate hotel. I watched him throw the dice along the ground, bouncing them against the side of a discarded cheese crate propped up for that purpose.

I must have caught Georgie's eye because he stopped talking mid-sentence, a guilty look moving across his face. "It's O.K., Georgie, you can keep going. I know this game and love it, too!"

I laughed, Georgie laughed; and the kids all giggled, relieved the play would continue.

Georgie was very smart. He explained the rules, the odds, and how to bet, using pebbles they had gathered on the lot as money.

Thelma had seen me playing craps with my brothers and some neighbors on the roof, yet until now, she hadn't paid too much attention. Now, thanks to Cousin Georgie, she experienced the thrill of the toss and learned how difficult it was to follow the game's lightning-fast betting action. I guess gambling was an inherited Freed trait!

Except for the occasional bathroom visit, we didn't see the children until almost eight in the evening, when the streetlights came on.

Mother was stimulated by the activity in the house. Her appetite perked up with a few forkfuls of my mother-in-law, Sali's, kraut sveckles, a dish of cabbage, onion, and noodles sautéed in butter. In the late afternoon, she managed to finish a cup of sugared tea and two of Gussie's apple fritters.

Her renewed interest in food gave us hope. Maybe Dr. Lippman was wrong, and she would come back from the brink. It was possible, wasn't it?

With school and work in the morning, the families didn't overstay on this night. The children who wished to say goodbye to Grandma Fannie did so; those who were not comfortable didn't, and that was alright, too.

It had been a good day for all, including Mother. She slept undisturbed for several hours, while Rose dozed on the settee, at the ready if needed. My daughters slept soundly, but Gussie and I woke many times during the night to check on Mother's breathing and general condition.

On Monday and Tuesday, the women worked as a team, attending to Mother, seeing to the children's needs, preparing meals and baked goods for the afterwork crowd. Coming directly from school, the older children were shooed outside to keep the house quiet while the littlest ones napped.

Evening passed playing cards, mostly rummy and poker. There was a sense of quiet celebration about the house. Mother didn't seem disturbed by the chatter of her grandchildren, who accepted the sickbed and their immobile grandmother as part of the landscape.

On Wednesday, the women couldn't entice Mother to eat or drink anything. She cried, seemingly in pain. Rose sent Thelma to Dr. Lippman's to ask for a house call.

He explained, "Fannie may be experiencing pain, or the sensation may be a phantom response to random brain activity." However, it didn't matter to him whether the pain was real or not; he administered a few drops of opium, soothing Mother immediately.

"The end of Fannie's life is near, maybe only a few hours away."

At that moment, Mother's death became an inescapable fact, one we could no longer deny. The festive air withered as a pall fell over the household. The children became quiet and introspective. It was as if a huge wave was coming to sweep us off the beach. It was surely coming, but no one could say when it would arrive.

As in other desolate times in her life, Mother summoned her last reserves, refusing to yield.

Haltingly, breathlessly, she began a discourse, an encapsulation of her life, in Hungarian. I was a thirty-six-year-old father of three, yet on this night, I was her Hungarian child. Albert, Morris, and I listened carefully. It had been years since we heard or spoke our native tongue.

It took all three to translate Mother's words.

"He was so handsome; he took my breath away." "His touch stirred my heart." "He washed the pox from my face." "Papa, please let Samuel in; he's knocking at the door." "Mama loved Samuel from the beginning." "An artist, tailoring at the finest level." "I loved him from the very first moment." "He was the only man I ever knew or loved." "He was my soul." "Mama's talc mixed with my tears at the station." "I'll be with them soon." "Samuel is waiting for me, I must go."

She was there, seeing Papa for the first time, saying goodbye in Nagy Karolyi, hearing Samuel's knock at the door. Papa was waiting for her.

Finally, she slipped from consciousness, her breathing shallow and rapid.

Sitting beside the bed, Morris leaned forward to rest his head against her hip and weep quietly.

She lay moribund until after midnight when Sam arrived from Southampton.

"Hello, Mama." We could hardly believe it, but she opened her eyes.

Charles tried to stifle a sob, but it only aggravated his coughing. Lou offered his handkerchief, putting his arm about Charlie's shoulder, a gesture of kindness not lost on the rest of us. Nora and Rose embraced and began to cry when Mother, perfectly lucid, smiled at Sam and looked at each of us in turn.

Albert motioned for us to gather more closely around the bed. Following his lead, we placed our hands upon her. Rose whispered in her ear, "We're all here with you, Mama. We love you, Mama."

We had risen to the occasion of this trial, all of us. In the end, we did what was natural and loving. In caring for Mother, we also cared for each other. Through the night, our hands stroked and patted her, never breaking the connection.

On the morning of Thursday, June 4th, the summer sun shone through the window and rested on her pale face. We stood at the bedside, enveloped by the mystery of the event.

She lay motionless, her face unstressed, at peace. At the top of each rattling crescendo, several seconds elapsed with no passage of air, no noise at all. During those pauses, each of us held our own breath, in harmony with her.

At 2:20 in the afternoon, her last exhale reverberated around the room. Mother had left this place, leaving us to accept the reality in the palpable silence of the moment. She had lived sixty-three years, two months, and four days.

Albert poured a small glass of apricot brandy for everyone in the room.

"We raise a glass to thank our Mama for giving us life. To honor her life's journey, her strength of character, her enduring optimism, the gift of her love. To say farewell to this exceptional woman: our creator, protector, champion, wellspring—our mother, Fannie.

Afterward

Fannie Bruder Freed was buried at the Mount Hebron Cemetery in Flushing, New York, on June 6, 1925. It was a sunny Friday morning.

My part in Fannie's story began with a simple family tree that grew into a forest of genealogical documents. I pored over immigration databases, railroad and maritime histories and schedules, newspaper articles, personal journals, diaries, maps, letters, photos. Then, there were New York, New Jersey, and Pennsylvania vital statistics and naturalization document searches. I corresponded with staff and researched the histories of the Sloan Hospital for Women, New York Infant and Hebrew Orphan Asylums, accounts of 19th Century midwifery. I consulted U.S. military records and spoke with trainmasters and historians of Tarrytown and Westchester County in New York and Carbon County, Pennsylvania.

Bits of data informed the back story: U.S. Archives, various Budapest websites, calendars, N.O.A.A. weather archives, New York and California cinema and recording industry databases. For hard details, there were cemetery documents, federal and New York State census reports, Hungarian village finders, Hungarian synagogue circumcision records, German/English and Hungarian/English dictionaries, world atlases, and interviews with as many living relatives as possible. I didn't start out to do all this; it just evolved, connecting one dot to another.

She did not invent the wheel, did not solve the mystery of the universe, nor discover a cure for cancer. She was an ordinary woman, born into ordinary circumstance.

She shared a deep and intimate love. She bore nine children, raising eight of them during decades fraught with religious persecution, national betrayal, world war, mass migration, technological advances, economic depression, disease, death, and poverty.

Her life speaks to the steadfastness of the human spirit. Its ability to adapt and renew, survive, and endure.

She reached out to me as I discovered the patterns of her life. I was compelled to tell her story, which I present as a gift to my own great-grandchildren, who will learn that Fannie lived, and her spark lives within them.

Diana Wiener, Rube Freed's granddaughter.

About the author

Brooklyn-born, Diana Wiener lived in Yonkers, New York. Together with her husband Sy, she mothered four children and has eight grandchildren. The focus of her 30's was family and community.

Diana became the first woman ever elected to Port Jervis, NY's Common Council, serving two terms. An entrepreneur at 42, her commercial interior design company employed 33. When Diana and Sy retired, they wintered for a decade in a Mexican enclave of artists. At 56, she was certified as a PADI Scuba Instructor!

For seven years, Diana posted political commentary, essays, and memoir on her blog, "My Century, So Far." In 2014, "What Having An Abortion In 1959 Was Like," received 700,000 BuzzFeed, HuffPost, Reddit, and Longform views.

Calliope published three of her essays in 2015, and *The New Guard* literary review re-published "Confined" in Volume X. She was also a regular at The Writer's Hotel conferences. A 1914 journal, written in her grandfather's hand, instigated ten years of genealogical research, inspiring the passion to write the account of her Hungarian great-grandmother's life; *The Wellspring, Fannie's Story*, a creative non-fiction narrative.

During the pandemic, Diana founded *The Buzz*, a newsletter that served her retirement community and lifted everyone's spirits-a story covered in *The New York Times*.

Book jacket author photo by Ella Monck.